NAGAVARMA'S

CANARESE PROSODY

NAGAVARMA'S
CANARESE PROSODY

EDITED WITH AN INTRODUCTION TO THE WORK AND AN ESSAY ON CANARESE LITERATURE

BY

REV. F. KITTEL.

B. M. S.

ISBN: 978-93-5128-808-4(PB)

First Published in 1875
Indian Reprint in 2017

Published by

Kalpaz Publications
C-30, Satyawati Nagar,
Delhi – 110052
E-mail: kalpaz@hotmail.com
Website: kalpazpublications.com
Ph.: +91-9212142040

Cataloging in Publication Data—DK
Courtesy: D.K. Agencies (P) Ltd. <docinfo@dkagencies.com>

Na˜gavarma, active 12th century, **author.**
Na˜gavarmana Kannadòa chandassu = Na˜gavarma's Canarese prosody / edited with an introduction to the work and an essay on Canarese literature by Rev. F. Kittel.
pages cm
English and Kannada.
Reprint. Originally published: Mangalore : Basel Mission Book & Tract Depository, 1875.
ISBN 9789351288084

1. Kannada language—Prosodic analysis. I. Kittel, F. (Ferdinand), 1832-1903, editor. II. Title. III. Title: Na˜gavarma's Canarese prosody.

PL4644.N325 2017 DDC 494.81416 23

A. Nâgavarma's Prosody[1].

The present edition of Nâgavarma's Prosody is based on a collation of the following Manuscripts:—

B. On paper, from Bĕṭṭigeri near Gadagu, to the east of Dhâravâḍa,—a very defective recension.

D. A lithograph from Dhâravâḍa (1865), belonging to the recension of B., but not to the same original.

H. A copy on paper from a MS. at Hubbaḷḷi near Dhâravâḍa. It forms a recension of its own. It uses the old letter ṛ (ಐ).

K. On olĕ (palmyra leaf), belonging to the Râja's library at Maisûr. Mr. Raṅgâčârya, Controller of the Mahârâja's palace, has been kind enough to send us its latter part for collation. See Additions. The said part belongs to the recension of M., but seemingly not to the same original.

L. On olĕ, from the Liṅgâita maṭha at Mâdevapura in Kŏḍagu (Coorg); a very incorrect MS., with a Commentary still more so. It apparently represents the same recension as Sb.

M. On paper. It has been kindly lent to us by Mr. B. Mallappa, Head of the Canarese department of the Mahârâja's school, Maisûr. It forms a recension of its own, and uses the letter ṛ.

O. One of the numerous fragments of recent date that are called Nâgavarma Čhandas. It is a collection of twenty-seven verses obtained at Maḍikeri (Mercara).

With the following four MSS. on paper B. L. Rice Esq., Bĕṅgaḷûr, has been kind enough to favour us:—

Ra. It belongs to the recension of H., and has, no doubt, been copied from the same original. It bears the Jaina heading "śrîvîtarâgâya namaḥ".

Rb. This interesting Jaina MS., though called a Prosody of Nâgavarma, shows no internal evidence whatever of belonging to him. Beginning with Pratishṭhĕ it gives 63 instances of 22 čhandas', the rules in verse, which at the same time form the instances, containing praises of the twenty-four known Jaina Tîrthaṅkaras, from Ṛishabhasvâmi to Śrîvîra. Cf. *e. g.* Ind. Ant. ii., 134 seq.

Rc. A recension of its own. It begins, for instance, with v. 3 of B. or v. 6 of M., an invocation of Sarasvatî; its v. 2 is D.'s last verse, H.'s v. 8, and M.'s v. 30; H.'s v. 6 is not in it; etc., etc.

Rd. A fragment of, or rather miscellaneous collections from Nâgavarma, with a few additions of its own; fifty-seven verses in all.

The following three olĕ MSS. have been kindly put at our disposal by Mr. Tirumalĕ Śyâmaṇṇa, Munshi of the Wesleyan Missionaries at Maisûr:—

---

1) Here and at other places where a reference to the text is made, every number to which the letter p. is not specially prefixed, refers to a verse.

Sa. An independent fragment, stating its contents as follows: Nâgavarma čhandas | kavitâlakshaṇa | shaṭpadikrama | shaḍvṛittanema (our v. 230) | shaṭprâsabagĕ (bagĕ= riti) | shaṭpratyaya | gaṇaprastâra | gaṇotpattisthâna | gaṇadevatĕ | gaṇaprayogaphala ‖.

Sb. Its recension resembles that of M., (K., L.), but is not identical with it. The editor, from fear less the olĕs might be damaged during the very damp monsoons at Mercara, returned it to its owner before annotating all its different readings; but nothing essential, he trusts, has been overlooked.

Sc. This the editor has used only for Nâgavarma's Genealogy. From the circumstance of its containing the genealogy it follows that it somehow belongs to the recension of M. (K., L., and Sb.)

From this list it appears that, not taking into account the fragments and MS. Rb., at least four different recensions are represented by the MSS., H., which, as will be seen, is probably the oldest; then M.; thereafter Rc.; and lastly B. The present edition is a collection of the essential portion of all the MSS., with a few additions concerning the Ragaḷĕs. Of the very numerous different readings, so far as they are quite unimportant, such have been adopted as are metrically right; wherever necessary, different readings are adduced. As the present edition is first of all intended for schools, some indecorous epithets of Nâgavarma's wife, to whom the instruction is given, and the superstitious first line of v. 22 have been altered. Such alterations appear in different type, as do also all editorial additions in Canarese[1)], and some spurious verses of recension B.; other spurious verses *e.g.* 318, 322, 326, 330, 334 and 337, are given in the letters of the text, as they have obtained a certain popularity, and others, as they are valuable. An alteration, which is not marked in print, regarding the genuine terms of Nâki, Nâkiga and Pinâki, and which further on will be treated of in particular, has been introduced chiefly to avoid perverse discussions at school; Piṅgaḷa or another similar word has been put instead. It is to be regretted that, through renumbering the verses of the MS. at the printing office, many of the numerical references in English have become incorrect; a list of them appears among the corrections. The Index contains all the terms of any interest.

What Dr. Weber says[2)] with regard to Kedâra's Vṛittaratnâkara, a prosody in Sanscrit, viz. that its great popularity becomes already satisfactorily evident from the floating condition of its text, holds good also with regard to Nâgavarma's Prosody; it is in fact the only Kannaḍa Čhandas.

1) Concerning them the wording of the last line of v. 45 and that of the instance of the Sîsa (270, 271) have been somewhat changed.

2) Über die Metrik der Inder, Indische Studien, viii., p. 206.

Nâgavarma's original work did not contain six Shaṭpadis, but only one, viz. the Sarashaṭpadi, as v. 340, in which he states that he has explained the chief uses of the devâksharas or of the feet formed of syllables of the devas. This shows that he had no knowledge of the other Shaṭpadis, for none of these are built on the devâksharas, whereas the Sarashaṭpadi originally was a devâkshara metre. Nâgavarma, on that account, put this his Shaṭpadi between the Eḷĕ and Akkarikĕ. Verses 318-338 of the text, therefore, so far as they are declared to be by Nâgavarma, are forgeries[1]. The same is to be said of verses 313 and 316 that are introductory to them. Here recension H., by adducing v. 316 (the only verse in which it alludes to the six Shaṭpadis) after its ch. 6 in an Appendix, clearly proves that they did not belong to the original text; and the indisputable text of H. (chapters 1-5), on this account, must have preceded those of the other recensions that adduce the spurious verses in the course of their texts. The whole recension of H. (chapters 1-6 and Appendix) appears to have been formed about 1300 A. D.[2] All that is contained in the Appendix of H., which comprises 27 miscellaneous verses (p. 130) but is not counted as a chapter, is not genuine; and H. fitly concludes its sixth or last chapter with v. 347 of the present text. In course of time a number of the said miscellaneous verses (and various others besides) were introduced into the text of other recensions, *e.g.* 14 of them that chiefly bear a superstitious character, into the first chapter of M. (p. 12, note 1; p. 130). It appears that no superstitious matter occurred in Nâgavarma's own composition, though three verses about the šubha and ašubha of the syllable-feet appear in the sixth chapter of H.[3]; for obviously on account of their having never belonged to the established text, the first of them occurs with some alterations, as M. i., 41; and the other two are identical with M. i., 40, 44 (our v. 36)[4]. So the 6th chapter of H. too, as it stands, is at least partly of a questionable character.

It is very remarkable that of the rules on Alliterations (42, 43, 50-55, 57, 59-61, 63 and 64) that are so essential to Canarese, verse 42 is found only in Sa., and v. 43 in the spurious supplement of H. and

1) It is strange that only three of the later Shaṭpadi instances (328, 335, 337) observe the rule (318-315) that each third line has a long syllable at its end, the others presenting at that place a short syllable that is to be looked upon as long; in these and in these alone the rule about the end of a Hemistich (27) seems to have been put into practice. 2) This was about the time when the later Shaṭpadis came into general use. 3) They are followed by two other verses (our 286=M. i., 76, and our 230=M. i., 69) that cannot be genuine; and then comes v. 347. 4) Regarding the state of M.'s first chapter further compare *e.g.* p. 24, note 3.

in B., M., Rc., whereas the other rules are only in the recensions of B. and Rc.; from which circumstance it follows first that Rc. is comparatively late, and secondly that Nâgavarma did not include the subject of alliterations in his prosody, although he always made use of the simple, here and there of the co-ordinate ones (cf. p. 21, note 2). It is worthy of notice that the Lalitapada (v. 183) which presents the final alliteration, is repeated in the supplement of H. (v. 11), and there bears the heading "*C*audanalakshaṇa" (Ra. *C*audalakshaṇa), as if it were a *C*atushpada (čau=čatush).

The recension of B. and that of the fragment Sa. are most probably not yet one hundred years old as there occurs in it a quotation from the Canarese Jaimini Bhârata (p. 125, note 1) which work belongs to about A. D. 1760. They have apparently used the Kavijihvâbandhana (on poetical composition, etc.)[1], Rc.[2] and M.[3]

The verses (37, 38) on the Refrain (B., Sa.) and the Verse-lines (B., M.) are certainly spurious[4]. The genuineness of a few other verses

1) See 34. p. 12. 42. p. 16. 65. 2) See 50-57. 59-61. 63. 64. 3) See *e. g.* vs. 16-21. Vs. 286 and 316 the Kavijihvâbandhana seems to have taken from one of the recensions. A remarkable instance with regard to the carefulness bestowed on recension H. is evinced by v. 29 being repeated in its supplement with a slight difference at its beginning, viz. ನಿಯುತಂ instead of ನಯುದಂ; ನಿಯುತಂ is the reading of M. (i., 63). The insignificant scholarship displayed in the recension of B. appears, for instance, from its verses regarding the formation of the Kanda. Everybody who takes the trouble of scanning Canarese Kanda verses, will find that the 6th foot of each Hemistich is to be either an Amphibrachys (◡—◡) or a Proceleusmaticus (◡◡◡◡). But the said recension whilst in no less than three verses (283, 287 and another not contained in the text) allowing the use of the Amphibrachys for the 6th place, does not even allude to the essential rule that a Proceleusmaticus may be its substitute. It is true, even Nâgavarma himself seems to have omitted to introduce this special rule, as v. 288 which contains it, cannot be genuine; for it occurs in the supplement of H., from which it has been transferred to the first chapter of M. (and Sb.; see p. 24, note 2, and corrections), and at the same time contains a form of the Na gaṇa that is foreign to Nâgavarma, and is probably a Tĕlugu Indra (=N) gaṇa. Under the impression that Nâgavarma could not have overlooked the rule regarding the Proceleusmaticus, the editor has tried, as No. 258 shows, to find it in v. 283, translating its conclusion as follows: "śaśipura (◡◡◡◡, *i. e.* makharipu), not being at 6 (vishayâdri, *i. e.* if śaśipura does not occur at 6), let purâri (◡—◡) be (there)." Against this translation (adri=meru), however, three objections must be raised, viz.: 1) that śaśipura (čandrapura) is an obscure word scarcely fit for expressing a name of *S*iva; 2) that Nâgavarma would have avoided the license of later writers to use the mutilated form of the Nominative (śaśipura instead of śaśipura*m*); and 3) that śaśipuravishayâdri has a different meaning in v. 287, though there some MSS. read śaśipurabâṇâdri. The reading of the verse ought to have been somewhat different (and it may have been so) to allow the editor's exposition. So the translation of the sentence as it stands is: "at śaśi, pura, vishaya and adri (*i. e.* the odd places) not being (*i. e.* let it not be! But at the even places) let purâri be!" 4) Nâgavarma never uses čaraṇa; verses 318-320, 324, 327, 331, 335, wherein the word occurs, do not belong to the original.

becomes slightly questionable on account of some grammatical irregularities[1]. A peculiarity is that the Ragaḷĕs (254 seq.) appear to be misplaced in the work; for, being not bound (at least for several centuries) to only five Mora-feet, they, as regards their form, ought to have followed the *Aryĕs*; their feet fall under the rules of the later Canarese Shaṭpadis. As to the Ragaḷĕs only v. 254 is original, and it says very little, the words "included within certain feet" in No. 243 being an editorial addition; after it in M. there is the dry remark: "one has to look for them" (in other works?). Concerning both the Ragaḷĕs and the later Shaṭpadis the authors of the rules have neglected to point out the number of feet as well as their different forms; and again none of them has called attention to the circumstance that no true Canarese foot is to begin with an Iambus. The editor, therefore, has supplied the necessary remarks in this respect.

According to verse 22 Nâgavarma took Piṅgala (Piṅgaḷa) as his guide in composing his work, calling it *C*handombudhi (23). This statement by itself leaves it somewhat doubtful whether he meant only the Sa*m*skṛita Piṅgala, or also the so-called Prâkṛita Piṅgala; but he more than probably, to some extent, meant both. It will prove advisable first to show his general plan as stated in his own words. He says there are "three and a half languages (bhâshâ), viz. Sa*m*skṛita, Prâkṛita, Apabhra*m*ša, and Paišâčika," (probably calling the last one "half a language" as being spoken only by barbarous tribes); "the bhâshâjâtis," he proceeds, "that are born of them, are those of all the 56 countries[2], *e.g.* (the countries called) Draviḍa (*i.e.* Tamiḷa)[3], Andhra, and Karṇâṭaka. There (*i.e.* in them, the 56 jâti languages) are the three kinds of Vṛittas, called sama, ardhasama and vishama; there (*i.e.* in them) are the 26 *C*handas', called Uktĕ, etc." If we follow H., the oldest of our recensions, Nâgavarma goes on to say (p. 23, note 2; v. 68): "Apart from them (the twenty-six *C*handas' and their Vṛittas) are the Jâtis (also common to all the countries), to which *e.g.* the Mâlâvṛittas, Daṇḍaka[4], Ragaḷĕ, and mâtrâgaṇaniyama Skandhaka (Kanda) belong[5]. Apart from

1) For instance, in v. 164 occurs ನೆಗಳದ instead of ನೆಗಳ್ದ; in v. 203 ನೆಗಳ್ತೆ is scanned ⏑—⏑ instead of ⏑⏑⏑, see p. 96 ನೆಗಳ್ವಂ = ⏑⏑—; v. 227 has ಅಱುಪಿದ instead of ಅಱುಪಿದಂ.

2) Shaṭpańčâšat sarva vishaya; for shaṭpańčâšat, in later works, generally čappanna is substituted. 3) Draviḍa (Drâviḍa), in South India, only means Tamiḷ; and all other meanings given by Northern writers and their followers to the word are highly perplexing to a Southerner. 4) These two classes are samavṛittas. 5) Ragaḷĕ (Raghaṭĕ) occurs in Tĕlugu as Ragaḍa; a Tĕlugu Daṇḍaka seems to belong to the Mora metres; the Kanda bears the same appellation in that language.

them (the Chandas' and Vṛittas? or the general Jâtis?) again are all those which are born of the languages of Karṇâṭaka, Andhra, Drâviḍa, Varâṭa, Lâṭa, Mâḷava, Gauḷa, Gurjara, Kaḷiṅga, Aṅga, Vaṅga, Keraḷa, Bâhḷika, Magadha, Ceri, Vâčâla, Pañčâla, Veṅgi (different from Andhra!), Tâḷava (Tauḷava?) and other countries; and they form the (particular) Jâtis of the languages of all the countries (sarvavishayabhâshâjâti), and (for Karṇâṭaka) are the following: Madanavati, Akkara, Caupadi, Gîtikĕ, Eḷĕ, Tivadi, Utsâha, Shaṭpadi (*i. e.* Sarashaṭpadi), Akkarikĕ, and Chandovata*m*sa."[1] After this the author states (v. 69, 70): "For each kind (jâti)[2], in a two-fold way, from Uktĕ to Utkṛiti, I will give (thee) instruction. In the two languages thus mentioned[3] (by me) I will hence let thee know concerning (what is common to) the languages etc. of all the countries (sarvavishayabhâshâdi)." Further, after the Ragaḷĕs, in verse 281 he says: "Thus, in this order, in all ways, I have informed thee concerning (what is common to) the languages etc. of all the countries; henceforth learn (also) the mode (anda) of the Kanda!" Then, after the Kanda and the other (Sanscrit) Mora-feet metres, he begins with the prose-heading: "I will (now) state the (particular) Jâti of the Karṇâṭaka country"; and proceeds in verse 296: "I have let (thee) know in full (what is common to) the languages etc. of all the countries; I will (now) relate the mode (anda) of the Karṇâṭaka language."

The above statement appears to say that in the Sa*m*skṛita, Prâkṛita, Apabhra*m*śa and Paiśâčika as well as in all the 56 Jâti languages (*i. e.* daughter-languages) there occur the three chief kinds of Vṛittas; and, as a different class, the Mâlâvṛittas, the Daṇḍaka (Vṛittas), the (mâtrâgaṇa) Ragaḷĕs and the mâtrâgaṇa Kanda, which are Jâtis (that are based on the prosody of the mother-languages, and occur also in all the languages). Different from these two classes are the (particular) Jâtis that have (independently) arisen in the languages of all the countries (and may to some extent occur in them).

So the division of all metres into the two classes: Vṛitta and Jâti,

1) An Ela metre, according to C. P. Brown's Dictionary a carol or catch, is also in Tĕlugu; Tĕlugu possesses also Akkara and Utsâha. 2) Here Jâti as in bhâshâjâti, must denote "kind", and be the same as "anda". 3) The "two-fold way" and the "two languages" seem to be identical; Sa*m*skṛita for the classical language, and Prâkṛita (in a general sense of the word) for all the languages, which, according to former Hindu notions, have arisen from Sa*m*skṛita. Nâgavarma appears to say that verses 72-295 of the text (so far as they are his) belong partly to the Sa*m*skṛita Piṅgala, partly to the so-called Prâkṛita Piṅgala.

that appears in Halâyudha and which had existed even for some time before him, occurs in Nâgavarma; although it is not exactly based on the difference between metres that are formed of syllable-feet and metres that are formed of Moras and Mora-feet (as is the case with Halâyudha, etc.)[1], for also the Mâlâvṛittas and Daṇḍaka vṛittas are counted with the Jâtis. In the secondary prose-paragraph of the text under No. 55 (that with slight differences occurs in MSS. B., D., and Rc.) the term "jâti" can only denote "kind" in a general sense[2].

Comparing the present text of Nâgavarma's work (including the 8 metres peculiar to Rb.: 144, 145, 146, 162, 169, 187, 192, 197) with the Saṃskṛita Chandas of Piṅgala as it lies before us in the 8th volume of Dr. Weber's excellent "Indische Studien," it appears that Nâgavarma's introductory verses 24, 26, 27 and 34 occur, with some modifications, in the first chapter of Piṅgala; instead of the six or seven cases in which according to P. a syllable may be long, N. with certain later writers (*e.g.* Kedârabhaṭṭa, W. 215), takes only five such cases for granted. P.'s general arrangement (with which that of Kedârabhaṭṭa agrees) has been quite inverted by N., P. beginning the profane metres (laukika čhandas) with the Gaṇačhandas, and N. with the Aksharačhandas; N. therefore brings in the Caesura (v. 39) just before the Aksharačhandas, as vs. 40-66 do not belong to the original recension. Further, P. introduces only 21 species of Samavṛittas, but N. 26. P. adduces for his species from gâyatrî to utkṛiti only 87 instances; N. for the very same no less than 136, and including the instances for Uktĕ-Supratishṭhĕ, altogether as many as 156.

The following table showing the numerical difference regarding the Samavṛittas of P. and N. may be acceptable[3]:—

Species.	Number of instances that occur in P.	in N.	in both P. and N.
gâyatrî	1	8	1 (96)
ushṇiḥ	1	11	none
anushṭubh	3	6	3 (111, 112, 113)
bṛihatî	3	9	2 (118, 122)
paṅkti	6	6	4 (126, 127, 128, 131)
trishṭubh	12	15	8 (132, 133, 135, 136, 138-140, 142)
jagatî	19	16	11 (147-152, 158-162)

1) Cf. ps. 22, 23; Weber ps. 288, 289. 2) After Tâḷavṛitta D. has still a Dindĕma vṛitta, called Diṇḍima vṛ. by Rc., and Mattebha (!) by B. 3) The garva, harivara (p. 26), ratânta (p. 27) of H., and the maṅgalikĕ (p. 48) of Rb. are not included.

Species.	Number of instances that occur in P.	in N.	in both P. and N.
atijagatî	6	8	3 (168, 169, 170)
śakvarî	6	5	3 (171, 172, 174)
atiśakvarî	4	6	2 (177, 178)
ashṭi	3	5	none
atyashṭi	7	7	5 (188-191, 193)
dhṛiti	3	4	2 (194, 195)
atidhṛiti	2	4	2 (199, 200)
kṛiti	2	4	none
prakṛiti	2	4	2 (206, 207)
âkṛiti	1	4	1 (211)
vikṛiti	2	3	1 (215)
saṅkṛiti	1	4	1 (218)
abhikṛiti	1	3	1 (221)
utkṛiti	2	4	2 (224, 225)
	87	136	54

Thus N.'s present edition has only 54 Samavṛittas in common with P. Of these 10 bear totally different names in P.'s work[1]; the names of 7 again differ to some extent[2]. A whole class of Samavṛittas, the Mâlâvṛittas, do not occur in P.[3]

Thirty-one of the Samavṛittas that are peculiar to P., are the following:—

1. Kumâralalitâ, ⏑ — ⏑ | ⏑ ⏑ — | — .
2. Hamsaruta, — — — | ⏑ ⏑ ⏑ | — — .
3. Mayûrasâriṇî, — ⏑ — | ⏑ — ⏑ | — ⏑ — | — .
4. Upasthitâ, — — ⏑ | ⏑ — ⏑ | ⏑ — ⏑ | — .
5. Ekarûpa, ⏑ ⏑ — | ⏑ ⏑ — | ⏑ — ⏑ | — .
6. Vâtormî, — — — | — ⏑ ⏑ | — — ⏑ | — — .
7. Vṛintâ, ⏑ ⏑ ⏑ | ⏑ ⏑ ⏑ | ⏑ ⏑ — | — — .
8. *S*yeṇî, — ⏑ — | ⏑ — ⏑ | — ⏑ — | ⏑ — .
9. *C*añčalâkshikâ, ⏑ ⏑ ⏑ | ⏑ ⏑ ⏑ | — ⏑ — | — ⏑ — .
10. Tata, ⏑ ⏑ ⏑ | ⏑ ⏑ ⏑ | — — — | — ⏑ — .
11. Kântotpîḍâ, — ⏑ ⏑ | — — — | ⏑ ⏑ — | — — — .
12. Navamâlinî, ⏑ ⏑ ⏑ | ⏑ — ⏑ | — ⏑ ⏑ | ⏑ — — .
13. Varatanu, ⏑ ⏑ ⏑ | ⏑ — ⏑ | ⏑ — ⏑ | — ⏑ — .
14. Jaladharamâlâ, — — — | — ⏑ ⏑ | ⏑ ⏑ — | — — — .
15. Gaurî, ⏑ ⏑ ⏑ | ⏑ ⏑ ⏑ | — ⏑ — | — ⏑ — .
16. Lalanâ, — ⏑ ⏑ | — — ⏑ | ⏑ ⏑ ⏑ | ⏑ ⏑ — .

1) I state the verses, adding P.'s names: 127, rukmavatî; 131, śuddhavirâj; 142, kuḍmaladantî; 169, kanakaprabhâ; 174, varasundarî; 193, avitatha (kokilaka); 194, vibudhapriyâ; 195, kusumitalatâvellitâ; 199, vismitâ; 206, dhṛitaśrî (śaśivadanâ). 2) 113, 147, 158, 160, 191, 211, 225. 3) The term of mâlâvṛitta does not occur in the St. Petersburg Lexicon.

17. Praharshaṇî,	– – –| ⏑ ⏑ ⏑| ⏑ – ⏑| – ⏑ –| –.
18. Gaurî,	⏑ ⏑ ⏑| ⏑ ⏑ ⏑| ⏑ ⏑ ⏑| ⏑ ⏑ –| –.
19. Kuṭilagati,	⏑ ⏑ ⏑| ⏑ ⏑ ⏑| – – ⏑| – – ⏑| –.
20. Asambâdhâ,	– – –| – – ⏑| ⏑ ⏑ ⏑| ⏑ ⏑ –| – –.
21. Aparâjitâ,	⏑ ⏑ ⏑| ⏑ ⏑ ⏑| – ⏑ –| ⏑ ⏑ –| ⏑ –.
22. Kuṭila,	– – –| – ⏑ ⏑| ⏑ ⏑ ⏑| ⏑ – –| – –.
23. Ṛishabhagajavilasita,	– ⏑ ⏑| – ⏑ –| ⏑ ⏑ ⏑| ⏑ ⏑ ⏑| ⏑ ⏑ ⏑| –.
24. *S*ailaśikhâ,	– ⏑ ⏑| – ⏑ –| ⏑ ⏑ ⏑| – ⏑ ⏑| – ⏑ ⏑| –.
25. Varayuvatî,	– ⏑ ⏑| – ⏑ –| ⏑ – –| ⏑ ⏑ ⏑| ⏑ ⏑ ⏑| –.
26. Va*m*śapatrapatita,	– ⏑ ⏑| – ⏑ –| ⏑ ⏑ ⏑| – ⏑ ⏑| ⏑ ⏑ ⏑| ⏑ –.
27. Atiśâyinî,	⏑ ⏑ –| ⏑ ⏑ –| ⏑ – ⏑| – ⏑ ⏑| ⏑ – ⏑| – –.
28. Vanamâlâ,	⏑ ⏑ ⏑| ⏑ ⏑ ⏑| – ⏑ –| – ⏑ –| – ⏑ –| – ⏑ –.
29. Suvadanâ,	– – –| – ⏑ –| – ⏑ ⏑| ⏑ ⏑ ⏑| ⏑ – –| – ⏑ ⏑| ⏑ –.
30. Vṛitta,	– ⏑ –| ⏑ – ⏑| – ⏑ –| ⏑ – ⏑| – ⏑ –| ⏑ – ⏑| – ⏑.
31. Aśvalalita,	⏑ ⏑ ⏑| ⏑ – ⏑| – ⏑ ⏑| ⏑ – ⏑| – ⏑ ⏑| ⏑ – ⏑| – ⏑ ⏑| ⏑ –.

Regarding the Pauses (yati) in N. it will be readily observed that those of vs. 126, 131-133, 136, 139, 147, 149-151, 158, 159, 206 and 211 do not agree with those pointed out for them by P. Several times the recensions of N. differ from each other with regard to the place of the Caesura (vs. 132-134, 153, 164, 171, 174, 175, 178, 179, 189, 198, 202, 214). Besides yati, N. has usir (breath), virati, virâma, viśrama, viśramaṇa, viśrânta, viśrâma. Where the Caesura is not indicated by him, he, like P., appears to mean that it is at the end of the line. (In Rb. I have met no reference to Caesura).

Dr. Weber's above-mentioned volume enables us also to compare the Samavṛittas of the present text with those contained in the Sanscrit Prosody, called Vṛittaratnâkara, by Kedârabhaṭṭa who lived before the 13th century, but after Halâyudha, who, as it appears, wrote his commentary on Piṅgala, the Mṛitasañjîvinî, towards the end of the 10th century (W. 184, 193, 206, 417). Sixteen Vṛittas that do not occur in P., but in Nâgavarma, and the Vṛittaratnâkara though partly bearing different names, are the following:—

1. Vičitra (95, also in H.), Kedâra's Somarâjî
2. Kumuda (97, also in H.), K.'s Ramaṇî
3. Mukuḷa (98, also in H.)
4. Madhumati (Sulabha in M., 108; not in H., but M. and Rb.)
5. Bhadraka (120, also in H.), K.'s Bhadrikâ
6. Maṇiraṅga (130, also in H.), K.'s Maṇirâga
7. *C*andrikĕ (137, also in H.), K.'s Bhadrikâ
8. Mâṇikya (141, not in H., but M.), K.'s *C*aikarûpa
9. Sumukhi (144, only in Rb.)
10. *S*rî (146, only in Rb.)
11. Nirupama (153, not in H., but M.), K.'s Priya*m*vadâ
12. Lalitapada (155, also in H.), K.'s Abhinavatâmarasa
13. *C*andrikĕ (156, not in H., but M.), K.'s *C*andravartman
14. Sukesara (Suraṅgakesara, 181, also in H.)
15. Jagadvandita (184, also in H.), K.'s Khagati
16. Pañčačâmara (187, only in Rb.)

From this list it seems to become certain that there is a very close connection between the Vṛittaratnâkara and the recension Rb.; see Nos. 4, 9, 10, 16; cf. verse 169; but three of its instances (145, 192, 197) are neither in Piṅgala nor Kedâra. M. has four forms of its own, Nos. 4, 8, 11, 13, that are in K.; but the names do not agree at all, except in some measure in No. 13; but cf. p. 54, No. 181. Recension H., in company with the others, shows nine forms of K., Nos. 1, 2, 3, 5, 6, 7, 12, 14, 15; but only four of them (3, 5, 6, 14) bear the same appellations.

About further differences in names and form it is to be remarked that there occurs a Hamsamâlĕ (110) for Ushṇih also in K., but its form is somewhat at variance (⏑⏑– | –⏑– | –); Mandânila (127) is Piṅgala's Rukmavatî, K.'s Campakamâlâ; Sândrapada (only in M., 142) is P.'s Kuḍmaladantî, K.'s Sândrapada, etc.; the Drutapada (154) has a somewhat different shape with K. (⏑⏑⏑ | –⏑⏑ | ⏑⏑⏑ | ⏑––); Mañjubhâshiṇi (-bhûshiṇi, 169) is P.'s Kanakaprabhâ, K.'s Mañjubhâshiṇî; Vanamayûra (174) is P.'s Varasundarî, K.'s Induvadanâ; Kanakâbjanîya (193) or Narkuṭaka (only in M., No. 181) is P.'s Avitatha or Kokilaka, K.'s Narkuṭaka; and Meghavisphûrjita (199) is P.'s Vismitâ, K.'s Meghavisphûrjita. How are such differences to be accounted for, side by side with the coincidences? Two remarkable circumstances, in this respect, are still to be taken notice of; the first is that K.'s Campakamâlĕ is N.'s Mandânila (127), whereas in Canarese the so common Campakamâlĕ (206, 230) is called by P. the Dhṛitaśrî (by others Pañčakâvaḷî, etc.), and is not in K.; the second is that another Vṛitta celebrated in Canarese, the Mahâsragdharĕ (210, 230)[1], is neither in P., nor in K. (although it is in recension Rb,). The Southerners seem to have worked with some independence.

The Drutapada of Nâgavarma (154) which, as has been remarked, is somewhat different from that of Kedâra, is indentical with the Drutapada of Varâhamihira (who lived from 505-587 A. D.)[2]; and further, N.'s Lalitapada (155) which is called Abhinavatâmarasa with K., bears the same name in Varâhamihira's Bṛihatsamhitâ. But then N.'s Candrikĕ (137) which is K.'s Bhadrikâ, is called Prasabha by Varâhamihira.

---

1) There is no Mahâsragdharâ in the St. Petersburg Sanscrit Lexicon. The Mahâsragdharâ has been employed in the Canarese čandraprabha, *e. g.* vi., 66, a Jaina composition of 1189 A. D.; and it is not an invention of Nâgavarma, as he *e. g.* in his Kâvyâvalokana (v., 84) cites a verse composed in it. The beginning of that verse is cited also in *S*abdamaṇidarpaṇa (Mangalore edition) p. 377 (ಶರವೇಯೊಳ್ etc.). Also the Abhinava Pampa Râmâyaṇa has the Mahâsragdharâ.

2) J. R. A. S., N. S., ii., 1, p. 407.

Continuing the comparison between the Saṃskṛita Piṅgala and Nâgavarma, it is found that of the Ardhasama vṛittas in P. none occurs in N., and that of the Vishama vṛittas in N. the Tripadonnati is not in P.

P.'s work is composed in short prose-sentences, the bulk of that of N. in verse. Where N. teaches the formation of a metre, he gives the verse the form of the metre in question. This peculiarity occurs also in the Vṛittaratnâkara (W. 207), in the commentary on Varâhamihira's Bṛihatsaṃhitâ by Bhaṭṭotpala who belongs to the 10th century[1], and in the Srutabodha by a Kâlidâsa[2]. N. employs, as has been stated above, various Alliterations, a circumstance that perhaps may be significant regarding his age, as the use of Alliterations has been considered to be a characteristic of later (Sanscrit) works[3]; all the Canarese works which N. quotes in one of his treatises, the Kâvyâvalokana, however, show at least the simple Alliterations; and the culture of Alliterations first for distinctly marking out the verse-lines and then also for giving pleasure to the ear, originally may have taken place in a conspicuous manner in the South. Of the licence of writers on Prosody later than Piṅgala, *e. g.* of Prâkṛita Piṅgala, Kedârabhaṭṭa, and Dâmodara (the source of whose work, called Vâṇîbhûshaṇa, is the Prâkṛita Piṅgala, and a certain copy in MS. of whose work dates either from 1633 or 1555 A. D.)[4], in allowing a short consonant to remain short before a double consonant the second part of which is a Repha (W. 224 seq.), nothing is found in Nâgavarma's original[5].

Nâgavarma, like Piṅgala, uses the syllables ma, ya, ra, sa, ta, ja, bha, na for the eight syllable-feet; but he goes further, giving each syllable-foot a peculiar name. In the present text the Molossus (– – –) is the earth (urvi, kshoṇi, kshmĕ, dharaṇi, dharĕ, dhâtri, bhû, bhûmi); the Bacchicus (⏑ – –) water (ambu, kuša, jala, toya, payas, salila); the Amphimacrus (– ⏑ –) fire (agni, anala, kṛišânu, jâtaveda, jâtavedas,

1) St. Petersburg Lexicon; J. R. A. S., N. S., ii., 1, 410. Weber 203, 205, 207. 2) Weber 166, 216; Colebrooke, p. 392. 3) Weber 201, 391. 4) The St. Petersburg Lexicon, s. v. Râghavadeva, states that Râghavadeva was the father of Dâmodara and the grandfather of *S*ârṅgadhara. Is this Damodara the author of the Vâṇîbhûshaṇa? *S*ârṅgadhara lived 1363 A. D.; Ind. Ant. i., 250, note. 4) The licence is met also in Tĕlugu; see the instances in Mr. Brown's grammar. The rules regarding Canarese sithilas, *i. e.* fleeting consonants, the observation of which appears in N.'s verses, are of a quite different character; see *S*abdamaṇidarpaṇa, rule 86 seq. This grammar, however, in rules 59, 60, acknowledges that in prosody some make use of the mentioned objectionable licence regarding the Repha; and with Canarese writers of the latest period it is not uncommon; in the period just preceding it the Repha was very often elided, *e. g.* prabhu became pabu; prauḍha, pauḍa. A curious word is pavâḍa with the Liṅgâitas (also in Tĕlugu), denoting a wonderful act done by a Jaṅgama to convince others of the truth of his tenets; it probably is pravrâḍ (pravrâj).

jvalana, jvâlĕ, teja, pâdapâšana, pâvaka, marudishṭa, mâruteshṭa, vahni, vaišvânara, šikhi, hutavaha, hutâšana); the Anapaestus (◡◡—) wind (anila, pavana, pavamâna, marut, maruta, mâruta, vâta, vâyu, švasana, samîraṇa); the Antibacchicus (——◡) the sky (ambara, âkâša, gagana, viyat, vyoma); the Amphibrachys (◡—◡) the sun (ambujamitra, arka, âditya, ina, kumudâri, kharakara, dinapa, dinâdhipa, divâkara, bhânu, bhâskara, ravi, saroruhamitra, sûrya); the Dactylus (—◡◡) the moon (abjâri, indu, kokanadavairi, čandra, vârijaripu, vidhu, šaši, šîtakara, sarojaripu, soma, himakṛit); and the Tribrachys (◡◡◡) heaven, a deity and Indra (aditijapura, animisha, amara, indra, indranilaya, indrapura, kuliša, kulišadhara, tridaša, diva, divija, divijapura, deva, devâdhipapura, nagahara, nâka, pura, šatamakha, sura, surapa, surapura, svarga). Regarding the term of Gaṇa that in the Saṁskṛita Piṅgala is restricted to the five Mora-feet, it is to be said that Nâgavarma, with Halâyudha (W. 335, 414, 415), uses it also for the syllable-feet; and, with the Prâkṛita Piṅgala (W. 291), also for all possible Mora-feet.

Besides N., like P., denotes long syllables by the syllable ga, or by the terms guru, četojâta, dîrghá, the Canarese binpu, vakra, and the Canarese kŏṅku; and short syllables by the syllable la, or by the terms laghu and the Canarese say (sayka, sayta, saytu, saypa).[1] But he calls long syllables also by the names of Rudra (aṅgajanmântaka, indudhara, îša, îšâna, îšvara, kapardi, kâmapradhvaṁsi, kâmahara, kâmântaka, čandradhara, triyambaka, deva, nîlakaṇṭha, puramathana, bhava, bhûtagaṇeša, madanahara, mârahara, rudra, šarva, somešvara, hara, himâṁšušekhara); and short ones by the names of Vishṇu (daityâri, murântaka, vaikuṇṭha, hari).

N. using a crooked perpendicular line (kŏṅku gĕrĕ, vakra) as the sign for a long syllable, and a straight perpendicular line (saytu gĕrĕ) as that for a short one, is a circumstance previously met with in the Prâkṛita Piṅgala and Vṛittaratnâkara (W. 215, 427).

N. agrees with P. in employing certain words to express numerical values; but a list of those used in our text (not excluding the spurious verses) will show a considerable difference[2]:—

1) Nija (=short) in vs. 42, 48 is spurious.

2) It will not be without interest to compare the list of Nijaguṇa yogi's Vivekačintâmaṇi, under the heading of gaṇitasajňĕ: 1. rûpa (P.), bhûmi, čandra. 2. yugma, yugaḷa, yuga, bâhu, pâda, paksha, nayana. 3. haranayana, agni, pura, vararatna. 4. kashâya, veda (P.), varṇa, âšrama, samudra (P.). 5. haravaktra, vrata, indriya (P.), bâṇa, vishaya, pâṇḍava, bhûta (P.). 6. ṛitu (P.), rasa (P.), skandha, mukha, vedâṅga, karma, varṇa, daršana, artha. 7. muni, giri, râjyâṅga, turaga, dhâtu, sabhâṅga, svara (P.), sâgara. 8. vasu (P.), diggaja, mada, karma. 9. randhra, nidhi, rasa, graha, ratha, bhakti. 0. bindu, šûnya, nâsti, anusvâra, gagana, pûrṇa. Herewith concludes the list.

1. khačara, garuḍa, pannagarâja, bhujaga, mṛigadhara, śaśi, sura

2. kara

3. pura, vahni, śikhibraja

4. ambudhi (P.'s samudra), ambunidhi, jalanidhi, yuga, vârdhi, śaradhi

5. kâmabâṇa, kâmâstra, bâṇa, bhûta (P.), vishaya

6. ṛitu (P.), kara, khara, rasa (P.)

7. agendra, adri, kulagiri, giri, turagavrâta, dineśahaya, naga, muni (P.'s ṛishi), yati (?), śaila, hayatati, hayanikara, hayavrâta

8. âśâgaja, kari, gaja, gajavraja, gajavrâta, danti, dikkari, digdanti, diś[1]), diśâkari, diśâgaja, diśĕ, nâga, madagaja, vasu (P.), hari

9. nidhi, randhra

0. ambara

11. rudra (P.), hara[2])

12. arka (P.'s âditya), dinakara, dinanâtha, dinapa, dineśa, divasakara, divasâdhipa, padminîmitra, bhânu, bhâskara, mârtaṇḍa, ravi, vidyâdhara

14. manu

15. paksha

16. dharaṇîśvara, mahîśvara, râja

20. râvaṇakara

Nâgavarma has the old significations for a verse-quarter: pada, pâda (with Piṅgala: pâda, iv., 10), in Canarese aḍi. Caraṇa and aṅghri, that are used by Kedâra to denote the same (W. 328), occur only in spurious verses. A Mora is called mâtrĕ by N.[3]); the name "kalĕ" used by Kedâra (W. 309), is not used by him.

It has been stated above as a peculiarity of N. that he gives names to the eight syllable-feet (aksharagaṇa); again differing from P. he calls the five Mora-feet (mâtrâgaṇa): giriša*m*, dhûrjaṭi, šarva*m*, purâri, makharipu[4]), these forms of Siva's names expressing at the same time the forms of the feet. (The foot na=⏑⏑⏑⏑, in v. 288, is not genuine).

1) In Piṅgala it denotes 10. 2) Bhaṭṭotpala has also Madanahara, W. 205.

3) The mentioning of mâtrĕs in the spurious verse 53 (Rc., B.) is inopportune. 4) Purâri does not occur in Halâyudha's Abhidhânaratnamâlâ, which Nâgavarma used for composing a Nighaṇṭu; but it occurs in the Trikâṇḍaśesha, a supplement to the Amarakosha, by Purushottama; makharipu is not with Halâyudha, and does not occur in the St. Petersburg Lexicon.

Such are the comparisons that chiefly suggest themselves with regard to the Saṁskṛita Piṅgala and Nâgavarma. It would be interesting to minutely compare also the so-called Prâkṛita Piṅgala, as some of the peculiarities of N. may possibly be found in it; but the editor is unable to adduce more than a few points. Dr. Weber[1] says that the Prâkṛita Piṅgala is a much later work than the Saṁskṛita P., and that its sûtras are composed in verse, and contain a great number of new *termini technici*. In it, as in Nâgavarma, the term "gaṇa" has a more general meaning; the Amphibrachys (⏑–⏑) is called ja and payodhara, a term that however is not in N.; and the âryâgîti bears the name of skandhaka, a circumstance that is met with also in N., his Kanda (a tadbhava of skandhaka) being the âryâgîti[2]. Mr. Colebrooke, in his article on Sanscrit and Pracrit Poetry (p. 412 seq.), remarks that besides the Jâti metres that are noticed in treatises on Sanscrit prosody, other kinds belonging to the class of metres regulated by quantity are specified by writers on Pracrit prosody. As instances of such metres he mentions the Dohâ, Gâhâ (gâthâ), Mahârâshṭra, Rola, Shaṭpadika, and others; but though as to names the Duvayi (295)[3], Gâdĕ (253) and Shaṭpadi of the present text may be compared, none of them appears to coincide as to form with any instances in Nâgavarma.

Nâgavarma knows only one kind of true Canarese metres: the devâkshara-feet metres[4], as he classes the Raghaṭĕ (Ragaḷĕ) with the Jâtis that are common to all the countries. He adduces two Samavṛittas (308, 309) among them, but theoretically their feet belong to the Canarese Mora-class. The Ragaḷĕs (a sort of Dvipada) are built on exactly the same principle as the later Shaṭpadis (318 seq.), that

1) Ps. 202, 203, 291, 295, 304. 2) As the skandhaka (or skandha, for the Canarese tadbhava is kanda) that is very common with Nâgavarma, is borrowed from the Prâkṛita Piṅgaḷa (W. 295) and was known to Varâhamihira (505-587 A. D., W. 294, 304), the beginning of the composition of the Prâkṛita Piṅgaḷa may have taken place in the 5th century. It is necessary to note this with regard to the Canarese works preceding Nâgavarma's, as also in them the kanda is frequently used, as one learns from the quotations in N. About the use of the âryâ-metre at a certain period (with *Â*ryabhaṭṭa, who was born 476 A. D., Varâhamihira, etc.) see W. 209. 3) Regarding the Duvayi's scheme as represented by verse 295, it has been omitted to adduce it in the text; it is as follows: ⏑⏑⏑⏑⏑⏑*⏑⏑⏑⏑ | – – | ⏑⏑– | ⏑⏑– | ⏑–⏑ | – ‖ ⏑⏑⏑⏑–*⏑⏑⏑⏑ | ⏑⏑– | ⏑–⏑ | – – | ⏑–⏑ | –. It would appear as if the foot preceding the long syllable in the end, were to be the purâri, a circumstance that would affect also the form of the scheme under v. 293. 4) This name is founded on v. 340 where N. says he has told the employment of the devâksharas.

nowadays are the commonest metres, but were unknown to N.; they contain a certain number of Moras, from three to five, in a certain number of feet that bear no particular name and may vary in form. The devâkshara-feet metres (296 seq.), however, are based on feet that, like the Saṃskṛita Mora-feet with N., have names which show the forms of the feet to be used, and form three classes. Regarding the employment of these feet to some degree a striking uncertainty exists, as the number of Moras, whether for the verse-lines or the whole verses, is not mentioned (cf. p. 97, note)[1]. To throw some light on the state of lexicography in South India at Nâgavarma's time[2] the three classes with their respective name-feet are quoted alphabetically—

I. Class: aja, jalasambhava, padmabhava, bisaruhajanma, bisaruhodbhava, brahma, vanajasambhava, sarasijabhava.

II. Class: adhokshaja, upendra, jaḷaruhodara, pŏḍĕ alara, madanapitṛi, mandaradhara, vanaruhodara, vishṇu, sarajijodara, hari.

III. Class: îśvara, kandarparipu, kâmântaka, kâmâri, bhujagapaksha, madanahara, rudra, śaṅkara, hara.

The name-feet are of:—

the first class: ajanĕ, dhâtṛi, nâki, bŏmmam, brahmâ, surapam;

the second class: kamsâri, govindam, narakâri, nâkigam, parahitam, muraripu, murahara, śrîpati, hṛidayeśam.

the third class: kandarpâri, kâmaripu, kâmântakam, gaṅgâdhîśam, girijâkântam, girijânâtham, čandramauḷi, trijagadguru, nîlakaṇṭham, puramathanam, pramathâdhipam, bhujagadhâri, bhûtâgraṇi, madanadhvamsi, madanaripu, vṛishabhalakshyam, śûladharam.

There remains still a word to be said about Chapter 6, containing the six Pratyayas. Nâgavarma introduces them with the words "hence I will nicely explain to thee, as well as I can, the six pratyayas." As the aphoristical text is rather corrupt, various different readings have been adduced. Recension M. (K.) introduces the pratyayas with the following šloka: prastâro nashṭamuddishṭameka-dvy-âdi-la-ga-kriyâ | saṅkhyânamadhvayogaš ča shaṭ-pratyayamiti smṛitaḥ ||. It can scarcely be doubted that this verse has been taken from Kedâra, the only difference between this verse and one in K. being that K.'s verse

1) Regarding the Madanavati, however, the number of Moras of which is certain enough, a verse is added in H., Ra. and M., stating to an inquirer that in this case there are 22 Moras; the metre of the corrupt verse looks somewhat like the Tripadi: ಗಣನಿಯಮಂಗಳ * ಗಣಿತಮೆ ನಲ್ಕಿದೆ | ಗಣಿತಮಿಪ್ಪದಿಪ್ಪತ್ತೆರಡು ಮಾತ್ರೆಗಳಕ್ಕುಂ | ಗುಣಯುತೆ ಮದನವತಿಗೆಂದುಂ. ||

2) Cf. the list of proper names for the long and short syllables, above p. xiv.

concludes "pratyayâ*h* shaṭ prakîrtitâ*h*" (W. 426). See also the remark on H.'s 6th Chapter above in p. v.

The following literal translation of Nâgavarma's traditional Genealogy is offered, as met with in MSS. L., M., Sb., and Sc. that as to age may form the second recension: "The Veṅgi country (said to be now the Northern Circars, but not identical with Andhra, see above p. viii.) was conspicuous as being a surpassing one in the world; and in the seven grâmas that are as if countless in that country, was (*or* is) the charming Veṅgipaḷu (*or* Veṅginagara). Vĕṇṇamayya, an equal of Vibhudeva, a clever man, was conspicuous in this world like Ambujabhava, always like a treasure of good qualities. Pĕṇṇamayya, a man of pure qualities, was as conspicuous as skilful....(He, Pĕṇṇamayya)....excelled Cupid in beauty, bore the form of Ambusambhava, and was a man of good conduct in the Kauṇḍiṇya gotra. For that vipra of extensive renown, for the dvijanma who was the beloved son of that man, there was a good wife who surpassed the virtuous Arundhatî; her name was Kauṇḍi kabbĕ. When to that Kauṇḍi kabbĕ and Vĕṇṇamayya who was conspicuous as a mine of glory, Dâmamayya was born in Cupid's form, he (Dâmamayya) being praised by the world became conspicuous. His (Dâmamayya's) modest wife abounding in world-famed good qualities, possessing a charming form, in every respect surpassed even Girijâtâ; her name was Kunda kabbĕ. To Kunda kabbĕ who was conspicuous in the said manner, and to Dâmamayya who was called a man of blameless qualities, the firstborn son was Vĕṇṇamayya, a person of world-praised renown, honoured by the dvijas, one of Manu's road. He (Vĕṇṇamayya) was conspicuous as gifted with perfect qualities, being called lord of *S*rîkântâ, a knower of all elegant arts (sakalakalâkovida), an unparalleled person, one of incomparable conduct, versed in the laukika and vaidika šâstras, and a man of many letters (anekâkshara). The wife of Vĕṇṇamayya who was called as stated, possessed good qualities, and shone as filled with such a devotion for her husband that she surpassed so to say even Dharaṇisutâ; her name was Poḷa (*or* Poti) kabbĕ. To that Poḷakabbĕ and Vĕṇṇamayya who was called a man advanced in science, the firstborn son became Nâgavarma who was gifted with the qualities of the poetrygem of Vâkšrîpati."

This our Nâgavarma is further called Kavirâjaha*m*sa in verses 1, 3, 16, (182, 194, 203, 222, ha*m*sa. 292,) 347. The numbers in brackets are to indicate that in those verses there exists some uncertainty as to whom the epithet is applied; and this circumstance leads us to an investigation into the meaning of the above-mentioned ambiguous terms of Nâki, Nâkiga and Pinâki.[1]

In page 96, according to H. and Ra., Nâki is a name of Brahmâ[2]; and Nâkiga one of Vishṇu; but according to recension M. Nâkiga is also identical with Nâgavarma, for it says in its reading of v. 22: "The prosody which Indudhara told to Umĕ, having been spread about on earth by Piṅgala, Nâkiga (Nâgavarma according to B. and Sa.) uttered the mode he learned from that čhandomburâśi (*i. e.* Piṅgala's work) to his own wife[3]."

In the text of the metres it is said that svâgata (139) is Nâkiga's (B., H., M.); lalitapada (155) is Nâkiga's (B., H.); ačyuta (164) is Nâkiga's (B., H., M.); jagadvandita (184) has been spread about by Nâkiga (B., H., M.); ha*m*sagati (214) is Nâkiga's (B., H., M.); tanvi (218) is Nâkiga's (B., M., Rc.); and the pure Canarese metre piri akkara (302) is of Nâkiga (H., M.). It might be inferred from this that all the said metres had been invented by Nâgavarma; but that would be wrong, as svâgata and tanvi belong to the Sa*m*skṛita Piṅgala. Nâkiga in these instances, however, cannot be meant for Vishṇu, but only for Nâgavarma[4].

His name, therefore, is also directly mentioned in some vṛittas; thus vanaja (121) is of Nâgavarma (B., H., M.); kusumâṅghripa (173) came from N. (B., H., M.); taraḷa (198) was invented (nirmita) by N. kavîndra (H., M.); and mattebhavikrîḍita (202) is N.'s (H., M.). Not one of these metres is in the Sa*m*skṛita Piṅgala. Nâgavarma, further, teaches the number of the vṛittas (222); and "he gifted with excellent qualities" (guṇâgraṇi) thė raghaṭâprabandha (254).

---

1) Nâki, a deity, occurs in the Abhidhânačintâmaṇi of Hemačandra who died 1172 A. D., and the Bhâgavatapurâṇa (7, 8, 36); but is not in Halâyudha's kosha. Nâkiga is neither in Halâyudha nor in the St. Petersburg Lexicon. According to the Canarese Gaṇasahasranâma (of about 1800 A. D.) Nâki is an epithet of *S*iva (2, 70). With regard to Dr. Burnell's interesting account of the Mṛityulâṅgala Upanishad in Ind. Ant. ii., 266 I remark that lâṅguli (perhaps another form of lâṅgali) is a name of *S*iva according to the same work (4, 2).

2) This appears further from a Kanda verse supplementary to the Utsâha (v. 339) which occurs in H. and Ra. at the end of ch. 5, and in which Nâki is explained to mean Aja gaṇa: ಮೃದುಮಧುರಮೆನಿಸುವೃತ್ತ್ವ | ಹದಂ ಧರೆಗೆ ನಾಕಿಯೆಂಬಜಗಣದಿಂದಂ || ಪ್ರದದಬಳೆ ಕಡೆಗೆ ಗುರು ಟೆ | ಲ್ವೊದವಿರೆ ಲಕ್ಷಣನಿಯುಕ್ತಮೆನೆ ಪೆಸರ್ವಡೆಗುಂ. ||

3) This verse appears in recension H. where it is the first verse of the work, in the following form: "Hear, my dear (wife), I am going to relate to thee that mode which the deva (*i. e.* śiva) told the devî, and which Piṅgala heard and told the ṛishis."

4) According to the rather arbitrary different readings of B. Nâkiga (and Nâki) occur also in some other metres. Nâkiga must have been a current term at Nâgavarma's time, for it occurs in v. 187 of the nânarthakâṇḍa of his vastukosha; but the verse is unfortunately quite corrupt in our copy.

N â k i occurs as genuine perhaps four times in the vṛittas: upendravajra (133) is in the manner which P i n â k i and Nâki stated (B., H., M.); šâlini (140) is Nâki's (H.); bhujaṅgaprayâta (149) is renowned like Nâki (B., M.)[1]; and nirupama (153) is unparalleled like Nâki (M.)[2]. Nirupama is not in the Saṁskṛita P. As Pinâki, *i. e. S*iva, and Nâki here occur as different in one and the same sentence, as above Indudhara and Nâkiga (Nâgavarma), it becomes probable that N â k i too stands for Nâgavarma.

In the rućira (163) that is in P., it is said that it is well ascertained by the way that was told by P i n â k i, *i. e. S*iva, to Girijĕ (B., H.) or Umĕ (M.) P i n â k i may perhaps be meant by the K a v i r â j a h a *m* s a of the verses that above, in connection with this term, appear in brackets; the metres of the verses, however, are n o t in the Sa*m*skṛita P.

K a v î š v a r a, k a v î n d r a, p r a b h u k a v î n d r a occur in vs. 147, 224, 252. It is a little dubious who is meant; but from v. 27 as well, which is genuine, and states that N â g a v a r m a k a v î n d r a, the s a y y a ḍ i (*i. e.* straight foot), taught the long and short syllables, as from v. 198 according to which the taraḷa was invented by N â g a v a r m a k a v î n d r a, it seems to follow that the terms in all the cases refer to Nâgavarma. S a y y a ḍ i occurs again in the indrava*m*ša (151, H., M.), the Canarese form of which was made by him.[3]

Two of such not unfrequent but strange v e r s e s t h a t p r a i s e t h e a u t h o r o f t h e v e r y w o r k in which they occur, are seen also in the course of N.'s prosody. The reading of the one (246) is quite unsettled; the other (249) says: "Possessed of excellent speech, born of the great lineage of *S* a t a p a t r o d b h a v a (*i. e.* Brahmâ), an ornament to the multitude of clever poets, unlimited in the appearance of good qualities (g u ṇ o d a y o d d â m a), parallel in understanding to *C*aturânana and Indra (H.; parallel to *C*aturânana, Indra and Vishṇu, B.) is N â g a v a r m a, unparalleled". A translation of the last verse of the work (347) is: "May this land that irradiates the sky and (its) margin, and the king (bhûmipa) be happily united for ever! May the land thrive! May Yama who plucks up the sole of (man's) foot, and adversity keep back! May the greatness of Nâgavarma's poetry become full by this *C*handas! May the meaning (mata) of the K a v i r â j a h a *m* s a be spread on earth!"

Verse 249 confirms the statement in the genealogy of recension M. that N â g a v a r m a was a B r â h m a ṇ a by birth; and verse 347 states that he

1) Ro. has Nâkiga. 2) Nâkiga in B. 3) Of the mandâkrânta (188) that is in P., it is said that it had become celebrated in the world by Kandarpa (Cupid; H., M.), *i. e.* probably by Nâgavarma who was like Cupid.

lived under a king, probably of Veṅgi, to which N. is stated to have belonged, and which was counted by him (according to H.) as one of the 56 countries still at the time when he wrote[1]. This land was once ruled by the Pallavas, probably a so-called Draviḍa race[2]. Their kingdom was called Veṅgîrâshṭra, and their capital was Veṅgîpura or Kaliṅganagara[3]. To the, strange to say, Sanscrit names of the (Jaina) rulers invariably the epithet "Varma" is added (cf. our Nâgavarma)[4]. A. D. 777 their dynasty was to some extent still extant; at that time Kuṇḍavvĕ (mother Kuṇḍĕ), daughter of the Pallava king, erected a Jaina temple in the north of *S*rîpura[5]. However 605 A.D. the *C*âlukya Vishṇu Vardhana II. had conquered the capital Veṅgîpura and founded the Râjamahendra dynasty[6]; and after 680 A. D. the *C*âlukya ruler of Kalyâṇapura on the Tuṅgabhadra, Vinayâditya, a relation of the Râjamahendra line, smote one of the Pallava râjas, as did also a king of the Kŏṅgu or *C*era dynasty[7]. About 1000 A. D. the kingdom Veṅgi passed to (the *S*aiva) Râjendra *C*oḷa, the then dominant sovereign of Southern India. A. D. 1175 Veṅgi vishaya had fallen under the sway of the Kâkateya dynasty of Ŏruṅgal[8]; Veṅgipaḷu has become a small hamlet.

Nâgavarma's *C*handas, especially in its present different recensions, is unfit to prove the religious notions of its author. From certain maṅgaḷa or nândi verses at the beginning of recensions B. and M., to which *e.g.* also verses 1-3 of the present text belong, it might be concluded he was a *S*aiva; but they are spurious, as none of them occurs in H., and only one of them, an invocation of Sarasvatî, is in Rc. But there are genuine passages enough to lead one of the present day to think that Nâgavarma was a follower of *S*iva. With Nâgavarma the term "deva," the originator of prosody according to H., denotes Rudra, and his wife devî is Umâ[9]. He calls a long syllable Rudra or deva, and a short one Hari; again he calls all Canarese feet that are long in form,

---

1) See above, p. viii. 2) Pallava may be another form of pŏllava or pŏlĕya *i. e.* a low man; cf. the Tĕlugu pallĕ, rustic, rude, low; paluva, wretched, vile. 3) Kaliṅga may be connected with kal, a stone. Oḍra, Uḍra (*i. e.* Orissa) means "of breakers"; ŏḍḍara desa the country of (the stone-) breakers; ŏḍḍa belongs to root: uḍ, ŏḍ, to break, the r in the word being the sign of the plural. The ŏḍḍa people (nom. pl. ŏḍḍar, gen. ŏḍḍara) are well-known tank-diggers that speak Tĕlugu. In Veṅgi probably the vowel e has originally been short.

4) Ind. Ant. iii., 152. 5) Ind. Ant. ii., 155 seq. 6) J. R. A. S., N. S., 2, 1, p. 253, 254; cf. Ind. Ant. i., 348. 7) Ind. Ant. ii., 156. 8) J. R. A. S., N. S., 2, 1, p. 252. 9) See above, p. xix., xx. Cf. Piṅgala's first, perhaps spurious verse, according to which Piṅgala obtains the prasâda of *S*iva.

Rudra; those of middle size Vishṇu; and the shortest Brahmâ; and lastly he gives names of Rudra to all the Sanscrit Mora-feet.[1] However as further on it will become quite certain that N. was a staunch Jaina, he in his prosody has simply hidden his convictions on account of the *S*aiva views, as it would appear, of the ruling dynasty; and not only that, but he has also flattered his king by adopting the above-mentioned course. For himself, nevertheless, he has made playthings of the deities; and must have laughed in his sleeve when using such convenient, but absurd phrases. It is interesting to observe that at Nâgavarma's time Vishṇu was condemned to be a short syllable, etc.; as it shows that the jealousy between *S*aivas and Vaishṇavas had already become notorious. In recension M. the concluding paragraphs of each chapter contain the words "the lotus-feet of śrîmad bhagavad arhat parameśvara," in which the "arhat" may possibly still point to a Jaina author.

By Mr. C. P. Brown's Tĕlugu Grammar of 1857, p. 295-322, we are enabled to throw a gleam of light on Nâgavarma's prosody. According to that work Tĕlugu Prosody comprises uniform metres (N.'s aksharačhandas) and changing metres (N.'s karṇâṭa mâ trâgaṇačhandas).

In the first there are used the 8 Sanscrit feet denoted by the letters Ma, Ya, etc., and the letters La (short) and Ga (long). Also Mahâsragdharĕ occurs among the uniform metres, of which a Ha*m*sayâna (seven trochees and a long syllable) is remarkable. N.'s Mallikâmâlĕ is called Mattakokila; and his Vanamañjari is Tĕlugu Mânini. Tĕlugu Taraḷa has its Caesura at 11, N.'s at 8; and in several other vṛittas the Caesura is different. Tĕlugu uses also the Kanda; "it is the metre employed by Nannayya bhaṭṭa in his *C*intâmaṇi, or treatise on Tĕlugu grammar"[2].

Regarding the changing metres or Upajâ ti metres Mr. Brown remarks that they originate in the Kannaḍa language. They comprise six Indra feet (⏑⏑⏑⏑;—⏑⏑; ⏑⏑⏑—; ⏑⏑—⏑;—⏑—;——⏑); two Sûrya feet (⏑⏑⏑;—⏑); and six *C*andra feet which are formed by adding a syllable

1) In his dictionary, the Vastukosha, Nâgavarma puts Rudra and his synonyms before Vishṇu and his, as Halâyudha had done before him in his Abhidhânaratnamâlâ. Professor Aufrecht says regarding Halâyudha's Kosha, p. v., that "he uses many artificial metres, which no other lexicographer has taken the liberty of employing for such a dry subject as a string of synonyms." But Nâgavarma has done exactly the same, using *e.g.* the mâlinî, indravajra, upendravajra, mandâkrânta, mahâsragdharâ, kanda, trivadi and akkara.

2) According to Brown's Dictionary, preface, p. x., he wrote about 1130 A. D.

to any Indra foot, and are used only in the Akkaras. (Did the Tĕlugu Vaishṇavas perhaps disagree about the Rudra gaṇas?)

Changing metres are 1) the Gîtis, viz. the Âṭa (first line 3. 3. 3 * 5. 5, second line 3. 3. 3. * 3. 3),[1] and the Teṭa (all the lines 3. 4. 5 * 3. 3); 2) the Sîsa; 3) the Dvipada (generally each line 5. 4 * 5. 3); 4) the Layas, viz. *e.g.* the Layagrâhi, or v. 276 of the present text; and the Layavibhâti, that is the Layagrâhi with its 39 Moras, but all its longs, except the two last, are resolved into two shorts each; 5) the Ragaḍa, N.'s Raghaṭâ; the names, however, for the instances are different; 6) the (mâtrâ?) Daṇḍaka or blank verse in a measured prose (six lines, each of which appears as ‒‒⏑.‒‒⏑.‒‒⏑.‒‒⏑); 7) the Taruvaja, an extension of the Dvipada, two Dvipada lines forming one Taruvaja line; 8) the Utsâha, or v. 339 of our text; 9) the Akkaras.

With regard to the Taruvaja (?), Utsâha and the Akkaras in general Mr. Brown thinks that they are "experiments in metre which have not obtained popularity", "are imitated from those in the Kannaḍa language, and have been introduced (into Tĕlugu); but have never become popular or common"; and concerning the Akkaras in particular he remarks: "the Akkara is used only by Nannayya bhaṭṭa (A. D. 1130), and one or two imitators. The poet himself uses only two varieties, which he calls by the one name Akkara". "The Akkara is in truth a Kannaḍa metre, and has been naturalized in very few Tĕlugu poems." He adduces the two varieties: madhya akkara and madhura akkara, names that correspond to N.'s naḍu akkara and ĕḍĕ akkara. The first, according to an instance from Nannayya's âdiparva, seems to contain 25 Moras in each line; the second, according to an instance from the same, 22; but as in Canarese there appears no rule regulating the number of Moras.

---

1) Comparing Mr. Brown's two instances of the Âṭa (p. 307, 309) it will be observed that they differ regarding the number of Moras. The instance of our text is 3. 3. 3 * 3. 4. 3 | 3. 3. 3 * 4. 3, exhibiting 16 Moras in the second line; whereas the above instance has only 15 in it. But our instance must be correct, as the numbers 4. 3 are very distinctly expressed in one of the lines of the original by "nagajâpriyya" (⏑⏑‒.‒⏑, an epithet of *S*iva); the other line in question is quite corrupt in our copy of the Kavijihvâbandhana.

B. An Essay on Canarese Literature.

I. The early period, from about 800 to 1300 A. D.

1. Means in hand.

The early period of Canarese (karnâṭa, kannaḍa) literature can be understood, to a pretty satisfactory extent, from Nâgavarma's čhandas, as seen above, and from the following works:—

1. The Sabdamaṇidarpaṇa of Kešava or Keši Râja, that forms a comprehensive grammar of the Canarese language as it lay before the author in the poetical works of the early poets, from which very numerous citations, directly or indirectly, are adduced. Our references are taken from the Maṅgaḷûr edition of the work. (Sbdm.)

2. The Kâvyâvalokana (-loka) of Nâgavarma, a Canarese treatise on poetical composition, the first two chapters (on olĕ) of which we have been favored with by Tirumalĕ Syâmaṇṇa, Munshi of the Wesleyan Missionaries at Mysore[1]. (Kvyl.)

3. The Samskṛita-Karnâṭa Nighaṇṭu of Nâgavarma, in many artificial metres, an olĕ MS. of which has been obtained from the Jaina library at Mûḍabidar on the W. coast, through the kindness of Dr. Burnell. The character used in the MS. is nearly identical with that of the Haḷagannaḍa specimen in Dr. Burnell's Vamšabrâhmaṇa, the only difference being the use of letter ṛ (ಐ).

4. The Jagannâtha Vijaya of Rudra (bhaṭṭa), a Canarese story of Kṛishṇa, on olĕ. (Jagv.)

5. The Rasaratnâkara of Sâlva, a Canarese treatise on poetical composition, an olĕ copy of which the Tirumalĕ Syâmaṇṇa has been kind enough to supply. (Rsr.)

6. The Višvakṛiti parîkshaṇa, 124 pages in Canarese, composed in A. D. 1873 by Hiraṇyagarbha, and lithographed at Dhâravâḍa (Dharwar). It contains specimens of two early Canarese works, and a few editorial remarks of value. (Vkp.)

---

1) In quoting it the 10 prakaraṇas of the 2 adhikâras (the first comprising 7, the second 3) have been counted successively by us, and the first number of the quotations refers to one of them. There may be a little irregularity in our counting as that of the MS. is out of order.

2. Kešava and Nâgavarma.

Kešava and Nâgavarma use in their writings the exact and finished style of their predecessors. It cannot be shown from their compositions that the so-called New Canarese existed at all in their time; Nâgavarma's prosody, in its present recensions, evinces some later grammatical licenses; but they certainly do not belong to him[1].

A peculiarity of Kešava is that he wishes the ancient consonant ḻ (ೞ), which for a long time has been quite out of use both in the oral and written language, to be retained and raised again to its due position, not only in cases of internal or external sandhi, but generally. How far Nâgavarma made use of the letter, is a question that cannot be satisfactorily decided on account of the questionable state of the MSS.; he maintains however its use in compounds[2], and writes khaḻga (instead of khaḍga, a sword)[3]. [I take the liberty here to add that from Nâgavarma's karṇâṭaka vyâkaraṇa in Sanscrit prose (Bhâshâbhûshaṇa) which L. Rice, Esq. is going to edit, and a MS. of which he very kindly sent me for a cursory inspection, it is certain that Nâgavarma treats of the letter ḻ (ೞ) also irrespectively of compounds; see 1, 10.]

To settle with any thing like certainty the time in which Kešava and Nâgavarma respectively wrote, is not very easy. It is certainly a strange circumstance that, in addition to many fragments, 42 whole verses occur as citations in the Sabdamaṇidarpaṇa[4], and that these are found

1) Abhinava Maṅga râja, the author of a Canarese Nighaṇṭu, says (i., 4) that he will pattern after the Canarese of Nâgavarma. Cf. Indian Antiquary, i., 345 seq. It is a very curious fact that the interesting verse about "Ancient Canarese" (Sbdm. p. xvii. seq.) that is quoted by Kešava, forms also a quotation in the Kâvyâvaloka (2, 23). Nâgavarma did precede the so-called H period, that appears already clearly in the Canarese Basava Purâṇa of A. D. 1369, where *e. g.* there occurs âdahĕm instead of âdapĕm (49, 30).

2) Kvyl. 5, 63. 98. 99. 3) Nighaṇṭu, Varga 12, 16; Nânârtha v. 100. The same form of the word appears in a rather old commentary in Canarese on Halâyudha's Abhidhânaratnamâlâ (2, 317), that regularly shows also ḻ (ೞ), instead of sh, before the consonant p, *e. g.* puḻpa (pushpa), a peculiarity that our MS. of Nâgavarma's Nighaṇṭu does not present. See Sbdm. p. 25. 4) p. 17 ಅರ್ಗಣವಾ; p. 18 ವರಸಂಧ್ಯಕ್ಷರ; p. 24 ಬಿಜಱ್ಕಂ; p. 67 ವಿಧುವಿಲ್ಲ; p. 73 ಇಲ್ಲಿ ಇದು; p. 75 ಅಸಿಯು; p. 78 ಪಟಗನ್ನಡ; p. 79 ಒಕ್ಕೈಗಸಿ; p. 81 ಎಳವೆಱಿತೆ; p. 81 ನಡುವಣ; p. 81 ಮರವಣಿಗೆಗಂ; p. 81 ಧರೆಯೊಳ್ ವೀರದ; p. 83 ಕಣ್ಸೋಲ; p. 84 ಪೊನ್ನುಳ್ಳ; p. 112 ಸುರತರು; p. 117 ಅವು ಪಿರಿಯುವು; p. 128 ಆಯಿರ್ದ; p. 130 ಕುಲಮುಂ; p. 130 ಮನದಿಂ; p. 136...ವಿನೋದದ; p. 166 ಮತ್ತಹಸ್ತಿ; p. 176 ಆರಕ್ತ; p. 188 ಉದಯಾ; p. 216 ಪಂದಳಿರ; p. 216 ಎನಿತುಂ; p. 221 ಕಡುವಿಲ್ಲ; p. 221 ಸೊಗಯಿಸು; p. 224 ಉರಗಂ ಕೊಂ; p. 224 ಕೇಱಿ; p. 224 ಅಱುದಿಂ; p. 225 ಪರಿಮರ್ದ; p. 230 ಗಳಿಯೊಡ; p. 231 ಬೆಳೆಗೆಯ್ದು; p. 233 ಗಂಡಿಗ; p. 234 ಮುಡಿವಳ್ಳ; p. 239 ಮಾಱಾ; p. 244 ಒಕ್ಕಲಿತಿ; p. 266 ಮುಟ್ಟಿತು; p. 267 ಅಸವಸ; p. 267 ಅಕೇರ್ದಂದು; p. 270 ನೆನೆಯುದ; p. 272 ವಾಯುಸ.

also in the first part of the Kâvyâvalokana which treats of grammar too, and further that of these verses in one case four, in another three, and in three other places two follow one another in the same succession in both works. One of the two authors therefore appears to have used the other's work. In the present recensions, Kešava's composition not unfrequently gives only fragments of verses as instances, whereas Nâgavarma always cites whole verses. I can mention only one Canarese early author as having been a common authority to both, viz. Ha*m*sarâja[1].

About the time of the two authors in general the following can be adduced. Nâgavarma, in his quotations, introduces a *C*âlukya čakreša as fighting[2]; a Jayasiṅga bhûpa whose elephant is fighting victoriously[3]; a Tailapa čakravarti in a very corrupt verse that contains, however, clearly the name of Raṭṭa haḷḷi[4]; a Vikramâṅka who orders a mahâdâna to be given[5]; the Pŏlakeši vallabha whose fortitude is praised[6]; a Suvarma nṛipa as fighting[7]; a Kŏṅguḷi (Kŏṅgaḷi?) varma who is gaining the victory over a body of horsemen[8]; a Mâdhava who is fighting[9]; and, in a verse that is also in the *S*abdamaṇidarpaṇa, a Vikhyâtayaša[10]. Also Kešava's quotations contain a Tailapa[11]; further a Vishṇu Vijayâditya[12], an Udayâditya[13], a Nṛipatuṅga[14], a Janodaya[15], a Nârasi*m*ha[16], and a Si*m*hasena kshitîša[17].

Pŏlakeši (Pulakeši), Jayasiṅga (Jayasi*m*ha), Tailapa and Udayâditya are names of kings belonging to the *C*âlukya dynasty; Tailapa belongs to the Kalyâṇa line, Udayâditya to that of Veṅgi; Jayasiṅga and Vijayâditya

---

1) *S*bdm. p. 377 (ತರಪೇೞಯ್); Kvyl. 5, 84. 2) Kvyl. 2, 46. The first half of this verse that does not include the name of *C*âlukya, occurs *S*bdm. p. 83 (ಪದನೆಱ್ಖರ). 3) 2, 37. 4) 4, 14. 5) 5, 84. 6) 9, 35. 7) 3, 38. 8) 5, 85. 9) 2, 38. 10) 3, 32; *S*bdm. p. 138: "To her and him Vikhyâtayaša was born, who as to kula and šala surpassed all on earth, cultivated justice, and was a peerless bull for the ocean of hostile armies". 11) p. 112: "The sword of Tailapa's arm was like Rudra (when being considered as) the fire of the (all-destroying) time". 12) p. 201 (cf. p. 90 where its beginning: ಅದವಿಷ್ಣು) according to a Jaina MS. received for collation from Mûḍabidar through the kind endeavours of Dr. Burnell: "Vishṇu Vijayâditya whose chest was like a cloud". 13) p. 175: "What a beauty! Udayâditya causes to be said of himself that Manu and he are the virtuous, that the celestial tree and he are the donors, that the ocean and he are deep". 14) p. 171, "Who will not bow to Nṛipatuṅga that bears the weapons as the first of kings, is conversant with politics, dignified, pure, munificent and heroic?" 15) p. 255: "I undertake to tell this to Janodaya". 16) p. 192: "Nârasi*m*ha is like lightning, like a lion, and like the flaming eye of Purahara". 17) p. 177: "King Si*m*hasena caused to be said of himself that he was life and riches, mother and father, the eye and the road."

occur in both the *C*âlukya lines[1]. Nṛipatuṅga may remind one of Vikrama deva or of Vîra deva, both of whom had the title "Kulottuṅga *C*oḷa."[2] Vikramâṅka[3] may be the mentioned Vikrama deva, (or may possibly be a mistake in writing for Vikramârka, "the ruby of the *C*âlukyas")[4]. Kŏṅguḷi (probably Kŏṅgaḷi *i.e.* Kŏṅgaṇi) varma and Mâdhava appear to belong to the *C*era dynasty[5].

Nâgavarma's quotations further mention a *C*oḷa dharitrîpâla[6]; and of Kešava it is stated that he has written a *C*oḷa pâlaka čaritra[7].

Nâgavarma was a native of Veṅgi[8]; Kešava probably of Kalyâṇa.[9] That the two poets were not contemporaneous with the mentioned kings, is beyond all doubt, as the verses in which they are alluded to, are quotations from the works of their predecessors that may have lived under those princes or afterwards.

The following are a few dates regarding the *C*âlukyas[10]: About 300 A.D. king Jayasi*m*ha of the *C*âlukya race began to subdue the Pallava dynasty[11] that ruled over a part of the South. The fifth king known after him was Pulakeši, 489 A.D. A hundred and twenty years later, 609 A.D., the *C*ălukya king Satyâšraya ruled at Kalyâṇapura[12], the capital of Kuntala deša; whilst his younger brother Vishṇuvardhana II. (Kubja Vishṇuvardhana) was king at Veṅgipura, the capital of Veṅgi deša (now the Northern Circars) which he had conquered A.D. 605. Fifty-two years afterwards, from 657-670 A.D. a Jayasi*m*ha ruled over Veṅgi; 707½-725½ Vijayâditya I. appears there; Vijayâditya IV. of Veṅgi occurs after 881 A. D. His successor, (about 900 A. D.), was Udayâditya.

Meanwhile the Kalyâṇa kingdom had been suffering much from the

---

1) Journal of R. A. S., N. S., i., 2, p. 253 seq.; Ind. Ant. ii., 175 seq.; Jayasi*m*ha also Ind. Ant. i., 157 (c. 478 A. D.); ii., 156. 297. There is an Udayâditya also among the Hŏysaḷas, Ind. Ant. ii., 299; and two Vijayâdityas are among the Kâdambas, i., 156; and a Vijayâditya râya (c. 750 A. D.) among the *C*eras, i., 362. 2) J. R. A. S., N. S., i., 2, p. 255. 3) Ind. Ant. ii., 155. 160. 361. 362; iii., 151 appear Vikrama râjas of *C*era. 4) Ind. Ant. i., 156. 5) Ind. Ant. 1872, 361. 6) Kvyl. 5, 121. 7) *S*bdm. p. xxii.; p. 408. 8) Nâgavarma's *C*handas v. 4 seq.; above p. xviii. 9) According to the Canarese Basava Purâṇa, etc. See further on. 10) J. R. A. S., N. S., i., 2, p. 251 seq.; Ind. Ant. ii., 175, 176. 11) As has been stated above p. xxi., its kingdom was called Veṅgi râshṭra, and the capital Veṅgîpura, and once Kaliṅganagara, Ind. Ant. iii., 152. A Pallama (Pallava) râya appears at Basava's time, Gaṇa sahasra nâma 8, 37. It has already been pointed out as something curious that the last term of the Pallava kings' names (except in one case) is "varma." Cf. the Kâdambas, Ind. Ant. i., 156, 366; the Tiruvâṅkoḍas (Travancoreans), Brown's Cyclic Tables p. 64; and Nâgavarma, Guṇavarma, etc. in the remarks on Nâgavarma's *C*handas. Paḷḷa is the name of a low tribe of people in the South. 12) Cf. Ind. Ant. ii., 94.

Raṭṭas or Raḍḍis (see above the Raṭṭa haḷḷi)[1]. 973 A. D. Taila bhûpa II. (Vikramâditya) restored the power of the Kalyâṇa dynasty which had been for some time usurped by the Raṭṭa kula. A. D. 1076 Tribhuvana Malla (Vikramâditya) became king, and reigned for 51 years[2]. 1150 A. D. Tailapa III. or Trailokya Malla ruled at Kalyâṇa; 1189 A. D. his successor, Someśvara deva IV., was dethroned by Bijjaḷa deva, who extinguished the Kalyâṇa dynasty, and founded the Kaluburigĕ dynasty[3].

In the mean time, about 1000 A. D.., Veṅgi had passed to Râjendra Coḷa, the then dominant sovereign of Southern India[4], whose brother

1) In Tamiḻ: Iraṭṭu; in Tĕlugu: Raḍḍi, Rĕḍḍi (Brown's explanations are: a Sûdra tribe; a Hĕggaḍi, i. e. a chief; a pĕdda yajamâna, i. e. a big master); in Kannaḍa: Raḍḍi, Rĕḍḍi. Reeve-Sanderson: a caste of original Tĕlugu farmers; the head man of a village; an affix to the name of stone-cutters (called ŏḍḍa) Cf. Ind. Ant. i., 361. 2) Ind. Ant. iii., 257. 3) According to the Canarese Canna Basava Purâṇa another establishment of Kaluburigĕ takes place (62, 30. 44), that may refer to the Muhammadan Bâhminî dynasty. At the same place the Purâṇa states that with Aḷiya Bijjaḷa (i. e. son-in-law-Bijjaḷa), the successor of Bijjaḷa, after he ruled for 60 years, this Bijjaḷa dynasty ceases. The Basava Purâṇa (5, 57) calls Bijjaḷa i. a Câlukya. According to Brown's C. T. p. 58 Bijjaṇa or Bijjaḷa deva was a Câlukya, and ruled from 1156-1168 A. D. His third successor was Someśvara deva (1176-1184 A. D.), after whom the name Câlukya begins to disappear. 4) 894 A. D. Âdityavarma, a Coḷa prince, had subdued the Kŏṅga or Cera dynasty, Ind. Ant. i., 360, 361. Taḷakâḍu on the Kâveri, about 35 miles S. E. of Srîraṅgapaṭṇa, had been one of its capitals. In the course of the 10th century it became the capital of the first or second sovereign of the Hŏysaḷa or Ballâḷa dynasty of Karnâṭa.—Ind. Ant. ii., 107, it is said that Kulottuṅga Coḷa, who appears already 1143 A. D., conquered the Tĕliṅgu âṇya (kingdom) 1171 A. D. (cf. Murdoch, p. 188, where a work about this event is mentioned); by him, somehow, Vîra deva Coḷa must be meant.—In the mentioned Canarese Basava Purâṇa appear as prior to, or contemporaneous with, Basava. (Cf. Canna Basava P. 55, 3 seq.): Kara Vîra Coḷa (44, 58; 26, 54; 54, 72; 9, 33); (Dharma) Coḷa of Karavûr (44, 58); Uttuṅga C. (44, 58; 11, 16); Râjendra C. (44, 58); Vikrama C., called also Narendra or Manujendra C. (44, 58; 27, 67); Vîra C. (44, 58; 22, 1 seq.; 25, 4); Kulottuṅga (Vara) C. (50, 1 seq.).— Mr. C. P. Brown in his Cyclic Tables adduces, sub A. D. 1108 and 1123, Vikrama Coḷa; 1118, 1149 and 1171 (here together with Kâkateya Gaṇapati of Ŏruṅgal) Kulottuṅga C.; 1233 Kulottuṅga Râjendra C.; 1279 Râjamahendri (and Karṇâṭaka? see Sbdm. p. xxii.) was ruled by Vîra Coḷa Mahârâja, younger son of Râjendra C.; whose son Râja râja had abdicated in favor of his brother this Vîra C.—"For some time before 1292 (or 1295) A. D. this (Ŏruṅgal) kingdom had been ruled by the queen dowager Rudramma Devî (a Devagiri princess), who seems to have entirely gained the affections of her people; she resigned in favor of her son Pratâpa Rudra deva, whose family-name was Kâkateya". Dr. Burnell's Vamśabrâhmaṇa, p. vii.—About Veṅgi deśa see also Ind. Ant. i., 348, where it is said that its capital Veṅgi was the residence of a Buddhist dynasty anterior to the foundation of the Eastern Câlukya kingdom about the end of the 6th century. Cf. J. R. A. S., N. S., iii., 1, p. 146. Regarding the establishment of Buddhism in the South the Mahâvamśa of about 460 A. D. (M. Müller's Sanscrit Literature, p. 267) states that 245 B. C. king Aśoka sent a Thero or Sthavira to Mahîśamaṇḍala (or Maisûr), and another to Vanivâsi (or Banavasi). Ind. Ant. iii., 273. In Tamiḻ Tera means a Bauddha. Terasa in Canarese is a member of a class of Liṅgâita gaṇas (Gaṇasahasran. 6, 4); Terasu in Tĕlugu is a leader or chief.

Vijayâditya became viceroy of Veṅgi deša. Râjendra Coḷa was succeeded by his son Vikrama deva, surnamed Kulottuṅga Coḷa. On the death of his uncle, the viceroy of Veṅgi deša, the king deputed his son Râja râja to assume the office; but after holding it for one year, 1078 A. D. he resigned it in favour of his younger brother Vîra deva Coḷa, who also assumed the title of Kulottuṅga Coḷa. His grants are found in great numbers from 1079-1135 A. D., when a partial restoration of the Câlukya line seems to have taken place. 1175 A. D. Veṅgi had already fallen under the sway of the Kâkateya dynasty of Ŏruṅgal.

As Nâgavarma and Kešava must have lived a certain number of years after the poets whom they quote, and who evidently had written on the feats of the Câlukya and Coḷa kings as connected also with the Veṅgi and Kalyâṇa lines (between 609-1189 A. D.), they cannot well have composed their works long before 1200 A. D.

The above-mentioned author of the Višvakṛiti parîkshaṇa (p. xxiv.), who evidently has concerned himself with the study of certain old Canarese works, states that he knows the Canarese novel Lîlâvati prabandha, from which, as he proves, Kešava has cited at all events two verses[1] and was composed more than a thousand years ago, so that it might date from about 870 A. D. (?). Another Canarese novel, called Candraprabha Purâṇa, was composed in A. D. 1189 by Argaḷa (Aggaḷa) deva. This seems to follow from the last verse of this work cited by Hiraṇygarbha: "When the 1111th year of the Saka nṛipa had arrived, on the 11th day of the bright lunar fortnight (sita) of the first lunar month (čaitra) of the well-known (prâkaṭa) Saumya year this pearl of composition was finished". These two circumstances contain a slight hint as to the age of the early Canarese writers.[2] Argaḷa is the

1) With regard to ಅಯ್ and ಅರಿ under rule 217. In this case Hiraṇyagarbha's recension of the grammar coincides with MS. No. iii. of the Maṅgaḷûr edition and with the Jaina MS. collated, that has been mentioned in p. xxvi., note 12. Vkp. p. 121. 2) Mr. C. P. Brown in his preface to his Tĕlugu-English Dictionary, 1852, repeats what he had stated two years ago in his Cyclic Tables (p. 58), viz. that the Mahâbhârata and Râmâyaṇa were translated into Tĕlugu in the days of Vishṇuvardhana (at first called Bĕṭṭa râya, hill-king), a Câlukya, A. D. 1120. His fuller statement in the Tables runs thus: "As the poet and grammarian Nannaya Bhaṭṭa, who wrote the Âdiparva in Tĕlugu, lived in the reign of (the Câlukya) Vishṇuvardhana, we are now in possession of the era when that author flourished: and at that period the Tĕlugu language had already attained classical perfection. The Mahâbhârata was commenced by the grammarian named above: but was continued by Erra Pragada, and completed by Tikkanna Somayâji: who likewise translated into Tĕlugu metre a great part of the Râmâyaṇa (i. e. Uttara Râmâyaṇa, preface to Dictionary). He (Tikka) died (according to a traditional verse) A. D. 1198". Mr. Brown before this (in his Essays) had placed

name of one of the fourteen Jaina Tîrthakaras, whose names will be given further on.

3. On Kešava in particular.

Regarding Kešava in particular it is curious that he twice uses as an instance[1] the word "ṭöppigĕ", a hat, cap, helmet, bonnet, which, if not so-called Dravidian, as it does not seem to be, is a tadbhava of the Hindusthâni "topi", "ṭopi", a word that is used nowadays in Tĕlugu, Malayâḷa, Canarese, etc. The first Mohammadan invasion of the Dakkaṇ took place A. D. 1294. If the word is not Dravidian and has reached the Dakkaṇ by that invasion, Kešava, especially if at the same time the word had been taken by him from a predecessor's composition, would fall rather late; but the term may have been introduced by traders and travellers long before 1294.

Kešava, as stated above (p. xxv.), teaches the use of the ancient letter ḻ (ೞ), and, to some extent at least, in conformity with what he found in the works of his predecessors or also in šâsanas (prayoga dṛishṭa, p. 37). In a copper grant of the Cera dynasty, dated 804 A. D., it is still regularly used[2]; in one of the Eastern Câlukyas of 1079 A. D. neither it nor the letter ṟ (ಱ), that is met with in MSS. even later than

Nannaya Bhaṭṭa at king Rudra Pratâpa Gaṇapati's time. About his other work, a Tĕlugu grammar in Samskṛita, Mr. Brown in his Dictionary says that it was written about A. D. 1130.—As the Vishṇuvardhana is called a Câlukya, he probably is the Vishṇu vardhana vii., surnamed Vîra deva Kulottuṅga Coḷa, who was viceroy over the once Câlukya kingdom Veṅgi (Râjamahendri?) A. D. 1079-1135, see p. xxix. Cyclic Tables p. 61 Mr. Brown adduces Bĕṭṭa râya, who took the title Bĕṭṭa Vishṇuvardhana, as one of the Höysaḷa Ballâḷas, and states he died A. D. 1134.—Mr. Brown, in his Preface, mentions another Râmâyaṇa in Dvipadas which is believed to have been written by Raṅganâtha for Kona Budha râja, son of Kona Viṭhal Bhûpati, and remarks that this version appears to be one of the oldest Tĕlugu poems. Simply on account of the names in italics we take the liberty to doubt this.—Regarding Tamiḻ literature it has been said that the oldest Tamiḻ works now extant are those which were written, or are claimed to have been written, by the Jainas, or which date from the era of the literary activity of the Jaina sect. The Jaina period extended probably from the 8th or 9th century A. D., to the 12th or 13th. The general opinion is that the grammar called the Tŏlkâvya (ancient composition, by Tṛiṇa dhûmâgni of Madhurâ) is the oldest work extant, and it has been placed about the 8th century A. D. The Tamiḻ Râmâyaṇa has been referred to the 11th century. See Classified Catalogue of Tamiḻ Books by Dr. J. Murdoch p. xxii., seq. Dr. Weber says the translation by (the Tamiḻ) Kamba (or Kampa of the Râmâyaṇa with the Uttarakâṇḍa) must certainly date, according to Wilson,... as far back as A. D. 885; Ind. Ant. i., 249. In this case, however, it apparently ought to be Jainic, which it does not seem to be; see Murdoch p. 194. The Tamiḻ Mahâbhârata seems to date from the 16th century, Murdoch, *ibid.* p. 190. 1) The instances do not appear to be interpolations. 2) In the Nâgamaṅgaḷa copper plates (Maisûr) of A. D. 776 its employment is regular; they too belong to the Ceras. Ind. Ant. ii., 776.

1428 A. D., are extant[1]; whether the absence of the two letters in this case is merely accidental, I am unable to say. I have not observed the ḻ as a letter of Alliteration in the fragment of the Lîlâvati as given by Hiraṇyagarbha; but from the instances in which it appears as such, its general use at a certain time can be firmly established[2], excepting cases of Sandhi of the older period.

It does appear more than probable that the author of the Canarese Basava Purâṇa[3], Bhîma, who finished his composition 1369 A. D.,

1) According to a communication from Dr. Burnell (1874). Also a Kalyâṇa-Câlukya plate of A. D. 608 does not contain the ḻ; if this be not accidental, it would point to the letter having become sooner obsolete towards the inland north (and perhaps also in Veṅgi, as Mr. Brown, in the preface to his Dictionary, does not seem to have known anything about the existence of the letter in Tĕlugu), the communication between this and the countries where it is still in use (Tamiḻ, Malĕyâḷa) having not been very frequent.

2) In Hiraṇyagarbha's fragment of the Candraprabha it may occur as letter of Alliteration in verse 69. 115. 144. 145 (?). 3) A few Lingâita notes rearding the founder of this Saiva sect, Basava, may prove acceptable. The Mala (i. e. great) Basava Purâṇa by Siṅgi râja says: "After 9 Nandas, after 10 Gupta kings, after 21 thrones of the Mŏrĕyas, and after 27 Kâdamba kings, the town of Paṭṭakal (i. e. royal insignia stone, about which place see Ind. Ant. iii., 257) had had 27 crownings of the assemblage of the Câlŏkya rulers. In it (the town) one of the Câlŏkya princes of the lineage of those and other kings, a rich merchant (vâṇija), an excellent follower of the Saivâgama has become râjyastha. He bears the name of Trailokyacûḍâmaṇi; his wife is Mahâlekhĕ; the prince born to them is Anumisha". When Anumisha, one day, is lost in a distant jungle, he is met by Anâdi Vṛishabha, who gives him his own liṅga. Vṛishabha in re-entering Kailâsa is stopped by the door-keepers Siṅgakeśa and Draviḍa (4, 11 seq.), whom for their rudeness Siva sends down to the earth. They go to Kalyâṇapura, "to the mighty, the chief of the sun-race of the Câlŏkyas (cf. Basava P. 5, 57, where too Bijjaḷa is stated to belong to the Câlŏkya anvaya) of the succession of the line of the kings' thrones; and the firstborn of them assumes the name of Bijjaḷa Karṇa deva (about Karṇa cf. J. R. A. S., N. S., i., 2, p. 261). When he has obtained the royal power (paṭṭa), Vṛishabha descends to the earth", and becomes the well-known Basava, the later premier at Bijjaḷa's court (Siṅgi râja 5, 1 seq.), whom two times he, Basava, calls "Keraḷa's king" (Basava P. 53, 83. 54). The same story in an abridged form occurs Canna Basava P. 57, 70 seq.: the wife here is Maharlekhĕ, the doorkeepers are Simhi kesari and Daviḍa (i. e. Draviḍa, Tamiḻa), the king is Kanyeśa (?) Bijjaḷa. Basava's father was Maṇḍigĕ Mâdirâja, an Arâdhya (Saiva) Brahman of Bâgavâḍi in the Karṇâṭaka deśa (Bas. P. ii., 45. 46). At the instigation of Basava and his friends Jagadeva, in company with Mŏllayya and Bŏmmayya, murders Bijjaḷa (Bas. P. 60, 60; 61, 6. 7; 61, 21 seq.; Can. B. P. 62, 26). Contemporaneous with, or prior to, Basava are, besides the Coḷa kings mentioned above p.xxviii.: 1) Allama deva or Allama prabhu, who as an incarnation of Gaṇanâtha went to the Bĕḷavala deśa (a portion of the Canarese country), entered the town Banavasŏ (i. e. wood-spring, bana-basĕ or basi, sanscritized vana-vâsi), the seat of the Kâdamba kings, (the ruins of which are still extant near the river Varadâ, nearly due east of Gokarṇa on the Western Coast; cf. Ind Ant. i., p. 157), where king Nirahaṅkâra (according to the Can. Bas. P.) or Mamakâra (according to the Prabhu liṅga lîlĕ) ruled with his wife Sujñâni or Mohini devi, whose beautiful daughter Mâyŏ he troubled very much, saw the above-mentioned Anumisha in his grave, and took his liṅga, and went to Kalyâṇapura to see Basava (Can. Bas. P. 6, 7 seq.; 57, 87;

means the Kešava or Keši râja in question, when he states (1, 10) that by the grace of Keši of Kŏṇḍagûḷi, Siri Paṇḍita, *S*ivaleṅka Mañčaṇa Paṇḍita, and Guru Mallikârjuna Paṇḍita he will utter his work. In the course of his Purâṇa Keši râja appears as one of the chief devotees of *S*iva at Kalyâṇapura in Bijjaḷa's and Basava's time, and is called *S*iva's clerk (senabova, 9, 42) and a *S*aiva dîkshâčârya (58, 4); further his disciples (šishya) are of a high standard (47, 35); he partakes, with many others, of a hideous *S*iva prasâda (59, 5); and at last Keši râja, the great one

62, 6 seq.; Prabhu liṅga lîlĕ, i., seq.; Prauḍha râya kâvya i., 47; cf Bas. P. 8). 2) Udbhaṭa (Udbhaṭṭa, Udbhuṭa) deva of Bhallakînagara, the guru of Bhoja râja (Bas. P. 57, 6 seq.; *C*an. Bas. P. 57; 51; 55, 46; 1, 29; together with Bâṇa, Keširâja, Mayûra, etc. in Brahmottara Kâṇḍa 1, 9; Gaṇa sahasra nâma 8, 16). 3) A Halâyudha (Bas. P. 25; *C*an. Bas. 57, 38; 1, 28 a Halâyudha occurs together with Udbhaṭa and other poets; *S*araṇa lîlâmṛita p. 3; Gaṇa s. n. 8, 36). 4) Sindu Ballâḷa (Bas. P. 24, 73; *C*an. B. P. 57, 30; Gaṇa. s. n. 8, 1). 5) Desiṅga Ballâḷa (*C*an. B. P. 57, 10). 6) Vîra Ballâḷa (Gaṇa s. n. 8, 47). 7) Kûna Pâṇḍya (Bas. P. 50; *C*an. B. P. 55, 33 seq.). 8) Kumâra pâlaka Gurjara (Bas. P. 54, 75; 44, 73; Gaṇa s. n. 8, 33). 9) Anantapâla nṛipâla (Bas. P. 55, 24). 10) A Gaṇapati king at Ŏruṅgal at Basava's death (*C*an. B. P. 62, 27), contemporaneous with a Guṇḍa Brahmayya (who is mentioned also Gaṇa s. n. 8, 32). 11) The (poet) Bâṇa (Bas. P. 54, 69).—The mentioning of the Hŏysaḷa king Vîra Ballâḷa of whom a šâsana is known that is dated 1193 A. D., and whose prime minister Râya deva had one written 1199 A. D. (Ind. Ant. ii., 298 seq.), is alone a sufficient proof that Basava belongs to the 12th or 13th century. Further Kumârapâla proves the same; towards the end of the 12th century he was converted by the celebrated Hemačandra, the Jaina Polyhistor, to the Jaina faith (Ind. Ant. ii. 15. 18. 19. 195. 241); Hemačandra died 1172 (Bombay J. ix, p. 224), Kumâra pâla 1166 A. D. Gaṇapati was a title of the Kâkateya kings of Ŏruṅgal; the earliest inscription of the Kâkateyas that has been met in Veṅgi deša, now the Northern Circars, bears date A. D. 1175, the latest 1336 (J. R. A. S., N. S., i., 2, p. 252; cf. our p. xxi.).—After so much it becomes clear that the following statement in the *C*an. Bas. P. (of 1585 A. D.) is a forgery, viz. that Basava (and Bijjaḷa râja) died "Tuesday, on the 11th day of the bright fortnight of the 12th month of the 707th year, called Raktâkshi, of the *S*âlivâhana *S*aka" (62, 18), *i. e.* A. D. 785. The *S*al. *S*. year 707 besides is not Raktâkshi, but Krodhana, Raktâkshi being the 706th (Brown's Tables, p. 44). The *S*aiva and Liṅgâita *S*araṇa lîlâmṛita (probably of the beginning of the 19th century) gives (p. 177. 178) the Râkshasa year of Kali 3911 as Basava's death; but this (according to Mr. Brown) is the Vikṛiti year, and corresponds to A. D. 810. —Prof. Lassen (Ind. Alt. 4, 622) says that Basava died 1168 A. D.; the same appears from Brown's Tables p. 5, who states ad A. D. 1160: "The Liṅgavanta creed is founded by Basava"; ad 1166: "Bijjaḷa râja of Banavasi gave certain lands to the Jaṅgamas, disciples of Basava"; and ad 1168: "Deaths of Bijjaḷa and Basava". These dates do not agree with the statement, that Bijjaḷa began to reign at Kalyâṇa in A. D. 1189; see above p. xxviii.—Cf. also the Gadagu grant with a figure of an ox or Basava, of A. D. 1213, Ind. Ant. ii., p. 297; and *ibid.* one of a similar character of perhaps A. D. 1057 (?); and two others dtto. dtto. p. 298: one of A. D. 1199; the other of a year between A. D. 1176-1182; and that of Vîra Ballâḷa of A. D. 1193. Vṛishabhalakshya or Vṛishabhadhvaja, however, is an epithet of *S*iva older than Kalyâṇa Basava's time.—Late Liṅgâita writers make a thorough Jaina of Bijjaḷa râya; but elsewhere he appears to have entertained rather fickle views, *e. g.* the Basava Purâṇa relates his having put up a Govinda pratimĕ at Prâtâpa Nârâyaṇapura (53, 31. 32).

(mahânta) goes with Basava to Saṅgameśvarapura (61, 9; Kappaḍi saṅgama, Kûḍal saṅgama, where Basava dieṣ)[1]. If the author of the *S*abdamaṇidarpaṇa is meant, he lived still A. D. 1168 (or, according to others, still after A. D. 1189).

Keśava or Keśi râja, an *A*rya and an âčârya of the Yâdava host (kaṭaka), was the son of the daughter of the poet Sumanobâṇa, and his father was the excellent Yogi Mallikârjuna deva[2]. This name reminds one of the just-mentioned *S*aiva Guru Mallikârjuna Paṇḍita, of Mallikârjuna *A*râdhya (*i. e. S*aiva Brâhmaṇa) of Amaraguṇḍa at Basava's time[3], and of the great Mallikârjuna Yogi who at the same time appears on *S*rîśaila, where he is met by Mâda arasa (râja) or Mâdi râja[4]. I cannot tell whether the Liṅgâitas count more than one great Mallikârjuna or whether the three names are to denote one and the same person; but it is evident that the grammarian's father bearing one of their liṅgas' names was one of the inducements for them to claim the renowned Keśava as belonging to their sect[5]. In Keṣava, however, no trace of Basava's sect is found.

1) The author of the *C*anna Basava Purâṇa (of 1585 A. D.), when praising a number of *S*aiva poets, mentions among them also Keśi râja (1, 17); the same does the author of the Râjaśekhara vilâsa (of 1657 A. D.) in 1, 17. The author of the Purâṇa further introduces at Basava's time the vîra śaiva âčârya Keśi râja daṇḍeśa (57, 49; cf. v. 34 where Keśi taṇdĕ, the father Keśi, occurs).—The author of the treatise Kavijihvâbandhana, a *S*aiva, calls himself an abhinava (modern) Keśi râja (1, 11. 12) or abhinava Keśava (3, 2. 3. 29), calls the author of the *S*abdamaṇidarpaṇa "Keśava" (1, 11), and quotes two verses of that grammar, his 3, 31 being *S*bdm. v. 34 on p. 45, and his 3, 30 occurring *S*bdm. p. 42, v. 30. In the said treatise "Keśava" occurs six times (1, 6; 2, 38. 39; 3, 2. 3. 29), and "Keśirâja" three times (1, 11. 12; 4, 40); so there remains not the slightest doubt about the identity; besides in the concluding sentences of the chapters the author is regularly named abhinava Keśi râja.—In the *S*aiva and Liṅgâita *S*araṇa lîlâmṛita the Keśi râja ayya (master) is mentioned among the poets of *S*iva (Bĕṅgaḷûr ed. 1871, p. 3); and in the Canarese Brahmottara kâṇḍa between the Saṃskṛita poets Bâṇa and Mayûra (1, 9).—In the *S*aiva and Liṅgâita Gaṇa sahasra nâma (of about 1800 A. D.) Keśi râja appears among the devotees at Basava's time (8, 8). 2) *S*bdm. p. 3. 408. 3) *C*an. Bas. P. 57, 17; Gaṇa s. n. 8, 14 (Amaraguṇḍa's Mallikârjuna taṇdĕ *i. e.* father); *S*araṇa lîl. p. 251 seq. 4) This yogi is treated of Basava P. chs. 19. 20. Before he entered on his ascetic life he was Malla arasa (râja) dharaṇîvallabha (19, v. 20). Ind. Ant. ii., 362 (cf. ii., 81) is a Malla deva i., that according to the system of dates there, lived somewhere between 746-878 A. D. and at whose time a Mallikârjuna svâmi lived; Malla deva ii. falls 878 A. D. Compare also *C*an. B P. 57, 43. 5) For this reason they have smuggled into the *S*abdamaṇidarpaṇa the Toṭa svâmi (p. 125; in the Mûḍabidar MS. and Maṅgaḷûr No. III. he does not occur), one of their own gurus, who belongs to the beginning of the 16th century; and in p. 57 the instance "Whom shall I praise but Gŏrava?" appears as "Whom shall I praise but the deva?" in the Mûḍabidar MS., though Gŏrava (a peculiar name of *S*iva) and the deva (according to Nâgavarma's *C*handas) in the end mean the same. The tendency of the Liṅgâitas of trying to impress their own seal on the celebrated works of other sects (Jainas) appears also to some extent from Nâgavarma's prosody; see above

To the proofs, given in p. xxi of the *S*bdm., that Kešava was a Jaina three others can now be added. The one occurs p. 132 in the instance "kramadĕ" to the rule about the ĕ of the instrumental, which word, according to two MSS. quite independent of each other,[1] is taken from a sentence about Jaina dîkshâ; the other is that, according to the same MSS. and one in the hands of Hiraṇyagarbha[2], in p. 255 two Kanda verses occur as instances to rule 217, that are quoted from the Jaina novel Lîlâvatî; and the third is that one of these forms a part of a praise offered to Jinešvara.[3] It is certain, Kešava would never have cited any passages of direct Jaina tendency, if he had been a Liṅgâita, or a member of the *A*râdhya Brâhmaṇas who were the first liṅga worshippers in Southern India, and could have avoided doing so (as he certainly could have done in all the instances concerned); for all who have had occasion to read Canarese Liṅgâita or *S*aiva works, will know of the bitter hatred and tales of cruel persecution of all that is Jaina exhibited in such works.[4] Besides, if Kešava had belonged to the Liṅgâitas or *S*aivas, he would at all events somehow have plainly professed his specific views, which is not the case. The very beginning of the grammar with simply a devotional verse to Vâgdevî seems to be characteristic for all Jaina compositions in Canarese.

4. On Nâgavarma in particular.

Nâgavarma is mentioned as a pattern-poet in the Canarese Rasaratnâkara of the Jaina kavi *S*âlva[5], and frequently quoted by

p. xxi. Their endeavours have been favored by the just-mentioned instance with Kešava, and as has been seen above, by some peculiarities with Nâgavarma. The Jainas made their peace with the Brahmans, and used also their pantheon; and the fact that with our two authors *S*iva is the deva, proves that at their time *S*ivaism was on the ascendency in the South, at least with the ruling powers, so that a compromise, playful and cunning on the part of the atheists, (for "deva" is a sort of slang) became expedient. See J. R. A. S., N. S., iii., 1, p. 146, where it is stated that A. D. 473 in Orissa (Oḍra) the Kešari family, worshippers of *S*iva, had raised themselves on the ruins of the Buddhist dynasty. Curtailing full quotations in the *S*bdm., see p. iv., may, at least partly, have happened from sectarian motives. *S*bdm. p. xxi. appears as an attack on the Brahmans: "O *S*iva, these people" etc.; it is advisable to give the original "O Trailokya *C*ûḍâmaṇi" instead of "O *S*iva". P. 110 occur the instances: "I am *S*iva", "I am Gauri", "I am Nandi", showing that certain *S*aiva tales became popular in the South at Kešava's time.

1) Mûḍabidar and Maṅgaḷûr No. iii. 2) Vkp. p. 121. 3) Lîlâvatî 1, 11; 3, 86. The Maṅgaḷûr edition has only all the verbal forms occurring in the verses. 4) Could the Liṅgâita Kalyâṇa Basava (Vṛishabha) have been got up to some extent in direct opposition to the Jaina Arhant Vṛishabha? 5) 1, 8. 12. 16 (Nâga); 2, 61.

him.[1] As will be seen further on, *S*âlva may have lived either at the time of Kâkateya Rudra Pratâpa Gaṇapati deva of Ŏruṅgal, or not long after it. This king ruled from A. D. 1292 (or 1295) to 1335.[2] *S*âlva says he has used all the lâkshaṇa granthas, but he will take up that of Nâga (*i. e.* Nâgavarma) who has been an ornament to the court (sabhâ rañjaka), and reproduce its contents in an abridged form.

The author of the Sa*m*skṛita-Karṇâṭa Nânârtharatnâkara[3], Devottama of the dvija va*m*ša, also a Jaina, states (1, 3) that among others[4] he has made use of the Abhidhânârtha of Nâgavarma (*i. e.* Nâgavarma's Nighaṇṭu) and of the *S*abdamañjari. If this last-mentioned vocabulary be the *S*abdamañjari by the above-mentioned Toṭa svâmi, Devottama would have lived about the middle of the 16th century[5].

Further the Kavijihvâbandhana[6] mentions Nâgavarma (1, 6), as does also the Nighaṇṭu of Abhinava Maṅga râja (verses 1. 4) or Kavi Maṅga (v. 540)[7]. The author of this vocabulary is called, in the final words of each chapter, "Abhinava Bâlasarasvati Maṅga râja," and speaks of his work as that "of Maṅga râja, that is named Bâlašâradĕ". This reminds one of the Tĕlugu Bâlasarasvatîya, the oldest commentary on the Nannaya Bhaṭṭîya of about A. D. 1130[8], by Bâlasarasvati. At all events this Maṅga râja does belong to the later writers, as the metre, Shaṭpadi, which he uses, sufficiently proves.

Nâgavarma, in his Kâvyâvaloka, alludes to old great poets (purâṇa kavîšvara, 10, 1). His quotations, like those of Kešava, often refer to

1) Probably N.'s Kâvyâvaloka, as all the quotations are rules belonging to kâvya; but that peculiar portion of the MS. is not in our possession. However two instances in our fragment (3, 89; 4, 89) are given by *S*âlva (1, 125; 2, 20). Two others (1, 48; 2, 24) occur in the *S*abdamaṇidarpaṇa (p. 264 ನಿಮಿರ್ದರ್ಪು; p. 91 ಮುದಗಜ); besides the firstmentioned quotations (1, 125; 2, 20) are found as such both in the Kvyl. (3, 39; 4, 89) and *S*bdm. (p. 136 ಏನೋಽದದ; p. 188 ಉದಯಾ). 2) Dr. Burnell's Va*m*ša Brâhmaṇa, p. vi., vii. Mr. Brown says he reigned 88 years, C. T. p. 66; cf. p. 30 and A. D. 1290. 1318. 1335.

3) Composed in 168 Sanscrit vṛittas. 4) Our MS. says nija Gopâli, Dhanañjaya, abhinava Jûda, Bhâguri, Jayantya, Amara, and Bala; the copy from which it has been taken, belonged to a Jaina of Mysore; amongst other praises by the Jaina owner occurs *e. g.* šrîmad-Bhaṭṭâkalaṅka-munayĕ nama*h*. This muni may be the srî bhaṭṭa Akalaṅka, the author of the Bhâshâmañjari on the Sanscrit-Canarese grammar *S*abdânušâsana; see *S*abdamaṇidarpaṇa, p. xiii. Regarding the inner evidences about Devottama's mata cf. verses 19, 44, 47, 48, 62, 64, 134, 150, 157, 160. 5) See p. xxxiii., note 5. The *S*abdamañjari, however, may be something different, perhaps even the Bhâshâmañjari of Akalaṅka or that of Samantabhadra (see further on). 6) See above p. xxxiii., note 1. 7) Cf. p. xxv., note 1. 8) See p. xxx., top of the note. Many assert that the commentator was a pupil of the ancient grammarian himself; Mr. Brown's Essay on Tĕlugu (1839), i., p. 10, and Preface to his Dictionary.

personages of the Bhârata and Râmâyaṇa[1]. Paragraph 4, 100 is curious; its translation is: "On earth the voices (dhvâna) of Nâgavarma, Guṇavarma and *S*ambavarma became highly renowned, so that the foremost of scholars (vibudhâgraṇi), who are called praised worthies, eulogized them". The conclusion of paragraph 7 is: "For an understanding of great glory that received eminent adoration in those assemblies, they would say of Nâgavarma that he was a second (abhinava) Sarvavarma";[2] and that of par. 9 is: "The assemblage of scholars with eulogy flatters the Paṇḍita Nâgavarma, saying that he spreads understanding which moves about in the selection of nectar, and that he is perfect in the quite mature šâstras, sweet in the happiness he possesses, and everywhere the beloved friend of the good". Further the final statement in par. 7 is: "This is the chapter on verbs in the šabdasmṛiti of the Kâvyâvaloka that has been composed by Nâga and the other Varmas (nâgâdivarma)". This remark probably refers to the three Varmas of 4, 100, who seem to have formed a trio, and to have worked together.

In Nâgavarma's Nighaṇṭu, the vastukosha, as the last verse (36) of the sâmânya kâṇḍa, occurs the very same verse that has just been quoted as the conclusion of par. 9 of his Kvyl.; the verse preceding it in the Nighaṇṭu is as follows: "Thus he who possesses sound qualities, good conduct, and a mind that is virtuous and fixed on one object, he the beloved son (*i.e.* pupil?) of Dâmodara (dâmodara priya suta)[3] and an ornament of the ear of poets (kavi karṇapûra), has told the sâmânya words, so that common people are enabled to understand them".[4]

If the Guṇavarma who has written a Canarese Harivaṁša[5] and is named by Kešava as one of his predecessors[6], be one of the three Varmas

1) For instance Râvaṇa (5, 88); Laṅkešvara (3, 16. 26); Dašânana (5, 84); Daityarâja (5, 101; 7, 2); Nîlagrîva (5, 84); Srî *C*andra bhûvallabha (6, 21); 5, 114 seems to refer to Kṛishṇa the shepherd and to put high attributes to him (pannagatalpa, kaṁsahara, etc.); Raghuvaṁša (5, 119); Rudra (2, 26); Rudrâvatâra (5, 62), Mâdeva, Mâdevî (5, 58).

2) Or *S*arvavarma. A *S*arvavarma is sometimes quoted by mistake as the author of the Kalâpa (or Kâtantra) grammar; M. Müller's Sanscrit Grammar, p. 4. 3) A Dâmodara who at all events lived before 1643 A. D., wrote the metrical composition Vâṇîbhûshaṇa, the source of which is the Prâkṛita Piṅgaḷa, and which endeavours to introduce the metres of this work into Saṁskṛita Prosody. See above p. xiii.; Weber. p. 208. Dâmodara is also a Jaina Tîrthaṅkara, Ind. Ant. ii., 140; and a name of Kṛishṇa. According to the genealogy in N.'s prosody, N.'s own father was Vĕṇṇamayya, p. xviii. 4) In these words he specially characterises himself as one of the propagators of vernacular literature in the South. 5) *S*bdm. p. 144. The Tĕlugu Harivaṁša was composed by Tikkanna Somayâji who died, it is said, A. D. 1198; See above p. xxix., and Mr. Brown's Preface to his Dictionary.

6) *S*bdm. p. 4.

and the fellow-poet of Nâgavarma, he and also Nâgavarma would have lived before Kešava; and it would also become certain, that they had preceded the reign of Pratâpa Rudra of Ŏruṅgal[1], if the Jagannâtha vijaya, which refers to Guṇavarma, is to be dated from that king's time (see p. xxxix.). However, having thus obtained the first hint regarding Nâgavarma's priority to Kešava, I may adduce an apparently direct testimony regarding it. Namely, that the two scholars should have quoted so many verses in common[2], independently of each other, is very improbable. Either Kešava has made use of Nâgavarma or vice versa. Such being the case one little circumstance seems to make it perfectly evident that the first, to some extent, copied Nâgavarma; viz. Kešava (p. 159), to show the use of the Dative in wishing a blessing (svasti) to somebody, quotes as an instance one of the two benedictory verses with which Nâgavarma concludes the ekârtha kâṇḍa of his Dictionary. Even the most cautious critic will grant that this circumstance is one of some weight. So we may safely assume that Kešava, in undertaking his work, wanted to write a more "comprehensive grammar" (vistâra vyâkaraṇa)[3] than in this case the mere skeleton in the first part of Nâgavarma's Kâvyâvaloka. The quotation in Kešava p. 18, beginning "varasandhyakshara", is very probably taken from the Kâvyâvalokana wherein (1, 14) it appears to form a statement of the author, and is immediately preceded by the Upendravajra verse that occurs Sbdm. p. 17.

As a curiosity it may be stated here, that our copy of the Kâvyâvaloka (4, 104) has the following verse: "Vâdirâja, who was the destroyer of the mass of Advaitavâdis that were like a troop of rutting elephants, and who was the lion on the mountain formed by the pre-eminent and pointed Syâdvâda, became renowned, so that the learned eulogized

1) p. xxxv. 2) p. xxv. 3) See Sbdm. p. xvi.; the reading there is corroborated by the Mûḍabidar MS. The grammatical quotation alluded to in that page is rule 16 of par. 6 of the Kâvyâvaloka; but does not belong to Kešava's original quotations, as it does not appear in the Mûḍabidar MS., though it is in all the others at hand.—By the way I may remark that the Mûḍabidar MS. does not contain the rules on the so-called passive voice, p. 299 seq., the verbal roots, p. 302 seq., and the Vocabulary, etc., p. 402-408. The second list of the somewhat obsolete words in the Maṅgaḷûr edition seems to be a forgery on account of No. 35 "baḷamardu", gunpowder, as according to Mr. Brown's Tables A. D. 1437 the Musalmans used no fire-arms, and only after the year 1510 cannon and musketry are mentioned in Indian history; unless it can be proved that a good number of years before 1437 gunpowder was known in India.

him." Could the Advaitavâdis be Sankarâčârya's followers?[1] Sankarâčârya belongs to the end of the 7th century A. D.

For his Dictionary Nâgavarma has used "Vararuči, Halâyudha, Sâšvata[2], Amarakosha, and others" (1, 2). If Halâyudha, the author of the vocabulary called Abhidhâna ratnamâlâ, and Halâyudha, that of the commentary on Piṅgala's Chandas sûtras called Mṛitasañjîvinî, be the same, Nâgavarma's authority would have lived under king Muñja of Campâ, A. D. 961-985[3]. It is worthy of notice, that Nâgavarma does not name Hemačandra who died 1172 A. D.[4] Nâgavarma's fame appears in v. 4: "When it is stated that Nâgavarma, the neck-ornament of poets, has composed it (the Nighaṇṭu) in Kannaḍa and so clearly that even a dull person may understand it; who would not like it?"

Nâgavarma, as appears very conspicuously from his Nighaṇṭu, was an avowed Jaina[5]; for, in i., 1 he begins by asking a blessing of Vardhamâna Jinendra, in the seventh verse he asks Vâṇî (Sarasvatî, the synonyms of whom he adduces) to correct his composition, and in the eighth verse he first of all gives the synonyms of Jinešvara, respectively Tîrthakara. His Kâvyâvalokana commences with a prayer to Višvešvara, followed by one to Sarasvatî devî (i., 1. 2), and contains already in our fragment several honorable allusions to Jainism[6].

5. On Rudra bhaṭṭa, etc.

It is much to be regretted that for the present it is quite impossible to fix the date of the above-mentioned Jagannâthavijaya[7]. It may be one of

1) Vâdirâja is *e. g.* a Bodhisatva with the Buddhists. The Vaishṇava dâsas of Uḍupu on the Western coast used to call their Madhvâčârya (A. D. 1121-1197, Dr. Burnell's Vamša Br. p. xxiv.), the Vâdirâja; see *e. g.* the introduction of the Abhimanyu kâḷaga. The Jaina Abhinava Pampa in his Râmačandra čarita Purâṇa (1, 24) says: "Srutakîrti (Srutikîrti), acquainted with the threefold knowledge, by means of the weapon of syâdvâda vidyâ, like Devendra, cut off the wings of the paravâdi mountains". 2) This name, however may be an adjective belonging to the next word. Sâšvata, a lexicographer, is the author of the Nânârtha kosha (Ujjvaladatta to Uṇâdi sûtra, see St. Petersburg Dictionary).

3) p. xi.; Dr. Weber's Indische Studien viii., p. 193 seq.; Indische Streifen i., p. 312 seq.; 358; ii., 227; Professor Aufrecht's Preface to his edition of the Abhidhânaratnamâlâ (1861). Compare the Halâyudha prior to or contemporaneous with Basava, above p. xxxii. 4) p. xix. 5) Cf. also the verse at the end of the sâmânya kâṇḍa, that will be quoted on p. xl. 6) Jinešvara 2, 52; Jaina gṛiha and prayer to Guṇabhadra deva 3, 5; Jaina dîkshâ 3, 27; Jinendra deva 3, 42; Jina dharma 5, 62; 6, 48.

7) p. xxxvii.

the earliest Canarese Brahmanical[1] compositions. It relates the stories of Kṛishṇa according to the Vishṇu Purâṇa (1, 21). The author calls himself Rudra (1, 21.22), and once Rudra bhaṭṭa (1, 16). Like those of Nâgavarma and Kešava, his work is written in archaic language, and in the čampû style which was, it appears, general with the early authors. He begins his composition by asking a blessing of Kṛishṇa (1, 1), then of *C*aturmukha (2), Umâpati (3), Mârtâṇḍa (4), Gaṇapati (5), and Vâṇî (6). Thereupon, as is customary with all modern poets, he praises Vâlmîki, Vyâsa, Bâṇa[2], Harsha[3], Mâgha and Kâḷidâsa (7-9)[4].

In 1, 17 he says, he will tell his story, the "šâradâbhra čandrâtapa Rudra Kṛishṇa kathâ", in such a manner that the learned will eulogize him. In "the story of Kṛishṇa, who belongs to Rudra whose lustre is like the moon of an autumnal cloud" the Rudra is either the poet himself, or perhaps a patron of his, or both may be meant. In one of the two last-mentioned cases Rudra Pratâpa Gaṇapati of Ŏruṅgal (about 1300 A. D.)[5] might be thought of, and an allusion to his name be found also in the above prayer, wherein Umâpati (Rudra), Mârtâṇḍa with the epithet pratâpodaya, and Gaṇapati occur successively. However that may be, it is a fact that a scholar, named Rudra bhaṭṭa, who lived under the said king, became the author of the *S*ṛiṅgâratilaka Pratâparudrîya in Sa*m*skṛita[6]; and strange to say the Jaina kavi *S*âlva[7], in his Canarese Rasaratnâkara, alludes to a Rasa-kalikâ of Rudra bhaṭṭa, and designates this person as one of the *A*ryas whose footsteps he will follow[8]. Here only one Rudra bhaṭṭa seems to be before us, who may have reproduced his Sa*m*skṛita composition in the Karṇâṭa language (just as Nâgavarma wrote in both languages, see above p. xxv.) and who perhaps may be also the author of the Jagannâtha vijaya.

1, v. 10 of Rudra is interesting, as, after the above-mentioned Sa*m*skṛita

---

1) The Tĕlugu Nannaya bhaṭṭa, probably a Brahman, wrote the *A*diparva of the Mahâbhârata about 1130 A. D.; see above p. xxix., seq. In Tĕlugu and Tamiḻ the Vishṇu Purâṇa seems to have been little regarded in earlier times. 2) Cf. Weber's Indische Streifen i., p. 312. 3) Cf. Ind. Ant. iii., 30. 4) Weber's Ind. Studien 8, 196. 415, etc.; "On the Râmâyaṇa" p. 81-87. 5) P. xxxv. 6) St. Petersburg Dictionary *s. v.* Rudrabhaṭṭa (Rudrakavîndra). 7) P. xxxiv. 8) 1, in the prose after v. 34; 1, 8. It is questionable whether he cites his work, or only mentions it as an authority; if the verse in question be a quotation, Rudra bhaṭṭa would be proved to be also a Canarese poet.—If it were not too unsafe a guide, as close imitations of ancient poets have been attempted by rather late poets, *e.g.* the author of the Râjašekhara vilâsa, the archaic language, style, etc. in the Jagannâtha vijaya would be decidedly in favour of supposing its author to belong to Rudra Pratâpa's time. He uses also the Mahâsragdhara; see above p. xii.

poets, follow the names of nine of his Karṇâṭa predecessors, that bear an archaic stamp; it runs thus: "In order that the world may praise this work, may it contain the imaginative power of *S*aṅkhavarma, the elegance of *S*ântivarma, the eminence of composition of Guṇavarma, the brilliancy of Manasija, the clever diction of Karṇama, the definition of Pampa, the knowledge (?) of *C*andra bhaṭṭa, the novelty of Pŏnnamayya, and the intelligence of Gajâṅkuša!" The first three names appear to refer to the above-mentioned trio: the *S*aṅkhavarma of our MS. is probably the *S*ambavarma of the Kâvyâvaloka[1]; *S*ântivarma may be a surname to express the endearing character of Nâgavarma, who states about himself in the Kâvyâvaloka at the conclusion of par. 7: "In this manner he who causes to rise the excellencies of poetry (kavitâguṇodaya) and possesses a peaceful mind (šântamana), has uttered this, so that the doubt regarding grammar, that is like a sea of darkness, disappears, and the assemblage of the learned quickly assents"[2]; and lastly Guṇavarma is the third of the company of friends. Rudra's work may have had somehow connexion with the black Jagannâtha pagoda in Orissa, the erection of which is said to have taken place between A. D. 1240-1299[3]. Our olĕ copy dates from a Prabhava sa*m*vatsara, probably A. D. 1807, and was written at Kiraṅgûr by a Narasimbhaṭṭa for a *S*rînivâsayya, the younger brother of Veṅkaṭapatayya.

It seems fit to state here that *S*âlva in his Rasaratnâkara (1, 8) mentions, as another of his authorities, Vidyânâtha, probably the author of the Pratâparudrîya, a work on the drama and rhetoric, in honour of Pratâpa Rudra Gaṇapati Kâkateya[4].

Regarding the *S*abdânušâsana, the Sa*m*skṛita-Karṇâṭa grammar

---

1) mba (ಂಬ) and *m*kha (ಂಖ) are easily mistaken one for the other in MSS.

2) This occurs just before the above-quoted passage (p. xxxvi.) in which Nâgavarma is called an abhinava Sarvavarma. The epithet "kavitâguṇodaya", in the Nighaṇṭu, occurs three times in connexion with him, at the end of the ekârtha-, nânârtha-, and sâmânya kâṇḍa. At the conclusion of the latter it is said: "This is the sâmânya kâṇḍa of the Abhidhâna vastukosha that has been composed by *S*rî Nâgavarma who causes to rise the excellencies of lovely (čaṅčura) poetry in clear and profound language, born of the good grace of the foot-lotus of Jina, and who is (therefore) praised by people in various ways." Another of his epithets is "čintâtîta prânta", he who has arrived at the state of being free from care, at the end of the ekârtha k. In his prosody he is named "guṇâgraṇi," above p. xix.; and "guṇodayoddâma," p. xx.

3) Brown's Tables, p. 6-8.

4) Mr. Brown's C. Tables, s. 1318 A. D., states that in the days of this king the Bhâskara Râmâyaṇa, the 7th book or uttara kâṇḍa, was written by Tikkanna; cf. his Essay on Tĕlugu Literature, ii., p. 24, 25. He revokes this statement already in his Tables, p. 58. 66, saying that the poet died 1198 A. D. See p. xxix.

in short prose sûtras like Nâgavarma's (p. xxv.)[1], mentioned in the Mangalore edition of the Sabdamaṇidarpaṇa (p. xiii., seq.)[2], it may be added here, that another MS. with its commentary, the Bhâshâmañjari, by the Jaina Srîbhaṭṭâkalaṅka, obtained by us through the favor of the Liṅgâita svâmi at Mâdevapura maṭha in Kŏḍagu (Coorg), says in its concluding šloka[3], that it was written by Kṛishṇa râja (1504-1529 A. D.), *i. e.* probably in his honour. If this statement be true, the Bhâshâmañjari would precede the king's reign by about a hundred years, and the Sabdânušâsana, its commentary, by about as many, so that its composition may probably be referred to Pratâpa Rudra's time; but it may be older.

6. Probable age.

To sum up, it seems probable that first Nâgavarma, then Kešava (Keši), and thereafter Rudra, flourished somewhere between the years 1000-1335 A. D. Sâlva probably lived a little after Rudra bhaṭṭa, or may belong to his later days. Kešava's time, if he be identical with the Keši of the Canarese Basava Purâṇa, would be about A. D. 1130-1180[4].

7. An alphabetical list of early authors.

The following is an alphabetical list of the early Canarese authors mentioned in Nâgavarma, Kešava, Rudra, Sâlva, Hiraṇyagarbha, etc. Where an asterisk is added to a name, it denotes that the person concerned may not have written in Canarese.

1) Nannayya bhaṭṭa's treatise on Tĕlugu Grammar (of about A. D. 1130) is written in Sanscrit verse. Brown's Grammar, p. 266. 304.

2) The Mûḍabidar MS. of the Sabdamaṇidarpaṇa is also accompanied with a commentary, but not that of Nishṭhûrasañjayya, a circumstance that shows the late age of this person; cf. Sbdm., p. xiv.

3) Its introductory šloka (after the Liṅgâita formula "šrîguru Basavaliṅgâya namah") is: "namah šrî Vardhamânâya višvavidyâvabhâsine | sarvabhâshâmayî bhâshâ pravṛittâ yan mukhâmbujât." The concluding one is: "Karṇâṭakavyâkaraṇam nabhasi vyayavatsare (*i. e.* A. D. 1526) | Kṛishṇa-bhûpena likhitam tatadâvegate kalau." There exists in Mûḍabidar a composition, as it seems on the Jaina religion, by Akaḷaṅka svâmi; Professor Wilson speaks of Akalaṅka, a Jaina teacher from Savaṇabaḷḷugoḷĕ, the Jaina village near Cinraipatam, as belonging to the 8th century. See also above p. xxxv. About the Jainas on the Western coast in Tuḷu, where Mûḍabidar is, see the article by Dr. Burnell in Ind. Ant. ii., 353. Through Dr. B.'s kindness in furnishing me with a catalogue I am enabled to mention some of the Jaina works extant at Mûḍabidar, and have also obtained a copy of the MS. of the Abhinava Pampa Râma Candra carita Purâṇa to which he alludes, *ibid.* p. 274, the MS. having been written about 440 years ago (š. š. 1350).

4) Keširâja was still alive when Basava died in 1168. If, however, the Bijjaḷa deva who died in the same year with Basava, did not begin to reign at Kalyâṇa before the year 1189 A. D., as stated in the Journ. R. A. S., N. S., i., 2, p. 252, Kešava is to be put somewhat later. See above p. xxxii.

1. Amṛitânandi*, a writer on good composition (Rsr. 1, 8; 1, after 42)[1].
2. Argaḷa (Aggaḷa) deva, a Jaina, who finished his Candraprabha Purâṇa A. D. 1189 (Vkp. p. 121)[2].
3. Asaga (Sbdm. p. 4).
4. Udayâditya, a writer on good composition (Rsr. 2, after 61).
5. Karṇama (Jagv. 1, 10)[3].
6. Kavirâjakuñjara, a Jaina, from whose Lîlâvatî prabandha at least two verses are quoted in the Sbdm. (1, 11; 3, 86). Perhaps A. D. 873. His real name is said to have been Nemičandra (Vkp. p. 121)[4].
7. Kâma*, or Kavikâma, appears together with Nâgavarma as a writer on good composition (Nâgavarma Kavikâmâdi mârga, Rsr. 1, after 8).
8. Kešava, or Keši râja, the author of the Sabdamaṇidarpaṇa, a Coḷapâlaka čaritra, Subhadrâharaṇa, Prabodhačandra, and Kirâta (Sbdm. p. 408).
9. Gajâṅkuša (Jagv. 1, 10).
10. Gajaga (Sbdm. p. 4)[5].
11. Gaṇešvara*, who, in company with others, wrote a Sâhityasañjîvana on good composition (Rsr. 2, after 61).
12. Guṇanandi (Sbdm. p. 4. 39)[6].
13. Guṇabhadradeva* (Kvyl. 3, 5)[7].
14. Guṇavarma (Sbdm. p. 4; Kvyl. 4, 100; Jagv. 1, 10), a contemporary of Nâgavarma, who wrote a Canarese Harivaṃša (Sbdm. p. 144).
15. Candrabhaṭṭa (Sbdm. p. 4; Jagv. 1, 10).
16. Nâgačandra Sukavîndra, whom Abhinava Pampa, the author of the Râmačandra čarita, is ambitious of imitating (ch. 16, towards

1) An Amṛitânanda yogîšvara is the author of an Akârâdi Nighaṇṭu (Mûḍabidar), that is asserted to be the Dhanvantari Nighaṇṭu (materia medica). 2) There are three MSS. at Mûḍab. called Candraprabha kâvya. Argaḷa or Aggaḷa is the name of one of the fourteen Jaina Tîrthakaras enumerated by Nijaguṇa yogi in his Vivekačintâmaṇi sub čârvâka šâstra; they are: Hemačandra (probably the scholar who died A. D. 1172), Nâgačandra, Nemičandra, Meghačandra, Mâghačandra, Ārhata, Ādinâtha, Aggaḷa, Pâršvanâtha, Saugata, Srutikîrti, Srîmati, Kâmarahita, and Munisvâmi. The names with spaces appear in the list of authors. 3) A Karṇavarma with a (Saṃskṛita) Nemanâtha purâṇa etc. at Mûḍab. 4) A (Saṃskṛita) Lîlâvatî pr. at M. 5) Nos. 9 and 10 may possibly mean the same person. 6) A Guṇanandi appears in the list of Jaina gurus of the Mercara plates that probably date from A. D. 466. Ind. Ant. i., 365. 7) If an author, he may be the Guṇabhadra âčârya, author of the (Saṃskṛita) Uttara Purâṇa, at M.

the end). This Nâgačandra is probably the author of the Canarese treatise on Jaina dharma, called Jinamunitanaya; 102 verses in the Kanda. Its v. 4 runs thus: "The virtue of the good who hear this (my composition), is the fortune of Nâgačandra who relates (it) and is praised by the poets. Do not think lightly of the saving šrî Jina dharma, thou that goest to emancipation (mokshagâmi), O son of Jina muni!" (Jinamunitanaya, these being the words with which each verse concludes).

17. Nâgavarma, or Nâga, the author of the Kâvyâvaloka, Nighaṇṭu, *C*handas, and a Karṇâṭaka vyâkaraṇa in Sanscrit[1].
18. Nemičandra, who has been stated to be identical with Kavirâjakuñjara (Vkp. p. 121)[2].
19. Pampa. See Hampa.
20. Pŏnna. Pŏnnamayya. See Hŏnna.
21. Manasija (*S*bdm. p. 4; Jagv. 1, 10), perhaps identical with the *C*ittaja of the Kavijihvâbandhana (1, 6; *S*bdm. p. xxv.).
22. Rudra, or Rudrabhaṭṭa, the author of the Jagannâtha vijaya and perhaps of the Rasakaḷikĕ.
23. Vidyânâtha* (Rsr. 1, 8), author of the Pratâparudrîya[3], between 1292-1335 A. D.
24. Vîraṇandi*, a Jaina (Abhinava Pampa 1, 26. 27)[4].
25. *S*aṅkhavarma (Jagv. 1, 10).
26. *S*ambavarma, a contemporary of Nâgavarma, probably identical with No. 25 (Kvyl. 4, 100).
27. *S*ântivarma (Jagv. 1, 10), probably a surname of Nâgavarma.
28. *S*âlva, the author of the Rasaratnâkara, a treatise on poetry and dramatic composition in three chapters: 1) šṛiṅgâra prapañča; 2) rasa vivaraṇa; 3) nâya nâyikâ vivaraṇa. He has consulted for his work Amṛitânandi, Rudrabhaṭṭa (rasakaḷikĕ), Vidyânâtha, Hemačandra, Nâgavarma, Kavikâma, Udayâditya, Gaṇešvara (sâhitya sañjîvana) and others. Among the Paurâṇika and Aitihâsika personages of his quotations occurs also a *C*andrahâsa (3, 13. 14), a circumstance that may point to the existence of a Canarese Jaimini Bhârata at his time, (different from

1) See note to Hampa, No. 34; and above p. xli. 2) At Mûḍabidar are a Gomaṭasâra mûla (Saṃskṛita) by Nemačandra, and a Tribhaṅgi paramâgama by Nemačandra siddhânti. (Nemačandra may be a slip of the Jaina writer's pen instead of Nemičandra.) 3) There is a Pratâparudra at M. 4) At M. is a *C*andraprabha kâvya mûla (or mâlâ?) by Vîranandîšvara.

that afterwards to be mentioned). His work, on account of its obscenities, is unfit for publication.

29. *S*rî Vijaya (*S*bdm. p. 4).

30. Samantabhadra* (*S*bdm. p. 125; Abhin. P. 1, 10)[1].

31. Sarvavarma*, a renowned predecessor of Nâgavarma (Kvyl. 7, at the end).

32. Sujanottamsa (*S*bdm. p, 4. 109. 112. 133. 164). The supposition has been expressed that he may be identical with Nemičandra (Vkp. p. 121).

33. Sumanobâṇa, a poet whose daughter was Kešava's mother (*S*bdm. p. 2).

34. Hampa, or Pampa (*S*bdm. p. 4; Jagv. 1, 10; see No. 16 of our list). One Abhinava Pampa, a Jaina, wrote a Râmačandra čarita Purâṇa, a Mûḍabidar copy of which is dated A. D. 1428 (see above p. xli., note 3). The work contains the following chapters (âšvâsa): 1. pîṭhikâ prakaraṇa; 2. Dašaratha janana; 3. Dašaratha kumârodaya varṇana; 4. Janaka Jina bhavana daršana; 5. Sîtâ svayamvara; 6. vana pravešа varṇana; 7. šarad varṇana; 8. čaraṇa yugala darpaṇa; 9. Sîtâ haraṇa; 10. Dašavadana vamša varṇana; 11. Laṅkâ dahana varṇana; 12. šrî Râma prayâṇa varṇana; 13. Balâčyuta puṇya prabhodaya; 14. Raghuvîra vijaya varṇana; 15. Sîtâ parityâga; 16. parinirvâṇa kalyâṇa varṇana[2]. It is not

1) Three works of a Samantabhadra (Samskṛita): Nyâya niščaya vârtikâlaṅkâra; Uktyânušâsana (?); Bhâshâmañjari are at M. 2) The author says (1, 40) he will tell the wonderful story of Râma which Gautama on the Vipula hill by the side of Vîrajina told the Magadhâdhipa who was a gaṇâgraṇi. He remembers all the great followers of Gautama's sudharma (1, 7), the šrutakevali Bhadrabâhu(v. 8), Bhûtabali, Puṣpadanta, Jinasena, Munîndra, Samantabhadra (v. 10), Kaviparameshṭhi, Pûjyapâda (v. 11; these last-mentioned three svâmis occur *S*abdamaṇidarpaṇa p. 125), Kuṇḍakundâčârya or Kŏṇḍa—(v. 12), Akaḷaṅka čandra (v. 13), Vardhamâna bhaṭṭâraka who caused the divyabhâshârasapûrṇašrutapayodhi to be obtained (v. 14. 15), Bâlačandra (v. 16. 17. 18), Meghačandra (v. 19. 20), *S*ubhakîrti (v. 21-23), *S*rutakîrti (once *S*rutikîrti, v. 24. 25), and Vîraṇandi siddhântika (v. 26. 27; cf. the Jaina siddhânta works, Ind. Ant. ii., 198).—The Kŏṇḍakundânvaya appears in a *C*era grant that belongs to 466 A. D., Ind. Ant. i., 365; a Kundâčârya occurs 522 A. D., Ind. Ant. ii., 131. Akalaṅka čandra may be the teacher of 788 A. D. mentioned in Ind. Ant. ii., 15. 16; cf. iii., 193; above p. xli. Bâlačandra occurs in the prose-sentence at the end of each chapter as being the guru of the author of the work. Meghačandra is one of the fourteen Tîrthaṅkaras mentioned above in p. xlii. Of *S*rutakîrti, also one of the above-mentioned Tîrthaṅkaras, it is said: "When *S*rutakîrti, the traividyavrati, by gatapratyâgata communicated the Râghava Pâṇḍavîya, he making it the surprise of the learned, manifested pure fame"; this work seems to be similar to the Râghava Pâṇḍavîya of Kavirâja (who perhaps belongs to the 11th century), as both appear to possess the peculiarity of giving two meanings when differently read, the last-mentioned presenting in the same words the story of the Râghavas

quite impossible that the original Hampa is identical with the Tamil Kamba or Kampa, the author of a Râmâyaṇa, as the Tamil letter k may represent an h; but in this case Kampa's work ought to be Jaina; see above p. xxx.

35. Hamsarâja, an author from whom a quotation is found in Nâgavarma (Kvyl. 5, 84) and in Kešava (Sbdm. p. 377)[1].
36. Hemačandra* (Rsr. 1, 8).
37. Hŏnna, or Pŏnna (Sbdm. p. 4), who is probably the same as Pŏnnam ayya (master) of Rudra (Jagv. 1, 10).

Two other Jainas may still be named, viz. Guṇačandra* and Devačandra. Guṇačandra, the author of a Pâršvâbhyudayamâghaṇandîšvara, may be identical with the Guṇačandra âčârya of Ind. Ant. ii., 131[2], occurring there under Pratâpa Ballâḷa whose second successor is Vîra Ballâḷa (1193-1199 A. D.)[3]. Devačandra wrote a Canarese Râjâvaḷi kathĕ according to Ind. Ant. iii., 154. To this period may further belong two well-known Jaina Canarese treatises: the Sâstrasâra, and the Dharmaparîkshĕ (by Vṛittavilâsa), copies of both of which are met with at Mûḍabidar[4]; and two Canarese Commentaries: the one on the Amarakosha, called Nâčirâji; and the other on Halâyudha's Abhidhânaratnamâlâ. This recension of the Abhidhânaratnamâlâ does not contain the stanzas referred to and quoted in Prof. Aufrecht's edition p. 98 seq.

Of the above-mentioned 40 names of early authors one only can with certainty be referred by me to a Brahman, viz. Rudra; his age, however, is still questionable. No. 1. 4. 5. 7. 11. 23 may perhaps be also Brahmanical.

---

and Pâṇḍavas (St. Petersburg Lexicon; Weber's Indische Streifen i., 352. 369. 371; Ind. Ant. i., 250). At Mûḍabidar are: Raghuvamša by Kîrtikavîšvara; Amoghavṛitti by Višâlakîrti svâmi; Jina yajña phalodaya by Kalyâṇakîrti. An Amalakîrti occurs Ind. Ant. ii., 131. Regarding Vîraṇandi see note to No. 24.—At Mûḍabidar are as works of Hampa kavi (whether Abhinava H. ?): Laghu purâṇa, Pâršvanâtha purâṇa, and Paramâgama. [Since writing the above we received the first 5 chapters of Abhinava Pampa's work in print from L. Rice, Esq. who is editing the whole. Mr. Rice remarks in his Prefatory Notice "the Mûla Pampa, as we learn from the Râma kathâvatâra, was a different person from Abhinava Pampa. It also informs us that the latter derived the materials for his poem from previously existing works, named Râmačaritra, Kumudendu Râmâyaṇa, Puṇyâšrava kathâsâra and others; whose authors were Câmuṇḍa râya, Nâgačandra (see above No. 16), Mâghanandi, Siddhânti Kumudendu, Nayasena and others". Mr. Rice is going to publish also, as he states, Nâgavarma's Bhâshâbhûshaṇa (a Canarese grammar in Sanscrit) and Sabdânušâsana.]

1) In Kešava there is a fragment, whereas the whole verse in the Mahâsragdharâ metre occurs in Nâgavarma. 2) Or with the Guṇačandra Bhaṭâra of the Kŏṇḍakundânvaya of the Cera grant of 466 A. D.; see above p. xliv. 3) See above p. xxxii.

4) They are archaic in style and language; the following šloka, used against Brahmanical antagonists, occurs in both: matsyaḥ kûrmo varâhaš ča nârasimhaš ča vâmanaḥ | râmo râmaš ča krishṇaš ča bauddhaḥ kalki dašâkṛitiḥ. Cf. Ind. Evangelical Review, i., 1, p. 67 seq.

That Rudra, though a follower of Vishṇu, mentions some of the renowned Jaina authorities of his time, is not to be wondered at, as he quotes them merely with regard to their style, a step most probably taken from his having no other choice, and which had no connexion with his religious views.

8. Some *S*aiva Paṇḍitas

As scholars at the time of the founder of their sect, Basava, the Liṅgâitas adduce the following (*S*aivas):

1. Malhaṇa or Maluhaṇa, a śiva kavi or šaiva kavîndra, whose companion was Maluhaṇî[1]. He is the author of a *S*ivastotra of forty verses in Sanscrit. (Regarding his age it is uncertain whether tradition places him before or contemporary with Basava.)

2. Paṇḍitârâdhya, also called Paṇḍiteša and Paṇḍita ayya (master), or simply Paṇḍita, a šiva kavi and *S*iva's dear paṇḍita. He was born at Sudkâkuṇḍa, and appears at the court of Anantapâla nṛipâla[2]. He is counted as one of the Liṅgâita Pańčâčâryas. His legend exists in Tĕlugu.

3. *S*rîpati paṇḍita or Siripati paṇḍita, called also simply *S*rîpaṇḍita, the siva kâvya[3].

4. *S*ivaleṅka Mańčaṇṇa (aṇṇa = elder brother) or *S*ivaleṅka Mańčayya (ayya = master), called also Leṅka Mańčideva, Mańčaṇa paṇḍita, Mańčaṇârya, Mańčârya and Mańčayya, *S*iva's collector of customs (suṅkiga)[4].

5. Mallikârjuna paṇḍita or Mallikârjuna ârâdhya of Amaraguṇḍa[5].

9. A few general remarks.

The Jainas of the beginning of the 5th century, in their works, treated the Brahmans with marked disrespect, saying *e. g.* that a *C*akravarti, a Baladeva or a Vasudeva could not be born in a Brahman or other mean family, but received birth in a noble family, a Kshatriya family, as in the family of Ikshvâku, or the Harivaṁša[6].

1) Bas. P. ch. 42; 50, 74; *C*an. B. P. 1, 29; 55, 44; Rajašekhv. 1, 17; Prauḍharč. ch. 9.

2) Gaṇasahasranâma 8, 14; Bas. P. 9, 43; *C*an. B. P. 1, 24. 29; 57, 18; 59, 21 seq.

3) Gaṇas. 8, 1; Bas. P. 1, 10 (see above p. xxxii.); 9, 43; 55, 24. 25.

4) Gaṇas. 8, 60; Bas. P. 1, 10; 9, 39; 53, 55; 57, 44.

5) Bas. P. 1, 10; *C*an. B. P. 57, 17 (where he appears just after Vemana ârâdhya; is this person the Tĕlugu Vemana who has written a šataka?). About Amaraguṇḍa cf. Sudhâkuṇḍa of No. 2.—As old šiva poets are enumerated by the Liṅgâitas *e. g.* the following: Kâḷidâsa, Bâṇa, Mayûra, Bhavabhûti, Halâyudha, Udbhaṭa, and a *S*aṅkara; see *C*an. Bas. P. 1, 29; Râjaš. 1, 17; etc., and above p. xxxii.

6) See M. Müller's Sanscrit Literature, p. 261.

Further proofs of their predilection for the Kshatriyas are Guṇavarma's Harivamśa, Pampa's Râmâyaṇa, and the quotations from the works of all the old Jaina authors, as they appear in Nâgavarma and Kešava (as shown above), in which frequent allusions to Kshatriyas of the Mahâbhârata, Râmâyaṇa and Southern dynasties occur. At Mûḍabidar are, besides the already mentioned works, a Râmačandra čaritĕ and a Hampaka Bhârata (by Caturakavitâguṇârṇava), both in Canarese; and Hiraṇyagarbha (p. 46) knows of a Jaina Râmâyaṇa purâṇa, Harivamśa p., Bhârata p., Râmâyaṇa and Parašu râmâyaṇa, all in the same language. The Lîlâvatî prabandha treats of the Jaina king Cintâmaṇi, whose son is Kandarpa deva and whose minister is Makaranda; and Argaḷa's Candraprabha purâṇa contains a novel about king Ajitasena[1]. No Canarese Itihâsa or Purâṇa by Brahmans seems to have existed before Rudra Pratâpa Gaṇapati (at whose time Brahmanical and Liṅgâita Canarese literature most probably came into existence); the Brahmanical Canarese Bhârata, Râmâyaṇa, etc., known nowadays, belong to a comparatively recent period.

Another peculiar feature of the first period of Canarese literature, as it appears in the Jaina works down to Sâlva, is the obnoxious taste for obscene matters, a taste that in all the branches of Canarese literature of all sects did not grow less in the following centuries, and is even nowadays certainly not on the decrease, which deplorable circumstance appears also in the republishing of both so-called religious and legendary books that contain impurities, and in adding commentaries that nourish the bad inclinations also of the hearts of the uneducated classes.

Some further circumstances in connexion with ancient Canarese literature still require particular consideration. The first is the to my knowledge total absence of all such true Canarese metres as are composed of certain Mora-feet without paying any regard to the forms and names of the feet, excepting only that none is allowed to begin with an Iambus (*i. e.* Ragaḷĕs and modern Shaṭpadis); another is that each verse-line, in its second letter, bears an Alliteration, this being the same for all the four lines; and a third that all the works are in Campu, *i. e.* are compositions in prose and verse (Vṛittas, Kandas, Akkaras, Tripadi). Besides, unacknowledged grammatical licences are nowhere met with; Tadbhavas, from Sanscrit, more or less occur in all the early compositions, the other vocables being Sanscrit and Canarese.

1) With Sâlva an Ajitasena nṛipa occurs in a quotation (2, 15).

II. The later Period, from about 1300 to 1872 A. D.

1. The Lingâita and *S*aiva period, about 1300-1500 (1490).[1]

The first part of this later period is characterised by the growth of Lingâitism, which between the years 1160-1168 A. D. or somewhat later had been established at Kalyâṇapura by the efforts of king Bijjaḷa's minister Basava, a Brahman by birth[2]. According to tradition soon after the founder's death the sect spread to Uḷavi, not far from the S. E. frontier of Govĕ (Goa); to Sŏnnalâpura or Sŏnnaligĕ (said to be the present Solâpura), *S*rîgiri, and the Malĕ râjya or Malĕ deša (hill-country) wherein Khâṇḍĕya, Hŏnnûr and in its vicinity Bâḷĕ haḷḷi are mentioned; and to Sivagaṅgĕ.[3]

This progress is said to have taken place within 60 years from Basava's death, *i. e.* between the years 1168-1228 A. D., under the rule of king Aḷiya Bijjaḷa of Kalyâṇa, the successor of Bijjaḷa. To Aḷiya Bijjaḷa, at the commencement of his reign, was said, according to the legend: "The royal insignia will be with thee for 60 years; afterwards the Râkshasa Pîtâmbara will be born of the race of the Turkas, and will rule successively for 770 years. They will cause this (Kalyâṇa) country to be called Turka âṇya (Turk kingdom), destroy Kalyâṇa, and build Kaluburigĕ. Thus, Turukâṇya will come into existence"[4]. Then the legend having related the growth of Liṅgâitism in a prophetic tone, says: "For sixty years after Basava's death Aḷiya Bijjaḷa will reign, and afterwards with an unequal force fight against the Turkas, and die, when the Turkas with great effort will destroy the glorious Kalyâṇa, rebuild Kaluburigĕ, kill cattle in Tripurântaka's temple, break Garuḍa's pillar, and build a mosque (masudi)"[5].

---

1) Regarding the year 1490 see further on the No. 15 of the list of authors. 2) His Liṅgâitism, which henceforth is to be understood as being meant in this article, is different from the worship of the lingadhâris which preceded it, and which is also still extant. This prior liṅga worship is specifically Brahmanical, and the Brahmans who wear the sacrificial thread and the liṅga, are called Ârâdhya Brâhmaṇas in the South. Basava abolished Brahmanical ceremonies, made the liṅga a common property to all, and relaxed caste-laws among his followers. 3) *C*an. Bas. Pur. (of A. D. 1585) 62, 31. 32. 35. 37. 38 seq. 4) Ditto. 62, 30; cf. 63, 41. 5) Ditto. 62, 44. The 770 years, according to the Purâṇa's system making Basava to die A. D. 785 (cf. above p. xxxii.), would close A. D. 1615, *i. e.* 51 years after the battle of Taḷakoṭĕ (1564), where Râma râja of Vidyânagara (Ânĕgundi), a prince of the house of Narasi*m*ha, was killed. After Râma's fall his family, for a time, took up its abode at *S*rîraṅgapaṭṇa, and *C*andragiri near Tirupati; 1610 *S*rîraṅgapaṭṇa became the seat of government of Râya ŏḍĕya (master) of Maisûr. About Vĕṅkaṭapati, one of the last of Râma's family (about 1591-1630 A. D.), see Ind. Ant. ii., 371. 1640 *S*rîraṅga, the son of *C*anna and the last râja of the Narasi*m*ha dynasty, made a grant to the English of the site of the city of Madras (*C*annapaṭṇa), and six years afterwards had to fly before the Sultân of

"When this Kalyâṇa has been destroyed, the Turka Râkshasas will ransack and strip its people. Then the ayyas Gummaṇa and Pĕmmaṇa, the vratis, having no place where to remain, will go and build a town in a good spot near *Sivagaṅgĕ*", calling it Gummaḷâpura, and found the Karṇâṭa land or kingdom, which is also called Sĕṭṭi nâḍu (land of the great merchants) or Pabuvâḍa (settlement of the prabhus), "where clever persons will be who are acquainted with all the purâṇas and âgamas of true and pure wisdom, and who know the Canarese and all the other šâstras"[1].

This Karṇâṭa kingdom[2] is probably identical with the Mahâ Karṇâṭaka, mentioned in the Canarese novel, called Kumâra (Kŏmâra) Râma čarita, the story of which begins at the time when Râma deva of Devagiri (Daulatâbâd) and the Ballâḷa râyas (of Haḷĕbîḍu or Dvârâsamudra) were flourishing[3], and therefore previous to the year 1306 A. D., when Râma was overcome by the Mohammadans. In 1310 Haḷĕbîḍu was for the first time taken by them. It was destroyed in 1326.

According to the just-mentioned Kumâra Râma čarita the devout Liṅgâita Siṅgi nâyaka or Mummaḍi Siṅga comes from Malĕpanti (Malĕpanta, Malĕpantha) in the Mahâ Karṇâṭaka to Râma deva of Devagiri[4], aids him in his fight against the Sultân (Suritâḷa)[5] of Ḍilli, sees him in captivity, returns to Malĕpanthi, protects Râma at Râyadurga, becomes governor, when after Râma's death feuds arise, causes his son Kampila, whom he had obtained by the favour of Kappili Somešа[6], to be crowned, and dies[7]. Kampila married Hari Amma, the daughter of Gujjâla Kâṭi nâyaka[8], who through the grace of Jaṭṭiṅga (Jaṭṭaṅgi, Jĕṭṭiṅgi, Jeṭṭiṅgi Râma, Râmeša liṅga) gives birth to Kumâra Râma[9].

Goḷakŏṇḍĕ who had invaded the Karṇâṭaka, *i. e.* the district on the Eastern coast which still bears that name for the Canarese dynasty of Vidyânagara having ruled over it since about 1490.—Pîtâmbara is a name of Kṛishṇa, and one of his epithets, *e. g.* in the Vaishṇava dâsa padas; the Râkshasa Pîtâmbara probably denotes a line of Vaishṇava rulers that, to Liṅgâitas, appeared as fiends and Turks, perhaps some of the Ballâḷas whose rule, about A. D. 1193, extended to the frontiers of Devagiri; see further on. Sixty-five years after Aḷiya Bijjaḷa, A. D. 1293, the Mohammadans took Kaluburigĕ, where 1347 they established the Bâhmînî dynasty. The year 1293 is obtained, if Basava died so early as 1168; but see p. xxxii.

1) *Can.* Bas. P. 62, 45-50. At Gummaḷâpura afterwards in the 16th century there appear Siddhaliṅga âčârya (Râghvâṅkač. 19, 88; *Can.* Bas. P. 63, 47) and Jaṅguḷi Vîrappa (*Can.* Bas. P. 63, 54). 2). Bas. Pur. 2, 28 it is said that to the S. W. of *S*rîgiri is Nandimaṇḍala; and v. 45 that to the W. of *S*rîgiri is the excellent Karṇâṭa deśa (where at Iṅgaḷĕšvara Bâgavâḍi the known Basava is born). 3) 1, 1-28; 3, 97. 4) 1, 1-28. 5) Suritâḷa, as the Liṅgâita works regularly call the Sultân, is explained to mean "he who takes arrack" (surĕ, and tâḷ, to take), *S*araṇalîlâmṛita, p. 174. 6) Compare Kampana Soma in Gaṇasahasranâma 2, 38. 7) 2, 1-67. 8) 1, 49-52. There is a Kâṭi Nâyaka of Suggalûr in *Can.* Bas. P. 62, 75; see Ind. Ant. ii., p. 307. 9) 3, 1-22.

Kampila occupies and fortifies the Hŏsa malĕ durga[1]; and young Râma marches out, and takes the forts of Toragal, Hânagal, Uččaṅgi durga, Niḍugal durga, Harihara, and coming to Penagŏṇḍĕ also Candragutti and Bĕḷagâvu[2]. Afterwards, when twelve years old, he marches against Jagatâpi of Gutti[3]; issues as victor from a fight about a Bŏlla (or Bolâni horse) with Ĕppattu râya, the son of Rudra Pratâpa Gaṇapati of Ŏruṅgal (A. D. 1295—1335); and on his return defeats several Tĕlugu Rĕḍḍis (Madana R., Malla R., Mača R., Kali R., Maduva R., and Nâyaka R.), and also the Mârigŏṇḍa or Mâra[4]. After his return to Hŏsamalĕ, on a hunt, he finds Kummaṭa durga, the Jaina inmates of which go away and build Kŏppaḷa (to the S. W. of Ânĕgundi), and fortifies it[5]; it is near the Tuṅgabhadra[6]. While his father is still alive, Râma is killed in a fight against the Turks, who had come from Ḍilli to destroy Kummaṭa[7]; and Kampila sends the head of his son to Kâśi's *Iśvara*.

Meanwhile, before the time of Basava of Kalyâṇa, the Ballâḷa or Hŏysaḷa dynasty had been established, whose capital was Haḷĕbîḍu (*i. e.* old settlement). The *Can.* Bas. Purâṇa relates that the first king, Hŏysaḷa, was crowned in *Sâl. S.* 800, the Vilambi year, *i. e.* A. D. 878.[8] Of his fourth successor Vishṇuvardhana it is stated that he made many religious gifts, invaded the whole earth as far as Bĕḷvŏla (generally called Bĕḷavala)[9], and washed his horse in the Kṛishṇavĕṇâ (near Sâtârâ); he was contemporary with Paramardi or Pĕrmâdi deva, *i. e.* the *C*âlukya king Vikramâditya II. of Kalyâṇa, who lived between A. D. 1076-1127, and died A. D. 1134.[10] Vishṇuvardhana's successor was one Narasi*m*ha with his wife Ečala devî, who was followed by Vîra Ballâḷa, who wrested the country of Kuntaḷa from the Yâdava dynasty of Devagiri, and fixed upon Lŏkkiguṇḍi (Lakkuṇḍi) as his capital. One of his grants (at Gadagu) that bears among others a figure of Basava and is connected with liṅgas, was made A. D. 1193; he ruled still 1199.[11] After him reigned Someśvara from A. D. 1233-1283, when his son

1) Beginning with this statement a very brief summary of the story is given in *Can.* B. P. 63, 77, where it is placed just before Harihara of Ânĕgundi, crowned A. D. 1336. 2) 23-92. For Uččaṅgi cf. Ind. Ant. ii., 302. 3) Ch. 4. 4) Ch. 5. 5) Ch. 7. 6) Ch. 8. 7) Chs. 10. 11. 8) 62, 51. The Vilambi year is right. As we have seen p. xxxii., the Purâṇa places Basava's death A. D. 785. After Hŏysaḷa follows Vinayâditya; then Eṛeyaṅga, Ballâḷa, (Udayâditya), and Vishṇuvardhana. 9) This name was given to the fertile district of the Canarese country in or about the centre of which are Gadagu, Ḍambaḷa and Lakkuṇḍi, belonging to the Dhâravâḍa Collectorate. See Ind. Ant. ii., 297; ii., 24; and above p. xxxi. 10) Brown's Tables p. 61. 11) For this see Mr. J. F. Fleet in Ind. Ant. ii, 296 seq.; cf. i., 156; ii., 131; iii., 264; and above p. xxxii.

Vîra Narasi*m*ha râya succeeded him, who may be the same whom Ferishta (the great Persian historian of the latter part of the 16th century) calls Bilal Dev (Ballâḷa king), and who lived still A. D. 1295.[1] As already remarked, Haḷĕbîḍu was taken by the Mohammadans A. D. 1310.

In connexion with the Ballâḷa râjas the *C*an. Bas. Purâṇa relates, that the Ballâḷa Vishṇu Vardhana erected a Vishṇu temple at Belûr or Velâpura[2]. Then, it proceeds to say: "When the ruler of the land, (the) Ballâḷa, asks for the accounts of Harîšvara, who is known as the chief of the family of the village-clerks (karaṇika) in the town called Haḷĕbîḍu, he having dropped (biṭṭu) the writing cloth (kaḍata), rubs his hands. When the king inquires: 'Let me know the meaning of this (thy strange movement)!', he says: 'When in the temple of Virûpâksha (at Pampâkshetra, *i. e.* Kalyâṇa on the Tuṅgabhadra)[3] a burning lamp having come into contact with the curtain cloth, it took fire, and I extinguished it. Hear!' Then the king says: 'The curtain cloth of what Virûpâksha temple? Where? What a wonder thou (art to me)!' and without delay" has further inquiries made, and sends Harîšvara to the said temple at Pampâkshetra to be there, where Hari aṇṇa (*i. e.* elder brother) recites verses in Ragaḷĕ metres concerning *S*iva's various hosts and the marriage of Girijâ (Girijâvivâha), and dies[4]. Then the legend goes on: "There is the sister's son of the great Harîšvara, who is called the šarabha bheruṇḍa of the poets of both languages[5], is decorated with various badges of honour, and whose name is Râghava. He goes to the town of Orugal (or Ŏruṅgal, *i. e.* one stone, ekašila), defeats the opponents there, receives from the Vîreša (idol) an excellent ornamental breast-plate, on his return goes to Velâpura, leaves his body in the fine grave, and without delay becomes

1) Brown p. 29. 61. 2) 62, 52. This Vishṇu Vardhana must be the above-mentioned one; cf. Ind. Ant. i., p. 40 seq. Ind. Ant. ii., 131 it is said: "š. š. 1039 (*i. e.* A. D. 1117) Bĕṭṭa (i. e. hill) Vardhana under the taunts of his favourite concubine, and the arguments of Râmânuja âcârya (cf. Brown p. 57; 61) . . . became a convert to the Vaishṇava religion, changed his name to Vishṇu Vardhana, . . . and set up panča Nârâyaṇas, viz. *C*ĕnniga Nârâyaṇa (Kṛishṇa) at Belûr, Kirti Nârâyaṇa at Taḷakâḍu, Vijaya N. at Vijayapura, Vîra N. at Gadagu," etc. This Bĕṭṭa Vishṇu Vardhana, according to Brown p. 61, died A. D. 1134; cf. also Murdoch, p. 66. Bĕṭṭa râya Vishṇu Vardhana, with Mr Brown, is once a *C*âlukya, ruling (at Kalyâṇa) from 1111-1139 A. D. (C. T. p. 58), and another time a Hŏysaḷa, dying 1134 A. D. (p. 4; 61). See above p. xxix., seq. According to another legend in Ind. Ant. ii., 174 seq. the fort and temple at Raee Velûr were built by a person called Bimardi (Paramardi?), between A. D. 1268-1277, and the idol belonged to *S*ambašiva, or was an *I*švara liṅga. About the *C*anniga at Belûr cf. Int. Ant. ii., 309. 3) Sometimes written Pŏmpâkshetra. 4) 62, 53-55. 5) Probably Sa*m*skṛita and Karṇâṭa; perhaps Tĕlugu and Karṇâṭa, as the poets of that time were accustomed to write in these two languages.

emancipated (bayal, lit. empty). There (at Velâpura) is the best of the Bammaṇas (Brâhmaṇas) and a vîra šaiva âčârya. His name is Padma arasa (*i. e.* râja)". He disputes with a Tibuvana (tribhuvana) tâta, defeats him, and makes him his own disciple, whereupon Biṭṭa Ballâḷa sends for Padma arasa, at his own expense has a large tank (kĕṛĕ) built by him, and gives the open space (bayal) that lies below the tank to the eighty-eight Bammaṇas of that place; and Padma arasa is called Kĕṛĕ Padma arasa, and becomes emancipated (bayal) in the open space[1]. Then, without any connecting remark, the legend proceeds: "The man of clean walk, Somešvara of Pâlkurikĕ, in the proper order performs the sixty-four šîlas, and with pleasure comes to Kaḷḷĕya, where he becomes truly emancipated in the *S*iva grave"[2]. A little further on appears Harabhakta of Anekañjanûr, a šaiva mendicant (âṇḍi), who composed a bhâshya on the Veda[3]. At the fine town of Paṭṭešvara one Râma ayya proves the truth of Liṅgâitism by throwing the Basava Paurâṇa into the fire without its being burnt[4]; and *S*iva kavîša at Bâyibidiri performs wonders before the Sultân (Suritâḷa)[5]. Shortly afterwards the very brief summary of the story of king Kampala and his son Râma or Râma nâtha occurs[6]; and then follows the coronation of Harihara of Ânĕgundi (Ânĕgŏndi) *S. S.* 1258, *i. e.* A. D. 1336, "who, in the neighbourhood of the Virûpâksha temple of Pampĕ, builds the town called Vidyânagara"[7].

Thus according to this portion of a still longer legend there lived under the Ballâḷas the Laiṅga poets: Harîšvara, Râghava, Padmarasa, Somešvara, Harabhakta, and *S*ivakavîša,

To obtain some more particulars regarding the age of these poets the Râghavâṅka čaritra is serviceable. It states: Harîšvara was at Hampĕ or Pampâpura, in the Kuntaḷa deša, on the banks of the Tuṅgabhadra, when Râghava was born to Harîšvara's sister Rudrâṇî and Mahâ deva bhaṭṭa, and Harîšvara became his guru[8]. When the poetical talents of Râghava begin to develop, he, after worshipping in the temple of the Virûpâksha liṅga, goes to Deva râja, king of Pampâpura, at whose court, at his express wish, he recites the story of Hariščandra to the great satisfaction of all present[9]; but for this offence against *S*iva his guru Harîšvara knocks out his teeth with one of his wooden shoes, which he receives back only after due repentance[10]. Henceforth Râghava excels in relating so-

1) 62, 56-58. 2) v. 59. 3) v. 63. 4) v. 68. 5) v. 72
6) Vide above p. xlix., seq. 7) 63, 2. 3. 8) 1, 1—2, 35. 9) Ch. 3. 10) Ch. 4.

manâtha satkâvyas, etc.[1], and once travels to Hŏysaḷa nagara to see king Narasimha Ballâḷa's minister Kĕṟĕ Padma arasa, who built the tank, defeated the Vaishṇava Tribhuvana tâta, and made him a vîra šaiva[2]. Having returned to Hampĕ and Hari arasa (*i. e.* Hari îšvara)[3], he hears that at the court of Rudra Pratâpa of Ŏruṅgal (or also Orugal) there are bad poets (kukavi) called eka-, dvi-, tri-sandhâgrâhis, whereupon he proceeds there, and is well received by the king[4]. He composes there the story of Vîrešvara in the Shaṭpadi metre, reads it at the court, gains the victory over his opponents[5], returns to Hampĕ, and at the command of his guru Hari deva[6] goes to Belûr where Padmarasa causes a grave to be prepared for him[7].

After so much it is evident that, according to tradition, the first Ballâḷa Vishṇuvardhana who died 1134 A. D., about 34 years before Basava, can have had no connexion with Harîšvara, or in other words that the king Biṭṭa Ballâḷa cannot be identical with the Bĕṭṭa Vishṇuvardhana Ballâḷa, as Harîšvara's contemporaries, Râghava and Padmarasa[8], live with him at the time of Narasimha Ballâḷa of Haḷĕbîḍu, Rudra Pratâpa of Ŏruṅgal, and Devarâja of Pampâpura (or Ānĕgundi, the later Vidyânagara). Rudra Pratâpa reigned between A. D. 1292-1335; Vîra Narasimha (or Ballâḷa deva) from A. D. 1283; and (Prauḍha) Devárâja from A. D. 1286-1328[9]. Harîšvara, therefore, cannot have lived any length of time before Vîra Narasimha or Biṭṭa Ballâḷa, *i. e.* before 1283, this year falling 115 years after Basava's death. Râghava's father comforts his wife, when still childless, by relating among other old stories how by parama Vṛishabhendra's favor Mâda arasa and Mâdalâmbikĕ had obtained the son Mala Basava (of Bijjaḷa's time), thus referring Basava to the past[10].

1) Chs. 13-15. 2) 16, 2. 5. 20. 3) Ch. 16 (continuation). 4) Ch. 17. 5) Ch. 18. 6) This name is given to Harîšvara also Canarese Brahmottara Kâṇḍa, 1, 9. 7) Ch. 19. 8) He is one of the *Šiva* kavis enumerated *Can.* Bas. P. 1, 29; *Saraṇalîlâmṛita* p. 3. 9) Brown p. 30. No other person but he can be meant. It appears that Harihara was the successor of this Devarâja, removing the seat of government from Kalyâṇa or Ānĕgundi a little further on to Vidyânagari. Dr. Burnell says, *Vamsabrâhmaṇa* p. viii: "Vulgar tradition attributes the foundation of Vidyânagara to him (Mayaṇa, the father of Sâyaṇa) or rather to Sâyaṇa himself (who was born A. D. 1295, and died 1386), and to the use of a hidden treasure; but the place seems to have existed before their time". — The surname "Biṭṭa" before Ballâḷa is probably connected with the above-stated tradition that in the Ballâḷa's presence Harîšvara "having dropped (biṭṭu) the writing cloth" etc. Biṭṭa Ballâḷa then denotes "the Ballâḷa in whose presence (the writing material) was dropped"; such is a common way of expression in Canarese. Whether the Purâṇa writer himself identified the Bĕṭṭa B. and Biṭṭa B. is a question that does not concern us here; however he would have done so, if Râmânuja (1127 A. D.) be meant by Tibuvana tâta. 10) Râghv. car. 1, 50.

Harîšvara, as stated above, wrote his poems in Ragaḷĕs, metres that are mentioned by Nâgavarma, but were not in use in very early times. His disciple Râghava, according to tradition, ushered in the period of the modern Shaṭpadi metres, in which nearly all the works of the later period, Liṅgâita as well as Brâhmaṇa, are written (generally a whole work, however so bulky, in only one class), and which are closely related to the Ragaḷĕs. At the time when Râghava was at Ŏruṅgal, during the reign of king Rudra Pratâpa, he composed, as indicated above, a tale of Vîrešvara in the (modern) Shaṭpadi metre at which he remarked: "Before (me) nobody has ever praised with these Shaṭpadis; by me they have also been invented (nirmita); therefore, oh! the name of virgin-poetry will be an ornament to this composition." "Such was his resolution; and he gave it that name".[1]

In recounting the poets of the later period who occur in the *C*an. Bas. Purâṇa, in the inverse order, it is expedient to introduce and begin with Bhîma or Bhîma arasa, the son of the famous *S*ivakavi[2] and the author of the Canarese Basava Purâṇa which he finished A. D. 1369,[3] and in the prologue to which he says he will perform his work also by the grace of sukavi Hari (Harîšvara) and his good son Râghava, who are ubhaya kavi šarabha bheruṇḍas[4]; after him we meet first *S*ivakavi deva (of Bâyibidiri or of Bâlačandra nagara)[5] who must be the above-mentioned father of Bhîma; then Harabhakta; then the kavi Somanâtha or Somešvara of Pâlkurikĕ to whom probably the Basava Paurâṇa at Paṭṭešvara belongs, as he is the author of a Basava Purâṇa (in Tĕlugu), of which Bhîma made free use when composing his Canarese work[6]; and thereupon the other two Liṅgâitas, Râghava and his uncle Harîšvara. When Bhîma was writing, Haḷĕbîḍu, the capital of the Ballâḷa râyas, had already been destroyed (A. D. 1326).

For the present it is still impossible to define the extent to which the so-called New Canarese appears already in the writings of the first representatives of the later period; but in the writers of the second half all its forms are met with.

The following is a list of Liṅgâita and *S*aiva (Ârâdhya Brâhmaṇa) authors and their works belonging to the first half of this period, to some degree tentatively arranged in a chronological order:

---

1) Râghavâṅka čaritra 18, 3. 2) Bas. P. 1, 17; *C*an. B. P. 1, 29; Râjaśekhav. 1, 18. 3) Ch. 61, 92. 4) Ch. 1, 11; cf. Râjaśekhav. 1, 79. 88. 5) Bas. P. 1, 17; Can. B. P. 1, 27. 6) Bas. P. 1, 14-16; cf. *C*an. B. P. 1, 29; Râghvč. 1, 18.

1. Harîšvara, a Liṅgâita, who in Ragaḷĕ metres wrote on *S*iva's various hosts (gaṇa) and the marriage of Girijâ, about 1290 A. D.

2. Râghava, the disciple of Harîšvara, about 1300 A. D. His topics were Hariščandra, *S*iva, Vîreša, Basava and Laiṅga devotees. The Anubhavašikhâmaṇi, a work of recent date (1768 A. D.), professes to be a composition of Râghava in a retouched form, the original having exhibited only (modern) *S*ara shaṭpadis. There is a tale of Nala in Dvipadas by one Râghava in Tĕlugu.

3. Somešvara, an Ârâdhya Brâhmaṇa of Pâlkurikĕ (in the Godâveri district), about 1300 A. D. His šataka, or 110 Canarese verses in the Mattebhavikrîḍita, contains some moral and other reflections on various subjects. He further composed, in Canarese, a *S*aiva and Liṅgâita gaṇa sahasra nâma or the thousand names of the pramatha gaṇa, Rudra gaṇa and bhakta gaṇa[1], the metre being Raghaṭĕ, Kanda and some vṛittas. In the Tĕlugu language he wrote a Basava purâṇa in Dvipadas[2], on which, as stated above, the Canarese Basava purâṇa by Bhîma kavi is founded (1369 A. D.). His liṅga was at Puligirinagari[3], and he died at Kaḷḷĕya. In a collection of verses lithographed at Dhâravâḍa (see further on No. 78) it is said: "Somanâtha kavi composed the Basava Purâṇa in Āndhra"; and in the Dîpakali čaritra (1, 5): "Pâlkurikĕ's Someša related the čaritĕ of *S*iva's šaraṇas (devotees)".

4. Harabhakta of Anekañjanûr, a Liṅgâita mendicant, about 1300 A. D., who composed a Bhâshya on the vedas.

5. *S*iva Kavîša, a Liṅgâita, probably the same who was once at Bâyibidiri[4], about 1330 A. D. He was the father of Bhîma kavi, the author of the Canarese Basava purâṇa. In the above-mentioned Dhâravâḍa lithograph, under No. 3, it is stated that "Somanâtha kavi composed the Basava purâṇa in Āndhra, and Bhîma in (Canarese) Shaṭpadi"; that "*S*aṅkara

1) 465 pramatha gaṇas, 171 rudra gaṇas, 28 yogâčâryas, 63 gaṇas (see the 63 devotees in Nijaguṇa's Purâtana Trivadi and in the Tamiḻ Pĕriya Purâṇa, Murdoch p. 81), 16 other gaṇas, 13 terasa gaṇas (cf. the terayyar, Murdoch p. xcix. see above p. xxviii.), 10 further gaṇas, 234 amara gaṇas. 2) Brown's Preface to his Dictionary (1852); he refers the Tĕlugu Purâṇa to 1300 A. D. 3) *S*ataka v. 1. Bas. P. 51, 76 seq. this town Puligiri (*i. e.* tiger-hill) is called Puligĕrĕ (*i. e.* tiger-line or tank), and its liṅga does a wonder for a šaiva Sova aṇṇa (*i. e.* elder brother Soma) whom Jainas had betrayed; cf. 9, 36; *Can.* B. P. 57, 85. The town is the present Hulikal paṭṇa (*i. e.* tiger-stone town).—The scheme for one of Somešvara's Ragaḷĕs, the verse containing two lines, is the following: ◡◡◡◡◡.◡◡◡◡◡.◡◡◡◡◡.◡◡◡ | ◡◡◡◡◡.◡◡◡◡◡.◡◡◡◡◡.◡◡◡ || 4) The Bidiri koṭĕ (*i. e.* fort) of *Can.* B. P. 63, 66 is probably the Bidar in the Nizâm.

ârâdhya kavîšvara completely told the story in Sanscrit[1]", and that "*S*iva kavi of Bâlačandranagara composed it with Vastuka".

6. Bhîma, the son of *S*ivakavi deva, who finished his Canarese Basava purâṇa 1369 A. D. It contains 61 chapters with 3623 verses in Shaṭpadi[2].

7. *S*aṅkara, an Ârâdhya Brâhmaṇa, who composed a Basava purâṇa in Sanscrit (see No. 5), may fall here.

8. Mallaṇa ârya (*i. e.* malla aṇṇa ârya, the great elder brother who is an ârya)[3] of Gubbi, a town in Maisûr, to the N. W. of Bĕṅgaḷûr, where, according to vulgar tradition, he lived about 500 years ago (*i. e.* c. 1370 A. D.), and in Canarese wrote the Vîrašaivâmṛita about *S*iva's twenty lîlĕs, and the Bhâvačintâratna[4]. The last-mentioned work he executed with varṇaka rîti, following an itihâsa in Tamiḻ by Piḷḷĕ Naynâr who was Vâgîša's teacher[5]. This Piḷḷĕ Naynâr was the son of a šiva vipra (*i. e.* ârâdhya Brâhmaṇa) of *S*rîkâḷi nagari, caused the king Inakulottuṅga *C*oḷa to become a *S*aiva, converted other Jainas and Bauddhas, *e. g.* at Tirumarakkaḍa and Tiruvâlavâ, invited by the queen Maṅgây akka (*i. e.* elder sister) of Madhurâ, the daughter of the *C*oḷa, went there, under the name of Jńânasambandhi healed and converted her husband Kûna Pâṇḍya who was hence called Saundara Pâṇḍya, and at the same time, at the king's court, defeated a large number of Jainas, eighteen thousand of whom were impaled on the red-hot šûlas which Kulaččari, the queen's šaiva guardian, minister and later virakta Mâṇikâčârya, had prepared[6]. The original name of Vâgîša or Tiruvâgîša, Piḷḷĕ Naynâr's disciple, was Pâršva paṇḍita; he first was a Jaina guru and Jina samaya mukhya at Tiruvâvalûr, suffered from dreadful colic, in despair followed the advice of his elder sister Tiruvalinâči to invoke *S*iva, was healed, became a *S*aiva, was very much persecuted by the Ârhatas, overcame them,

1) There are many Liṅgâitas (*S*aivas) in the Paurâṇika legends who bear that name. See *e. g.* Gaṇasahn. 8, 13. 45. 49; Bas. P. 9, 39; *C*an. B. P. 1, 17. 29; 57, 4. 20; *S*araṇalîlâmṛita p. 280. In the Râjašekharavilâsa (of A. D. 1657) 1, 17 a *S*aṅkara is mentioned together with (Gubbi's) Mallaṇârya, Harîšvara, etc.; Gaṅgâdhara Maḍivâḷešvara, in a note on p. 20, says that the poet *S*aṅkarâcârya (whom does he mean?) composed a Basava Purâṇa in Sanscrit. 2) In the Journal of the Bombay Branch of the Royal Asiatic Society, if my memory does not deceive me, of 1865, is a summary of the sectarian legends and tenets of the Basava P. and *C*anna B. P. by the late Rev. G. Würth. 3) Râjašekharav. 1, 17; sanscritised the name is "Malhaṇa". 4) Gaṅgâdhara ad Râjašekh. 1, 17. Vulgar tradition may have put Mallaṇa too early. The Bhâvacintâratna has been reproduced in the Râjašekharavilâsa; (1, 78). 5) Râjašekh. 1, 77. 78. 88. 6) *C*an. B. P. 55, 33. 34; Bas. P. ch. 50; 25, 4; 11, 15. 16; 9, 48; Prauḍharâya č. ch. 18. Mâṇikâčârya is the Tamiḻ Mâṇikavâčaka, the author of the šaiva work Tiruvâčaka; Murdoch p. lxxxix and p. 89.

destroyed many Jina pratimĕs and bastis (vasati), and had as a disciple the renowned Naḥpûti[1]. Mallaṇârya wrote a Râmastavarâja in Tĕlugu, an allegory, representing the body as a city and the soul as its inhabitant, a sort of yogaŝâstra[2].

9. Perhaps to this period belongs the *C*aturâsya Nighaṇṭu by Kavi Bŏmma (Brahmâ), 100 verses in Kanda, comprising old Canarese terms and Tadbhavas. As it is less systematic and detailed than No. 14 and 15, it appears to have preceded them. Each verse concludes with "oh *C*aturâsya!" The author's mata is not indicated in our MSS. Bŏmma is a very common proper name in Liṅgâita legends.

10. Siṅgi râja or Siṅgi râja âčârya, the author of the Mala Basava čaritra[3] or Hara kathâ ŝaradhi, 48 chapters with 1807 verses in Shaṭpadi. It contains stories similar to those of the Basava and *C*anna Basava Purâṇa. The author, on account of his Vârdhika shaṭpadi, cannot be the Siṅgi râja who belonged to the gaṇas at Basava's time[4]; but is one of the eleven persons who together are mentioned in verse 13 of the first chapter of the Râghavâṅka čaritra, viz.: Hari deva (Harîŝvara), Kĕṟĕ Padmarasa, Râghava deva, Jakkaṇâčârya, *C*âma arasa, Bhîma arasa, Mŏggĕ âčârya, Kalmaṭha âčârya, Siṅgi râja âčârya, Pâlkurikĕ Soma, and Mahâdeva ayya. The first three and Bhîma are already known to us. Jakkaṇâčârya, together with Harîŝvara and Râghava, appears in verse 17 of the first chapter of the Râjaŝekharavilâsa of A. D. 1657; according to the Prauḍha râja čaritra[5] he lived in company with *C*âma arasa and Kalmaṭha âčârya at the court of Prauḍha narendra or Prauḍha devendra of Vidyânagara (Ânĕgundi), whose minister he was[6], and where he overcame the Vaishṇava Mukkunda pĕddi (*i. e.* three hill headman)[7]. The Prauḍha narendra is the (Mummaḍi) Prauḍha, who ruled

1) *C*an. B. P. 55, 35; Bas. P. ch. 49; 27, 69; Prauḍhar. *C*ar. 7; according to Bas. P. 9, 48 Kulaččari or Kulasčari appears to be contemporaneous with Basava; cf. also Gaṇasahasran. 5, 11. About Kulottuṅga *C*oḷa see p. xxviii., seq.; about Kûna Pâṇḍya or Saundara P. the various dates assigned to him Ind. Ant. ii., 16. 107. 131. 263. Kûna Pâṇḍya seems to belong to the 12th century. Cf. also Brown's Tables sub 1118 A. D. Vâgîŝa's tale agrees best with that of the Tamiḻ poet Appa (*i. e.* father) who "though born of *S*aiva parents, entered a Jaina monastery. Having subsequently been attacked by disease in the stomach, his sister persuaded him that it was a punishment for his apostacy, and he returned to *S*aivism. The Jaina king is fabled to have vainly attempted to put him to death by throwing him into a limekiln, etc. With Sambandha (*i. e.* our Jńânasambandhi) and Sundara (another ŝaiva poet) he laboured zealously to propagate *S*aivism in S. India". Murdoch, p. lxxxiii. 2) Brown's Preface. 3) Mala (*i. e.* great) Basava is the founder of the sect, and is sometimes called so to distinguish him from his nephew čanna or čikka Basava; see *e. g.* *C*an. B. P. 1, 15; 6, 17; Râghv. čar. 1, 50. 4) Gaṇasahasran. 8, 1; *C*an. B. P. 55, 50; 57, 50. 5) 1, 41. 6) Cf. 1, 12. 7) 1, 39 seq. Jakkaṇârya is mentioned as the alleged builder of various temples, Ind. Ant. i., 44; ii., 296. Grand works are not always very old; thus, for instance, the huge Jaina statue at Kârkaḷa dates only from 1432 A. D. (see Ind. Ant ii., 353) or from about Jakkaṇârya's time.

at Vidyânagara from 1450 (or 1456) to 1477 A. D.[1] In the Canna Basava Purâṇa he appears as belonging to the lineage of the kings Harihara and Bukka, and at his court is also the above-mentioned Mŏggĕ âčârya, here named Mŏggĕ Mâyi deva[2]. "In his race" follows Virûpâksha râya (A. D. 1488)[3], whom Narasaṇa râya (Narasiṁha râya) drives away, and then takes the town (A. D. 1490)[4].--On account of the persons with whom Siṅgi is associated in the verse of the Râghava čaritra, it seems very probable that he lived somewhere between 1330-1477 A. D. Is he perhaps the Siṅgi of the Kumâra Râma čaritra?[5]

11. *C*âma arasa, a Liṅgâita, who lived at the court of the just-mentioned Prauḍha râya, 1450-1477 A. D., composed the Prabhu liṅga lîlĕ, *i. e.* the life of Prabhuliṅga who bears also the names of Prabhu deva, Allaṁa prabhu, and Gŏhešvara (guhâ-îšvara) liṅga. It consists of 25 chapters with 1111 verses in Shaṭpadi[6]. Allama prabhu is an incarnation of *S*iva's gaṇanâtha, and born on earth to Nirahaṅkâra and Sujñânî. To examine Allama's mind *S*iva's wife sends to the earth her own tâmasa guṇa, the Mâyĕ[7], who is born of Mohinî devî, the wife of king Mamakâra prabhu of the town Banavaše in the Bĕḷavala deša[8], and when a beautiful virgin is severely tempted by Allama, whom she loves very much[9]. But Allama is not in earnest; according to the short tale in the *C*anna Basava P.[10], "he laughs at her in contempt, (leaves her), comes (to the grave) of Anumisha (above p. xxxi.), takes the liṅga out of (his) hand, by his instruction gives liberation (mukti) to Gŏggayya[11] and Muktâyi (whom he happens to meet there), and thence goes to Basava at Kalyâṇa, where he ascends the šûnya pîṭha which till then had been taken care of by Basava". At last he goes to *S*rîšaila, where he dies a little before Basava[12]. In Tĕlugu there is a translation of the Prabhu liṅga lîlĕ by Pidupati Somayya[13]; the Tamiḻ translation is by *S*ivaprakâša dešika of the 17th century[14].

1) Brown's Tables, p. 31. 57. 2) 63, 6. 38. 3) 63, 39; Brown, p. 57. The intervening kings—Vîra R., Mallikârjuna R., and Râmačandra R.—are not mentioned in the Purâṇa. 4) 63, 39. 5) See above p. xlix., seq. 6) Prauḍha râya č. 21, 30 seq., where *C*âma's authorship of the work is spoken of. 7) Prabhul. 2, 36-41. 8) 3, 1 seq. 9) 5, 1 seq. 10) 57, 87. 88; 62, 8 seq.; see above p. xxxi. 11) Cf. Bas. P. 58, 6. 12) *C*an. B. P. 62, 17. 13) Brown's Preface. 14) Murdoch, p. 70.—Regarding the term "Allama" I perfectly agree with Mr Brown, when he says in his Dictionary s. v. ಅಲ್ಲಮ "the name Allama . . . probably is borrowed from Allah, or from 'Alamm' a mysterious word used in the Koran for the deity. . . . . The Musulman name for God was known in India before the Jaṅgama (Liṅgâita) religion arose." The identity of the two names is in fact suggested in the Monešvara Purâṇa, 9th chapter. Compare the story of the guru of Virûpâksha paṇḍita, the author of the *C*anna B. P.; Bâbâ Nânak, the founder of the Sikhs, and the Allah Upanishad in Dr. Burnell's Pahlavi Inscriptions (1873), p. 15. Dr. Burnell mentions *ib.* p. 7 that a Christian was Dewan of Vijayanagara (Vidyânagara) about 1445 (under one of Prauḍha râya's next predecessors, Gaṇḍa deva, 1434-1454; Brown, p. 57 and 1457 A. D.). The Jesuit C. J. Beshi was the Dewan of *C*undâ Sâib, the Nabob of the Carnatic, till 1740.

2. The Vaishṇava, Liṅgâita and *S*aiva period, from about 1500 (1490)-1874.

12. Kumâra Vyâsa, a Vaishṇava, freely translated the first 10 Parvas of the Mahâbhârata into Canarase, using the Shaṭpadi metre. He says (1, 6): "The Vîra Nârâyaṇa (an idol at the town of Gadagu)[1]) is the poet, the writer is Kumâra Vyâsa". Then he invokes Gadagu's Vîranârâyaṇa (v. 7), and calls himself his slave (v. 9). His 11th verse runs as follows: "Under the burden of the (probably Jaina) poets of the Râmâyaṇa the king of serpents was pressed down; in the mass of Râma-tales there was no interstice to place one's feet. Will he (Kumâra Vyâsa) take into account the inferior poets? Do not think: 'it is enough!' Is he not like (Vyâsa's son) *S*uka? Does not the poet Kumâra Vyâsa make dance the others, and laugh (at them)?" This author, according to the preface of Kṛishṇa râja's Bhârata, wrote, as it seems, at or about the time of the coronation of Kṛishṇa râja, who was king at Vidyânagara from A. D. 1504-1529[2]). The translation of the first ten Parvas of the Mahâbhârata into Tamiḻ by Villiputtûra dates from about the 16th century[3]).

13. Timmaṇa's Bhârata, in Shaṭpadi, of about A. D. 1504-1506. It is called Kṛishṇa râja Bhârata. Its preface calls Kṛishṇa râja the son of Narasa nṛipâla (also the son of Narasendra, Narasa narapâlaka, Narasi*m*ha, Narasaya)[4]), and relates that Timma nṛipa was born in the Tuḷu va*m*ša, that his son was *I*švara kshitinâtha[5]), and that the son of *I*švara was Narasa bhûvara (at Vidyânagara from A. D. 1490-1495) whose wife was Nâgamâmbĕ[6]). "When Kṛishṇa, the son of Narasa, gloriously rules with joy, he immediately hears the (Canarese) Bhârata kathâ (that seems, therefore, to have become just ready at that very time), looks at his poets, calls Timmaṇa, the son of Bhânu kavîndra, and says: 'First Kumâra Vyâsa has nicely related ten parvas....Now relate thou the remaining parvas of the Bhârata!' Thereupon Timmaṇa, the son of Bhânu bhaṭṭa"

1) See above, p. li., note 2. 2) Brown's C. T. p. 57. 59. 62. 3) Murdoch, p. ci. 190.
4) *Can*. Bas. P. 68, 39 appears the form "Narasaṇa"; see above p. lviii., and further on No. 15.
5) Cf. Brown's remark to Aĉyuta D. R., C. T., p. 57. 6) Or, according to Brown's C. T., p. 62, Nâgala devî. Narasa had two other wives: Tippakshi and Voyambikĕ, the second of which bore him two sons named Raṅga and Aĉyuta. To Tippakshi and Nâgala devî there were born Vîra Narasiṅga and Kṛishṇa. A. D. 1495 Vîra Narasiṅga became king, and ruled till 1504; his son was the afterwards so unfortunate Râma râja who wedded his niece, the daughter of Kṛishṇa râja who reigned from 1504-1529. Kṛishṇa râja was followed by Narasa's son Aĉyuta râja, from 1530-1541, when Râma râja came to the throne, and 1565, when seventy years of age, was overcome in battle and killed by the Muhammadans. The *Can*. Bas. P. (63, 59) states that "Narasaṇa's son (*i. e.* no doubt his family) reigns for 51 years", *i. e.* till 1541, and that "Aĉyuta is the last who is crowned", which probably means "is the last who dies with the crown on his head". See Brown's C. T., p. 57. 62. 16.

instructs Narasaya Kṛishṇa râya, and recites the rest of the work in the same metre (bhâmini shaṭpadi). In the concluding verse attached to each chapter the son of Devakî is constantly named Věṅkaṭeša or Věṅkaṭa-šailanâtha, Věṅkaṭagiryadhîša, Věṅkaṭâdrîšvara. Kṛishṇa râya was also the celebrated patron of Tělugu literature[1].

14. About this time or perhaps somewhat earlier the Vocabulary of old Canarese terms, Tadbhavas and a few Tatsamas, called the Kabbiga kaipiḍi, may have to be placed, if it has been composed with the object of supplying a real want; and so it appears, for if it had been written after the next to be mentioned famous and somewhat fuller vocabulary by Toṭa ârya, it would scarcely have obtained the good name it still bears. Its author is Liṅga, first minister of the râya of Uggěhaḷḷi, son of the Brahman Virûpâksha and a follower of the Virûpâksha liṅga at Pampâpura (2. 3. 99); he has written it to help in understanding the old and renowned Sivakavis. 100 verses in Shaṭpadi.

15. Toṭa Ârya's Canarese Vocabulary[2], the Sabdamañjari, 120 verses in Shaṭpadi, belongs to the beginning of the 16th century. Like the Kabbiga kaipiḍi it gives the meanings of some Tatsamas, Tadbhavas and old Canarese words. The Canna Basava purâṇa relates (63, 40, seq.) that only a short time after the death of Prauḍha râya of Vidyânagari (*i. e.* after A. D. 1477)[3] who is succeeded by Virûpâksha and the usurper Narasaṇa (Narasimha), a decline of Liṅgâitism or of the "Vîra Saiva âčâra" happened, and "anâčâra" (*i. e.* Vaishṇavism) began to prevail. At that time Nirañjana Gaṇešvara was born on earth of Gosala Canna-basavešvara, and was called Siddheša; he went to the garden (toṭa) of Kaggěrě, and there by his šivadhyâna became a great man, receiving the appellations of Toṭa Siddhaliṅga, Toṭa Yati, Toṭa Ârya.

16. The Canarese prose-versions of the Pañčatantra may be dated from the beginning of the 16th century, if the style of language that forms the only test regarding the age of the versions we have seen, be not misleading. Mr. Brown in the Preface to his Dictionary says that its Tělugu translation in verse was done by the Kshatriya Baisarâju Veṅgaḷarâju perhaps in A. D. 1500. The version edited at Běṅgaḷûr in 1865 by Mr. J. Garrett—who states that "to make it more complete, the Sanscrit šlokas and Canarese padyas have been included", and that "the Editor has had the advantage of consulting two excellent copies contained in the Library of the College of Fort St. George"—appears

1) Brown's C. T. p. 59. 2) 1, 2. above p. xxxv. 3) See above p. lvii.

to be from about the beginning of the 19th century. The Canarese verses in it, partly free translations of šlokas, are in Shaṭpadis, Kandas, Sîsa, an unsettled Gîta, and a few Vṛittas. One of the last-mentioned, named *Câmara*, is peculiar, each of its quarters consisting of –⏑.–⏑.–⏑. –⏑.–⏑.–⏑.–⏑.–; it is in fact the Ha*m*sayâna of Tĕlugu prosody; see above p. xxii.

17. To the beginning of the 16th century also, appears to belong *I*švara kavi, son of Kaččuṭeša, the modern Keši râja and author of the Kavijihvâbandhana[1]; for he teaches the use of the Tĕlugu vaḍis, *i. e.* ornaments (in verse), a subject hitherto apparently foreign to Canarese prosodical treatises, but alluded to in one of the first works of the specific Vaishṇava dâsas, whose literary period is beginning, at this time. Kanaka dâsa, the author of the Mohanataraṅgiṇi, states (1, 20) that he will compose his work according to prâsu and vaḍi; and *I*švara says (ch. 2) he will teach both these in Canarese, "the vaḍi according to the Āndhra (Tĕlugu) mârga, as they use it only in Tĕlugu"; then he mentions five more common kinds out of twenty: svara vaḍi, *i. e.* the repetition of the first vowel of the first foot at the same place through one or more lines, especially at the places of Caesura, v. 28; sarasa vaḍi, *i. e.* the use of the consonants č, čh, j, jh together with š, sh, s as initials of feet; ĕkkaṭi vaḍi, *i. e.* the same use made of only one consonant, for instance, k; sa*m*yuktâkshara vaḍi, *i. e.* the same use made of double consonants; and varga vaḍi, *i. e.* the same use made of consonants that belong to one class. *I*švara, no doubt, used the Tĕlugu Appa kavi[2]. His work, superstitious and occasionally very obscene, according to our MS., contains four chapters, i. about the gaṇas and their šubha, ašubha, rasa, diš, varṇa, vâhana, ĕṇĕ or maitrya, vaira, nakshatra, guṇa, graha,

---

1) See above p vi. 2) Appa kavi's rule concerning the Sîsapadya (v. 269) as it has been communicated to me, is the following kanda: ಸುರಪತುಲಾಬ್ಜು ರಿಪ್ಯೈಭಾ | ಸ್ಥರುಲಿರುವ್ವರುಗೂಡನೊಕ್ಕಟ ರಣಮುಶೀಲ್ಗುಂ || ಬರುಗುನವಿನಾಲುಗಡುಗುಲ | ವಿರಮಮುಪ್ಪೈರೆಂಟರೆಂಟವೆಳಯುಗವಲಯುನ್ || To confirm that the form of the Sîsapadya of our text represents the true Tĕlugu metre of that name, I adduce a verse of Appa kavi in that metre as communicated to me, which is composed only of short syllables, 36 for a line:

Karivaradaparamakṛipadharaṇidharasuravinutakanakavasananarahari * garuḍagamana
naḷinakarapadanayanadaḷitakharadanujačayanarasakhavaraguṇanidhi * šaradhišayana |
paramapadanilayahariparamapurushaprakṛitikibaruḍanininunigamani * vahamupaluku
niratamunuhṛidayamunaninudalatunanumanupumaniyanaghačaritajala * danibhavanuva ||

About the age of Appa kavi Mr Brown, in his first Essay on Tĕlugu (1839), p. 11 says the poet lived some ages after Nannayabhaṭṭa who is placed 1130 A. D.; and in his grammar (1857) he states (p. 357) Appa kavi was posterior to the Tĕlugu Naishadha (that dates from about 1400 A. D., see further on, No. 23).

kula, devatĕ and phala; ii. about the prâsus and vaḍis; iii. about the šubha and ašubha aksharas, their kula, the classification of bâla svaras and kumâra svaras, the svara kâlas and svara liṅgas, the alpa and mahâ-prâṇas, the kavitâpatinâmâksharas and kavitâkanyakânâmâksharas and the daša kûṭas (combinations), and the adhidevatĕs; iv. mentions the nakshatrâdhidevatĕs, the bhâvas, thirty-six alaṅkṛitis, nine liṅgas, two sandhis, six prâsus, seven vibhaktis, three kâlas, three purushas, and ten nighaṇṭus as subjects that poets ought to know; then he enumerates the sixteen arrows of Cupid, the adhidaivas of the pushpâstra, the mohabheda, the kâmakalâ nâmas and sthânas, the darpakakalâ nâmas, the čandrakalâs, the strîkalâ sthânas, gives a description of four viṭas, the vairâksharalekhanakrama, and lastly of the Shaṭpadi lakshaṇa. The work, excepting the Sîsa instance of the Tĕlugu and the Shaṭpadi lakshaṇa, is written in Kandas and Samavṛittas.

18. According to an obscure (perhaps spurious) dâsa hymn of only three verses, found among a number of miscellaneous dâsa hymns in our possession, the Vaishṇava dâsa Purandara Viṭhala of Paṇḍaripura may have been living at Vijayanagara (Vidyânagara) in a vilambi saṃvatsara, on phâlguṇa bahuḷa čauti šrîvâra. This year may be the vilambi year 1538, when Ačyuta deva ruled, who succeeded Kṛišhṇa râya in 1529 and died in 1541. If the pada be genuine and the explanation right, Purandara would probably stand in close connexion with the Baṅgâḷi *C*aitanya who from 1510-1516 "roamed all over India preaching Vaishṇavism"[1]. At the same time a slight doubt arises whether

1) Cf. Varâha dâsa's words: "This is the dâsas' lot: they fill all the countries". Ind. Ant. ii., 312. *C*aitanya was born A. D. 1486, and died 1534. Ind. Ant. ii., 1. 3. At nearly the same period we find the Hindu Bâbâ Nânak in the Pañjâb, who was born 1469 and died 1539 A. D. He was "the first teacher and founder of the Sikh tenets, and laboured to reform the lives and religion of his countrymen, to break through the tyranny of priestcraft, outward ritual, and caste". He travelled in India, and visited also Makka and Medinah in Arabia. Ind. Ant. iii., p. 295 seq. Nânak, *C*aitanya, and Purandara lived under Muhammadan rule and influence; and besides Purandara was preceded at one of the seats of his labours, Vidyânagara, by a Christian Dowan (about 1445 A. D., see above p. lviii.). "It is remarkable", says Dr. Burnell in his Pahlavi Inscriptions (Mangalore, 1873), p. 14, "that all the greatest reformers in S. India were born near Persian (Christian and Manichaean) settlements; *S*aṅkarâčârya (7th century) near Cranganore (Kŏḍuṅgalûr in Malayâḷa), Râmânujâčârya (12th century) near Madras (at the ancient Christian settlement at Mayilâpura or San Tomé), and Madhvâčârya (12th century) at Kalyâṇa (in the Tuḷu country, where before the 6th century there was a Christian bishop). The only original S. Indian poet is the Tamiḻ Tiruvaḷḷuvan (about the 9th century, Murdoch p. xxiii.), but he was a native of San Tomé, and of very low caste; in his sister, Auvayâr's poems Christian influences are evident to a casual reader. In Tiruvaḷḷuvan's poem (the Kuṟaḷ, *i. e.* poem

three songs regarding the pûjâ at Uḍupu on the Western Coast, that clearly bear the mudrikâ of Purandara, are not an interpolation; for in the description of that pûjâ the firing of guns (kovi), the jack-fruit of the Franks (pâraṅgi palasu), and the mango of Goa (Govĕ mâvu) are mentioned, a circumstance that seems not to be much in favor of the author having lived so early as the year 1538[1]. However another obscure and at the same time mutilated little hymn, belonging to the collection, seems to corroborate the statement of the first-mentioned hymn which it immediately follows, for it appears to point out Purandara's death as having occurred in a raktâkshi saṁvatsara, in pushya bahuḷa atiśaya amavâsyĕ, which may be A. D. 1564, the very year when the Vijayanagara dynasty was destroyed by the Muhammadans[2]. The two hymns appear among the additions. Purandara is known as the author of many Vaishṇava dâsa padas in Ragaḷĕs.

19. Perhaps partly contemporaneous with, but independent of Purandara, was Kanaka, the Vaishṇava dâsa of Kâginĕlĕ. This appears from his Mohanataraṅgiṇi, in which he does not refer to any Kṛishṇa dâsas by name, but simply to Madhva guru (of Uḍupu, 1121-1197 A. D.)[3]

written in Kuṛaḷs or distichs) the indications of such influences are less precise, but still apparent. The resemblances between Christianity and the S. Indian modifications of the old Vedânta are numerous and complete, especially if the systems of Mânî and the Gnostics are considered", etc.; p. 15: "We have, indeed, long winded romances of how Śaṅkara, Râmânuja, and Madhva conquered all their opponents of different sects in disputations, but though all of them must have met Christians, there is not a word about them anywhere; it looks as if they were purposely ignored. That the Hindus have always been an imitative people, and ready to borrow foreign ideas, is proved by an enormous mass of evidence; *e. g.* writing was certainly adopted by them from foreigners; their astronomy and medicine (partly at all events) are of Greek origin; the Sikhs and similar sects are the result of intercourse with Muhammadans; and the Brahmasamâj derives its leading doctrines from Christianity. Mr. Fergusson considers that the Hindu architecture is of Greek origin."

1) A. D. 1519 Hindus had begun to use musquetry and cannon. Brown's C. T. sub 1519. See above p. xxxvii. French expeditions to India commenced 1604; but the name "Frank" (foreigner) may have been introduced before that time by the Arabs. Goa was seized by the Portuguese A. D. 1510, and it is not impossible that within 54 years (1510-1564) the grafted mangoes of Goa had become a common article of commerce on the Western Coast.

2) Purandara cannot have flourished in the 15th century, as has been supposed to be the case in the valuable article "Lieder Kanaresischer Saenger" by Dr. Moegling in the Zeitschrift der Morgenlaendischen Gesellschaft, xiv., 3, 502 seq., 1860. The Kṛishṇa râya mentioned there is more than probably not the personage to whom oral tradition refers Purandara; cf. Brown's C. T. p. 59. The Kṛishṇa râja whom people speak about and who died 1529, had as minister Appâji, who seems to have served already either his father or brother Narasiṅga râja. See Tennâla Râma Kṛishṇa's story in Canarese, and Tamiḻ (Murdoch, p. 204. 207). Kṛishṇa râja, 1504-1529, was also the patron of the Tĕlugu writer Allasâni Pĕddanna; Brown's C. T. p. 14.

3) See Dr. Burnell's Vaṁśabrâhmaṇa, p. xiv. Râmânuja appears 1127 A. D., Weber's Râmâyaṇa p. 110.

and the great tarki Râmânuja (1, 2), calling himself the best of the dâsas (2, 1). If he was a beḍa (fowler), as oral tradition says, he certainly could also sing and write; for many are the Kṛishṇa songs he has composed in Ragaḷĕs; besides these he wrote a Kṛishṇa bhaktisâra, of 108 verses in Shaṭpadi, and a rather voluminous work, the Mohanataraṅgiṇi (1, 37). The last-mentioned composition contains 42 chapters with 2705 verses in one Ragaḷĕ metre[1]. It contains various Paurâṇika stories about suras, asuras, and Kṛishṇa, addressed to his wife. He remarks (2, 1): "He who has composed the work, is Kanaka, the best of the dâsas; she to whom he has related (it), is the prudent young woman. The author of the work is Âdikeśava (a Narasimha idol, 42, 76) of Kâginĕlĕ; if one hears the work, virtue is obtained" (cf. 1, 25). In 2, 13 he makes an attempt to enumerate the countries of Ancient India, and unhesitatingly mentions also the Hŏysaṇa (Hŏysaḷa) and Cauṭa countries, the last one very probably being the territory of the Jaina dynasty of that name on the Western Coast, obscure members of which are still living (see further on No. 37). In v. 1, 18 he says: "I praise the good Kavîśvaras who translate the good Purâṇas"; from which it would appear that in his time Vaishṇava Purâṇas were translating into Canarese, a circumstance that partly guides one in chronological attempts.

20. The Bhârata Nighaṇṭu falls after the time of Kumâra Vyâsa, as the author states in the initial verse: "I will carefully explain the meaning of the words for which the kavirâja Kumâra Vyâsa, in the Bhârata, has become famous." 62 kanda verses.

21. The Liṅgâita Virûpâksha paṇḍita finished his Canna Basava Purâṇa A. D. 1585 (63, 77). He was a disciple of Siddha Vireśa of the Hiri maṭha (chief or old convent) at Vidyânagara (1, 21 seq.), about 20 years after the town's capture by the Muhammadans. Of his teacher he says that he became the guru of seven hundred vara Khalindaras (fakîrs?), went to Makhya (Mekka), caused rain (maḷĕ) to fall at the time of a drought, was revered by the Suritâḷa (Sultân), and hence was called Maḷĕ Malleśa,[2], *i. e.* the great rain-master (1, 18. 19). The work contains 63 chapters consisting of 2898 verses in Shaṭpadi.

22. To about the same time may belong the Canarese Râmâyaṇa by Kumâra Vâlmîki, who dedicated his work to the Narasimha idol of Tŏravĕ (1, 10; 113, 66. 67) in the district of Solâpura. He praises

1) Its scheme is two times: 4.4.4.4*4.4.4. 2) A Maḷĕ râja appears Bas. P. 44, 52; 54, 74; Can. Bas. P. 55, 44; Râgh. Caritra 1, 49.

"Kumâra Vyâsa, the author of the beautiful Bhârata in Canarese" (1, 18; 113, 70). His work comprises 113 chapters with 5148 verses inShaṭpadi, and has no Uttara kâṇḍa.

23. From the end of the 16th century probably dates also the translation of the Bhâgavata Purâṇa. Towards its conclusion it is said in the true Vaishṇava dâsa style: "The good poet Câṭu Viṭhala nâtha has made the Canarese translation." It contains 11,298 verses in Shaṭpadi. The abridgment in prose of the Bhâgavata in Tamil dates from the end of the 18th century; the Tĕlugu was done about 1408 A. D. by Bŏmmĕra Poturâju, who lived under Siṅgama nâyuḍu (chief) who was the mûlapurusha (founder?) of the Veṅkaṭagiri saṁsthâna, and was contemporaneous with the bard Srînâtha who composed the Naishadha or story of Nala[1].

24. The same may be said of the work called Kṛishṇa lîlâbhyudaya (1, 16), a saṅgraha of the daśama skandhas of the Mahâbhâgavata (1, 17), 51 chapters with 2543 rather refined verses in Shaṭpadi. It is of the Vaishṇava dâsas' time, the author remembering the guru Madhva munipa, (called also) Ânandatîrtha ârya (1, 10). The same, regarding its authorship, appears from the following two verses: "In the shining country Pĕnugoṇḍa (where at that time the wrecked dynasty of Vidyânagara still existed)[2] is an excellent man belonging to the Brâhmaṇas of the great grâma of Kaḍagatûr, a person of peerless good conduct, a handsome (aḷagu) ârya, a big Vaishṇava, a Canarese of the Northern district, a worshipper of the feet of guru Madhva muni, and a descendant of the Jâmadajñâvatsa gotra. His son is the good Vĕṅkârya Timma arasa ârya. His firstborn son am I, Vĕṅkaya ârya; and my mother is Seshâmbĕ, the crest-gem of young women, true to her husband, good, with lotus-eyes, and of an comprehensive understanding. I am the brother of Nârâyaṇa ârya of pure knowledge, and bear the name of Hari dâsa. Depending on Hari's grace, I have become an author; Vĕṅkaṭa Sauri (*i.e.* Kṛishṇa at Tirupati with the hill of Vĕṅkaṭagiri)[3] is the lord of this work" (1, 21. 22; 51, 26. 27).

1) Murdoch, p. 111; Brown's Preface to his Dictionary. The Tĕlugu fragmentary Padma Purâṇa and Vishṇu Purâṇa are by Vĕnnŏla Kanṭi Sûrayya (Br.'s Preface), and were done after the Bhâgavata and Prabhuliṅgalîlĕ (Br.'s Essay i., p. 8). 2) See also above p. xlviii. and No. 41, note. 3) Mr. Brown in his C. T., p. 2, says the Tirupati temples were built 1040 A. D. Ziegenbalg's Malabarische Götter, p. 112, it is stated that the temple at Tirupati was built by the Tŏṇḍamân Âdŏṇḍai, an illegitimate son of a Coḷa king. According to Ind. Ant. ii., 107 this king was Kulottuṅga Coḷa who conquered the Tĕlugu country, and appears between 1143 and 1171 A. D.; see above p. xxi., xxix. Ziegenbalg, p. 58 (cf. 112. 110. 117) it is said that Tirupati was taken from the Saivas by Râmânuja (12th century).

25. Nijaguṇa yogi, an Ârâdhya Brâhmaṇa (*S*aiva), falls somewhere between 1522-1657 A. D., though vulgar tradition says, he lived 900 years ago in the Maisûr country as a petty king[1]. He is mentioned by Shaḍakshari of No. 27 in his Râjaśekhara vilâsa (1, 16) of 1657 A. D.; his approximate date will be known from foot-note 2. Six works are ascribed to him, viz. 1., a Kaivalya paddhati, chiefly on yoga, 174 Ragaḷĕ songs in the Vaishṇava dâsa style and under eight headings; 2., an Anubhava-sâra; 3., a Paramânubhava bodhĕ; 4., a Paramârtha gîtĕ, in which a guru instructs his pupil in the Vedânta, using a sort of Lalita Ragaḷĕ (two times 4.4.4.3, also with final alliteration); 11 paragraphs with 1469 verse-lines; 5., Purâtana tripadis, 77 verses in Tripadi regarding the sixty-three Purâtanas (*S*aiva devotees, see above p. lv.); 6., the Vivekaćintâmaṇi, a *S*aiva concordance of the Vedas, sûtras, purâṇas, etc., in *C*ampu, the prose greatly preponderating; this work has been translated into Tamiḻ[2].

1) Compare the Nijaguṇa mahârâja of *C*an. Bas. Purâṇa 57, 56. 2) Murdoch's Catalogue, p. 74. It is there called a "small treatise"; but in Canarese it comprises 10 prakaraṇas, and the Bĕngaḷûr printed edition contains 564 pages of 19 lines each. The tradition that N. lived 900 years ago is stated and acquiesced in by Gaṅgâdhara Maḍivâḷeśvara Tûramarî, Canarese Translation Exhibitioner E. D., in his Saṭikarâjaśekhara, Belgaum, 1871. Significant as to Nijaguṇa's age, however, is what he says himself in the first prakaraṇa of his concordance under the heading "sûtra vićara", Bĕngaḷûr edition, p. 22, viz. that there is the *S*âbara bhâshya for the Pûrvamîmâmsâ or the Jaimini sûtra; the Bhâṭṭa of Bhaṭṭâćârya, a vârtika for the Mîmâmsâ śâstra; and for the *S*âbara bhâshya the vyâkhyâna called Prâbhâkara, a matântara by Prabhâkara guru, a disciple of Bhaṭṭâćârya; further that *S*aṅkara guru Bhagavatpâdâćârya composed the Vedânta bhâshya on the Uttara mîmâmsâ; and that Vivaraṇâćârya wrote a Vivaraṇa regarding this Bhâshya; that regarding the same *S*aṅkara bhâshya a vṛitti, the Pańćapâdikâ, the Râmânandîya, the Brahmavidyâbharaṇa and many other vyâkhyânas were done by *S*aṅkara's disciples; and that also regarding the *S*aṅkara bhâshya Vâćaspatimiśra wrote the vyâkhyâna called Bhâmatî; "for it (what?) is the vyâkhyâna called Kalpataru; for it is the ṭîkâ called Kaustubha".—As puṇya-kshetras he mentions (p. 421) also Jagannâtha, Viṭhala, *S*eshâćala (*i. e.* Vĕṅkaṭagiri), Kâńći, Kalyâṇa; as a śaktipîṭha also that of Hŏnnâmbĕ at *S*ivagaṅgĕ, and that of Mahâlakshmi at Kŏllâpura. Regarding Vâćaspatimiśra see Ind. Ant. i., 297 seq.; 354; ii., 71 seq.; iii., 81 seq.; Aufrecht's Halâyudha, p. iv. The *S*abarabhâshya is mentioned Ind. Ant. i., 309. (A Râmânanda belongs to the end of the 14th century, Weber's Râmâyaṇa p. 110).—Dr. Burnell has kindly furnished the following notes in a letter dated Tanjore, 20th October, 1874: "As regards the Pûrvamîmâmsâ, the *S*abarabhâshya is the oldest known Commentary. The C. by Bhaṭṭâćârya is the Tantravârttika of Kumârila Bhaṭṭa who lived in the 7th century A. D. Prabhâkara Bhaṭṭa's atheistic Commentary is not known to be in existence. As regards the Uttaramîmâmsâ, *S*aṅkarâćârya lived at the end of the 7th century A. D. (see p. ii. of the Preface to the 1st Vol. of my edition of the Sâmavidhânabrâhmaṇa). The Vivaraṇa I cannot identify. The Pańćapâdikâ is by Pâdapadma said to have been a disciple of *S*aṅkara. Râmânanda's C. has been printed by Dr. Roer; the date is uncertain. The Brahmavidyâbharaṇa (by Advaitânanda) is an abridgment of it by a pupil. The Kalpataru (by Amalânanda) was written in the reign of king Kṛishṇa (? of Vijayanagara at

26. The Praudha râya *C*aritra too may belong to the end of the 16th century. Of this there would be no doubt, if the author, when calling Maḷĕ Mallešа his guru (for instance at the end of the chapters), means that this person was still living or that he had been educated by him[1]. The Liṅgâita author was "Adṛiša appa (father), a disciple of Maḷĕ Mallešа, and the son of Aṇṇa appa who belonged to the karĕ kula of the merchant-chiefs (dešâi) of the Paragaṇĕ (Perguna) of Kollâpura in the Bijâpura prânta" (21, 38-41; 1, 25). The work contains 21 chapters with 1113 verses in Shaṭpadi, and tells how Jakkaṇârya related to king Praudha of Vidyânagara (A. D. 1450-1477)[2], whom he served as minister and who evinced an inclination towards Vaishṇavism, various *S*aiva stories, that are mostly, if not throughout, more detailed accounts of the legends which are sometimes only alluded to in the course of the tales of the Basava and *C*anna Basava Purâṇas[3].

27. A. D. 1657 the Liṅgâita Shaḍakshari deva completed his Râjašekhara Vilâsa (14, 184), seventeen years after *C*annapaṭṇa (Madrâs) was founded by the English. The work forms a Liṅgâita novel in which Râjašekhara, the son of the šaiva king Satyendra *C*oḷa of Dharmavatipura, is playing the chief role, and is valuable only for its fine, though very often voluptuous, diction[4]. Except some verses in Ragaḷĕs, it is in the pure *C*ampû of the first Canarese period, as also with regard to grammar. Besides this work Shaḍakshari wrote a *S*abara-šaṅkara vilâsa and a Vṛishabhendra vijaya in Canarese; and a Kavikarṇarasâyana, a Bhaktâdhikya, and a *S*ivâdhikya in Sanscrit[5]. His Râjašekhara vilâsa is based on a *S*aiva work called Bhâvačintâratna by Mallaṇârya (of Gubbi, 1, 78)[6]. In the preface he remembers first his own guru *C*ika vîra dešika, then Basava, *C*anna Basava,

---

the beginning of the 16th century). The Kaustubha (by Appayya Dîkshita of the N. Tanjore District) was written at the end of the 16th or beginning of the 17th century. Nijaguṇa cannot possibly have lived before the middle of the 17th century....To be sure, Appayya Dîkshita was a great promoter of the *S*aiva religion, and sought to make *S*iva=the Brahma of the Vedânta. I am much surprised at the omission of the *S*aiva C. on the Vedânta sûtras, that by Nîlakaṇṭha. It was certainly in existence about 1500 A. D."—Mr. Brown, in his C. Ts., places Appayya Dîkshita 1522 A. D.; the year may refer to his first public appearance.

1) See above p. lxiv. 2) See above p. lvii. 3) In 1, 31 I meet the expression "Tiguḷa âṇya" together with Karṇâṭa, Drâviḍa, etc.; Tiguḷâṇya occurs also *C*an. Bas. P. 62, 6; see also Ind. Ant. ii., 24. 4) Its leading scenes appear in the Maṅgaḷûr Anthology, Basel Mission Press, 1874. 5) Gaṅgâdhara Maḍivâḷeśvara, p. 1.
6) See above p. lvi.

Allama, (Toṭa) Siddhaliṅga yati[1], further (of the Purâtanas) *e.g.* the Mâdiga (chuckler) *C*annayya who ate with *S*iva[2], Mârayya who played at dice with *S*arva[3], the Beḍa (fowler) Kaṇṇappa of Appuḍuvûr in the Kâḷahastigiri district who plucked out his own eyes and gave them to Bhava[4], Kŏḍagûsu of Koḷûr who offered milk to Abhava[5], Dîpa kali who built a fort for *S*ivâdhava, spending his whole property in his name[6], and then also Nijaguṇa yogi (6-16)[7]. After them he thinks of Reṇuka ârya (ârâdhya), Râma ârya (or Ekorâma tandĕ *i.e.* father), Paṇḍita ârya, Maruḷa ârya, Mâyi deva[8], Jakkaṇa ârya[9], Malhaṇa ârya[10], Mallaṇa ârya (of Gubbi)[11], *S*aṅkara[12], Harîśvara[13], Râghava[14], Keśirâja[15], Soma (of Pâlkurikĕ)[16], (Kĕṛĕ) Padma[17], Bhîma[18], and Bhoja (17-19), especially praising Hari deva (Hariśvara) again in v. 20, 79 and 88. Then he gives also his genealogy (53-68): Reṇukeśa (Revaṇa prabhu, Revaṇa ârya, Reṇuka âčârya) was born of the îśa (liṅga) at Kŏllipâki[19] as a Jaṅgama, instructed Kumbhaja (Agastya)[20] and other munis, went to Laṅkĕ, fulfilled the wish of Vibhîshaṇa, frustrated the plans of the Siddhas, (came to Kalyâṇapura and) frightened (king) Bijjaḷa, gave sight to a man called Tĕlliga, (went to Vishṇu Kańči and) caused the trembling of Vishṇu's idol to cease, released from bondage many females, fulfilled the wish of Vikramârka, crushed Kharpara, preserved the Yaksha, married daughters of kings[21], and (thus he) Revaṇa prabhu obtained

1) See above No. 15. 2) *C*an. Bas. P. 55, 12. 3) Bas. P. 9, 41. 4) Bas. P. 9, 36; ch. 18. His history occurs also in Tamiḻ; Murdoch, p. 77. 5) Bas. P. 9, 38; ch. 14; Can. Bas. P. 57, 39. 6) Gaṇa sahasra nâma 5, 4; Bas. P. ch. 16. 7) See No. 25.
8) Bas. P. 58, 10, at the time of Basava. 9) See above No. 10. 10) See above p. xlvi. 11) See above No. 8. 12) Above No. 7. 13) Above No. 1.
14) Above No. 2. 15) Above p. xxxiii. 16) Above No. 3. 17) Above p. lii.
18) Above N. 6. 19) Kŏllipâkîśa was Reṇuka in the Drâpâra, Revaṇârya (Revaṇârâdhya, Revaṇa siddheśvara, Revaṇa siddha) in the Kali age (Pańčâčârya vamśâvaḷi, taken from the Sanscrit Supra bhedâgama, 1, 18); Revaṇa's guru-throne is at Kadaḷîpura or, in Canarese, Bâḷĕhaḷḷi (1, 1 and conclusion, which place was founded by one of his disciples, *C*an. Bas. P. 62, 35 seq.). He is the first of the five âčâryas or ârâdhyas who are considered to be the founders of the liṅga worship. The second is Maruḷa (or Maruḷa Siddha), born of the Siddhavaṭa, whose throne is at Ujjiniyâpura or Ujjini (2, 1 seq.). The third is Paṇḍita, born at *S*udhâkuṇḍa (see above, p. xlvi.), and his throne is at *S*rîśaila (3, 1 seq.). The fourth is Ekorâma (or Ekorâma tandĕ), born at Drâkshârâma kshetra, and his throne is at Ketâra. The fifth is Viśva, born of the Viśveśa liṅga, and his throne is at Kŏllipâki (4, 1 seq.). The *C*anna Bas. P. enumerates four, leaving out Viśva (59, 21-30). Revaṇa is probably meant in the śâsana adduced Ind. Ant. i., 80 seq. (Kanna, Bamma, Nimba are names not unfrequently met in Liṅgâita books). An Ekântarâma of Abbalûr appears Bas. P. 49, 2 seq.; cf. Gaṇasahasran. 8, 48; Gaṇas. 8, 53 a Mârayya of Kŏllipâki is mentioned. 20) In the Tamiḻ Siddhântaśikhâmaṇi of the 17th century the contrary is stated. Murdoch p. 71.
21) King Râjendra *C*oḻa (about 1000 A. D., see above p. xxi.) gave his daughter in marriage to Revaṇa siddha, says the *C*an. Bas. P. 55, 23.

the son Rudramunîšvara; and when 1400 years were completed[1], Reṇukâčârya re-entered the îša at Kollipâki. Rudramunîndra[2] showed forth *S*iva's greatness everywhere, gaining victory over the kshudra matas. In his lineage (vaṁša) Uddâna šivayogi was born, whose spiritual son was Annadânîša dešika[3]. His disciple was Revaṇasiddha dešika, who lived in the maṭha of Danugûr (or Anugûr). His disciple was *C*ikavîra, whose disciple was Shaḍakshari who composed the work[4].

28. To the middle of the 17th century probably belongs also the Râghavâṅka *C*aritra, or the tale about the above-mentioned[5] poet Râghava, by *C*ikka Nañješa, who was a disciple (karakamalasambhava) of Pañčavaṇṇigĕ Siddha Nañješa, the lord of the guru-throne at Pûvalli pura (Hubbaḷḷi, near Dhâravâḍa), who was the spiritual son of Kuruvatti Nañješvara, who was the spiritual son of Annadânîša (of Shaḍakshari's genealogy; 1, 21. 22)[6]. *C*ikka Nañješa remembers, besides others, Prauḍha narendra, and Jakkaṇârya, *C*âmarasa, Vîraṇâčârya, and Nirvâṇi Boleša, who lived at his court (1, 12. 13), and also Toṭa ârya (19, 94; No. 15). The work contains 19 chapters with 1495 verses in Shaṭpadi.

29. From this time may date also the Liṅgâita translation of the Brahmottara Purâṇa or *S*ivakathâmṛitasâra, made with the help of guru *S*ânteša liṅga, and containing 32 chapters with 1885 verses in Shaṭpadi. Our MS. offers no key to fix the time of its composition, except its mentioning Hŏmpâvâsa Hari deva (Harîšvara), its Shaṭpadi and the

1) 700 of these peculiar 1400 years appear in Liṅgi râja 4 after v. 34 (cf. *C*an. Bas. P. 63, 41. 42) in words that are put into the mouth of *C*anna Basava deva, saying to Vṛishabha, who returns without his liṅga from Anumisha to Kailâsa (see above p. xxi.), regarding his former births: "Was not Indrajit (Râvaṇa's son) 700 years ago in the womb of Maṇḍodari (Râvaṇa's wife), and was born? When thou tiedst the royal insignia of sacred ashes to (his) body, grace was obtained by me. Do not fear, lord of Kûḍal saṅgama (or Kûḍal, at the Kṛishṇa river)! I am the handmaid of thy handmaid". Counting back from 1160 A. D. (about the time of Basava) Râvaṇa would have lived 460 A. D.; and counting back from the year 785 A. D., in which Basava died according to the *C*an. Bas. P. (see above p xxxii.), Râvaṇa's time would fall 85 A. D. according to Liṅgâita views. 2) He appears at *C*anna Basava's time (about 1168 A. D.) and immediately after his death again. His famous disciple was Muktimuni; Muktimuni's disciple was Digambarasu Muktimuni who founded Bâḷĕhaḷḷi near Hŏnnûr in the Malĕ deša. *C*an. Bas. P 62, 35 seq.; see above p. xlviii.

3) Mentioned in the Râghavâṅka Kâvya, 1, 21; 19, 96. 4) Gaṅgâdhara Maḍivâḷešvara says that he died at Ĕḷĕndûr (where at the period of Toṭa Siddhaliṅga the King *C*anna ŏḍĕya was a good Liṅgâita, Can. Bas. P. 63, 55), and that up to this day his relations are at Kŏllipâki, Danugûr to the South of Bĕngaḷûr, and Ĕḷĕndûr (Yaḷandûr). 5) p. li. 6) There is a Siddha Nañješvara at Toṭa ârya's time; *C*an. Bas. P. 63, 47. A Pañčavaṇṇigĕ *C*anna Mallikârjuna appears *S*araṇalîlâmṛita p. 5.

late style of its language. A Tamiḻ translation of the Brahmottara kâṇḍa Varatuṅga by Râma Pâṇḍya has been referred to about the 12th century[1].

30. Also the **Bhaktirasâyana** by **Sahajânanda** whose paramâtma seems to have been *S*iva and whose guru was šrîmatparamaha*m*saparivrâjakâčârya šrî **Saččidânanda**, may possibly be referred to about 1650 A. D. The first Saččidânanda (of five of that name) of *S*ṛiṅgeri is the seventh guru before the present one (called Nṛisi*m*ha Bhârati)[2], and he may be meant on account of para. 31; cf. however paras. 46-48. The work is a prayer in 108 Shaṭpadi verses of inferior merit.

31. The popular treatise on pantheism, called **Anubhavâmṛita**, was composed by **Raṅganâtha** (*S*rî Raṅga), a son of Mâliṅga of the Sahavâsi family, a pupil of srîmatparamaha*m*saparivrâjakâčârya **Sahajânanda** guru, and an ardent follower of the Mallikârjuna liṅga of the lovely *S*rîgiri or *S*rîšaila, or of *S*rîgirîšvara (1, 1-3; 18, 27-36). Sahajânanda may be identical with the author of the just-mentioned Bhaktirasâyana. I see no valid objection to assigning the composition to about 1680 A. D.; and in fact vulgar tradition makes it 200 years old. It numbers 13 chapters with 856 verses in Shaṭpadi.

32. A rather bulky Liṅgâita work (our MS. is not properly numbered), the **Akhaṇḍešvara** (*S*iva) **vačana**, called also the Shaṭsthala âčâraṇa and treating on all the various highly mystical topics of the Liṅgâita sect, may date from this time. The form of the vačanas seems to be Ragaḷĕ; the author is not mentioned, but the style is modern. The **headings** of the 9 chapters are: guru kâruṇya sthala, liṅga dhâraṇa sth., vibhûti sth., rudrâkshĕ sth., bhakti sth., tûrya nirâlamba sth., prasâdi sth., prâṇa liṅgi sth.; the **six sthalas** can mean: shaḍ akshara (o*m* nama*h* šivâya), shaḍ dhâtu, shaṭ karma, shaḍ indriya, shaḍ bhâva, shâḍ liṅga.

33. The following three little treatises (like which there are very many), according to their language, ideas and form, may belong to this time: 1. The vedântic treatise of 15 vačanas, called **Pañčîkaraṇa**, each vačana concluding with the words: "Is it not so, oh *C*idânanda sadguruprabhu?" 2. The 7 **Liṅgâvadhûta vačanas**, each one concluding either with: "Oh *S*aṅkara, Nañjuṇḍešvaraprabhu!", or with: "Oh Kûḍal's *C*annasaṅgamadevaprabhu!" (Kûḍal is the place where Basava died). 3. The **Saṅkaratatva**, 7 Ragaḷĕ verses told by a *S*aṅkara deva.

---

1) Murdoch p. 82. 2) Mysore Kṛishṇa râja's list of the *S*riṅgeri gurus; the **title** put to Saččidânanda appears in the list, p. 18, as belonging to the *S*ṛiṅgeri svâmis.

34. About 1760 A. D.[1] falls the popular composition of the Canarese so-called Jaimini Bhârata[2] by Lakshmîša of the Bharadvâja family, a son of Aṇṇama of Devapura (Amarapura, Surapura; 1, 11; 34, 40. 41. 47)[3], containing 34 chapters with 1907 verses in Shaṭpadi. Its easy style is a curious mixture of old and new forms, a peculiarity that more or less pervades all the works of the later period. There exists also a Tĕlugu translation of the Jaimini Bhârata which is very popular; it is sometimes mentioned as pañča ḍabbu, "mere fiction", which name is given to apocryphal poems that are not grounded on any classical tradition, as the Mai Râvaṇačaritra, *S*atamukha Râmâyaṇa, Kṛishṇârjunasa*m*vâda, and Gaṅgâ Gaurî sa*m*vâda[4].

35. The Vaishṇava dâsa songs of Varâha Timmappa are also to be referred to about 1760 A. D. This appears from one of the hymns that bears his mudrikâ, in which a person of *S*ivabĕḷḷi Mâgaṇĕ (a division of a district) is introduced as having gone with his family to the Mûḍugiri (Tirupati), to tell the Kṛishṇa idol there his deplorable state that began under a Vibudhendra yati in the Pramâdi sa*m*vatsara (A. D. 1759) on čaitra šuddha pañčami, when Gopâlayya of Sâgara was the karaṇika of the hobaḷi (a division of a district). The country then fell into the hands of the Navâb deva, and the devotees of *S*iva fled from Eṇupura. The manager of the hobaḷi, that belongs to Kanyânagara, was then Mudrâḍi Anantayya, a man of tyrannical temper. The father of the family, unable to bear the persecution, runs away, halts at Somešvara-koṭĕ, crosses the Ghaṭṭa in coming to Bhîmakaṭṭĕ and seeing Muḷḷubâgil svâmi, etc., etc. A.D. 1760 the Navâb Hyder made himself master of the kingdom of Maisûr.

36. To the same time may belong the Vaishṇava dâsa songs by Viṭhala and Madhva; the first calling himself an abhinava (new) Purandara[5], and the second remembering "the feet of the excellent

1) H. Narasimmiah, proprietor of the Vičâradarpaṇa Press, Beṅgaḷûr, in his prospectus (1873) regarding a new edition of Lakshmîša's work, says the poet executed his work about 180 years ago. Mr. Narasimmiah has no doubt made to his own opinion proper inquiries before printing the statement. Some say, for instance, the Munshi Tirumalĕ *S*yâmaṇṇa of the Wesleyan Missionaries at Maisûr who knows the family very well, that the work is not even 100 years old.

2) The Sanscrit work is a Paurâṇika composition, and seems to have been in existence already before the 7th century; see Weber's Ind. Streifen ii., 392; Ind. Ant. iii., 23. 25; above p. xliii.

3) This place, named also Devaṇâpura, is in the Bâṇâvâra Tâlûk of Maisûr.

4) See further on, No. 45, a Canarese composition of the same name.

5) Ind. Ant. ii., 308; the Viṭhopačaritra mentioned there, does not belong to Viṭhala dâsa. See further on.

Purandara dâsa" in his Abhimanyu kâḷaga[1], a composition in Ragaḷěs of 43 pages in MS. There is a *C*itrasenakâḷaga prasaṅga by Madhva dâsa of Kuḍuma pura (Uḍupu?)[2], taken from the Bhârata, in 355 Yakshagâna verses[3].

37. A. D. 1761 the Jaina Surâla, according to his own final statement, wrote the story of the nymph Padmâvatî devî for *C*ěnnamma devî of the râṇivâsa (queen's house) of *S*rîčandrašekhara *C*ikkarâya *C*auṭa of Puttikâpura (probably Puttûr, not far from Maṅgaḷûr), the present *C*auṭa ex-râyas[4], according to this work (1, 84), belonging to the Kâdambas. The story has 12 chapters with 1671 verses in a Ragaḷě metre.

38. Very probably from A. D. 1768 dates the Anubhavašikhâmaṇi; for the author, Râmačandra, a devotee of the Virûpâksha liṅga at Hampě, states (24, 59) that he finished his work in the Sarvadhâri sa*m*vatsara, by which must be meant 1768 A. D., and not 1828, as our copy was written in 1844. In verse 9 he asks a blessing of jagadguru Mallikârjuna, Paṇḍitârâdhya, Onnama âčârya who is an avatârašishya of Aghahara (*S*iva), and *S*aṅkarâčârya in the maṭha of *S*ṛingaripura on the southern bank of the Tuṅga; and in chapter 9 he relates a story about *S*aṅkarâčârya defeating the Jainas at Kâši. The mention of *S*aṅkarâčârya, the founder of *S*ṛiṅgeri, is a circumstance very rarely met with in Canarese compositions. Regarding himself the author says: "The purohita of my house is Bŏmmi baṭṭa of Jâḍa (weaver) Hěbbaḷḷi. When Pědda arasa of the Gautama gotra, of the great Āṅgirasa Āyâsya pravara, of the Baudhâyana sûtra of the Yaju*h* šâkhě of our Yajurveda invested me with the sacrificial thread (muñji), he readily and cheerfully gave me instruction regarding the thread (yajñopavîta) and the gâyatri; and by this grace of the guru I set forth the Anubhavašikhâmaṇi. The kâraṇika Govinda Sâmba of Mayyûrapura is my maternal uncle and guru, who took my hand, taught (me), and showed (me) the road to good poetry". His own father was Râmačandra, the karaṇika of the village Kurutukoṭě of the paragaṇě of Krutapura (1, 10-12). The work contains *S*aiva legends first told by Gautama muni to

1) Ind. Ant. ii., p. 309. 2) Ibd. p. 310. 3) Yakshagâna, a term not in the St. Petersburg Lexicon, in Canarese and Tělugu, denotes "a melody". Mr. Brown s. v. says: Yakshagâna is "poetry written rather to suit an air than according to the strict rules of prosody". But such licence is not to take place in Canarese, as it includes all the metres; respectively Mora-metres, that are fit for being chanted: Kandas, Ragaḷěs, and Shaṭpadis. As a work composed in the Yakshagâna style, he mentions *e. g.* a Sîtâkalyâṇa. Cf. the Sîtâkalyâṇa of our list, No. 52. 4) See above p. lxiv.

Gambhîra râya of Ratnagiri paṭṇa in Kâšmîradeša, who in the end with his town went to Kailâsa; and then, under the appellation of Gambhîrarâjačaritra, by Satyašivayogîndramunì to Uttamarâja of Kântâvatipura in the North, who obtained the same benefits from them. Chapter 24, 22 the author states: "When I saw this poetry that, with joy, had been composed in *S*ara shaṭpadi by Râghava, the spiritual son of Hampĕ's Harihara[1], I learned its meaning by the guru's grace, and composed it in Bhâmini, Vârdhika, and *S*ara shaṭpadi". He observes 24, 58 that the benefits derived from hearing his composition are similar to those derived from hearing the Bhâgavata and Purâṇas, probably meaning Canarese translations of them.

39. To the later days of the Vaishṇava dâsas seems to belong the Nalačaritra,—9 chapters with 481 verses in Shaṭpadi,—the author of which calls his Kṛishṇa the *C*anniga râya (*i. e.* Raṅganâtha) of Varapura, for instance, 1, 2. 3. The two Tĕlugu translations are mentioned above under Nos. 2 and 23.

40. Here we venture to place also the Nijaliṅga šataka, 100 verses in Shaṭpadi in praise of *S*iva, the language resembling that of the padas of the Vaishṇava dâsas. Each verse towards its end contains the words: "Oh Nijaliṅga bhavabhaṅga!" The last verse says that the author's liṅga has its abode at Kadrubhavapura (Pampâpura?) on the shore of the Tuṅgabhadra[2].

41. About 1800 A.D. the Liṅgâita Sarvajña's Vačanas in Tripadi may have been composed, with such headings as guru karuṇa paddhati, liṅga p., ishṭa liṅga p., bhakta p., jñâna p., etc.[3] MSS. of them vary to a great extent: a Bĕṅgaḷûr edition (1872) contains 105 verses, a Dhâravâḍa one (1866) 225; whereas one of our MSS. (A.) has 398 verses, although a chapter on kâlajñâna is wanting, 33 verses of which are contained in another incomplete MS. (B.). This chapter also is not in the other recensions. A. contains forty riddles (ŏgaṭu, ch. 21)[4] and

1) See above p. liv., where it is stated by the author of the Râghavâṅkačaritra that Râghava has invented the Shaṭpadis. He means the modern Shaṭpadis, that are unconnected with Nâgavarma's devâkshara-feet, as is seen from Râghavâṅka č. 19, 82 seq., where he adduces patterns in short letters of the Vârdhikya, *S*ara, Kusuma, Bhoga, Bhâvani (!) and Parivardhini, and introduces another kind, the Uddaṇḍa shaṭpadi, which regarding the number of Moras is exactly like the Vârdhika of our text (337), whereas his Vârdhikya pattern in our two MSS. lacks two Moras in each hemistich; but the Vârdhikya in which he has composed his work, quite agrees with our rule 337. 2) v. 81 contains the Hindusthânî term "lâčâr", needy. Nijaliṅga is also a proper name of men, see *e. g.* Bas. P. 59, 1; Gaṇasah. 8, 10. 3) Cf. Ind. Ant. ii., 23. 4) There are also riddles in Tamiḻ, Murdoch p. 208.

a story of 15 verses told by the author regarding himself (ch. 22), neither of which is in the other recensions. According to the said story Sarvajña was the illegitimate son of the *S*aiva Brâhmaṇa Basava arasa of Mâsûr (in the zillah of Dhâravâḍa), and had been born of a widow, a Mâḷava woman, whom his father, in returning from a pilgrimage to Kâši to obtain a prasâda for a male child, had met in the potters' street at Ambalûr, and upon whom he had bestowed his specific *S*ivaprasâda. Sarvajña's prophetical sentences are, we think, based upon the kâlajñâna in the *C*anna Basava Purâṇa (63, 60 seq.); but he goes further, stating that before the great Liṅgâita ruler who is to come also according to the *C*an. Bas. P[1]. to restore the Kalyâṇa dynasty, called Basavanta deva or Vîra Vasavanta, Raṅgadurga (also: Raṅgapaṭṇa, Raṅgapura, *S*rîraṅga)[2] will be taken by people with trowsers and hats (ṭŏppigĕ), an event that cannot well refer to *S*rîraṅgapaṭṇa A. D. 1610 becoming the seat of government of the Maisûr dynasty in succession to that of Vidyânagara in that place; but probably refers either to its being taken by Haidar in 1761, or by the English in 1799.

42. From the beginning of the 19th century may date also the Kumâra Râma *C*aritra composed by the Liṅgâita Raṅgayya, son of the pañčâḷa (artificer) *C*anna Bhujaṅga of the Canarese country, in which he

---

1) It says, he will be born in kali 4683 in the svabhânu sa*m*vatsara (*i. e.* either 1582 or 1583 A. D.), will go to the town that bears the name of Basava and is in the midst of Eṇṇĕkâveri, and after the final destruction of the Narasi*m*ha dynasty by the Turkas will come to Vidyânagari, take possession of the Bâliyâ bhaṇḍâra, and rebuild Kalyâṇa; 63, 64-70. (The Purâṇa dates from A. D. 1585). 2) Raṅgadurga, etc. is very unlikely to mean the island *S*rîraṅga opposite Tiručinâpaḷḷi in the Kâveri, that contains two pagodas, one of Vishṇu or *S*rîraṅga, and one of *S*iva or Jambukešvara. The following to some extent only probable dates may be mentioned: 1565 A. D., after king Râma's defeat, his general and minister of Vidyânagara, took the government. 1572 Tirumalĕ, a brother of Râma, held the rule for some time at Pŏnugŏṇḍa (see above No. 24) and at *S*rîraṅgapaṭṇa, and then was succeeded by *S*rîraṅga. 1585 or 1591 Vĕṅkaṭapati followed, since 1594 at *C*andragiri, 11 miles from Tirupati (cf. Ind. Ant. ii., 371), during whose reign *S*rîraṅgapaṭṇa was once besieged by the nâyaka Vîrappa of Madhurâ who, however, was driven home; but 1610 Râja ŏḍĕya of Maisûr conquered that city, and made it his capital. 1630 Vĕṅkaṭapati was followed by Râma. 1640 *S*rîraṅga ruled, who made a grant to the English of the site of the city of Madras, that after his father was called *C*annapaṭṇa; 1647 he was conquered by the Sultân of Goḷakŏṇḍa, and became a fugitive (see above p. xlviii.); and 1663 the Vidyânagara dynasty ended with him. 1677 Vĕṅkaṭa deva mahârâja ruled Tiručinâpaḷḷi. 1687 the first Mŏgal force entered the Carnatic; 1710 Sâdat ulla khân became its first Navâb; 1736 Tiručinâpaḷḷi got into the power of *C*andâ sâheba, the son-in-law of the Navâb of Ârkâḍu. 1741 Tiručinâpaḷḷi was taken by the Mâhrâṭṭas. 1750 *C*andâ sâheba appears again as a rival Navâb of the Carnatic, 1757 with the French blockaded his rival and the English at Tiručinâpaḷḷi, etc.

remembers the Vighnarâja idol at Tagaḍûr (8, 8. 9)[1]. It contains 11 chapters with 1915 verses in the same Ragaḷĕ metre that Kanaka dâsa used for his Mohanatarangiṇi. For its contents see above p. xlix. seq., and compare further on para. 66.

43. Probably about the same time the *S*ivašaraṇalîlâmṛita was composed, that contains stories regarding Lingâita devotees, based on the Basava and *C*anna Bas. Purâṇas. It has 11 chapters with 4220 Yakshagâna verses according to the Bĕngaḷûr printed edition (1871), from which, however, our MS. differs to a considerable extent. The author is *C*annappa ayya of the town of Niḍugal, to the South of Hampĕ, the Southern Kâši, where the Virûpâksha linga is (p. 5. 279).

44. Here may be mentioned as probably belonging to the same time, the Monešvara Purâṇa, by an author who says that he knows nothing concerning the rules of poetical composition, making obeisance to Gangâdhara gurunâtha (1, 9. 11). It is a story about a Mona (or Mauna, 7, 11. 32; 8, 6), who does very extraordinary feats, *e. g.* raising people from the dead (as many Lingâitas at and since Basava's time are declared to have done) being a trifle to him. He was born to a kammâra (blacksmith) Kallappa[2] or Hâvappa and his wife Hâvakka of Hâvinâḷpura in the grâma of Goṇâḷ near Surapura (1, 19; 2, 8. 9), and was an incarnation of Mona linga. Kumâra Mona kills the king's son; to those who endeavour to seize him, he appears as Mona phakîr, assumes his original form, and restores the prince to life. In course of time he goes to Kâši (3, 45), and afterwards appears at Bîjâpura where the Muhammadans rule under a Pâčča, who do not worship any idols in the great Masûti (mosque) there, but teach the Kurân (4, 18-25). Mona assuming the guise of a mad Mona dîn or Mona phakîr enters the mosque, calls out "Allallâhâyahâ", approaches the Mulla who is reading the Kurân, and by his magic power causes one of his shoes to fall from above down on the Kurân as if it fell from heaven by *S*iva's power. For this offence he is killed by the Pâčča's order, but remains alive, whereupon he is adored as Mona Pâčča (ch. 4). Then there is a Gangappa phakîr who is like a son of Monesa (Mona 5, 38), and other phakîrs that stand in close relation to him: Siddhasâheba phakîr (7, 31), Bâbâ ph., Pañča ph., and Bâla ph. (8, 4-11). Chapter 9 occurs, amongst other similar comparisons

1) At Tagaḍûr there lived, about Toṭa Ârya's time (see above, No 15), a Lingâita Prabhu, *C*an. Bas. P. 63, 33; about the same time there lived a Nañja râya, v. 55, probably of Maisûr (A. D. 1401-1432). 2) A Kalli, Kallayya, Kalla of Hâvinâḷpura of an earlier time appears Bas. P. 9, 44; 55, 26; 58, 7; *C*an. Bas. P. 57, 6 (Hûvina Hâḷ); cf. Gaṇasah. 8, 26. 39.

e. g. that "amîn" is the same as "mona", also the declaration that the term "Allama" is identical with "Allah". The Monešvara of the story, whosoever he may have been, must have lived somewhere between the years 1489-1686, when the Bijâpura kings ruled.

45. The Gaṅgâ Gaurî Samvâda too I place here, though with some diffidence. It relates how *S*iva in company with Nârada going to seek for another wife, after much hardships found Gaṅgâ, brought her home, put her on his head and Gaurî on his knee, and for his own and the world's amusement caused both to fight together. It contains 5 chapters with 835 Ragaḷĕ verses, and professes to have been first told (at Bijjaḷa's time) by Nîlammĕ to her husband Basava at Kalyâṇapura. It has been stated already that a composition of the same name exists in Tĕlugu[1].

46. The Jñânasindhu, a large treatise on Vedântism for the masses, by *C*idânandâvadhûta, whose guru was *C*idânanda (Saččidânanda) Bhârati who was in the Ayodhyâpura (*S*ṛiṅgeri) on the bank of the Tuṅgabhadra (1, 1-25). The negligent language of the work compels one to refer it to this late period, and to suppose that this *C*idânanda Bhârati was the last guru of this name at *S*ṛiṅgeri[2], the immediate predecessor of the present one, according to the *S*ṛiṅgeri guru list that A. D. 1854, after the death of Saččidânanda Bhârati, was composed by Kṛishṇa râjendra of Maisûr, son of *C*âma râja, who was set aside in 1832 and died in 1868. The Jñânasindhu, therefore, probably dates from about 1830. 46 chapters with 3486 Shaṭpadi verses.

47. Probably a few years prior to the Jñânasindhu *C*idânanda himself composed the *C*idakhaṇḍânubhava sâra, wherein he says he intends to make the meanings of the Upanishats or the Vedânta popular (2, 3. 10. 11). 8 chapters with 537 verses in Shaṭpadi.

48. The Haribhakti rasâyana, another kind of Vedântic treatise for the people, also bears *C*idânanda's name, who states (1, 16) he does not know the parama rahasyas told by the Vedântas, nor what the Kâpilas say, nor the way in which the Pâtañjalas and *S*âṇḍilyas roam, nor the various Âgamas and Paurâṇas; he will speak by the grace of the sadguru. But in the concluding verses of the first four chapters he asserts that he has given the essence of all the Âgamas and Paurâṇas; and, in the end of the fifth, also that of the whole Âmnâya (vedic texts). 5 chapters with 301 Shaṭpadi verses.

1) See above No. 34. 2) See above Nos. 30. 31. The Saččidânanda mentioned there cannot well be of so late a date, as he was the guru of Sahajânanda, whose pupil, it seems, was Raṅganâtha.

49. The Anubhava rasâyana by Krishṇa râja of Maisûr, mostly in prose, evinces the style of a tract, and may have been written in opposition to Mission tracts. It was printed at Bĕṅgaḷûr in 1865.

50. A translation of the Sukasaptati, or seventy tales of a parrot, was made by a servant of Basava kshitîśa, who says that Kŏḍagi pura's Nârâyaṇa will bless those who hear it (1, 17). 70 chapters with 2937 verses in Shaṭpadi.

51. A. D. 1830 the Viṭhopa (Viṭhoba) Caritra, also called Viṭhala Caritra, was composed at Kundâpura on the Western coast by Vĕṅkaṭeśa bhaṭṭa and one of his friends[1], describing how a Brahman child that was to be sacrificed for the attainment of riches, was saved by the interference of Viṭhala (Krishṇa) of Paṇḍari nagara. 70 Ragaḷĕ verses.

52. About A. D. 1830 a Sârasvata Brahman, called Gĕrsappĕ Sântayya, who was Principal Sadaramîn at Maṅgaḷûr (Kshemapura) where he died about 25 years ago[2], began to compose a number of tales on subjects taken from the Bhârata and Râmâyaṇa in Yakshagâna metres, to be used at dramatic performances (nâṭaka)[3]. Such compositions bear the name of prasaṅgas. Of Sântayya's compositions may be mentioned: the Bhîshma parva, Droṇa parva and Karṇa parva; an Ekâdaśî prasaṅga; a Jarâsandha kâḷaga (fight), a Surathasudhanva kâḷaga; a Saubhadrâ kalyâṇa; a Sîtâ kalyâṇa[4], wherein the author's idol is called Kshemapurîśa, 84 pages in MS.; Sîtâviyoga Lavaṇasamhâra, which the author designates as belonging to the Prâkrita Râmâyaṇottara[5], calling his idol Kshemapuranivâsa and Kshemapureśa, 80 pages in MS.; and the Râvaṇadigvijaya, from the Uttarakâṇḍa of the Râmâyaṇa, wherein the author appears as a devotee of Vĕṅkaṭa of Kshemapura or of Kshemapureśa, his Gaṇeśa being at Sarapura, 65 pages in a Maṅgaḷûr lithograph.

53. Similar productions, probably of the same age, are: the Lavakuśa kâḷaga of the Nâṭaka Râmâyaṇa, 453 Yakshagâna verses, at the end of which Srîraṅga whose abode is at Kaṇpuri, is invoked, a Dhâravâḍa lithograph, 1867; and the slaughter of Kîčaka by Bhîma, etc. from the Yakshagâna Virâṭparva, the author of which invokes the Îsa

1) This statement which annuls the supposition expressed in Ind. Ant. ii., 808, is taken from a MS. that since came to hand. 2) Mr. Bâḷappa, a Sârasvata, and Sanscrit teacher at the Government School at Maṅgaḷûr, has been kind enough to give us these particulars.

3) The Nâṭaka Râmâyaṇa in Tamiḷ is referred to the 18th century; Murdoch p. 199.

4) Above No. 86, note 8. 5) The Tĕlugu Uttara Râmâyaṇa, that superseded the older versions, was written by Pushpagiri Timmanna about A. D. 1790; Brown's Preface.

(liṅga) that dwells at Sarasijabhavapura or Ajapura, 423 verses in a Dhâravâḍa lithograph of 1867.

The works we are now going to enumerate, have all been composed in the 19th century, and some of the authors are likely to be still alive. They form some of the publications of Bĕṅgaḷûr and Dhâravâḍa native presses, from A. D. 1864-1872; the lithographs from Dhâravâḍa simply ruin the eyes.

Publications of Bĕṅgaḷûr:

54. Tĕnnâla Râmakṛishṇa hâsyarasa kathâ, 20 stories in prose regarding the jester Râmakṛishṇa, who was attached to the court of Kṛishṇa râja of Ânĕgŏndi (1504-1529) whose minister was Appâji. It exists also in Tamiḻ (Murdoch p. 207).

55. Bâlagraha, a superstitious treatise on children's diseases.

56. Betâḷa (Vetâḷa) pañčavimšatikathâ, in prose, a translation of the twenty-five tales related by the Betâḷa (goblin) to Vikramârka.

57. Sânanda gaṇešvara kathâ, in Yakshagâna verses, based on the 56th chapter of the Canna Bas. P. The ṛishi Pûrṇavitta obtains from Siva his son Sânanda who takes all the inhabitants of Yamapura to Sivapura[1].

58. Hamsa vimšatikathâ, in prose, translated by S. Kṛishṇayya. This series of twenty amorous stories narrated by a Hamsa, has been translated also into Tĕlugu verse (Brown's Preface).

Publications of Dhâravâḍa:

59. Kathâsâgara, 53 stories in prose, composed by Mânavi Vîrappa of Bhrûpura (Hubbaḷḷi) in A. D. 1851.

60. Kâmadahana Ratipralâpa Dundumĕ (dundumĕ=wanton or bombastic composition), 27 verses.

61. Kṛishṇapârijâta, 128 pages, in Yakshagâna verses,—a love affair between Kṛishṇa's wives, arising on account of a pârijâta flower brought by Nârada to Kṛishṇa,—by Aparâḷa Tammaṇṇa of the Râyačûr district.

62. A Kṛishṇa lîlâ of 16 verses.

63. A Kṛishṇa lîlâ Dundumĕ, 25 verses, the last of which mentions šrîguru of Kundagŏḷḷa.

64. Kṛishṇârjuna Dundumĕ, 142 verses, as it appears by Kali Basava Liṅgayya who, invoking the favor of the guru of Kunda-

1) The same is told of Siddharâmeša, the friend of Canna Basava. Can. Bas. P. 59, 12.

gŏḷḷa, composed the work by the wish of Kĕñčendra and Sirasa of Bhrûlatâpura (Hubbaḷḷi), sons of Timmendra and Mâjavva.

65. Kaivalyapaddhati gîtâ[1], in Yakshagâna verses, a sort of Lainga dâsa padas, frequently referring to Liṅgâita legends, by one Ĕragambaḷi Siddha varaliṅga or Shaḍakshari deva (?). 70 pages.

66. Kŏmâra Râma kathâ, an episode from the work mentioned above No. 42, in an enlarged form and Yakshagâna verses, treating of the vile desires of Ratnâjî, one of Kampila râya's wives, for her husband's son, the hero Râma. 58 pages.

67. Jalašilpi pallîšakunâdi šakuna, or omens regarding the building of tanks, wells, etc.; and omens connected with lizards, etc. 32 pages in prose.

68. Dîpa Kali čaritra, or the story of the šivabhakta Dîpa Kali of Kañčipura in Čoḷamaṇḍala[2], based on Basava P. 16, apparently by an Ambuligĕ Čanna Mallîša. 1, 5 he says: "Pâlkurikĕ's Somešа uttered the story of the Siva šaraṇas (devotees), and Bhîma kavi uttered the Basava Paurâṇa". 9 chapters with 1058 Shaṭpadi verses.

69. Dhanañjaya Nighaṇṭakâ, a Canarese ṭîkâ professedly on 202 verses of Dhanañjaya; but 21 verses only are given in full.

70. Draupatî mânaharaṇa Dundumĕ, 67 verses, by a disciple of Čŏkka Siddheša of Bhrûlatâpura (Hubbaḷḷi).

71. Dhâravâḍa Varelavarṇana Dundumĕ, 33 verses about the Varelas, a class of people at Dhâravâḍa.

72. Nuli Čandayya šârada, a praise of the Liṅgâita Nuli Čandayya of Basava's time (Bas. Pur. 58, 7). 25 verses.

73. Pallî saraṭâdi šakuna, or omens of lizards, chameleons, etc.[3] 20 pages in Sanscrit and Canarese, taken from a Bombay publication.

74. Vîra Saṅgayya Dundumĕ (cf. Bas. P. 58, 2), a sort of Liṅgâita love story, by Sâli Čanna Basava of Tantupura (Dhâravâḍa).

---

1) The Dhâravâḍa editor, on the title-page, says it is a gîtâ sung by Shaḍakshara svâmi; he perhaps means the author of the Râjašekhara vilâsa, see above p. lxvii. The first verse is as follows: "As all šâstras declare, thou art the spotless guru for all and all, I have understood by (or under) the name of Ĕragambaḷi Siddhavaraliṅga; oh Hara, thou hast made dîkshâ to me; by (or under) the name of vara Shaḍakshari deva thou hast let me know the anubhava of the Siva šâstra." In the Maṅgaḷa verses on page 70 Čanna Vṛishabha of the Tarabet maṭha of Tantupura is mentioned, called in one of the following verses Dhâravâḍa's Čan. Vṛishabha. Tantupura is a translation of Dhâravaḍâ. 2) The person is mentioned also in Gaṇasahasranâma 5, 4. 3) I possess two treatises on fate in MS., one is called Navaratna čintâmaṇi in Canarese; the other is a Nakshatra tilaka, Sanscrit and Canarese. The first-mentioned seems to belong to the 19th century.

75. Vetâḷa pañčavimšakathâ, in a translation quite different from that of No. 56.

76. Vaidya šâstra, expressly prepared for the press.

77. Vaidyâmṛita, translated from the Marâṭhî.

78. *S*araṇu Basava Ragaḷĕ and *S*araṇa Basava Ragaḷĕ Kanda. The first of these Liṅgâita praises forms 100 verses, each of which ends in "*S*araṇu Basava"; of the second (p. 26 seq.) it is not easy to determine the end, as it is printed together with matter that seems to be different[1]. On page 36 the following words occur (see above Nos. 3. 5. 6. 7): "I will mention the names of the poets who praised the Basava purâṇa;... Somanâtha kavi composed the Basava Purâṇa in Ândhra, and Bhîma in (Canarese) using the Shaṭpadi metre;... *S*aṅkara ârâdhya, the lord of the poets (kavîšvara), was pleased to tell the story fully in Sanscrit; *S*iva kavi of Bâlačandra nagara composed it with vastuka;... and then the *C*atura Basava liṅga (the author probably meaning himself) has elegantly written the granthârtha by the grace of Yatipura's Siddheša".

79. *S*ivapârijâta, or the story how Pârvatî rejected Vishṇu and married *S*iva, throwing on his neck the pârijâta garland. 3 chapters in Yakshagâna verses in 18 pages.

80. *S*ivabhakti sâra, 107 verses in Shaṭpadi, by *S*ivadhyâna Râmayya, the chief disciple of Gaṅgâdhara Bhârati svâmi.

81. *S*ivarâtrî kathâ, or a story about a cruel fowler[2] who at night unconsciously threw some Bilva leaves on a neglected liṅga, when *S*iva's messengers came and invited him to come to Rajatâdri (Kailâsa). 101 verses in Shaṭpadi dedicated by the author to guru Govinda.

82. Simhâsana battîsuputtaḷĕ, or thirty-two stories told by thirty-two puppets of Vikrama râja's throne to Bhoja râja, in prose, translated from the Marâṭhî by one *C*anna Basava and Basava Liṅga.

83. Sudhâma čaritra, a story of Kṛishṇa's friend Sudhâma, 6 chapters with 148 Shaṭpadi verses. 1, 3 yati, vaḍi, and prâsu are mentioned.

84. Subodhâmṛita, a collection of 22 miscellaneous stories in prose.

85. Subhâshitagrantha mâlâ, a collection of alphabetically arranged Sanscrit verses with a Canarese translation. 72 pages.

---

1) The small volume of 48 pages wherein it occurs, contains also an Akaharamâlâ in praise of *S*iva, this word forming the end of each of the 51 verses, ascribed to *S*aṅkarâčârya. It begins: adbhutavigraha amarâdhîšvara | agaṇitaguṇagaṇa amitašiva || 1 || ânandâmṛita âšritarakshita | âtmânanda mahešà šiva || 2 || Also a Mahimna stava by Pushpadatta has been printed at Dhâravâḍa, 42 verses in Sanscrit with a Canarese translation.

2) Cf. Bas. P. 58 v. 3 šivarâtrĕ Saṅgayya, v. 6 šivarâtrĕ Saṅkaṇṇa.

86. Saumini kathâ, 98 verses in Shaṭpadi. The author is Basava Liṅga, the son of Maḍivaḷa of Kundagōḷḷa. The Brahman woman Saumini walks in a dissolute way, is driven away into the jungle and lives there with a fowler with whom she eats flesh and drinks brandy, so that when she dies, Yama curses her to be born again as a miserable low-caste woman. As such she once follows the pilgrims to Gokarṇa, where she quite accidentally offers a Bilva leaf to a liṅga, and therefore is taken to Kailâsa.

87. Hubbaḷḷi varṇana Dundumĕ, 9 verses of a low character.

88. Hubbaḷḷi markaṭa Dundumĕ, 5 stupid verses. The author is a son of Canna Vṛishabha (Basava) and belongs to the Tarabetsâli maṭha of Dhâravâḍa (see above No. 65, note)[1].

In the above list are no doubt many omissions, though it contains all the generally known and read native productions so far as they have not been executed by Christians. I have given what I happened to have at hand. May the present volume form a small contribution towards a History of Canarese literature! Its defects will doubtless be excused by all who know the difficulties connected with first attempts of a similar character.

Of Tamiḻ literature it has been said by Dr. Caldwell that "it is the only vernacular literature in India which has not been content with imitating the Sanscrit, but has honorably attempted to emulate and outshine it." But my own impression is that the more Canarese vernacular literature becomes known, the more evident it becomes that it will fully bear comparison with any other vernacular literature of the South.

Mercara, 19th October 1874. **F. Kittel.**

1) Canna Basa appa and Basa Liṅga appa, Dhâravâḍa's Deputy Educational Inspector (Dipûṭi Ijyukeśanal Inaspĕkṭara), ventured on a translation of Shakespear's Comedy of Errors (Kâmeḍi âph Yarasa), and anno. 1871 had it printed at Dhâravâḍa under the title "A wonderful story that will cause to laugh who do not laugh."

CORRECTIONS

REGARDING THE PREFACE AND ESSAY.

Page V, *line* 27, from top, supply a comma after "occurs".

P. X, *note* 1, *not* "śaiśvadanâ", *but* "śaśivadanâ".

P. XIII, *l.* 21, f. t., *not* "1633", *but* "1643".

P. XVII, *l.* 15, f. t., *not* "sarajijodara", *but* "sarasijodara".

P. XVIII, *l.* 14, f. t., *not* "Kaundinya", *but* "Kauṇḍinya".

P. XXIV, No. 5, *not* "the Tirumalĕ", *but* "Tirumalĕ".

P. XXV, *l.* 23, f. t., *not* "found also", *but* "found as such also".

P. XXVIII, *note*, *l.* 20, from bottom, strike out the stop after "Basava".

P. XXIX, *l.* 19, f. t., *not* "two verses[1]) and was", *but* "two verses[1]), was".

P. XXXI, *l.* 4, f. t., *not* "from the instances", *but* "only from instances".

P. XXXI, *note*, *ls.* 3-4, f. b., *not* "where king Nirahaṅkâra (according to the *Can.* Bas. P.) or Mamakâra (according to the Prabhuliṅgalīlĕ) ruled with his wife Sujńâni or Mohini devi", *but* "where king Mamakâra ruled with his wife Mohini devi".[1])

P. XXXIV, *note*, *l.* 6, f. b, *not* "became", *but* "had become".

P. XXXV, *note*, *l.* 16, f. b., *not* "Two others", *but* "Two others in the Rasaratnâkara".

P. XXXIX, *note*, *l.* 1, f. b., *not* "Mahâsragdhara", *but* "Mahâsragdharâ".

P. L, *l.* 3, f. t., *not* "Penagŏṇḍĕ", *but* Pĕnagŏṇḍĕ".

P. LVIII, *note*, *l.* 2, f. b., *not* "*Cundâ*", *but* "*Candâ*".

P. LX, *l.* 1, f. t., *not* "recites", *but* "relates".

P. LX, *l.* 18, f. t., *not* "of some Tatsamas, Tadbhavas", *but* "of some Tatsamas, of Tadbhavas".

P. LXV, *l.* 18, f. t., *not* "The same, regarding its authorship, appears from the following two verses", *but* "The same appears from the following two verses regarding its authorship".

P. LXV, *l.* 27, f. t., *not* "an comprehensive", *but* "a comprehensive".

P. LXIX, *l.* 16, f. t., *not* "Boleśa", *but* "Boḷeśa".

P. LXIX, *note*, *l.* 1, f. t., *not* "Liṅgi", *but* "Siṅgi".

P. LXX, *l.* 2, f. t., *not* "Varatuṅga by", *but* "by Varatuṅga".

P. LXX, *l.* 27, f. t., *not* "shâḍ", *but* "shaḍ".

---

1) The curt sentence in the *Can.* Bas. P. allows also the meaning of the Prabhuliṅgalīlĕ. See p. LVIII.

ನಾಗವರ್ಮಛಂದಸ್ಸು

NĀGAVARMA'S PROSODY

ಶ್ರೀರಸ್ತು!

(INTRODUCTION)

(ಪೀಠಿಕೆ)

1. This work of the Kavirâjahamsa, for its excellence, commands the esteem even of Kâḷidâsa.

ಚಂಪಕಮಾಲಾವೃತ್ತಂ

ರಚಿತ-ಪದ-ಪ್ರಸನ್ನ-ಪರಿಪೂರ್ಣ-ರಸಾವಹಮರ್ಥ-ಯುಕ್ತಮಾ
ಗುಚಿತ-ಪುರಾಣ-ಮಾರ್ಗ-ಪದ-ಪದ್ಧತಿ-ಬಂಧುರ-ಬಂಧಮೊಂಬಿದಂ ।
ರಚಯಿಸೆ, ವಾಚ್ಯ-ವಾಚಕ-ವಿಶೇಷ್ಯ-ವಿಶೇಷಣ-ಲಕ್ಷ್ಯ-ಲಕ್ಷಣ-
ಪ್ರಚುರತೆ ಕಾಳಿದಾಸನುಮನೋಳಿಸಿತೀ ಕವಿ-ರಾಜಹಂಸನಾ. ॥ 1[1] ॥

---

1) Before this verse there are 6 Maṅgaḷa verses (stanzas) in M. and Sb. of which v. 6 (an invocation of Bhâratî) is also in Sa. as v. 3, in Rc. as v. 1, and in B. and D. as v. 3; and of which v. 1 is also in B. and D. as v. 2. H. Ra. Rb. and Rd. contain no Maṅgaḷa verses. H. and Ra. begin with simply stating that Nâgarvarma told his wife, he was going to teach her prosody as he had learned it, viz. according to what Piṅgaḷa heard when the deva (no name) was telling prosody to the devî, and afterwards told the Ṛishis (the reading differing from that of v. 22 of the text, the English heading of which is to be compared); Rb. begins with the Pratishṭhâ, resp. v. 80 of the text; Rd. with a verse after our verse 84, that has not been adduced in this edition. See note to v. 84.

2. **At the request of the learned the work has been composed.**

ಕಂದಂ

ಬಲ್ಲರ ಬಗೆಯಂ ಕಲ್ತವ
ರೆಲ್ಲಂ ಮುಂಗೊಂಡೊಱಲ್ದು ಕೇಳಲ್ಕೀತಂ ।
ಬಲ್ಲನೆನಲ್ಕೆಱವಿಕ್ಕಿದ
ಬೆಲ್ಲದ ಪೊಲಪೂರ್ವಮಾಗೆ ಪೇೞ್ದಂ ಕೃತಿಯಂ. ‖ 2[1] ‖

3. **Only a poet like the author can write with elegance.**

ಕರಮಸ್ತ್ರಾಕ್ಷರಮುಚಿತಾ
ಕ್ಷರಮವಲಂಬ-ಪ್ರಸನ್ನ-ಮತಿ-ಮಧುರಮಲಂ ।
ಕರಣ-ಯುತಮೆನಿಸೆ ಪೇೞಲ್
ಧರೆಯೊಳ್ ಕವಿ-ರಾಜಹಂಸನೊಬ್ಬಂ ಬಲ್ಲಂ. ‖ 3[1] ‖

4. **Nâgavarma's genealogy[2].**

ಜಗದೊಳಗಿದೊಂದು ಮಿಗಿಲೆನೆ
ನೆಗೞ್ದಿರ್ದುದು ವೆಂಗಿವಿಷಯಮಾ ವಿಷಯದೊಳಾ ।
ಳ್ಗಗಣಿತಮೆನೆ ಸಪ್ತಗ್ರಾ
ಮಗಳೊಳಮಾ ವೆಂಗಿಪೞು ಕರಂ ಸೊಗಯಿಸುಗುಂ[3]. ‖ 4 ‖

ಆ ವೆಂಗಿಪೞುವಿನೊಳ್ ವಿಭು
ದೇವ-ಸಮಾನಂ ವಿದಗ್ಧನಂಬುಜಭವನಂ ।
ತಾವಗಮೊಳ್ಗುಣ-ನಿಧಿಯಂ
ಶ್ರೀ ವಸುಧೆಯೊಳೆನಿಸಿ ವೆಣ್ಣಮಯ್ಯಂ ನೆಗೞ್ದಂ. ‖ 5[4] ‖

ವೇದದೊಳನುಗತರೆನಿಸುವ
ವೇದಗಳೊಳ್ ನಿಪುಣನಾಗಿ ನೆಗೞ್ದಂ ಗಂಭೀ ।
ರೋದೋಂ[5]ತತೆ ಪರಿವೇಷ್ಟಿತ
ಮೇದಿನಿಯೊಳ್ ವೆಣ್ಣಮಯ್ಯನಕಲಂಕ-ಗುಣಂ. ‖ 6 ‖

1) In Sb. and M. verses 8 and 9. 2) This is in Sb., Sc., M. and L.; the text is a true copy of Sc. 3) Sb. and M.:——ವಮಾ ವೆಂಗಿನಗರಮುಂ ಸೊಗಯಿಸುಗುಂ. 4) This verse is only in Sc. 5) In Sb. and M.: ವಾದಿನೊಳಗಣಿತವೆನಿಸುವ | ಮೇದಿನಿಯೊಳ್ ನಿಪುಣರೆನಿಸಿ ನೆಗೞ್ದರ್ದರಿಗೊ | ಲ್ದರ, and then a large blank. ವೇದಗಳೊಳ್ is certainly wrong; perhaps ವಾದಗಳೊಳ್?

ಸಕಲ-ಜ್ಞಾನ-ವಿನಿಂದಿತ-
ನಿಕರ-ಗುಣಾವಿಪ್ರಭವ-ಮನೋಭವ-ರೂಪಾ ।
ಧಿಕನಂಬುಸಂಭವ-ಮೂರ್ತಿ-
ಪ್ರಕರು ಕೌಂಡಿನ್ಯ-ಗೋತ್ರ-ಮಂಗಲ-ಚರಿತಂ. || 7[1] ||

ವಿತತ-ಯಶಂಗಾ ವಿಪ್ರಂ
ಗೆ ತತ್-ಪ್ರಿಯಂ ಸಂಭವಂ ದ್ವಿಜನ್ಮಂಗೆ ಗುಣಾ ।
ನ್ವಿತೆ ಸತಿ ಸಜ್ಜನಿಕೆಗರುಂ
ಧತಿಗೆ ಮಿಗಿಲ್, ಕೌಂಡಿಕಬ್ಬೆಯೆಂಬಳ್ ಪೆಸರಿಂ. || 8[2] ||

ಆ ಕೌಂಡಿಕಬ್ಬೆಗಂ ಮಹಿ
ಮಾಕರನೆನೆ ನೆಗಳ್ದ ವೆಣ್ಣಮಯ್ಯಂಗಮನಂ ।
ಗಾಕಾರಮಾಗಿ ಪುಟ್ಟಿಯೆ,
ಲೋಕ-ಸ್ತುತನಾಗಿ ದಾಮಮಯ್ಯಂ ನೆಗಳ್ದಂ. || 9[3] ||

ಆತನ ಕುಲ-ವನಿತೆ ಜಗ-
ಖ್ಯಾತ-ಗುಣ-ವ್ರಾತೆ ರೂಪ-ಲಾವಣ್ಯ-ರಸೋ ।
ಪೇತೆ ಗಿರಿಜಾತೆಗಂ ಮಿಗಿ
ಲೇತಱೊಳಂ, ಕುಂದಕಬ್ಬೆಯೆಂಬಳ್ ಪೆಸರಿಂ. || 10[4] ||

ಎನೆ ನೆಗಳ್ದ ಕುಂದಕಬ್ಬೆಗ
ಮನಿಂದ್ಯ-ಗುಣನೆನಿಪ ದಾಮಮಯ್ಯಂಗಂ ಭೂ- ।
ವಿನುತ-ಯಶಂ ದ್ವಿಜ-ವಂದ್ಯಂ
ಮನು-ಮಾರ್ಗಂ ವೆಣ್ಣಮಯ್ಯನಗ್ರ-ತನೂಜಂ. || 11[5] ||

ಶ್ರೀಕಾಂತಾ-ಪತಿ ಸಕಲ-ಕ
ಲಾ-ಕೋವಿದನದ್ವಿತೀಯನತುಳ-ಚರಿತ್ರಂ ।
ಲೌಕಿಕ-ವೈದಿಕ-ಶಾಸ್ತ್ರನ
ನೇಕಾಕ್ಷರನೆನಿಸಿ ನೆಗಳ್ದ ಚತುರಸ್ರ-ಗುಣಂ. || 12[6] ||

1) In Sc. and L.; the Repha in ಪ್ರ is not counted. 2) In Sc. and L. 3) In Sc. and L. 4) In Sc. and L. 5) In Sc. and L. Instead of ಕುಂದಕಬ್ಬೆಗಂ L. reads ಕುಂದುಕಜ್ಜಿಗಂ, as it reads in v. 9, instead of ಕೌಂಡಿಕಬ್ಬೆಗಂ, ಕೊಂಡಕಜ್ಜಗಂ. 6) Only in Sc.

ಅಂತೆನಿಪ ವೆಣ್ಣಮಯ್ಯನ
ಕಾಂತೆ ಗುಣಾಕ್ರಾಂತೆ ಧರಣಿ-ಸುತೆಗಂ ಮಿಗಿಲೆಂ ।
ಬಂತೊದವಿದ ಪತಿ-ಭಕ್ತಿಯಿ
ನಂತೆಸೆದಳ್ ಪೋಳಕಬ್ಬೆಯೆಂಬಳ್ ಪೆಸರಿಂ. || 13[1] ||

ಆ ಪೋಳಕಬ್ಬೆಗಂ ವಿ
ದ್ಯಾ-ಪರಿಣತನೆನಿಪ ವೆಣ್ಣಮಯ್ಯಂಗಂ ವಾಕ್- ।
ಶ್ರೀಪತಿ ತತ್ತಗು . . . .
ಣೋಪೇತಂ ನಾಗವರ್ಮನಗ್ರ-ತನೂಜಂ. || 14[2] ||

5. **All good poets will be pleased with this brilliant work.**

ಪ್ರಾಸಾನುಪ್ರಾಸಕ್ಕಿದು
ಲೇಸಾಗಿ ಪೆಸರ್ಕಡಂಗೆ ಕನ್ನಡದಿಂ ಪೇ ।
ಳ್ದಾ ಸೂರ-ಕರ-ವಿಲಕ್ಕೆಯ
ನಾ ಸುಕವಿ-ಪ್ರಕರಮಱಿದು ಮೆಚ್ಚುಗುಮಲ್ತೇ? || 15[3] ||

6. **The author's desire has been to produce a good treatise.**

ಚಂಪಕಮಾಲಾವೃತ್ತಂ

ನವ-ರಸಮುಣ್ಮೆ ಮಾತು ಪೊಸತಾಗಿರೆ, ದೇಶಿಯದೇಶಿವೆತ್ತುದಂ
ಬ ಪೊಲಿರೆ, ಜಾಣ್ ಮನಂಗೊಳಿಸೆ ಪೊಣ್ದಿರೆ ತೋರ್ಪ ಕೃತಿ-ಪ್ರಬಂಧಮಂ ।
ಕಿವಿಗಿನಿದಾಗೆ, ನಿಚ್ಚ ಪೊಸತಾಗೆ, ಮನೋಹರಮಾಗೆ ಪೇಳ್ದ ಸತ್-
ಕವಿ ವರ-ರಾಜಹಂಸನನೆ, ಪೇಳಲೊಡರ್ಚಿದನೀ ಪ್ರಬಂಧಮಂ. || 16[4] ||

---

1) In Sb., Sa., M. and L. Instead of ಪೋಳಕಬ್ಬೆ L. has ಪೊಳಲಕಜ್ಜಿ. Sb. and M.'s reading is: ಅಂಕೆನಿಪ ವೆಂಗಿಮಯ್ಯನ | ಕಾಂತೆ ಗುಣವ್ರಾತೆ ಧರಣಿಸುತೆಗಂ ಮಿಗಿಲೆಂ|| ಬಂತಿಪ್ಪಳ್ ಪತಿ-ಭಕ್ತಿಯ | ನಾಂತೆ ಸೆವಳ್ ಪೋಳಿಕಬ್ಬೆಯೆಂಬೀ ಪೆಸರಿಂ|| . 2) In all the four manuscripts. L.'s corrupt reading is: ಆ ಪೊಳಲಕಜ್ಜಿಗಂ ವಿ | ದ್ಯಪಣ್ಣಗೆ ವೆಂಪಣಗೆ ವೆಣ್ಣಮ್ಮೆಯ್ಯಗಂ ವಾಕ್ಕಿಗಂ|| ಶ್ರೀಪತಿಕವಿಕಾರಕ್ನಗು | ಣೋರಾಜಿತಂ ನಾಗವರ್ಮನಗ್ರತನುಜಂ|| Sb. and M. read thus: ಆಕೆಯ ನಿಜ-ಕಾಂತನು ಮಹಿ | ಮಾಕರನೆನಿಪ ವೆಂಣ್ಣ (M. ವೆಂಗಿ) ಮಯ್ಯಂಗಂ ವಾಕ್- || ಶ್ರೀ ಕಮನೀಯಂ ತಶ್ವ-ಗು | ಣಾಕರನೆನೆ ನಾಗವರ್ಮನಗ್ರ-ತನೂಜಂ|| . Then in Sb. and M., as their verses 16 and 17, follows an uninstructive praise of the renowned Nâgavarma (somewhat mutilated). 3) A corrupt reading of this verse occurs in M. and Sb.; the one given is that of Sa. 4) In M., Sa., Sb., B. and D. After it 4 verses (containing reflections of the poet in a mutilated form) that are in M. and Sb., two of which occur also in L., and the last in D. and B., have been left out, the course of instruction beginning with v. 17 of the text.

7. An illiterate poet is a blind man.

ಕಂದಂ

ಛಂದಮನಱಿಯದೆ ಕವಿತೆಯ
ದಂದುಗದೊಳ್ ತೊೞಲಿ ಸುೞಿವ ಕುಕವಿಯೆ ಕುರುಡಂ; ।
ಮುಂದೆ ಕವಲ್ದಟ್ಟೆಯಿರ
ಲ್ಕಂದುಮಣಂ ಪದಮನಿಡಲದೇಂ ಗೆಯ್ದಪನೋ? ॥ 17[1] ॥

8. Or he is a mere howler like a bear screaming for its sore eyes.

ಮಾನಿತ-ಪದಮುಂ ಪದ-ಸಂ
ಧಾನಮನರ್ಥ-ಪ್ರತೀತಿಯುಂ ಕವಿ-ಹೃದಯ- ।
ಸ್ಥಾನಮನಱಿಯದದೇಂ? ಕಣ್-
ಬೇನೆಯ ಕರಡಿಯ ವೊಲೊಱಲುವಂ ವಾಚಕನೇ! ॥ 18[2] ॥

9. A sign of inexact poetry.

ಹಱಿ-ಗವಿಗಳ ಕಬ್ಬಂಗಳ
ಪೊಱ-ಗಳಿದ ಹೊಲಿಗೆ ಬಿರ್ಚಿದೊಡೆಲ್ಲಂ ।
ಬಱಿ ತಾಱಿಗ ಬೀಱಿಗವೆ
ತ್ರಱಿ ತತ್ತ್ರಱಿವೆಕ್ಕಸಕ್ಕವಸ್ತಂ ವ್ಯಸ್ತಂ. ॥ 19[3] ॥

10. Forced poetry is unsuccessful.

ಮೞೆಯಿಲ್ಲದೆ ಪೊಯ್-ನೀರಿಂ
ಬೆಳಗುಮೆ ಧರೆ? ಮಱುಗಿ, ಕುದಿದು ಶಾಸ್ತ್ರದ ಬಲದಿಂ ।
ದಳುಪಿಂ ಪೇೞ್ದೊಡಮದು ಕೋ
ಮಳಮಕ್ಕುಮೆ? ಸಹಜಮಿಲ್ಲದಾತನ ಕಬ್ಬಂ! ॥ 20[4] ॥

11. He who knows how to handle one pattern-metre well, for instance, Jagatī (v. 124 seq.), cannot be called arrogant for thinking himself able to become deeply versed in prosody (?).

ಜಗತೀ-ಛಂದದ ಬಲುಮೆಗೆ
ಬಗೆವೊಡೆ ಪಡಿ-ಛಂದಮೆನಿಸಿ, ಬುಧ-ಜನದ ಮನಂ ।

1) In M., Sa., Sb., B. and D. 2) In M., Sb., B. and D. 3) In M., Sb., B. and D. D. reads: ಪೊಱಗೊಳಗಕ್ಕರದ--ತಾಱಿಗೆ; D.: ಬೀಱಗ; Sb.: ಬೀಱುಗ; Sb. and M.'s last line: ತಱ ತತ್ತ್ರಱವೆಕ್ಕಸಿಕ್ಕನಸ್ತ ವ್ಯಸ್ತಂ. 4) In M., Sb., B. and D.

ಬುಗುವಂತಿರೆ ಪೇಳ್ದ, ಬಳಿ
ಕ್ಕಂ ಗುಣ್ಪಿಂ ಪರಿವೆನೆಂಬವಂಗೆಂಟೆರ್ದೆಯೋ? || 21[1] ||

12. **Nâgavarma teaching his wife, to a great extent, made use of the prosody that had been propagated in the world by Pingaḷa [and had been told by Indudhara to Umĕ].**

ಇಂದು-ನಿಭಾನನೆ, ಮಂಗಳ-
ಛಂದಂ ಪಿಂಗಳನಿನವನಿಯೊಳ್ ಪರಪಿದೊಡಾ ।
ಛಂದೋಂಬು-ರಾಶಿಯೊಳ್ ಮಿಗೆ
ತಂದದ ನಿಜ-ಸತಿಗೆ ನಾಗವರ್ಮಂ ಪೇಳ್ದಂ. || 22[2] ||

13. **He recommends his work, the ĉhandombudhi, to his wife.**

ವಿಧು-ಬಿಂಬಾನನೆ, ಛಂದೋಂ
ಬುಧಿಯೆಂಬುದಿದೆನ್ನ ಪೆಸರ ಛಂದಮಿದುಂ, ಕೇಳ್, ।
ಬುಧ-ಸಮಿತಿ ಮೆಚ್ಚೆ ಪೇಳ್ದೆಂ
ಮಧುರ-ಗುಡ-ಪ್ರಚುರ-ವಚನ-ರಚನೆಗಳಿಂದಂ. || 23[3] ||

---

1) In Sa., Sb., M., B. and D. The reading given is nearly B.'s; D. has: ಬಳಿ | ಕೆ ಗುಣಂ ಪರಿವೆನೆಂಬವಂಗೆಂಟಿರ್ದೆಯೋ; M. and Sb.: ಬುಗುವಂತಿರೆ ಪೇಳ್ದವನೊಳ್ಳಿಹ ಕಬ್ಬಿಗ ಪೇಳ್ದನೆಂಬವಂಗೆಂಟಿರ್ದೆಯೋ, a reading against the metre; B. has: ಬಳಿ | ಕ್ಕಂ ಗುಣ್ಪಂ ಪರಿವನೆಂಬವಂಗೆಂಟಿರ್ದೆಯೋ. Sa.'s reading is peculiar: ಜಗತೀ ಛಂದದ ಬಲ್ಮೆಯ | ಮಿಗಿಲೆನಿಪದೆ ಛಂದಮೆನಿಸಿ ಬುಧ-ಜನದ ಮನಂ-|| ಬುಗುವಂತಿರೆ ಪೇಳ್ದೊದೆ ಕ | ಬ್ಬಿಗನೊರ್ವಂ ಪರಿಯುನೆಂಬವಂಗೆಂಟಿರ್ದೆಯೋ ||. 2) In Sa., Sb., M., D., B.; cf. H. Ra. under v. 1. Sb. and M. more correctly as to grammar:-- ಯೊಳ್ ಕಲ್ತಂದಮನಾತ್ಮೀಯ-ಸತಿಗೆ ನಾಕಿಗನುಸುರ್ದಂ. This reading gives Nâgavarma the name of Nâkiga. This last word, according to some MSS., recurs also in vs. 111. 115. 137. 147. 153. 181. 215. 236 (instead of ಕರ್ತೃ-) where the text has Pingaḷa. V. 131, line 3, the MSS. have: "In the way which Pinâki and Nâki uttered"; Nâki alone, according to some MSS., occurs also v. 121 (instead of ಲೋಕದೊಳ್) and v. 151 (ನಾಕಿಯುಂತೆವೋಲ್ instead of ಪಿಂಗಳೋಕ್ತಿಯೊಳ್). See Nâkiga (Vishṇu) No. 273, b. 3) In Sa., Sb., M., D. (as the concluding verse of the work), H. and Ra. v. 3, Rc. v. 2. ಗುಡ only in Sa., the others have ರಸ.

A. THE SYLLABLE-FEET[1]

ಅಕ್ಷರಗಣಂಗಳ್

I. CHAPTER

ಸಂಜ್ಞಾಧಿಕಾರಮೆಂಬ ಪ್ರಥಮಾಶ್ವಾಸಂ

1. The syllables or syllabical marks of the syllable-feet

ಅಕ್ಷರಗಣಾಕ್ಷರಂಗಳ್

14. The ten syllables of great distinction (ಲ=laghu, ಗ=guru). See verse 28, etc.

ಕಂದಂ

ಒಗೆದವು ಮ-ಯ-ರ-ಸ-ತ-ಜ-ಭ-ನ-
ಲ-ಗಾಕ್ಷರಂ, ಕೌಸ್ತುಭಾದಿ-ನಾನಾ-ವಿಧ-ವ ।
ಸ್ತುಗಳೊಡನೆ ಪಯೋಂಬುಧಿಯೊಳ
ಗೊಗೆದಂತಿರೆ, ಚಂದ್ರ-ವದನೆ, ಛಂದೋಂಬುಧಿಯೊಳ್. || 24[2] ||

2. The five long syllables and the two signs to mark the quantity of syllables

15. The sign for a metrically long (guru) syllable is a crooked perpendicular line; that for a metrically short (laghu) syllable is a straight perpendicular line. (The forms appear in A. Weber p. 203. 215. 416.) Instead of the first-mentioned sign Europeans use a horizontal line (—), and instead of the other a turned up half Bindu (◡). The European signs have been adopted for this Edition.

---

1) This heading is not in the manuscripts. Observe, from the beginning, that the syllable-feet are formed of unalterably fixed syllables occurring at fixed places. There is another kind of feet which is formed of a certain number of Moras (mâtrâ), a Mora being the quantity of a short syllable; such feet are called Mâtrâ Gaṇas. The Kanda verse (v. 269 seq.), for instance, consists of Mâtrâ Gaṇas, as do also all true Canarese metres. 2) In Sa., Sb., M., D., B., Rc. 3, H. and Ra. v. 4.

ಬರೆದೆಯ್ದುಱ ಲೆಕ್ಕಮನಾ
ದರದಿಂ ಗುರು-ಲಘು-ವಿಭೇದಮಂ ಭಾವಿಸು ನೀಂ! ।
ಗುರು ಪಿಂತೆ ಕೊಂಕಿ ತೋಱುವ
ಗೆರೆ; ಮುಂತಣಾ ಸ್ಮೈತುಮಪ್ಪ ಗೆರೆ ಲಘು. ಕೇಳದೀ! ॥ 25[1] ॥

16. A syllable, though short by itself (sayyakkara), within a verse becomes metrically long when followed by a double-consonant (ŏttakkara), counting as much as a syllable followed by a double-consonant in a word.

ಗುರುವಕ್ಕುಂ, ಮುಂತೊತ್ತ
ಕ್ಕರಮಾಗಿರೆ, ಪಿಂತೆ ನಿಂದ ಸ್ಮೈಯಕ್ಕರಮುಂ; ।
ಗುರುವೊತ್ತುಗಳಿಂದಪ್ಪುದು
ನಿರಂತರಂ. ಚಾರು-ರೂಪ-ಭಾಸಕ-ಸತಿಯೇ! ॥ 26[2] ॥

17. Besides, a double-consonant (daḍḍakkara) formed by a consonant being followed either by the Bindu or the Visarga; then the end of a Hemistich (padântya, the length of which however ought to be always clearly expressed in practice); and a long vowel (dîrgha) are metrically long (guru).

ಬಿಂದು ವಿಸರ್ಗಂ ವ್ಯಂಜನ
ಮೊಂದಿದ ದಡ್ಡಕ್ಕರಂ, ಪದಾಂತ್ಯಂ, ದೀರ್ಘಂ ।
ಬಂದೊಡಱ, ವನಜ-ಮುಖಿ, ಗುರು
ಮೆಂದುಂ ಸ್ಮೈಯಡಿಯ ನಾಗವರ್ಮ-ಕವೀಂದ್ರಂ. ॥ 27[3] ॥

3. The figurative names for the eight syllable-feet, and for long and short syllables

18. By mixing long and short syllables three by three, the eight syllable-feet (akshara gaṇa) are obtained. An enumeration of their figurative names: dharaṇi, jala, agni, marut, vyoma, ravi, śaśâṅka, indranilaya.

---

1) In Sa., Sb., M., B., D., H. and Ra. v. 5, Rc. v. 4, Rd. v. 4. B., D., Rc. have ಸ್ಮೈತುಮಪ್ಪ; M., Sa. ಸ್ಮೈಕಮಪ್ಪ; Ra. ಸ್ಮೈತನಪ್ಪ; Rd. ಸ್ಮೈಪನಪ್ಪ. H. ಸ್ಮೈಕನಪ್ಪ. 2) In Sa., Sb., M., B., D., H. Ra. v. 7, Rc. v. 6, Rd. v. 3, O. v. 3. Sa., M., Sb. ಸ್ಮೈಯಕ್ಕರ; H. and Ra. ಸ್ಮೈತಕ್ಕರ; Rb. ಸ್ಮೈಪಕ್ಕರ: Rc. ಪೈಯಕ್ಕರ. D. and B. ನಿಂದು ತೋರ್ಪಕ್ಕರ. 3) In Sa., etc., H. Ra. v. 8, Rc. v. 7, Rd. v. 2, O. v. 2.

ಗುರು-ಲಘು-ಮಿಶ್ರಂ ಮೂಱೆ
ಕ್ಕರದಿಂ ಗಣಮಿಡು, ಲತಾಂಗಿ, ಬಗೆದೆಂಟು ತೆಱಂ; ।
ಧರಣಿ-ಜಲಾಗ್ನಿ-ಮರುದ್-ವ್ಯೋ
ಮ-ರವಿ-ಶಶಾಂಕೇಂದ್ರನಿಲಯಮಿವು ಗಣದ ಪೆಸರ್. || 28[1] ||

19. **Figurative names for Guru (triyambaka, rudra, or any other synonym) and Laghu (murântaka, hari, or any other synonym). Instead of the figurative names for the eight syllable-feet the eight letters, mentioned already in verse 23, are also used.**

ನಯದಿಂ ಗುರುವೆಂಬುದು, ಕೇಳ್,
ತ್ರಿಯಂಬಕಂ; ಲಘು ಮುರಾಂತಕಂ, ಮೃಗ-ನಯನೇ! ।
ಮ-ಯ-ರ-ಸ-ತ-ಜ-ಭ-ನ-ಲ-ಗ-ಸಂ
ಚಯಮೆಂಬುದು ನಿಯಮದಿಂ ಗಣಾಕ್ಷರಮಕ್ಕುಂ. || 29[2] ||

4. The way of calculating the eight syllable-feet

ಪ್ರಸ್ತಾರಕ್ರಮಂ

20. **A first rule (the same as verse 325), the form of which appears to be this:**

— — (Spondeus)
◡ — (Iambus)
— ◡ (Trochaeus)
◡ ◡ (Pyrrhichius)

ಗುರುಗಳನಿಟ್ಟವಱಾದಿಯ
ಗುರುವಿಂದಂ ಕೆಳಗೆ ಲಘುವನಿಡು! ಮುಂತೆ ಸಮಂ ।
ಗುರು; ಮಾಱಣೆ[3] ಪಿಂತೆ; ನಿರಂ
ತರ-ಲಘುಗಳನೆಯ್ದುವನೆಗಂ, ಮೃಗ-ನಯನೇ! || 30[3] ||

1) In Sa., etc., H. Ra. v. 12, Rc. v. 5, Rd. v. 13, O. v. 7. Ra. H. have, as their v. 13, a Kanda verse of their own: ಎಂತೆಂತು ನುಡಿಯೆ ವಿಸ್ಮಯ | ಮಂತಂತೊದವಿಪುದು ಹೃದಯದೊಳ್ ಪೇೞದೆನಾ|| ದ್ಯಂತನೆರೆ ನಿನ್ನ ನಿಜವೃ | ತ್ತಾಂತಮನೆನಗಱಿಯೆ ಪೇೞ್ದುದತಿಕೌತುಕಮಂ|| 2) In Sa., Sb., M., B., D., H. Ra. v. 9, Rc. v. 8, Rd. v. 5, O. v. 4. 3) In Sb., M., B., D., Rd. v. 12 (instead of ಮಾಱಣೆ it has ಪೂರಣೆ).

21. The grand rule with three steps:

First	*Second*	*Third*
1	1 2	1 2 3
1. —	1. — —	1. — — —
2. ◡	2. ◡ —	2. ◡ — —
3. —	3. — ◡	3. — ◡ —
4. ◡	4. ◡ ◡	4. ◡ ◡ —
5. —	5. — —	5. — — ◡
6. ◡	6. ◡ —	6. ◡ — ◡
7. —	7. — ◡	7. — ◡ ◡
8. ◡	8. ◡ ◡	8. ◡ ◡ ◡

ಮತ್ತೇಭವಿಕ್ರೀಡಿತಂ

ಗುರುವೊಂದುಂ ಲಘುವೊಂದನೆಂಟು-ಬರೆಗುಂ ಪ್ರಸ್ತಾರಿಸಂತಾದಿಯೊಳ್
ಗುರು-ಯುಗ್ಮಂ ಲಘು-ಯುಗ್ಮಮುಂ ಬರೆ ಚತುಃಸ್ಥಾನಂ-ಬರಂ ಮಧ್ಯದೊಳ್! ।
ಗುರು ನಾಲ್ಕುಂ ಲಘು ನಾಲ್ಕುಮೆಯ್ದೆ ಬರೆ ನೀನ್ ಅಂತ್ಯಂಗಳೊಳ್! ಸಂತತಂ,
ನಿರವದ್ಯೇ, ಅತಿಚಾರು-ಪಂಕಜ-ಮುಖೀ, ಪ್ರಸ್ತಾರಮಿಂತೀ ಕ್ರಮಂ! ॥ 31[1] ॥

5. The names and forms of the eight syllable-feet. cf. v. 27

22. A short verse with the figurative names (changing according to the selection of corresponding synonyms), i. e.

— ◡ ◡, śaśi	◡ — —, jala
◡ — ◡, sûrya	— ◡ —, vahni
◡ ◡ —, vâyu	— — ◡, gagana
— — —, dharĕ	◡ ◡ ◡, nâka

ಕಂದಂ

ಆದಿಯ ಮಧ್ಯಾಂತದೆ ಗುರು
ವಾದಡೆ ಶಶಿ-ಸೂರ್ಯ-ವಾಯು; ಗುರುವಿರೆ ಧರೆ; ಮ ।

1) In Sa., etc., H. Ra. v. 14, Ro. v. 9, Rd. v. 11. M., Rd. read ನಾಲ್ಕನೆಯ್ದೆ. M. (vs. 65. 66) has two other verses after our v. 30, together with Sb., and H. Ra. v. 10 and v. 11; the second one is also in Ro. as v. 13; they are as follows: ಗುರುವಿನಡಿ ಮೊದಲ ಲಘುವಂ | ಬರೆ ಮುಂತಂ ಕೂಡೆ ತತ್ಸಮಂ ಬರೆ ಪಿಂತಂ || ಗುರುವಿಂದಂತೀವೃತ್ತಂ | ದೊರೆಯುತ್ತೆಯ್ದಿಡೆ (Ra. ದೊರೆಯದಿರೆಂತೆಯ್ದಿ) ಸರ್ವ-ಲಘುವಪ್ಪಿನೆಗಂ ||65|| ಮೂಱು ಗುರುವಿಟ್ಟು ಮೊದಲೊಳ್ | ತೋಱಿರೆ ಲಘು ಪಿಂತೆ (Ra. ಮುಂತೆ) ಮುಂತೆ ಸಮನಾಗಿಯೆ (Sb. ಸಮನಾದಿಯು, Ro. ಸಮನಾರಿಯು, Ra. and H. deficient) ಟಿ || ಸ್ಫೋಱಿಸು ಗುರು-ಲಘುವಂ ಮಿಗ (Ro. ಸ್ಫೇರಿಸುವಂ ಲಘು ತಮಿಗಂ, Sb. ಸ್ಫೋಱಿಸುಗುಂ ಲಘುವಂಮಿಗ) | ಲಾದವು ಗುರು ಪಿಂತೆ ಮುಂತೆ ಸಮನೆಂಟು-ವರಂ (Ro. ತಾದವು ಗುರು ಮುಂತೆ ಪಿಂತೆ_) || 66 ||

ತ್ರಾದಿಯ ಮಧ್ಯಾಂತದೆ ಲಘು
ವಾದಡೆ ಜಲ-ವಹ್ನಿ-ಗಗನ; ಲಘುವಿಂ ನಾಕಂ. || 32[1] ||

23. A longer verse of the same description.

— — —, dhâtri	— — ◡, vyoma
◡ — —, toya	◡ — ◡, âditya
— ◡ —, śikhi	— ◡ ◡, abjâri
◡ ◡ —, mâruta	◡ ◡ ◡, nâka

ಮತ್ತೇಭವಿಕ್ರೀಡಿತಂ

ಗುರು ಮೂಱಾಗಿರೆ ಧಾತ್ರಿ; ಮುಂತೆರಡು ಬಿಣ್ಪಿಂ ತೋಯಮಾದ್ಯಂತದೊಳ್
ಬರೆ ವಕ್ರಂ ಶಿಖಿಯೊಂದು ಕೊಂಕು ಕಡೆಯಿಂದಾ ಮಾರುತಂ; ವ್ಯೋಮಮೊ|
ಪ್ಪಿರೆ ಬಿಣ್ಪಿಂತೆರಡಾದಿಯೊಳ್; ನಡುವೆ ಕೊಂಕಾದಿತ್ಯನಬ್ಜಾರಿ ತ
ಳ್ತಿರೆ ವಕ್ರಂ ಮೊದಲಲ್ಲಿ; ಮೂಱು ಲಘುವಿಂ ನಾಕಂ, ವಿಶಾಲೇಕ್ಷಣೇ! || 33[2] ||

24. A verse with the syllable-names, viz.

— — —, Ma gaṇa	◡ — ◡, Ja gaṇa
◡ ◡ ◡, Na gaṇa	— ◡ —, Ra gaṇa
— ◡ ◡, Bha gaṇa	◡ ◡ —, Sa gaṇa
◡ — —, Ya gaṇa	— — ◡, Ta gaṇa

ಕಂದಂ

ಗುರು ಲಘು ಮೂಱಿರೆ, ಮ-ನ-ಗಣಂ;
ಗುರು ಲಘು ಮೊದಲಲ್ಲಿ ಬರಲು, ಭ-ಯ-ಗಣಂ; ಮತ್ತಾ |
ಗುರು ಲಘು ನಡುವಿರೆ, ಜ-ರ-ಗಣಂ;
ಗುರು ಲಘು ಕಡೆಯಲ್ಲಿ ಬರಲು, ಸ-ತ-ಗಣಮಕ್ಕುಂ. || 34[3] ||

25. The figurative names and the syllable-names, (to which the European names have been added at the end), *i. e.*

1) In M. and Sb. The verse is not perfect regarding grammar (ಗಗನ= ಗಗನಂ). 2) Sa., Sb., etc., H. Ra. v. 15, Ro. v. 10, Rd. v. 10, O. v. 6. 3) In D., B. and O. v. 20. It is identical with v. 14 of the Kavi Jihvâ Bandhana; it is defective regarding grammar.

— — —, Ma gaṇa, Earth (bhûmi, dhâtri, dharĕ, dharaṇi, urvi, etc.), *Molossus*

◡ — —, Ya gaṇa, Water (jala, toya, etc.), *Bacchicus*

— ◡ —, Ra gaṇa, Fire (agni, śikhi, vahni, anala, etc.), *Amphimacrus* (*Creticus*)

◡ ◡ —, Sa gaṇa, Wind (vâta, mâruta, vâyu, marut, etc.), *Anapaestus*

— — ◡, Ta gaṇa, Sky (ambara, vyoma, gagana, etc.), *Antibacchicus*

◡ — ◡, Ja gaṇa, Sun (arka, âditya, sûrya, ravi, etc.), *Amphibrachys*

— ◡ ◡, Bha gaṇa, Moon (śaśi, abjâri, śaśâṅka, indu, etc.), *Dactylus*

◡ ◡ ◡, Na gaṇa, Heaven (nâka, indranilaya, deva, indra, etc.), *Tribrachys*

ಮ-ಗಣಂ ಭೂಮಿಯೆನಿಕ್ಕುಂ,
ಯ-ಗಣಂ ಜಲ, ರ-ಗಣಮಗ್ನಿ, ಸ-ಗಣಂ ವಾತಂ, |
ತ-ಗಣಾಂಬರ, ಜ-ಗಣಾರ್ಕಂ,
ಭ-ಗಣಂ ಶಶಿ, ನ-ಗಣ ನಾಕಮಂಬುಜ-ವದನೇ! || 35 [1] ||

26. Special cases in which the several syllable-feet are used (at the beginning of a verse), viz.

— — — in blessing (âśirvâda)

◡ — — in coming to war (parabalamuttigĕ)

◡ ◡ — in suffering pain or being sick (kleśavyâdhi)

— ◡ — in showing courage (dhairya)

◡ — ◡ in showing fear (bhîta)

— ◡ ◡ in being happy and liberal (toshatyâgi)

— — ◡ in sacking (dhâḷiyiḍuvikĕ)

◡ ◡ ◡ in desiring (kâmi)

1) After this verse (defective in grammar, but also in H. and Ra.'s VII.) there follow in M. and Sb. 23 verses about gaṇa-phala-vṛitti, *i. e.* the good or bad consequences connected with the use of the syllable-feet, and about gaṇa-lakshaṇa, *i. e.* the colour, presiding deity (adhidaiva), caste (kula) and good or bad character of the several feet. Only 8 of the verses are in Rd.; in Ra. and H. some of them are given in a supplement after chapter 6, that does not bear the signature of belonging to the original work; Rc. has 5 of them after our v. 32. D. and B. have 8 of them after the same verse; one of them occurs also in the Kavi Jihvâ Bandhana as v. 15, and as v. 1 in Rd. and O. In O. there are 4 of them. One that is in B., D., Sa., and Rc. as v. 12, is in none of the others. Verse 35 of our text shows a peculiar character, and has, therefore, been adduced; it is in all the MSS. Rd.'s reading (v. 14) of it has been adopted, as it brings in all the feet. The Kavi Jihvâ Bandhana, in its v. 51, states that when one is in doubt about the foot with which to begin a verse, the deva-foot *i. e.* ◡◡◡ (Tribrachys) is always very good. Here is the verse: ಭಾವಿಸೆ ಪದ-ಪದ್ಯಂಗಳ | ಗಾವಗ ಮೊದಲಲಿ ಗಣಕ್ಕೆಯುದುವಿದುವೆಂನದೆ (the ದೆ ought to be long, but then there would be 5 Moras to the foot) || ದೇವ-ಗಣವಿಟ್ಟು ಮುಂದ | ಕ್ಕಾವ ಗಣಂ ಬಂದಡುತ್ತಮಂ, ಕಮಲ-ಮುಖೀ! || 51 || This verse, with a very slight alteration, occurs as v. 30 in D. and B. D. and B. also say that a poem ought to contain śrî (at its beginning): ಶ್ರೀಕಾರಂ ಸ್ವೀಕಾಗಿರೆ, | ಲೋಕ-ತ್ರಯದಲ್ಲಿ ಕೀರ್ತಿ-ವಡೆದುದು ಪದ್ಯಂ; || ಶ್ರೀಕಾರಮಿಲ್ಲದ ಪದಂ | ಲೋಕದೊಳದು ಸಲ್ಲದೆಂದನಾ ಫಣಿವರ್ಮಂ. || 28 ||

ಶಾರ್ದೂಲವಿಕ್ರೀಡಿತಂ

ಆಶೀರ್ವಾದದೊಳುರ್ವಿಯುಂ, ಪರ-ಬಲಂ ಮುತ್ತಿರ್ದೊಡಾ ತೋಯಮುಂ,
ಕ್ಲೇಶ-ವ್ಯಾಧಿಗೆ ವಾಯು, ಧೈರ್ಯ್ಯಕನಲಂ, ಭೀತಂಗಮಾದಿತ್ಯನಾ ।
ತೋಷ-ತ್ಯಾಗಿಗೆಯಿಂದು, ಧಾಳಿಯಿಡುವಂಗಂದಂಬರಂ, ಕಾಮಿಗಂ
ಭಾಸ್ವದ್-ದೇವ-ಗಣಂಗಳೆಂದಱಿಪಿದಂ, ಪಂಕೇಜ-ಪತ್ರೇಕ್ಷಣೇ! ॥ 36 ॥

6. The Refrain

27. If there occurs a refrain (pallava) in true Canarese poetry, it is to be in the feet (gaṇa) of the verse (pada) to which it is attached.

ಕಂದಂ

ನಲ್ಲಳೆ, ಪದಮಿಡುವೆಡೆಯೊಳ್
ಪಲ್ಲವದೊಳ್ ಪದದೊಳುಭಯ-ಗಣ-ಸಮನಾಗಲ್, ।
ಸಲ್ಲಲಿತ-ಕೀರ್ತಿಯಾದಪು
ದಲ್ಲದೊಡಾ ಕೃತಿಗೆ ಹಾನಿ ತಪ್ಪದೆ ಬರ್ಕುಂ. ॥ 37[1] ॥

7. The Verse-lines

28. A verse in one of the syllable-feet metres consists of four lines (čaraṇa, also pâda, pada), a fault in which would be injurious to the honor and feelings of the king (in whose service the poet is), poet, writer and reader.

ಚರಣಂಗಳ್ ನಾಲ್ಕುವಱೊಳ್,
ಪರಿಕಿಸೆ, ಕರ್ತಂಗೆ ಕವಿಗೆ ಲೇಖಕನಪ್ಪಂ ।
ಗಿರದಕ್ಕುಮಪಾಯಂಗಳ್;
ಚರಣಾಂತ್ಯದೊಳೋದುವಂಗೆ, ಪಂಕಜ-ನಯನೇ! ॥ 38[2] ॥

8. The Pause

29. The pause or Caesura (yati) of a verse forms, so to say, a place for taking breath.

ಯತಿಯೆಂಬುದು ಗಣ-ನಿಯಮ-
ಪ್ರತತಿಗುಸುರ್ದಾಣಮಂತದಂ ದಾಂಟಲ್ಕಾ ।

1) Only in Sa., B. and D. 2) In Sb., M., B. and D.

ಯತಿ ಕೆಡುಗುಂ; ದಾಂಟಿದೊಡಾ
ಯತಿ ಕೆಡೆ, ಕವಿತಾಭಿಮಾನಮೇನ್ ಎಸೆದಪ್ಪುದೋ? || 39[1] ||

9. Faults in Poetry

30. The following eighteen faults (dosha) are to be avoided: asad artha, viparîta kalpanĕ, abhavya, dushkara, grâmya, nîrasa, aprauḍhatĕ, apratîti vačana, dussandhi, viślesha, nashṭa samâsa, naya nâśa (?), rîti viphala (?), dullakshaṇa, hâsya vâč, vishama, asaumya (?), anojĕ (?).

ಮತ್ತೇಭವಿಕ್ರೀಡಿತಂ

ಅಸದರ್ಥಂ ವಿಪರೀತ-ಕಲ್ಪನೆಯಭವ್ಯಂ ದುಷ್ಕರಂ ಗ್ರಾಮ್ಯ-ನೀ
ರಸಮಪ್ರೌಢತೆಯಪ್ರತೀತಿ-ವಚನಂ ದುಸ್ಸಂಧಿ ವಿಶ್ಲೇಷ-ನ |
ಷ್ಟ-ಸಮಾಸಂ ನಯ-ನಾಶ-ರೀತಿ-ವಿಫಲಂ ದುಲ್ಲಕ್ಷಣಂ ಹಾಸ್ಯ-ವಾಗ್-
ವಿಷಮಾಸೌಮ್ಯಮನೋಜೆಯೆಂಬಿವಿನಿತುಂ ದೋಷಂಗಳಷ್ಟಾದಶಂ. || 40[2] ||

---

1) In Sa., Sb., M., B., D., H. Ra. v. 11, Ro. v. 17. Nâgavarma, like Piṅgaḷa (VI., 1: yatir viččhedaḥ), does not give any particular rules regarding the Caesura; but further on (from v. 124), when adducing the various Sanskṛit metres, he uses to point out the places where it is to be put. Halâyudha, in his commentary on the Piṅgala Chandaḥ Sûtras, cites the following ślokas from a yatyupadeśopanishat: ಯತಿಃ ಸರ್ವತ್ರ ಪಾದಾಂತೇ * ಶ್ಲೋಕಾರ್ಧೇ ತು ವಿಶೇಷತಃ * | ಸಮುದ್ರಾದಿ-ಪದಾಂತೇ ಚ * ವ್ಯಕ್ತಾವ್ಯಕ್ತವಿಭಕ್ತಿಕೇ * || 1 || ಕ್ವಚಿತ್ ತು ಪದಮಧ್ಯೇ ಪಿ * ಸಮುದ್ರಾದೌ ಯತಿರ್ ಭವೇತ್ * | ಯದಿ ಪೂರ್ವಾಪರೌ ಭಾಗೌ * ನ ಸ್ಯಾತಾಮೇಕವರ್ಣಕೌ * || 2 || ಪೂರ್ವಾಂತವತ್ ಸ್ವರಃ ಸಂಧೌ * ಕ್ವಚಿದೇವ ಪರಾದಿವತ್ * | ದೃಷ್ಟವ್ಯೋ ಯತಿಚಿಂತಾಯಾಂ * ಯಣಾದೇಶಃ ಪರಾದಿವತ್ * || 3 || i. e. "The Caesura always (occurs) at the end of a quarter (pâda, of a verse); then, especially, at (the end of) the half of a verse; and then also at the end of the words (which are marked out in the rules) by such words as 'samudra' (words that signify certain numbers). (The end of a word marked out by 'samudra', etc.) may show either a direct case-inflection or an indirect one (i. e. one which is in a state of sandhi with the following word) (v. 1). At the places (marked out by) 'samudra', etc., however, the Caesura, now and then, may occur also in the midst of a word; but only in the case when the word's first and second part (produced by the Caesura) have no claim to one and the same letter (v. 2). A vowel which has been produced by sandhi, is (generally) looked upon as forming the end of the preceding word, seldom as forming the beginning of the next one; such a half-vowel (of ಇ, ಉ and ಋ, for instance: ದಧ್ಯತ್ರ, ಮಧ್ವತ್ರ, ಪಿತ್ರರ್ಥಂ=ದಧಿ-ಅತ್ರ, ಮಧು-ಅತ್ರ, ಪಿತೃ-ಅರ್ಥಂ), however, with regard to Caesura, is always considered as forming the beginning of the next word". (v. 3.) But Gaṅgâdâsa, in his Chandomañjari, states that Sveta, Mâṇḍavya and other Munis did not acknowledge any rules of Caesura. See A. Weber, Indiche Metrik, p. 222. 364.

2) Only in Sb., M. and L. The reading of them all is very corrupt, and the words in English letters with a sign of interrogation are mere guesses arrived at by comparing the letters of the three different readings.

10. Alliteration in three classes

31. Alliteration (prâsa, prâsu) as it is to occur in each verse of Canarese poetry, generally speaking, is the custom of putting the second letter of the first line or quarter (pâda) in the same place of the other quarters.

ಕಂದಂ

ಪಾದದೊಳೆರಡನೆಯಕ್ಕರ
ಮಾದರದಿಂದಾವುದಾದುದದನಱಿತದಱಿಂ ।
ಪಾದದೊಳಿಡುವಡದಕ್ಕುಂ,
ಭೇದೋಕ್ತಿ-ಕ್ರಮ-ವಿಚಾರಿ, ತೋರ-ಪ್ರಾಸಂ. ॥ 41[1] ॥

32. The six kinds of alliteration of the *first* class and their names, viz.

The alliteration formed by:

1. short letters (nija) is the *Lion* (siṅga, hari);
2. long letters (dîrgha) is the *Elephant* (gaja, kari);
3. the Bindu (and the preceding Consonant) is the *Bull* (vṛishabha);
4. the (final) Consonant (vyañjana, of the preceding word and the initial one of the following word) is the *Monster* (śarabha);
5. the Visarga (with the Consonant that precedes it) is the *Goat* (aja);
6. double Consonants (daḍḍakkara, ŏttu) is the *Horse* (haya, turaṅga).

ಹರಿ ಕರಿ ವೃಷಭ-ತುರಂಗಂ
ಶರಭಮಜಂಗಳುಮೆನಿಪ್ಪ ಷಟ್-ಪ್ರಾಸಕ್ಕುಂ; ।
ತರುಣಿ, ನಿಜ-ದೀರ್ಘ-ಬಿಂದುವಿ
ನಿರದೊತ್ತುಂ-ವ್ಯಂಜನಂ-ವಿಸರ್ಗದಿ ಬರ್ಕುಂ. ॥ 42[2] ॥

---

1) This is only in Re. as v. 21. The Kavi Jihvâ Bandhana has the following as its v. 4 of chapter II.: ಮೊದಲಕ್ಕರದಿಂ ಮುಂತಣ | ದದು ನೋಡಲ್ ಪ್ರಾಸದಕ್ಕರಂ; ತತ್-ಪ್ರಾಸಂ|| ವಿದಿತಂ ನಾಲ್ಕುಂ ಪಾದ | ಕ್ಕದಯಿಸುಗುಂ ವರ್ಣವೊಂದೆ ಪದ-ಪದ್ಯಕ್ಕಂ.|| 2) This occurs only in Sa., and is the same as Kavi Jihvâ B. II., 5. After it Sa. has some explanations in prose to be quoted in the note to v. 42, from which it will be seen that it is slightly doubtful whether the Bindu of No. 3 and the Visarga of No. 5 belong to the first or second syllable. The Kavi Jihvâ Bandhana's instance for the Bull: ಒಂದಂಜ — ಕೊಂದಂಗ — ನಂದಂಗಿ — ಬಂದಂಶಿ is somewhat dubious by itself; but when compared with its instance for the Goat, *i. e.* ಪಾಶಃಸಂ—ವಾಸಃಪ—ನಾಶಃಪಂ—ಲಾಸಃಪಿ, it becomes certain that that work refers the Visarga as well as the Bindu to the second syllable; instances, however, of these two kinds are rare. Observe that what, in the next note, by Sa., is called "dushkara prâsa" (ದುಷ್ಕರಪ್ರಾಸ), the Kavi Jihvâ Bandhana (II., 24) calls "dustara prâsa" (ದುಸ್ತರಪ್ರಾಸ), its instance being: ಪ್ರಸ್ತುತ—ನ್ಯಸ್ತಪ—ದ್ವಿಸ್ತರ—ಹಸ್ತಂಶಿ. Here the Visarga is supplanted by "s" (ಸ್).

ನಿಜದಿಂ ಬಂದೊಡೆ ಸಿಂಗಂ;
ಗಜ ದೀರ್ಘಂ; ಬಿಂದು ವೃಷಭ; ಮೆಂಜನ ಶರಭಂ; ।
ಅಜನು ವಿಸರ್ಗಂ; ಹಯಮುಂ
ಬುಜ-ಮುಖಿ, ದಡ್ಡಕ್ಕರಂಗಳಿವು ಷಟ್-ಪ್ರಾಸಂ. ॥ 43 ॥[1]

33. An instance of the *Lion*. (By the presence of a good poet who is like the full moon, the Ambrosia sea of poetry begins to swell.)

ಸಕಳ-ಕಳಾ-ನಿಧಿ-ನಿಕಟದೆ
ಸುಕರ-ರಸ-ಪ್ರಕಟ-ಕಾವ್ಯಮೆಂಬಮೃತ-ಪಯೋ ।
ಧಿ ಕರಂ ಪೆರ್ಚುಗುಮಲ್ಲದೆ
ಕುಕವಿ-ಬುಧ-ಪ್ರಭೃತಿಯಿದಿರೊಳೇಂ ಪೆರ್ಚುಗುಮೇ? ॥ 44 ॥[2] ಇದು ಸಿಂಗಪ್ರಾಸು.

34. An instance of the *Elephant*. The alliteration-syllable, though short by itself, may be long also on account of a following double-consonant. (Only a good poet has access to the Parnassus.)

ಆರಾರೇಱಿರ್ ಶಾಸ್ತ್ರ-
ಶ್ರೀ-ರೋಹಣ-ಗಿರಿಯನಲ್ಲಿ ನವ-ಕವಿತಾ-ಚಿಂ ।
ತಾ-ರತ್ನಂ ದೊರಗುಮೆ ಕೇ
ಜೋ-ರೂಪ-ಕೃಪೆಯಿರದಂಗೆ ಧರಣೀ-ತಳದೊಳ್? ॥ 45 ॥[3] ಇದು ಗಜಪ್ರಾಸು.

---

1) This ungrammatical verse is in Sb., M., O. v. 10, H. and Ra.'s supplement, Ro. v. 18, Rd. v. 16, B., D. After it, in all the manuscripts, though differing much regarding the wording, also in Sa., a verse, on the good and evil resulting from the use of the several alliterations, occurs that has not been given in the text. Verses 43—48 are instances adduced by the Editor. There are instances only in B. and D., and they are taken word for word from the Kavi Jihvâ Bandhana (II., 7-12). Sa.'s Prose-sentences alluded to in the note to v. 41, are as follows: ಸಿಂಹಪ್ರಾಸಕ್ಕೆ ಲಕ್ಷಣಂ । ಸರಸಿಜಜ । ಉರುಹ । ಇದು ದೇವಗಣಂ॥ ಗಜಪ್ರಾಸಕ್ಕೆ ಲಕ್ಷಣಂ । ಪಂಕಜ । ಕಿಂಕರ । ಇದು ಭಗಣಂ॥ ವೃಷಭಪ್ರಾಸಕ್ಕೆ ಲಕ್ಷಣಂ । ಧರಾಧರ । ಮರಾಳ । ಇದು ಸೂರ್ಯಗಣಂ । ತುರಂಗಪ್ರಾಸಕ್ಕೆ ಲಕ್ಷಣಂ । ಮತ್ತಚಕೋರಲೋಚನೆ । ಚಿತ್ತಜರಾಜಧಾನಿ । ಇದು ಲಕ್ಷಣದಲ್ಲಿ ಭಗಣಂ॥ ಶರಭಪ್ರಾಸಕ್ಕೆ ಲಕ್ಷಣಂ । (ನೀರೊಳ್) । ಕಶ್ತ್ಯೇಶ ಯಿ । ತ್ರ್ಯಕ್ತಂಪಕಗಂಧ । ಇದು ಆಕಾಶಗಣಂ । ನಾಂದಿಯ ಮೊದಲಿಗೆ ಸಲ್ಲದು॥ ಅಜಪ್ರಾಸಕ್ಕೆ ಲಕ್ಷಣಂ । ಸ್ವಃಕಾಂತಾ । ಇದೆ ದುಷ್ಕರಪ್ರಾಸವೆಂಬುದು । ಇದು ನಾಂದಿಯ ಮೊದಲಿಗೆ ಆಗದು ॥ ಇಂತು ಪ್ರಾಸಲಕ್ಷಣಸ್ವರೂಪವನರಿ॥ As it appears Sa.'s Bull is wrong. The Kavi Jihvâ Bandhana's instances, as to method and name, correspond to those of the text; here follow the beginnings: Lion ಸದಮ; Elephant ಮೊರಾರಿ; Bull ಬಿಂದಂಜ; Monster ಸನ್ಮಾರ್ಗ; Goat ಪಾಶಃಸಂ; Horse ಸಗ್ಗದ. There is, however, the possibility, though very slight, that Sa.'s scheme of the Elephant is the true pattern for the Bull, and his scheme of the Goat that for the Goat, viz. that the Bindu or the Visarga of the rule, against the Kavi Jihvâ Bandhana, refers to the end of the first syllable. 2) Râjaśekhara I., 25. 3) Râjaśekhara I., 29.

35. An instance of the *Bull*. (King, come and see the beautiful garden!)

ಆ ನಂದನಮಂ, ವಿಜಿತ-ಮ
ಹಾನಂದನಮಂ, ನಿಜಾಂತರಾಳಾಶ್ರಿತ-ಲೋ |
ಕಾನಂದನಮಂ, ತೋಷಿತ
ಮಾ ನಂದನಮಂ ನಿರೀಕ್ಷಿಸಲ್ ನಡೆ, ನೃಪತೀ! || 46[1] || ಇದು ವೃಷಭಪ್ರಾಸು.

36. An instance of the *Monster*. (The Elephant and her young one in the hot season.)

ಬಾಯ್ವಿಡುತೆಯ್ದಿದ ಮಱಿಯಂ
ತಾಯ್ವಿಡಿ ನಡೆ ನೋಡಿ, ಬಾಡಿ, ತಾಪಂ ಮೊದಲಿಂ |
ದೆಯ್ವಡಿ ನೆಗಳ್ದಿರೆ, ತೆಗೆದೇಂ
ಕೆಯ್ವಿಡಿದೂದಿದುದೊ ಸೋಷ್ಣ-ಜಲಮಂ ಬಸುಱಿಂ? || 47[2] || ಇದು ಶರಭಪ್ರಾಸು.

37. An instance of the *Goat*.

ನೀಂ ನಿಃಶಂಕೆಯನೀ! ದೇ
ವಾ ನಿಃಶರಣ-ಜನರಿಂಗೆ ಶರಣಾಗೀಗಳ್! |
ಕೇಳ್, ನಿಃಶಮಮಂ ಪರಿಹರಿ
ಸೀ ನಿಃಶಾಪ-ಪ್ರಸಾದಮಂ, ಕರುಣಾತ್ಮಾ! || 48 || ಇದು ಅಜಪ್ರಾಸು.

38. An instance of the *Horse*. (The Jasmin buds among the young Mango leaves are like the stars, and the black bees alighting on them like the coming darkness of the evening.)

ಮಲ್ಲಿಗೆ ಮಾ-ಮರದೆಳೆ-ದಳಿ
ರಲ್ಲಿ ಮುಗುಳ್ತಡಱಿ; ಮುಗುಳ್ಗಳೆಸೆದವು ಸಂಧ್ಯಾ- |
ಸಲ್ಲಲಿತ-ತಾರಕಾಳಿಯೊ
ಲಲ್ಲಿಳಿವಾಱಿಡಿಗಳಿಳಿವ ತಮಮೆನಿಸಿರ್ಕುಂ. || 49[3] || ಇದು ಅಶ್ವಪ್ರಾಸು.

39. Without Alliteration Canarese poetry is worthless.

ನುತ-ಶಬ್ದಾಲಂಕಾರದೊ
ಳತಿಶಯಮದು ಕನ್ನಡಕ್ಕೆ ಸತತಂ ಪ್ರಾಸಂ; |
ಕೃತ-ಕೃತ್ಯಮಪ್ಪುದೆಲ್ಲರ
ಮತದಿಂದದು ತಪ್ಪೆ, ಕಾವ್ಯಮೇಂ ಶೋಭಿಪುದೇ? || 50[4] ||

1) Rajaśekhara X., 5. 2) Rājaśekhara V., 40. 3) Rājaśekhara II., 41. 4) Rc. v. 20, and D., B.

40. The six kinds of alliteration of the *second* class and their names:

1. The *praised* alliteration consists of the consonants (letters) of conjunction (or suitableness, sambandhâkshara, yogâkshara), as it seems of the consonants which in the first class (verses 42-49) have been assumed to be peculiarly suited to form the alliteration, viz. consonants not only cognate i. e. classified under the same head, but identical, in this case possessing also *one and the same vowel* (vinuta prâsa, suprâsa).
2. The first *peaceful*[1] one consists of the mentioned consonants of conjunction, these having not one and the same vowel (śânta pûrva prâsa, śânta prâsa).
3. The second peaceful one or *that of classified consonants* consists of consonants that are not the same, but fall under the same head, with vowels according to one's convenience (varga prâsa). For another peaceful alliteration that, however, ought not to be imitated, see the note to v. 330.
4. The *proximate* one consists of the unclassified, but proximate consonants ś, sh, and s, the vowels falling under no rule (samîpa prâsa).
5. The *successive* one occurs when the syllable of alliteration is frequently repeated throughout the whole verse, with vowels as convenient (anugata prâsa, anuprâsa; cf. the Sanskrit "vṛitti").
6. The *final* one happens when an alliteration is put also at the end of each quarter or line (pâda), this alliteration being not the same as the initial one (anta prâsa).

ವಿನುತ-ಪ್ರಾಸಂ ಶಾಂತೋ
ಪನತಂ ವರ್ಗೋದಿತಂ ಸಮೀಪ-ಗತಂ ಮ ।
ತ್ತನು-ಗತಮಂತ-ಗತಂ ಸಂ
ಜನಿತಂ ವಿಭಪ್ರೋಕ್ತಿಯಿಂದಿವಂತಾಱು ತೆಱಂ. ॥ 51[2] ॥

41. An instance of the *praised* alliteration or of No. 1. Mâtrĕ = Mora; see, previously, the note to A., p. 7.

ಮನೆಗಿಂದು ಬರ್ಕುಮೆಂದಾನ್
ಅನೇಕ-ವಿಧ-ವಸ್ತು-ವಾಹನಂಗಳನೊಸೆದಿಂ ।
ಬನೆ ಪಸರಿಸ್ಸಿ, ಕುಳ್ಳಿರ್ದೆಂ.
ಜನೇಶನಿಂತೇಕೆ ಕಳೆದು ಪೋದನೊ? ಪೇಳಾ! ॥ 52[3] ॥ ಇದು ವಿನುತಪ್ರಾಸಂ.

---

1) "Peaceful" means to say that, though there be no uniformity, there is harmony.
2) Ro. v. 22, B., D. 3) Ro. 23, B., D. See the beginning of the next verse which expressly states that this verse forms an instance of the vinuta prâsa.

ಎಂಬುದು ವಿನುತ-ಪ್ರಾಸಂ;
ಸಂಬಂಧಾಕ್ಷರದೊಳೆಲ್ಲ ಮಾತ್ರೆಗಳುಂ ತ |
ಳ್ತಿಂಬಾಗೆ ಬೆರಸಿ, ಶೋಭಾ
ಡಂಬರಮಂ ಪಡೆಗುಮುಚಿತ-ಕಾವ್ಯೋಕ್ತಿಗಳೊಳ್. || 53[1] ||

42. Definition of the first *peaceful* alliteration or of No. 2, pointing out the distinction between this and No. 1. In No. 2. the letters are yogâksharas, but the vowels no ekasvaras.

ಬೆರಸಿರೆ ಮುಂದುಂ ಯೋಗಾ
ಕ್ಷರಂಗಳೇಕ-ಸ್ವರಂಗಳಿಂ, ಸುಪ್ರಾಸಂ |
ನೆರೆದು,—ವಿಪರ್ಯಾಸ-ಕ್ರಮ
ಮಿರೆ, ಸತತಂ ಶಾಂತ-ಪೂರ್ವಮಕ್ಕುಂ ಪ್ರಾಸಂ. || 54[2] ||

43. Definition of the second peaceful alliteration, that of *classified consonants*, or of No. 3.

ಶಾಂತ-ಪ್ರಾಸದ ಭೇದಮ
ದಿಂತಕ್ಕುಂ; ವರ್ಗದಕ್ಕರಂಗಳ್ ನಾಲ್ಕುಂ |
ಶಾಂತಮಿರೆ, ಪೇಳ್ದ ತಾಣದೊ
ಳಂತಕ್ಕುಂ ಪ್ರಾಕ್ತನೋಕ್ತ-ವರ್ಗ-ಪ್ರಾಸಂ. || 55[3] ||

44. An instance of No. 3.

ಸಕಲ-ಜನ-ವಿನುತನಂ, ಶತ
ಮಖ-ಸದೃಶ-ವಿಶಾಲ-ವಿವಿಧ-ವಿಭವೋದಯನಂ, |
ಸುಗುಣ-ಗಣ-ಯುತನನರಿ-ಬಲ-
ವಿಘಟನನಂ ಕಂಡನಣುವನಾ ರಾಘವನಂ. || 56[4] || ಇದು ವರ್ಗಪ್ರಾಸಂ.

45. Definition of the *proximate* alliteration or of No. 4.

ಇದು ಸದ್ವರ್ಗ-ಪ್ರಾಸ
ಕ್ಕುದಾಹೃತಂ. ಕುಱಿತ ಶ-ಷ-ಸ-ವರ್ಣ-ತ್ರಯಮುಂ |
ವಿದಿತ-ಪ್ರಾಸ-ವಿಯುಕ್ತಾ
ಸ್ಪದದೊಳ್ ನಿಲೆ ಪೇಳ್ದೊಡದು ಸಮೀಪ-ಪ್ರಾಸಂ. || 57[5] ||

1) Rc. v. 24, B., D. 2) Rc. v. 25, B., D. 3) Rc. v. 26, B., D. 4) Only in D., B.
5) Rc. 27, D., B.

46. An instance of No. 4.

ಶಶಧರ-ಬಿಂಬಾನನೆಯಂ,
ಝಷಕೇತನ ಮಾತೆಯಂ, ಸರೋಜಾಂಬಕೆಯಂ, |
ಬಿಸ-ವಿಶದ-ವರ್ಣೆಯಂ ಕಂ
ಡೊಸೆದಂ ಬನದೊಳಗೆ ಜನಕ-ತನುಜೆಯನಣುವಂ. ‖ 58[1] ‖ ಇದು ಸಮೀಪಪ್ರಾಸಂ.

47. Definition of the *successive* alliteration or of No. 5.

ಎಂದಿಂತು ಸಮೀಪ-ಪ್ರಾ
ಸಂ ದರ್ಶಿತಮಾಯ್ತು. ಮತ್ತನುಪ್ರಾಸಮುಮಂ |
ಸಂದಿಸಿದೆಣೆಯಕ್ಕರವೊಂ
ದೊಂದಱೊಳಳವಡೆಯುಸುದೊರ್ಡನುಗತಮಕ್ಕುಂ. ‖ 59[2] ‖

48. An instance of No. 5.

ಜನ-ವಿನುತನನಘನನುಪಮ
ನನುನಯ-ಪರನರಸನಿನಿಸು ನೆನೆನೆನೆದು, ಮನೋ |
ಜನಿತ-ಮುದನನಿಲ-ತನಯನ
ನನೃತ-ವಚನ-ರಚನನಂತಿರೆನೆ ನುಡಿದನವಂ. ‖ 60[3] ‖ ಇದು ಅನುಗತಪ್ರಾಸಂ.

49. Definition of the *final* alliteration or of No. 6.

ಇಂತಿದನುಪ್ರಾಸಂ. ಪಾ
ದಾಂತದೊಳೆಂದಾವುದಾನುಮಿಟ್ಟಕ್ಕರಮಂ |
ಮುಂತಣ ಪಾದಾಂತಂಗಳೊ
ಳಂ ತಡೆಯದೆ ಪೇಳ್ದೊಡಂ ತದಂತ-ಪ್ರಾಸಂ. ‖ 61[4] ‖

50. An instance of No. 6. See v. 226; 234; 257 seq.; 272 seq.

ಅತಿ-ವಿಶದ-ಯಶೋ- ವೃತ್ತಂ,
ನತ-ಸಕಲಾರಾತಿ-ಜನ-ವಿತಾನಂ, ಮತ್ತಂ |
ವಿತತ-ಶ್ರೀ-ಸಂಪತ್ತಂ,
ಶತಮಖ-ಸದೃಶಾನುಭಾವ-ವಿಭವಂ-ಚಿತ್ತಂ. ‖ 62[5] ‖ ಇದು ಅಂತಪ್ರಾಸಂ.

51. The four kinds of alliteration of the *third* class, occurring along with the ten simple alliterations (prâsa) and the successive (anuprâsa) and final one (antaprâsa).

1) Only in D., B. 2) Rc. 28, D., B. 3) Rc. 29, D., B. 4) Rc. 30, D., B. 5) D., B.

ಪ್ರಾಸಾನುಪ್ರಾಸಾಂತ-
ಪ್ರಾಸಂಗಳ್ ಮೂಱುಂ ಇವತಿಶಯಂಗಳ್. ಮತ್ತಂ ।
ಪ್ರಾಸಾಭಾಸಂ ಮಾಱುಂ;
ಭಾಸುರ-ಕಂಜಾಯತಾಕ್ಷಿ, ಕೇಳ್, ಅದನೊರೆವೆಂ. || 63[1] ||

Alliterations

1. in which, instead of only one, two letters (2nd and 3rd) are made to rhyme (dviprâsa, according to the Kavi Jihvâ Bandhana: dvivarṇa prâsa);
2. which take place twice (or oftener) within a quarter, viz. near the beginning and midst (or at other places) of it (dvandva prâsa);[2]
3. in which three letters (2nd, 3rd and 4th) are made to rhyme (triprâsa or trivarṇa prâsa);
4. which, in the same shape, occur at the end and at the beginning of each quarter (antâdiprâsa).

ದ್ವಿ-ಪ್ರಾಸಂ, ಸುಭಗಂ ದ್ವಂ
ದ್ವ-ಪ್ರಾಸಂ, ಕಾವ್ಯ-ರಚನೆಗುಚಿತಮೆನಿಪ್ಪ ।
ತ್ರಿ-ಪ್ರಾಸಂ, ಸಲೆಯಂತಾ
ದಿ-ಪ್ರಾಸಂ, ಬೇಱಿ ನಾಲ್ಕು ತೆಱನಾಗಿರ್ಕುಂ. || 64[3] ||

52. An instance of the Dviprâsa or No. 1.

ಅರಸರೊಳೆಲೆ ನೀಂ ಸರಸರ
ನರಸಿ ಮೆಱೆವೊಲಾಡುತಿರ್ಪ ನಿನಗಿದು ಗುಣವೇ? ।
ಅರಸರ ಸರಸವ ಬಲ್ಲರೆ?
ಸರಸವನಾಡರಸರಲ್ಲದವರೊಳ್, ಮಗಳೇ! || 65[4] || ಇದು ದ್ವಿಪ್ರಾಸಂ.

53. An instance of the Âdyanta Prâsa or No. 4.

ವಿಮಲರ ಮಿತ್ರಂ, ವಿಮಲಂ,
ವಿಮಲ-ವಿನತ-ಮೂರ್ತಿ, ವಿಮಲರೊಳ್ಗತಿ-ವಿಮಲಂ, ।
ವಿಮಲ-ನ್ಯಾಯದೆ ವಿಮಲಂ,
ವಿಮಲ-ರುಚಿ-ಮಯಂ, ನಿರಂತರಕ್ಕಂ ವಿಮಲಂ. || 66 || ಇದು ಆದ್ಯಂತಪ್ರಾಸಂ.

11. A short Survey of the subjects to come.

54. According to Nâgavarma's opinion there are 3½ mother-languages (Samskṛita, Prâkṛita, Apabhramśa and Paiśâćika) and 56 daughter-languages (Draviḍa, Andhra, Karṇâṭaka,

1) Ro. 31, D., B. Instead of ಮಾಱುಂ Ro. and D. have ಮೂಱುಂ, B. has ನೋಡಂ; ಮಾಱುಂ, i. e. new form too, is a guess.

2) This kind may be called "co-ordinate alliteration." Cf. Lalita (v. 217), Krauñća pada (v. 221), Vanalatê (v. 226), the Mâlâvṛittas (vs. 233. 234), the Raghaṭês (v. 254 seq.), and the Akkarikê (v. 308). 3) Ro. 32, D., B. 4) D., B., Kavi Jihvâ Bandhana II., 20.

etc.) in India. In each of these languages occur the Vṛittas (turns, forms or specimens) of the akshara gaṇa čhandas, *i. e.* metres with a fixed scheme of the 8 Syllable-feet (akshara gaṇa). This **Akshara gaṇa *Chandas*** (v. 71 seq.) falls under three heads, viz.

1. Sama vṛittas, *i. e.* metres the four lines or quarters (pâda, pada, čaraṇa) of which have the same gaṇas in the same places, their vedic types (čhandas) being 26;
2. Ardha sama vṛittas, *i. e.* metres in which such is the case only in half the number of lines (1 and 3, 2 and 4 being equal);
3. Vishama vṛittas, *i. e.* metres in which, though each line is composed of the Syllable-feet, all lines, more or less, differ from each other.

Besides there are the **Mâtrâ *Chandas'*** (v. 250 seq.), *i. e.* metres that are to contain a certain number of Moras (a Mora being the quantity of a short syllable) in each line, and, at the same time, some syllables bearing a fixed form.

Further there are the **Mâtrâ gaṇa *Chandas'*** (v. 254 seq.), *i. e.* metres which, also when consisting of feet that, in form, are equal to the Syllable-feet, do not require that the same forms of feet recur at the same places, but in which the feet, throughout or in certain places, contain the same number of Moras (mâtrâ). The mâtrâ gaṇas (Mora feet) often show forms that are not found among the eight Syllable-feet. The two classes of Mora metres form the so-called **Jâti metres**, *i. e.* metres peculiar to the Bhâshâ jâtis, the daughter-languages.

ವಚನಂ

ಅದೆಂತೆಂದೊಡೆ ಸಂಸ್ಕೃತಂ ಪ್ರಾಕೃತಮಪಭ್ರಂಶಂ ಪೈಶಾಚಿಕಮೆಂಬ ಮೂಱುವರೆ[1] ಭಾಷೆಗಳೊಳ್ ಪುಟ್ಟುವ ದ್ರವಿಡಾಂಧ್ರ-ಕರ್ಣಾಟಕಾದಿ-ಷಟ್ಪಂಚಾಶತ್-ಸರ್ವ-ವಿಷಯ[2]-ಭಾಷಾ-ಜಾತಿಗಳಕ್ಕುಂ. ಅಲ್ಲಿ ಸಮಮರ್ಧಸಮಂ ವಿಷಮಮೆಂದು

---

1) Only Ro. reads ಚತುರ್ ಭಾಷೆ. 2) Great arbitrariness is shown in enumerating the čappanna deśas or shaṭpančâśad vishayas (56 countries); complete enumerations are also seldom to be met with in Canarese; generally books mention some above forty, and then conclude with ಮೊದಲಾದ (etc.). Here follows the list of the commentary of L., alphabetically arranged by the Ed.:-ಅಂಗ, ಅಂಧ್ರ, ಆರ್ಯ, ಏಕಪಾದ, ಓಡ್ರ (ಒಡ್ಡರ ದೇಶ), ಕರ್ಣಾಟ, ಕಳಿಂಗ, ಕಾಂಬೋಜ, ಕಾಶ್ಮೀರ, ಕಾಳವ, ಕುಂತಳ, ಕುಕುರ, ಕುರಂಗ, ಕೇರಳ, ಕೊಂಕಣ, ಕೊಂಗು (ಕೊಂಗ), ಕೊರಹ (ಮಹಾಕೊರವ), ಕೊಲ್ಲಾಳ, ಗಾಂಧಾರ, ಗುರ್ಜರ, ಗೌಳ, ಘೋಣಮುಖ, ಚೋಳ, ಚೀನ, ತುರುಷ್ಕ, ತುಳುವ, ತೆಲುಗ (ತೆಲುಂಗ), ದ್ರಾವಿಡ (ದ್ರವಿಳ), ನೇಪಾಳ, ಪಲ್ಲವಕ, ಪಾಂಚಾಳ, ಪಾಂಡ್ಯ, ಪಾರಿಯಾತ್ರಕ, ಬಂಗಾಳ, ಬರ್ಬರ, ಬಾಹ್ಲಿಕ, ಬೆಳವ, ಭೋಟ, ಮಗಧ, ಮಧ್ಯ, ಮಲಹ (ಮಲೆಯ), ಮಲೆಯಾಳ, ಮಹಾರಾಷ್ಟ್ರ, ಮಾರವ, ಮಾಳವ, ಲಂಬಕರ್ಣ, ಲಾಳ, ಲುಬ್ಧಕ, ವಂಗ, ಸಿಂಗಳ (ಸಿಂಹಳ), ಸಿಂಧು (ಸೈಂಧವ), ಸಿಂಹಪ್ರಾಣ (ಸಿಂಹಪ್ರಾಣ), ಸಂಕರ, ಸ್ತ್ರೀದೇಶ, ಹಂಮೀರ, ಹೈವ.—In other enumerations for some of the countries are substituted the following: ಅಮರಕ, ಕಂಬೋಜ, ಕರಾಳ, ಕಿರಾತ, ಕುರು, ಕೊಡಗು, ಕೋಸಲ, ಕಾರ್ಪೂರ, ಖರ್ಪರ, ಘೃತ್ಯಟಿ, ಚೇರಿ, ಜಾಲಂಧ್ರ, ತುರುಕಾಣ್ಯ, ತ್ರಿಗರ್ತ, ದ್ವೀಪ, ನಿಷಧ, ಪಾಟಾಲ, ಬರಮ, ಬಲ್ಲಾಳ, ಬೋರಟ, ಮತ್ಸ್ಯ, ಮಾಟ, ಮುರು, ಮ್ಲೇಚ್ಛ, ಯವನ, ವರಾಳ, ವಾಚಾಲ, ವಿದರ್ಭ, ಶೂರಸೇನ, ಸೌರಾಷ್ಟ್ರ, ಸೌವೀರ, ಹೂಣ, ಹೈಹಯ. A Tamiḻa list is as follows (Rottler s. v. ದೇಶ): ಅಂಗ, ಅರುಣ, ಅವಂತಿ, ಆಂಧ್ರ, ಲಾಟ, ಒಡ್ಡಿಯ, ಕರುಷ, ಕಳಿಂಗ, ಕಣ್ಣಡ, ಕಂನಾಡ, ಕಾಶ, ಕಾಶ್ಮೀರ, ಗಾಂಧಾರ, ಕಾಂಬೋಜ, ಕಿರಾತ, ಕುರುಗು, ಕುಡಗ, ಕುಂತಳ, ಕುರು, ಕುಲಿಂದ, ಗೂರ್ಜರ, ಕೇಕಯ, ಕೇರಳ, ಕೊಂಕಣ, ಕೊಲ್ಲ, ಕೋಸಲ, ಶಕ, ಸೌವೀರ, ಶಾಲ್ವ, ಸಿಂಗಳ, ಸಿಂಧು, ಚೀನ, ಶೂರಸೇನ, ಚೋಡ, ಚೋನಗ, ದ್ರಾವಿಡ, ತುಳುವ, ತೆಂಗಣ, ನಿಡದ, ನೇಪಾಳ, ಬಬ್ಬರ, ಪಲ್ಲವ, ಪಾಂಚಾಲ, ಪಾಂಡಿಯ, ಪುಲಿಂದ, ಪೋಡ (ಬೋಡ), ಮಗಧ, ಮತ್ಸ್ಯ, ಮರಾಡ, ಮಲೆಯಾಳ, ಮಾಳವ, ಯವನ, ಯುಗಂಧರ, ವಂಗ, ಬಂಗಾಳ, ವಿದರ್ಭ.

ವೃತ್ತಂ ಮೂಱು ತೆಱನಕ್ಕುಂ. ಅಲ್ಲಿ ಉಕ್ತೆ (ಉಕ್ತ, ಉಕ್ತಿ), ಅತ್ಯುಕ್ತೆ, ಮಧ್ಯಮೆ, ಪ್ರತಿಷ್ಠೆ, ಸುಪ್ರತಿಷ್ಠೆ, ಗಾಯತ್ರಿ, ಉಷ್ಣಿಕ್, ಅನುಷ್ಟುಭ್, ಬೃಹತಿ, ಪಂಕ್ತಿ, ತ್ರಿಷ್ಟುಭ್, ಜಗತಿ, ಅತಿಜಗತಿ, ಶಕ್ವರಿ, ಅತಿಶಕ್ವರಿ, ಅಷ್ಟಿ, ಅತ್ಯಷ್ಟಿ, ಧೃತಿ, ಅತಿಧೃತಿ, ಕೃತಿ, ಪ್ರಕೃತಿ, ಆಕೃತಿ, ವಿಕೃತಿ, ಸಂಕೃತಿ, ಅತಿಕೃತಿ, ಉತ್ಕೃತಿ ಎಂದು, ಇರ್ಪತ್ತಾಱುಂ ಛಂದಂಗಳಕ್ಕುಂ.[1] || 67 ||

55. **Besides (the Vṛittas, beginning with the Uktĕ type and ending in the Utkṛiti type) there are the Mâlâvṛittas (vs. 232-234), the Daṇḍaka (v. 231, and the Ardhasama and Vishama Vṛittas, vs. 235-249). (Then follow) the Raghaṭĕs (v. 254 seq.), the Mâtrâryĕs (v. 289 seq.), the Tripadi (v. 299), the *C*atushpadi (v. 309), the Shaṭpadi (vs. 313-338), the Ashṭapadi (v. 277 seq.), the Gaṇaniyama Kanda (vs. 284-288), the *S*aṅkhâvṛitta (?), the Tâḷavṛitta (? cf. vs. 254, 274, 279, 280) and other *Jâtis*, viz., (v. 68), the Akkaras (v. 302 seq., the *C*aupadi=the *C*atushpadi), the Gîtikĕ (v. 312), the Eḷĕ (v. 307, the Tivadi=the Tripadi), the Utsâha (v. 339, the Shaṭpadis), the Akkarikĕ (v. 308), the *C*handovatamsa (v. 310).**

ಅವಱಿಂ (ಎಂದೊಡೆ ಇರ್ಪತ್ತಾಱುಂ ಛಂದಂಗಳಿಂ) ಪೊಱಗೆ ಪುಟ್ಟುವ ಮಾಲಾವೃತ್ತ-ದಂಡಕ[ಂಗಳುಂ]-ರಘಟೆ (ರಗಳೆ)-ಮಾತ್ರಾರ್ಯಾ-ತ್ರಿಪದಿ-ಚತುಷ್ಪದಿ-ಷಟ್ಪದಿ-ಅಷ್ಟಪದಿ-ಗಣನಿಯಮಕಂದ-ಶಂಖಾವೃತ್ತ-ತಾಳವೃತ್ತ-ಆದಿ-ಜಾತಿಗಳ್[ಉಂ]ಉಂಟು[2], ಅವಾವುವೆಂದೊಡೆ

ಕಂದಂ

ಮದನವತಿ, ಅಕ್ಕರು ಚೌ
ಪದಿ ಗೀತಿಕೆಯೇಳೆ ತಿವದಿಯುತ್ಸಾಹಂ ಷ ।

1) In all the MSS. 2) Instead of ಪೊಱಗೆ ಪುಟ್ಟುವ Sa. has only ಪೊಱಗೆ; Re., D., B. have ಪೊಱಗಣ (cf. v. 285) Ra. and H. read: ಅದಱಿಂ ಪೊ.... ಮಾಳವೃತ್ತ-ದಂಡಕ-ರಗಳೆ-ಮಾತ್ರಾಗಣನಿಯಮಸ್ಕಂಧಕಾದಿ (skandhaka=kanda)-ಜಾತಿಗಳಕ್ಕುಂ. ಅವಱಿಂ ಪೊಱಗೆ ಮತ್ತಂ ಕರ್ನಾಟಕ-ಅಂಧ್ರ-ದ್ರಾವಿಡ-ವರಾಟ-ಲಾಟ-ಮಾಳವ-ಗೌಳ-ಗುರ್ಜರ-ಕಳಿಂಗ-ಅಂಗ-ವಂಗ-ಕೇರಳ-ಬಾಹ್ಲಿಕ-ಮಗಧ-ಚೇರಿ-ಪಾಟಾಲ-ಪಾಂಚಾಲ-ವೆಂಗಿ-ತಾಳವಾದಿ-ದೇಶ-ಭಾಷೆಗಳೊಳ್ ಪುಟ್ಟುವವೆಲ್ಲಂ ಸರ್ವವಿಷಯಭಾಷಾಜಾತಿಗಳಕ್ಕುಂ. ಅವಾವುವೆಂದಡೆ, and then v. 68. An observation is to be made here, viz. that regarding these last prose-lines an important difference occurs in the MSS.; M. and Sb. after 66 read only: "ಅವಱಿಂ ಪೊಱಗೆ ಪುಟ್ಟುವ ಅವೆಂತೆಂದೊಡೆ", and then all at once introduce v. 68. This reading, though deficient (as *e. g.* it does not include all the Jâti *C*handas'), essentially alters the classification, so that the Mâlâvṛitta and Daṇḍaka that belong to the Sama Vṛittas, the Ardha Sama Vṛittas, and Vishama Vṛittas do not come under the head of the Jâtis, as they, in fact, ought not to do. For the true Jâtis are those metres that are formed of Mâtrâ gaṇas. See W. p. 289: ವೃತ್ತಮಕ್ಷರಸಂಖ್ಯಾತಂ ಜಾತಿರ್ ಮಾತ್ರಾ-ಕೃತಾ ಭವೇತ್ । The syllables in square brackets are proffered by us for correction.

ಟ್ಟದಿಯಕ್ಕರಿಕೆ ಕರಂ ಚೆ
ಲ್ವೊದವಿದ ಛಂದೋವತಂಸಮಬ್ಜದಳಾಕ್ಷೀ! || 68[1] ||

56. The author is going first to impart knowledge regarding each of the 26 normal forms (jâti) of the Sama Vṛittas, from Uktô to Utkṛiti, in a two-fold manner (as the rules concern Samskṛita as well as Prâkṛita).

ಒಂದೊಂದು ಜಾತಿಗಿಂಮಡಿ
ಯಿಂದಂ, ತಾನ್ ಉಕ್ತೆಯಾದಿಯಾಗಿರೆ, ಸಂಪೂ ।
ರ್ಣೇಂದು-ಮುಖಿ, ತಿಳಿಯ ಪೇಳ್ವೆಂ,
ಸಂದುತ್ಕೃತಿಯೆಯ್ದುವಿನೆಗಮಿಂತೀ ಕ್ರಮದಿಂ. || 69[2] ||

57. He says that his first instruction will concern the metres common to the two great divisions of languages (the Samskṛita and Prâkṛita), it thus being given concerning the languages etc. of all the countries. (Cf. vs. 281. 296.)

ಇಂತಱಿಪಿದುಭಯ-ಭಾಷೆಯೊ
ಳಂ, ತೊಡರದೆ, ಸರ್ವ-ವಿಷಯ-ಭಾಷಾದಿಗಳಿಂ, ।
ಮುಂ-ತಿಳಿಪಿದಪೆಂ ನಿನಗಾನ್,
ಅಂತರಿಸದೆ. ಕೇಳ್ ಇದಂ, ಪಯೋ-ರುಹ-ವದನೇ! || 70[3] ||

ಗದ್ಯಂ

ಇದು ಸಮಸ್ತ-ಸುರಾಸುರೇಂದ್ರ-ಮುನೀಂದ್ರ-ಮಣಿ-ಮಕುಟ-ಘಟಿತ-ಶ್ರೀಮದ್-ಭಗವದರ್ಹ-ಪರಮೇಶ್ವರ-ಪಾದಾರವಿಂದ-ದ್ವಂದ್ವ-ಮಕರಂದ-ಮತ್ತ-ಮಧುಕರಾಯಮಾನ-ವಿಬುಧ-ಜನ-ಮನಃ-ಪದ್ಮಿನೀ-ರಾಜಹಂಸ-ನಾಗವರ್ಮ-ವಿರಚಿತ-ಛಂದೋಂಬುರಾಶಿಯೊಳ್ ನೆಗಳ್ದ ಸಂಜ್ಞಾಧಿಕಾರಂ ಪ್ರಥಮಾಶ್ವಾಸಂ.

---

1) H., Ra., Rc., Sb., M., D., B. Regarding the Vṛittas (*i. e.* Mâtrâ Vṛittas) that appear among the true Canarese Jâtis, verses 276, 308 and 309 can be pointed at. 2) Rc. 34, M., Sb., D., B., Ra., H. 3) Rc. 35, M., etc.; not in Ra., H. After this verse, in M. and Sb., there is: ಕರ್ಣಾಟಕಾಂಧ್ರದ್ರವಿಡದೇಶಭಾಷೆಗಳೊಳ್ ಪುಟ್ಟುವವೆಂತೆಂದೊಡೆ, whereupon follow 3 verses regarding the Shaṭpadi, 4 verses regarding the Kanda, and 1 verse regarding the Anushṭubh (śloka), all of which are out of place here, as they are repeated at the places where these metres are separately treated of.

II. CHAPTER: THE SAMA VṚITTAS

ಸಮವೃತ್ತವಿವರಣಮೆಂಬ ದ್ವಿತೀಯಾಶ್ವಾಸಂ

58. The instruction regarding the Sama Vṛittas begins; the verses that contain the rules (pada), being at the same time the instances.

ಕಂದಂ

ಶ್ರೀಪದಮಂ ಸಮವೃತ್ತ-ನಿ
ರೂಪಣ-ಸಮಯದೊಳೆ ತಂದು, ಪದನಿಟ್ಟೆನಿದಂ; ।
ಚಾಪಳ-ಲೋಚನೆ, ಬಹಳಾ
ಳಾಪದೊಳೇಂ? ಕೇಳೆ, ಕೆಳದಿ, ನಿನಗಭ್ಯುದಯಂ! ‖ 71[1] ‖

1. Uktŏ (ukti, uktam). In this type (ċhandas) each quarter (pâda) consists of 1 syllable; by putting short syllables instead of the long ones of the instance, 1 other vṛitta, *i. e.* ◡, is possible

ಉಕ್ತೆಯೆಂಬ ಛಂದಸ್ಸಿನೊಳ್ 1 ಅಕ್ಕರಂ ಪಾದಮಾಗಿ ಪುಟ್ಟುವ 2 ವೃತ್ತಂಗಳೊಳಗೆ

59. An instance: —, the Śrî. (H., Ra. also: ◡; la li | la li ‖).

ಶ್ರೀವೃತ್ತಂ

ಶ್ರೀ
ಶಂ ।
ಕಾಂ
ತೇ. ‖ 72[2] ‖

2. Atyuktŏ. In this type each quarter consists of 2 syllables; 4 vṛittas are possible, viz. a Spondee – –; an Iambus ◡ –; a Trochee – ◡; and a Pyrrhich ◡◡

ಅತ್ಯುಕ್ತೆಯೆಂಬ ಛಂದಸ್ಸಿನೊಳ್ 2 ಅಕ್ಕರಂ ಪಾದಮಾಗಿ ಪುಟ್ಟುವ 4 ವೃತ್ತಂಗಳೊಳಗೆ

60. An instance: – –, the Geya.

ಗೇಯವೃತ್ತಂ

ಶ್ರೀಯಂ
ದೇಯಂ ।

1) H., Ra., Rc., Sb., M., D., B. 2) The vṛitta names are stated separately only in Rc.

ಪೇಯಂ
ಗೇಯಂ. || 73 ||

61. A second instance: ⏑ – , the Diganta.

ದಿಗಂತವೃತ್ತಂ

ಅಗೋ
ಪಗಂ ।
ದಿಗಂ
ತಗಂ. || 74[1] ||

3. **Madhyamē.** Quarters of 3 syllables; 8 vṛittas possible, viz. ⏑⏑–; –––; –⏑–; ⏑⏑⏑; –⏑⏑; ––⏑; ⏑––; ⏑–⏑. These form the eight gaṇas mentioned in the first chapter, v. 31 seq.

ಮಧ್ಯಮೆಯೆಂಬ ಛಂದಸ್ಸಿನೊಳ್ 3 ಅಕ್ಕರಂ ಪಾದಮಾಗಿ ಪುಟ್ಟುವ 8 ವೃತ್ತಂಗಳೊಳಗೆ

62. An instance: ⏑⏑ – (wind), the Pravara.

ಪ್ರವರಂ

ಪವನೋ
ದ್ಭವದಿಂ ।
ಪ್ರವರಂ,
ಪ್ರವರೇ! || 75 ||

63. Another instance: ––– (earth), the *Syâmânga*.

ಶ್ಯಾಮಾಂಗಂ

ಭೂಮಿ-ಪ್ರೋ
ದ್ದಾಮಂ, ಕೇಳ್, ।
ಶ್ಯಾಮಾಂಗೀ,
ಶ್ಯಾಮಾಂಗಂ. || 76 ||

1) H. has also: ––, the Garva; and: ⏑⏑, the Harivara.

64. A third instance: — ⏑ — (fire), the Pâvana.

ಪಾವನಂ

ಪಾವಕೋ
ದ್ಭಾವದಿಂ, ।
ಶ್ರೀವಧೂ,
ಪಾವನಂ. || 77 ||

65. A fourth instance: ⏑ ⏑ ⏑ (heaven), the Paramĕ.

ಪರಮೆ

ಸುರರ
ನೆರವಿ ।
ನೆರೆಯೆ,
ಪರಮೆ. || 78[1] ||

4. Pratishṭhĕ Quarters of 4 syllables; two times the eight gaṇas *i. e.* 16 vṛittas are possible[2]

ಪ್ರತಿಷ್ಠೆಯೆಂಬ ಛಂದಸ್ಸಿನೊಳ್ 4 ಅಕ್ಕರಂ ಪಾದಮಾಗಿ ಪುಟ್ಟುವ 16 ವೃತ್ತಂಗಳೊಳಗೆ

66. First instance: — ⏑ — | —, the Devaramya.

ದೇವರಮ್ಯಂ

ಗಲಗ । ಗಂ (ಅಗ್ನಿಯೂ ಗುರುವೂ) || 79 ||

1) Ra., H. also: ⏑ — —, the Ratânta. 2) Instead of the verses of the MSS, (all of which contain, if required, nothing but a dry enumeration of the gaṇas of the concluding long and short syllables, and of the names, together with some epithets for Nâgavarma's wife) only the names and the *rules* (not forms) in letters have been given under this heading. This method, to some extent, will be followed also further on. It is, in fact, Piṅgaḷa's own method; similarly Rb., in the first line, generally adduces the letters and names, and then a praise; sometimes this method appears also in the other MSS. It may be added here that the true readings of the verses containing the rules are lost in some indefinable measure, as would appear especially from Rb., wherein the verses have their own, quite peculiar wording, and show a strong Jaina tendency. The Janodaya, for instance, appears in Rb. as follows: ಏನೇಳ-ಗಂ ಜನೋ ದಯಂ । ಸುನಾಮದಿಂ, ಜಿನೇಶ್ವರಾ. || Rb.contains also less instances.

67. Second instance: – ⏑⏑ | –, the Saundara.

ಸೌಂದರಂ

ಗಲಲ । ಗಂ (ಚಂದ್ರನೂ ಗುರುವೂ) ‖ 80 ‖

68. Third instance: ⏑ – ⏑ | –, the Janodaya.

ಜನೋದಯಂ

ಲಗಲ । ಗಂ (ಸೂರ್ಯನೂ ಗುರುವೂ) ‖ 81 ‖

69. Fourth instance: ⏑⏑ – | –, the Mṛiganetra.[1]

ಮೃಗನೇತ್ರಂ

ಲಲಗ । ಗಂ (ಲಘುಯುಗ್ಮವೂ ಗುರುಯುಗ್ಮವೂ) ‖ 82 ‖

70. Fifth instance: ⏑⏑⏑ | ⏑, the Surataru.

ಸುರತರು

ಲಲಲ । ಲಂ (ಸ್ವರ್ಗವೂ ಲಘುವೂ) ‖ 83 ‖

71. Sixth instance: – – ⏑ | –, the Kâmodbhava.

ಕಾಮೋದ್ಭವಂ

ಗಗಲ । ಗಂ (ವ್ಯೋಮವೂ ಗುರುವೂ) ‖ 84 ‖[2]

72. Seventh instance: – – – | –, the Prema.

ಪ್ರೇಮಂ

ಗಗಗ । ಗಂ (ಭೂಮಿಯೂ ಗುರುವೂ) ‖ 85 ‖[3]

1) M. calls it Mridunetra. 2) In M. and Sb; Ra., H. call it Kâmânga. 3) Only in Rc. The MS. called Rb. begins all at once with Pratishṭhĕ, and its only instance for it is the Janodaya.

5. Supratishṭhĕ. Quarters of 5 syllables; four times eight *i. e.* 32 vṛittas possible

ಸುಪ್ರತಿಷ್ಠೆಯೆಂಬ ಛಂದಸ್ಸಿನೊಳ್ 5 ಅಕ್ಕರಂ ಪಾದಮಾಗಿ ಪುಟ್ಟುವ 32 ವೃತ್ತಂಗಳೊಳಗೆ

73. **First instance:** — ◡ — | ◡ —, **the Nandaka.**

ನಂದಕಂ

ಒಂದು ಪಙ್ಕ್ತಿಯೊಳ್
ನಿಂದೊಡಂ ಲ-ಗಂ, ।
ಸೌಂದರಾಂಗಿ, ಕೇಳ್,
ಸುಂದ ನಂದಕಂ. ‖ 86 ‖

74. **Second instance:** — ◡ ◡ | — —, **the Kâñčanamâlĕ.**

ಕಾಂಚನಮಾಲೆ

ಮಿಂಚುವ ಚಂದ್ರಂ
ಗಂಚೆಯ ರುದ್ರರ್ ।
ಸಂಚಿಸೆ, ವೃತ್ತಂ
ಕಾಂಚನಮಾಲೇ. ‖ 87[1] ‖

75. **Third instance:** — — ◡ | ◡ —, **the Tilaka.**

ತಿಲಕಂ

ವ್ಯೋಮಂ, ಹರಿಯಿಂ
ದೇ ಮಾರಹರಂ ।
ತಾಮಾಗೆ, ಸತೀ,
ನಾಮಂ ತಿಲಕಂ. ‖ 88[2] ‖

76. **Fourth instance:** ◡ — ◡ | — —, **the Nanda.**

ನಂದಂ

ದಿನೇಶನಿಂದ
ತ್ತ ನೀಲಕಂಠರ್, ।

1) ರುದ್ರ ಅಂದರೆ ತ್ರಿಯಂಬಕ, ಅಂದರೆ ಗುರು. See v. 29. 2) ಹರಿ ಅಂದರೆ ಮುರಾಂತಕ, ಅಂದರೆ ಲಘು; ಮಾರಹರ ಅಂದರೆ ಗುರು. See v. 29.

ತನೂದರೀ, ನಿ
ಲ್ಕೆ, ನಂದಮಕ್ಕುಂ. || 89 ||

77. **Fifth instance: ⏑ ⏑ ⏑ | ⏑ —, the Sarasiruha.**

ಸರಸಿರುಹಂ

ಬರೆ ನ-ಲ-ಗಂ,
ಸರಸಿರುಹಂ, |
ವರವರನಾ,
ಪರಮ-ಜಿನಾ! || 90 ||

78. **Sixth instance: — ⏑ ⏑ | ⏑ —, the Prema.**

ಪ್ರೇಮಂ

ಸೋಮ-ಹರಿಯುಂ
ಕಾಮಹರನುಂ |
ತಾಮಿರೆ, ಪೆಸರ್
ಪ್ರೇಮಮಬಲೇ! || 91[1] ||

6. Gâyatri. Quarters of 6 syllables; eight times eight *i. e.* 64 vṛittas are possible

ಗಾಯತ್ರಿಯೆಂಬ ಛಂದಸ್ಸಿನೊಳ್ 6 ಅಕ್ಕರಂ ಪಾದಮಾಗಿ ಪುಟ್ಟುವ 64 ವೃತ್ತಂಗಳೊಳಗೆ

79. **First instance: — ⏑ — | ⏑ — —, the Sâlini.**

ಶಾಲಿನಿ

ಜ್ವಾಲೆ ತೋಯಮೇಳ್ತಂ
ದೋಳಿವೆತ್ತೊಡಕ್ಕುಂ |
ನೀಲ-ಕುಂತಳೇ, ಕೇಳ್,
ಶಾಲಿನೀ-ವಿತಾನಂ. || 92 ||

1) Of these six instances only 2, 3 and 5 are in Rb.; 5 gives Rb.'s reading.

80. **Second instance:** ◡ ◡ ◡ | ◡ – –, **the Udâtta.**

ಉದಾತ್ತಂ

ನ-ಯ-ಗಣದಿಂದಂ
ನಿಯತಮಿದಕ್ಕಂ, ।
ಪ್ರಿಯ-ಲಲನೇ, ಕೇಳ್,
ನಯದಿನುದಾತ್ತಂ. ‖ 93 ‖

81. **Third instance:** – ◡ ◡ | ◡ – –, **the *Saśikânta.***

ಶಶಿಕಾಂತಂ

ಶೀತಕರ-ತೋಯಂ
ದ್ಯೋತಿಸಿರೆ, ನೀಲಾ ।
ಬ್ಜಾತ-ನಯನೇ, ಕೇಳ್,
ಓತು, ಶಶಿಕಾಂತಂ. ‖ 94 ‖

82. **Fourth instance:** ◡ – – | ◡ – –, **the Vičitra.**

ವಿಚಿತ್ರಂ

ಪಯೋ-ಯುಗ್ಮದಿಂದಂ,
ಪಯೋ-ಜಾಯತಾಕ್ಷೀ, ।
ಪ್ರಯೋಗ-ಪ್ರಸಿದ್ಧಂ,
ನಿಯುಕ್ತಂ ವಿಚಿತ್ರಂ. ‖ 95 ‖

83. **Fifth instance:** – – ◡ | ◡ – –, **the Tanumadhyē (or Tilaka)**

ತನುಮಧ್ಯೆ (ತಿಲಕಂ)

ವ್ಯೋಮಾದಿ-ಜಲಾಂತಂ
ತಾಮಾಗೆ, ನಿತಾಂತ- ।
ಶ್ರೀಮಾನಿನಿ, ನೀಂ ಕೇಳ್,
ನಾಮಂ ತನುಮಧ್ಯೇ. ‖ 96 ‖

84. Sixth instance: ◡◡– | ◡◡–, the Kumuda (or Mukuḷa, Mukura).

ಕುಮುದಂ (ಮುಕುಳಂ, ಮುಕುರಂ)

ಅನಿಲ-ದ್ವಿತಯಂ
ಘನಮಲ್ಲಿಯುಮಂ ।
ಬಿನವೊಂದಿರೆ, ಕೇಳ್,
ವನಿತೇ, ಕುಮುದಂ. || 97 ||

85. Seventh instance: – – – | ◡◡–, the Mukuḷa (or Kumuda).

ಮುಕುಳಂ (ಕುಮುದಂ)

ಉರ್ವ್ಯಗ್ರಂ ಮರುತಂ
ಪರ್ವಿರ್ದಂದಬಲೇ, ।
ಸರ್ವಾದ್ಯಂತದೊಳಂ
ನಿರ್ವ್ಯಾಜ್ಯಂ ಮುಕುಳಂ. || 98 ||

86. Eighth instance: ◡◡◡ | – – –, the Sulalita.

ಸುಲಲಿತಂ

ಕುಲಿಶ-ಭೂ-ಯುಗ್ಮಂ
ನೆಲಸಿದಂದಕ್ಕುಂ, ।
ಜಲಜ-ಪತ್ರಾಕ್ಷೀ,
ಸುಲಲಿತಂ ವೃತ್ತಂ. || 99[1] ||

7. Ushṇih. Quarters of 7 syllables; (16×8 *i. e.*) 128 vṛittas possible

ಉಷ್ಣಿಕ್ ಎಂಬ ಛಂದಸ್ಸಿನೊಳ್ 7 ಅಕ್ಕರಂ ಪಾದಮಾಗಿ ಪುಟ್ಟುವ 128 ವೃತ್ತಂಗಳೊಳಗೆ

87. First instance: ◡◡◡ | ◡◡– | –, the Sadamala (čitra, vičitra).

ಸದಮಲಂ (ಚಿತ್ರಂ, ವಿಚಿತ್ರಂ)

ತ್ರಿದಶ-ಪವನೇಶರ್
ಪುದಿದು ನಿಲೆ ಪಾದಾಂ ।

1) Of these eight instances only 4, 5 and 6 occur in Rb.; it, H. and Ra. call 5 the Tilaka, and Rb. calls 6 the Mukuḷa. M.'s and Sb.'s name of 6 is Mukura; Ra.'s, H.'s, D.'s and B.'s Kumuda. 7 appears as Kumuda in M. and Sb.; in Ra., H. there is a blank.

ತದೊಳಱಿ, ವಿದಗ್ಧೇ, |
ಸದಮಲ-ವಿತಾನಂ. || 100[1] ||

88. **Second instance: — ◡◡ | — ◡◡ | —, the Amaḷa (Kamala in M.).**

ಅಮಳಂ (ಕಮಲಂ)

ಇಂದು-ಯುಗಂಗಳ ಮುಂ
ದಿಂದುಧರಂ ಬರೆ ತಾ |
ನೆಂದುಮಿದರ್ಕೆ ಪೆಸರ್,
ಸೌಂದರಿ, ಕೇಳ್, ಅಮಳಂ. || 101 ||

89. **Third instance: — ◡◡ | — ◡ — | —, the Virâma (Vinamra in H.).**

ವಿರಾಮಂ

ಶೀತಕರಾಗ್ನಿ-ಚೇತೋ-
ಜಾತ-ಹರರ್ಕಳಿರ್ದಂ |
ದೇ, ತೊದಳೋವಳೇ, ನಾ
ಮಾತಿಶಯಂ ವಿರಾಮಂ. || 102 ||

90. **Fourth instance: — — — | — ◡◡ | —, the Citra.**

ಚಿತ್ರಂ

ಧಾತ್ರೀ-ಚಂದ್ರೇಂದುಧರಂ
ಸೂತ್ರಾರ್ಥಂ-ಬೆತ್ತ ಗಣಂ |
ಧಾತ್ರೀ-ಪೂಜ್ಯಂ; ಪೆಸರಿಂ
ಚಿತ್ರಂ, ಪಂಕೇಜ-ಮುಖೀ! || 103 ||

91. **Fifth instance: — ◡ — | ◡ — ◡ | —, the Vibhûti. (Three Trochees and a long syllable.) Cf. the 10th instance.**

ವಿಭೂತಿ

ತೇಜಮರ್ಕನೀಶನಿಂ
ದೋಜೆ-ವೆತ್ತು ಬಂದೊಡಂ |

---

1) M. reads: ಸದಮಲ-ವಿಚಿತ್ರಂ. Rb. begins ಇರೆ ನ-ಸ-ಗ ಚಿತ್ರಂ | ಸರಸಿರುಹ-ನೇತ್ರಾ; the rest is quite corrupt, but does not contain the name of the metre, so that Rb. calls it čitra.

ಭೋಜ-ಪತ್ರ-ನೇತ್ರೆ, ಕೇಳ್
ಈ ಜಗದ್-ವಿಭೂತಿಯಂ! || 104 ||

92. Sixth instance: ⏑⏑–|–⏑–|–, the Sarala.

ಸರಳಂ

ಮರುತಂ ಜಾತವೇದಂ
ಹರನಂ ಕೂಡಿ ಬಂದಂ ।
ದರವಿಂದಾಯತಾಕ್ಷೀ,
ಸರಳಂ ವೃತ್ತ-ನಾಮಂ. || 105 ||

93. Seventh instance: ⏑⏑–|––⏑|–, the Komala.

ಕೋಮಳಂ

ಸ-ತ-ಗಂಗಳ್ ಕೂಡೆ ಪ
ದ್ಧತಿಯಿಂ ಚೆಲ್ವಾಗಿರಲ್ ।
ಸತತಂ, ಪಂಕೇರುಹಾ
ಯತ-ನೇತ್ರೇ, ಕೋಮಳಂ. || 106[1] ||

94. Eighth instance: ⏑⏑⏑|–⏑–|–, the Naraga (H., Ra. Saraga).

ನರಗಂ

ನ-ರ-ಗಮೆಂಬ ವರ್ಣಗೋ
ತ್ಕರಮೆ ಪಾದಮಾಗು ।
ತ್ತಿರೆ, ಶಶಾಂಕ-ವಕ್ತ್ರೇ,
ನರಗ-ನಾಮ-ವೃತ್ತಂ. || 107 ||

95. Ninth instance: ⏑⏑⏑|⏑⏑⏑|–, the Sulabha (or Madhumati). (Three Pyrrhichs and a long syllable.)

ಸುಲಭಂ (ಮಧುಮತಿ)

ನ-ನ-ಭವ-ಯುತದಿಂ,
ವನ-ರುಹ-ವದನೇ, ।

1) Other readings are: ಪದ್ಧತಿಯಂ, ಪದ್ಧತಿಯುಂ, ಕೂಡಿಪದ್ಧತಿಯಿಂ.

ನಿನಗೞುಪುವೆನಾಂ,

ಜನ-ನುತ-ಸುಲಭಂ. || 108 ||[1]

96. **Tenth instance:** — ◡ — | ◡ — ◡ | —, **the Sunâma.** The same as the 5th instance.

ಸುನಾಮಂ

ರ-ಜ-ಗಂ. || 109 ||[2]

97. **Eleventh instance:** — ◡ — | — ◡ — | —, **the Haṁsamâlĕ.**

ಹಂಸಮಾಲೆ

ರ-ರ-ಗಂ. || 110 ||[3]

8. **Anushṭubh.** Quarters of 8 syllables; (32×8 *i. e.*) 256 vṛittas possible

ಅನುಷ್ಟುಪ್-ಛಂದಸ್ಸಿನೊಳ್ 8 ಅಕ್ಕರಂ ಪಾದಮಾಗಿ ಪುಟ್ಟುವ 256 ವೃತ್ತಂಗಳೊಳಗೆ

98. **First instance:** — — — | — — — | — —, **the Vidyunmâlĕ.** (Four Spondees.)

ವಿದ್ಯುನ್ಮಾಲೆ

ಪಿಂತುರ್ವೀ-ಯುಗ್ಮಂಗಳ್ ಬರ್ಕುಂ,
ಮುಂತೀಶಾನ-ದ್ವಂದ್ವಂ ತೋರ್ಕುಂ; |
ಸಂತಂ, ನೀಂ ಕೇಳ್, ಅಂಭೋಜಾಕ್ಷೀ-
ಕಾಂತೇ, ವಿದ್ಯುನ್ಮಾಲಾ-ವೃತ್ತಂ. || 111 ||

99. **Second instance:** — ◡◡ | — ◡◡ | — —, **the Citrapada.** (Two Dactyls and a Spondee.)

ಚಿತ್ರಪದಂ

ಇಂದು-ಯುಗಂಗಳ ಮುಂದುಂ
ಬಂದು ಹರ-ದ್ವಿತಯಂಗಳ್, |
ನಿಂದೊಡೆ, ಚಿತ್ರಪದಂ ನಾ
ಮಂ, ದಳಿತಾಂಬುಜ-ನೇತ್ರೇ! || 112 ||

---

1) Rb. calls it Madhumati; its first half is: ಮಧುಮತಿ ನ-ನ-ಗಂ | ಮಧುಕರ-ರುಚಿ-ರಸಂ||

2) This is only in M.

3) Also this only in M. Of the eleven instances only 1, 5 and 9 are in Rb.; 2 is not in H., Ra., B.; 9 not in Ro., Ra., H.

100. Third instance: — ◡ ◡ | — — ◡ | ◡ —, the Mâṇavaka.

ಮಾಣವಕಂ

ಕಾಂತೆ, ಶಶಿ-ವ್ಯೋಮ-ಲ-ಗಂ
ಮುಂತಿರೆ, ನೀಂ ಕೇಳ್, ಕೆಳದೀ, ।
ಭ್ರಾಂತಿಯೊಳೇಂ, ಪಿಂಗಳನಿಂ
ದಂತೆ ಪೆಸರ್ ಮಾಣವಕಂ. || 113 ||

101. Fourth instance: ◡ — ◡ | — ◡ — | ◡ —, the Cirampramâṇika (Pramâṇika). (Four Iambus' i. e. ◡ — | ◡ — | ◡ — | ◡ —)

ಚಿರಂಪ್ರಮಾಣಿಕಂ (ಪ್ರಮಾಣಿಕಂ)

ಜ-ರ-ಲ-ಗಂ. || 114[1] ||

102. Fifth instance: — ◡ — | — ◡ — | — — —, the Sṛitânanda (Sṛitânanta, Subhânanta).

ಶೃತಾನಂದಂ (ಶೃತಾನಂತಂ, ಶುಭಾನಂತಂ)

ರ-ರ-ಗ-ಗಂ. || 115[2] ||

103. Sixth instance: ◡ ◡ ◡ | — ◡ — | ◡ —, the Sumâlati.

ಸುಮಾಲತಿ

ನ-ರ-ಲ-ಗಂ. || 116[3] ||

9. Bṛihati. Quarters of 9 syllables; (64×8 i. e.)
512 vṛittas possible

ಬೃಹತಿಯೆಂಬ ಛಂದಸ್ಸಿನೊಳ್ 9 ಅಕ್ಕರ ಪಾದಮಾಗಿ ಪುಟ್ಟುವ 512 ವೃತ್ತಂಗಳೊಳಗೆ

104. First instance: — ◡ ◡ | — ◡ ◡ | — ◡ —, the Utsuka. (Two Dactyls and an Amphimacrus.)

ಉತ್ಸುಕಂ

ಇಂದು-ಯುಗಂಗಳ ಮುಂದೆ ಬಂ
ದೊಂದಿರೆ ವಹ್ನಿ ಪದಾಂತದೊಳ್, ।

1) M. gives two instances, both of different words but of the same feet, calling the one Pramâṇika, the other Cara(?) pramâṇika. H., Ra.'s instance has the name of Pramâṇika; Ro.'s, D.'s, B.'s Ciram pramâṇika. 2) M., H., Ra. Sṛitânanda; Ro., D. Sṛitânanta; B. Subhânanta.
3) Only in M. Of the six instances only two, the Mâṇavaka and Vidyunmâlĕ, are in Rb., and one that is too corrupt to find out the metre and name.

ಸುಂದರಿ, ಪಿಂಗಳನಿಪ್ಪದಿಂ
ಸಂದುದಿದುತ್ಸುಕ-ನಾಮಕಂ. || 117 ||

105. **Second instance:** — ᴗ — | ᴗ ᴗ ᴗ | ᴗ ᴗ —, **the Halamukhi (Halâmukha, Halâyudha).**

ಹಲಮುಖಿ (ಹಲಾಮುಖಂ. ಹಲಾಯುಧಂ)

ರಂ-ನ-ಸಂ ಹಲಮುಖಿಯಿರಲ್,
ಕಿಂನರೇಶ್ವರನೆ ಸಲಿದಾ |
ರಂನ-ಧಾರೆಯಲಿ ಗುಣ-ಸಂ
ಪಂನ-ಪದ್ಮ-(ನಿಭ-ನಯನಾ!) || 118[1] ||

106. **Third instance:** — ᴗ ᴗ | ᴗ — ᴗ | ᴗ ᴗ —, **the Udaya. (Trochee, Pyrrhich, Trochee, Pyrrhich, and a long syllable.)**

ಉದಯಂ

ಕೋಕನದವೈರಿ-ದಿನಪಂ
ಗಾ ಕಡೆಗೆ ವಾಯು ನಿಲೆ, ಕೇ |
ಳಾ, ಕಮಲ-ಲೋಚನೆ, ಪೆಸರ್
ಬರ್ಕುಮಿರದೆಂದುಮುದಯಂ. || 119 ||

107. **Fourth instance:** — ᴗ — | ᴗ ᴗ ᴗ | — ᴗ —, **the Bhadraka.**

ಭದ್ರಕಂ

ರೌದ್ರವಹ್ನಿ-ಸುರ-ಪಾವಕಂ
ಕ್ಷುದ್ರಮಲ್ಲದಿರೆ, ನಾಮದಿಂ |
ಭದ್ರಕಂ, ಸರಸಿಜಾನನೇ,
ಸದ್ರುತಂ ಲಯ-ಪದ-ಕ್ರಮಂ. || 120[2] ||

---

1) This is Rb.'s reading; that of all the other manuscripts is decidedly wrong, they introducing here the Bhadraka form (4). Rb. says the same as Pingala (VI., 9): ಹಲಮುಖೀ ರ್ನ್ಸೌ (i. e. ರ-ನ-ಸ) || H., Ra. have Hakâmukhi; Ro. Halâmukha; D., B., M. have Halâyudha. Ro., D., B. and M. repeat their form of 2 not only as that of 4, but after Bhujagaśiśu also as that of a Śrîvilâsini. 2) ಲಯ means "tempo" of which three are counted: ದ್ರುತ, quick; ಮಧ್ಯಮ, middle; ವಿಲಂಬಿತ, slow.

108. **Fifth instance:** – ◡ – | ◡ ◡ – | ◡ ◡ –, **the Vanaja.**

ವನಜಂ

ಪೋಗದಗ್ನಿ ಮರುತ್ತುಗಳಿಂ
ಯೋಗವಮಾಗಿರೆ, ಭಾವಿಸು, ಭೂ ।
ಭಾಗದೊಳ್, ಮೃಗ-ಲೋಚನೆ, ಕೇಳ್,
ನಾಗವರ್ಮನಿನೀ ವನಜಂ. || 121 ||

109. **Sixth instance:** ◡ ◡ ◡ | ◡ ◡ ◡ | – – –, **the Bhujagaśiśusṛita (— — pada, — — pari; — —sṛita only in M.).**

ಭುಜಗಶಿಶುಸೃತಂ

ಸ್ತಜಯಿಸೆ ನ-ನ-ಮಂ, ಮತ್ತಂ,
ಗಜಪತಿ-ಗಮನೇ, ವೃತ್ತಂ ।
ತ್ರಿಜಗದೊಳಿದು ಸಂಸಿದ್ಧಂ,
ಭುಜಗಶಿಶುಸ್ಸೃತಂ ನಾಮಮಂ. || 122 ||

110. **Seventh instance:** ◡ ◡ ◡ | ◡ ◡ ◡ | – ◡ –, **the Vinuta.**

ವಿನುತಂ

ನ-ನ-ಯುಗಮಿರೆ, ಪಾದಪಾ
ಶನ-ಗಣಮಿರೆಯೆನ್ನ ಕೋ ।
ಕನದ-ನಯನೆ, ಲೋಕದೊಳ್
ವಿನುತಮಿದುವೆ ನಾಮದಿಂ. || 123[1] ||

111. **Eighth instance:** ◡ ◡ ◡ | ◡ ◡ – | ◡ – –, **the Mayûra.**

ಮಯೂರಂ

ನ-ಸ-ಯಂ. || 124[2] ||

112. **Ninth instance:** ◡ – – | ◡ – – | ◡ – –, **the Bṛihati.**

ಬೃಹತಿ

ಯ-ಯ-ಯಂ. || 125[2] ||

---

1) **Not in H., Ra.; Ro. Vidruma.** 2) **Only in M.; its last words of v. 123 are:** ಕೇಳಿಂತ ದಕ್ಕಂ । ನಿಲಂತಾ ಬೃಹತ್ಯಾಖ್ಯವೆಂದುಂ. **Of the nine instances only Halamukhi and Utsuka are in Rb.**

10. Pankti. Quarters of 10 syllables; (128×8 *i. e.*) 1024 vrittas possible. (Hence the *Caesuras* are pointed out by the author)

ಪಂಕ್ತಿಯೆಂಬ ಛಂದಸ್ಸಿನೊಳ್ 10 ಅಕ್ಕರಂ ಪಾದಮಾಗಿ
ಪುಟ್ಟುವ 1024 ವೃತ್ತಂಗಳೊಳಗೆ. (ಪಂಕ್ತಿ ಮೊದಲ್ಗೊಂಡ ವೃತ್ತಗಳಲ್ಲಿ
ಯತಿಯನ್ನು ತೋಱಿಸಲಾಗಿದೆ)

113. First instance: — — — | ⏑ ⏑ ⏑ | ⏑ * — — | —, **the Paṇavaka; Caesura at 7 (giri).**

ಪಣವಕಂ

ಭೂ-ನಾಕಾಂತದೊಳಿರೆ* ತೋಯೇಶಂ,
ತಾನೆಂದುಂ ಪಣವಕ-*ನಾಮಂ, ಕೇಳ್! ।
ನೀನಿಂತೀ ತೆಱನಱಿ*ದೋದೆಂದುಂ,
ಮೀನಾಕ್ಷೀ, ಯತಿ ಗಿರಿ*ಯೊಳ್ ನಿಲ್ಕುಂ. || 126 ||

114. Second instance: — ⏑⏑ | — — — | ⏑⏑ — | — *, **the Mandânila; (Caesura at the end of the Quarters).**

ಮಂದಾನಿಲಂ

ಶೀತಕರೋರ್ವೀ-ಮಾರುತ-ಚೇತೋ *
ಜಾತ-ಹರು ಬಂದಿರ್ದೊಡಮಿಂತೀ * ।
ಭೂತಳಕೆಲ್ಲಂ ಸಂದುದಿದೆತ್ತಂ *,
ನೀತಿ-ಯುತೇ, ಮಂದಾನಿಲ-ವೃತ್ತಂ *. || 127 ||

115. Third instance: — — — | — * ⏑⏑ | ⏑⏑ * — | —, **the Matta; Caesura at 4 (yuga).**

ಮತ್ತಂ

ಮುಂನಂ ಧಾತ್ರೀ-*ಶಶಿ-ಪವ*ನೇಶೋ
ತ್ತುಂಸಂ; ನಿಲ್ಕುಂ * ಯತಿ ಯುಗ*ದೊಳ್; ಸೇ ।
ವ್ಯಂ ನವ್ಯಂ ಭೂ*ತಳಕಿದು *, ಪೂಜ್ಯಂ;
ಭಿಂನಾಬ್ಜಾಕ್ಷೀ *, ಪೆಸರಱಿ *! ಮತ್ತಂ. || 128 ||

116. **Fourth instance: — ⏑⏑ | — ⏑⏑ | — ⏑⏑ * —, the *C*itrapada; Caesura at 9 (randhra). (Three Dactyls and a long syllable.)**

ಚಿತ್ರಪದಂ

ಚಂದ್ರ-ಗಣಂ ಬರೆ ಮೂಱಿಡೆ*ಯೊಳ್,
ಚಂದ್ರಧರಂ ಬಳಿಕಾ ಕಡೆ*ಯೊಳ್; |
ರಂಧ್ರ-ಯತಿ-ಸ್ಥಿತಿ ಪಂಚಮ*ದೊಳ್,
ಚಂದ್ರ-ಮುಖೀ, ನಿಲೆ, ಚಿತ್ರಪ*ದಂ. || 129[1] ||

117. **Fifth instance: — ⏑ — | ⏑⏑ * — | ⏑⏑ — | — *, the Maṇiranga; Caesura at 5 (bhûta).**

ಮಣಿರಂಗಂ

ಪಾದಪಾಶನ-*ಮಾರುತಯುಗ್ಮಂ*,
ಪಾದದಂತದೊ*ಳೀಶ್ವರನಿರ್ಕುಂ*; |
ಕಾದಲೇ, ಯತಿ*ಭೂತದೊಳಿರ್ದುಂ*
ದೋದಿ ಕೊಳ್ಳಬ*ಲೇ! ಮಣಿರಂಗಂ*. || 130 ||

118. **Sixth instance: — — — | ⏑⏑ * — | ⏑ — ⏑ | — *., the Kalyâṇa; Caesura at 5 (bâṇa).**

ಕಲ್ಯಾಣಂ

ಕ್ಷೋಣೀ-ವಾಯು-ದಿ*ನೇಶ-ರುದ್ರನುಂ*;
ಬಾಣ-ಸ್ಥಾನದೊ*ಳಾಗಿ ವಿಶ್ರಮಂ*, |
ಜಾಣಿಂ ನಿಲ್ತಿರೆ*, ಸಂದುದಲ್ತೆ ಕ*
ಲ್ಯಾಣಂ, ಪಂಕಜ-*ಪತ್ರ-ಲೋಚನೇ*? || 131[2] ||

11. Trishṭubh. Quarters of 11 syllables; (256×8 *i. e.*) 2048 vṛittas possible

ತ್ರಿಷ್ಟುಪ್ ಎಂಬ ಛಂದಸ್ಸಿನೊಳ್ 11 ಅಕ್ಕರಂ ಪಾದಮಾಗಿ ಪುಟ್ಟುವ 2048 ವೃತ್ತಂಗಳೊಳಗೆ

119. **First instance: — — ⏑ | — — ⏑ | ⏑ — * ⏑ | — —, the Indravajra; Caesura at 8 (others at 5).**

ಇಂದ್ರವಜ್ರಂ

ವ್ಯೋಮ-ದ್ವಯಂ ಭಾನು-ಕಪ*ರ್ದಿಯುಗ್ಮಂ
ತಾಮಾಗಿರಲ್ಕೆಂಟನೆಯೊಳ್*ವಿರಾಮಂ; |

---

1) ಪಂಚಮದೊಳ್ = elegantly. 2) Of the six instances only Mandânila is in Rb.; its other instance bears the name of Bhûmâlê, but is quite corrupt.

ಈ ಮಾಳ್ಕೆಯಿಂದೋದಿದೊಡಿಂ*ದ್ರವಜ್ರಂ
ನಾಮಂ, ವಿಲೋಲಾಂಬುರುಹಾ*ಯತಾಕ್ಷೀ! || 132 [1] ||

120. Second instance: ⏑—⏑ | ——⏑ | ⏑—*⏑ | ——, the Upendravajra; Caesura at 8.

ಉಪೇಂದ್ರವಜ್ರಂ

ದಿನಾಧಿಪಂ ವ್ಯೋಮ-ರವೀ*ಶಯುಗ್ಮಂ
ಘನಂ ನಿಲಲ್ಕೆಂಟನೆಯೊಳ್*ವಿರಾಮಂ; |
ಸನಾತನೋಕ್ತಂ ಬಹು-ಕೀ*ರ್ತಿ-ಯುಕ್ತಂ,
ಘನಸ್ತನೀ, ಕೇಳ್, ಅದುಪೇಂ*ದ್ರವಜ್ರಂ. || 133 [2] ||

121. Third instance: —⏑— | ⏑—*⏑ | —⏑— | ⏑*—, the Sainika; Caesura at 5 (others at 8). (Five Trochees and a long syllable.)

ಸೈನಿಕಂ

ಪಾದಪಾಶನಾ*ರ್ಕ-ಪಾವಕಂ ಲ-*ಗಂ
ಪಾದಮಪ್ಪಿನಂ * ವಿರಾಮಮೆಯ್ದೆ*ಐಂ |
ಮೇದಿನೀ-ವಿಕಾ*ಸಮಾಗಿ ನಿಂದೊ*ಡಾ
ಮೋದ-ರೂಪೆ, ಕೇಳ್*, ಇದಿಂತು ಸೈನಿ*ಕಂ. || 134 [3] ||

122. Fourth instance: —⏑⏑ | —⏑⏑ | —⏑⏑ | ——*, the Dodhaka; Caesura at the end of the Quarters (pada). (Three Dactyls and a Spondee.)

ದೋಧಕಂ

ಇಂದು-ಗಣಂಗಳ ಮೂಱುವಱಿಂದಂ *
ಮುಂದೆ ಗುರು-ದ್ವಯಮಾಗೆ, ವಿರಾಮಂ * |
ಬಂದು ಪದಾಂತದೊಳಿರ್ದೊಡೆ, ಸಂಪೂ *
ರ್ಣೇಂದು-ಮುಖೀ, ಬಗೆ! ದೋಧಕ-ವೃತ್ತಂ. || 135 ||

123. Fifth instance: —⏑— | ⏑⏑⏑* | —⏑— | ⏑—, the Rathoddhatē; Caesura at 6 (rasa).

ರಥೋದ್ಧತೆ

ಮಾರುತೇಷ್ಟ-ದಿವಿ*ಜಾಗ್ನಿಯುಂ ಲ-ಗಂ
ಸಾರೆಯಾಗೆ, ರಸ*ದಲ್ಲಿ ವಿಶ್ರಮಂ |

1) D., B., Rc. have "Caesura at 5" (in a numeral); H., Ra., M. "Caesura at 8". 2) Ra., H. "Caesura at 5". 3) H., Ra. and M. "Caesura at 8"; the others "Caesura at 5".

ದೂರಮಲ್ಲದಿರೆ*, ಕೇಳ್, ರಥೋದ್ಧತೋ
ದಾರ-ನಾಮಮೆಸೆ*ಗುಂ, ರಥೋದ್ಧತೇ! || 136 ||

124. Sixth instance: ⏑⏑⏑ | ⏑⏑⏑ | –⏑*– | ⏑–, the *C*andrikĕ; Caesura at 6 (diś).

ಚಂದ್ರಿಕೆ

ಅಮರ-ಯುಗಮುಮಗ್ನಿ*ಯುಂ ಲ-ಗಂ
ಕ್ರಮದಿನೊಡನೆ ಬಂದು *ನಿಲ್ಕೆ, ವಿ |
ಶ್ರಮಣಮೆಸೆಯೆ ದಿಕ್-ಪ್ರ*ದೇಶದೊಳ್,
ಕಮಲ-ವದನೆ, ಚಂದ್ರಿ*ಕಾಹ್ವಯಂ. || 137 ||

125. Seventh instance: ––– | –*⏑⏑ | ⏑⏑*⏑ | ⏑–, the Bhramaravilasita; Caesura at 4 (?).

ಭ್ರಮರವಿಲಸಿತಂ

ಏಮಾತುರ್ಮ್ *ಶಶಿ-ದಿವಿ*ಜ-ಲ-ಗಂ
ತಾಮೆತ್ತಂ ಬಂ*ದಿರೆ, ಯತಿ-*ಚತುರೋ |
ದ್ದಾಮಂ ವೃತ್ತಂ*, ವರ-ವದ*ನ-ಯುತೇ,
ನಾಮಂ ಶ್ರೀಮದ್-*ಭ್ರಮರವಿ*ಲಸಿತಂ. || 138 ||

126. Eighth instance: –⏑– | ⏑⏑⏑ | –⏑*⏑ | ––, the Svâgata; Caesura at 8 (diśâgaja).

ಸ್ವಾಗತಂ

ಏಗಳುಂ ಯತಿ ದಿಶಾ-ಗ*ಜದೊಳ್ ನಿಂ
ದಾಗಳಗ್ನಿ ದಿವಿಜೇಂದು *ಹರರ್ ಸಂ |
ಯೋಗಮಾಗಿರೆ, ಪಯೋರು*ಹ-ವಕ್ತ್ರೇ,
ಸ್ವಾಗತಂ ನೆಗಳ್ದ ಪಿಂಗ*ಳನಿಂದಂ. || 139 ||

127. Ninth instance: ––– | ––⏑ | –*–⏑ | ––, the *S*âlini; Caesura at 7, as śaila is the same as parvata *i. e.* 7. (Giri is often = 8.)

ಶಾಲಿನಿ

ಭೂಮಿ-ವ್ಯೋಮದ್ವಂದ್ವ-ರು*ದ್ರದ್ವಯಂಗಳ್
ತಾಮೆತ್ತಂ ಚೆಲ್ವಾಗೆ, ಶೈ*ಲಂಗಳೊಳ್ ವಿ |
ಶ್ರಾಮಂ ನಿಲ್ವಂದಕ್ಕುಮು*ದ್ಗಂಧ-ಶಾಲೀ,
ಶ್ರೀಮದ್-ಗಂಧಂ ಶಾಲಿನೀ-*ನಾಮ-ವೃತ್ತಂ. || 140 ||

128. Tenth instance: — — — | ◡ ◡ — | ◡ — ◡ | — —, the Mâṇikya (=Caikarûpa); Caesura not pointed out.

ಮಾಣಿಕ್ಯಂ

ಮ-ಸ-ಜ-ಗ-ಗಂ. || 141[1] ||

129. Eleventh instance: — ◡ ◡ | — — ◡ | ◡ ◡ ◡ | — —, the Sândrapada.

ಸಾಂದ್ರಪದಂ

ಭ-ತ-ನ-ಗ-ಗಂ. || 142[1] ||

130. Twelfth instance: — — ◡ | — — ◡ | — — ◡ | — —, the Layagrâhî. (Three Antibacchicus' and a Spondee.)

ಲಯಗ್ರಾಹಿ

ತ-ತ-ತ-ಗ-ಗಂ. || 143[1] ||

131. Thirteenth instance: ◡ ◡ ◡ | ◡ — ◡ | ◡ — ◡ | ◡ —, the Sumukhî.

ಸುಮುಖಿ

ನ-ಜ-ಜ-ಲ-ಗಂ. || 144[2] ||

132. Fourteenth instance: ◡ ◡ ◡ | — ◡ — | — ◡ — | ◡ —, the Nîtikĕ (Gîtikĕ?).

ನೀತಿಕೆ

ನ-ರ-ರ-ಲ-ಗಂ. || 145[2] ||

133. Fifteenth instance: — ◡ ◡ | — — ◡ | ◡ ◡ ◡ | — —, the Śrî.

ಶ್ರೀ

ಭ-ತ-ನ-ಗ-ಗಂ. || 146[2] ||

1) These instances are only in M. 2) These are only in Rb. Besides these 3 there are in Rb. the verses 132, 133, 135, 136, 138, 139, 140.

12. Jagati. Quarters of 12 syllables; (512 × 8) *i.e.* 4096 vṛittas possible

ಜಗತಿಯೆಂಬ ಛಂದಸ್ಸಿನೊಳ್ 12 ಅಕ್ಕರಂ ಪಾದಮಾಗಿ ಪುಟ್ಟುವ 4096 ವೃತ್ತಂಗಳೊಳಗೆ

134. First instance: ⏑⏑⏑ | —⏑⏑ | —⏑⏑* | —⏑—, the **Drutapūrvavilambita; Caesura at 9 (randhra).**

ದ್ರುತಪೂರ್ವವಿಲಂಬಿತಂ

ನ-ಭ-ಭ-ರಂಗಳವೊಂದಿರೆ * ಪಾದದೊಳ್,
ಶುಭಕರಂ ಯತಿ ನಿಲ್ತಿರೆ * ರಂಧ್ರದೊಳ್, ।
ಪ್ರಭು-ಕವೀಂದ್ರ-ಸಹಾಯದಿ * ನಾದುದಿಂ
ತಿಭ-ಗತೀ, ದ್ರುತಪೂರ್ವವಿ*ಲಂಬಿತಂ. ॥ 147 ॥

135. Second instance: ⏑⏑— | ⏑⏑— | ⏑⏑— | ⏑⏑—*, the **Toṭaka; Caesura at 12 (divasādhipa). (Four Anapaests.)**

ತೋಟಕಂ

ಪವಮಾನ-ಚತುಷ್ಕ-ಯುತಂ, ಯತಿಯುಂ *
ದಿವಸಾಧಿಪರೊಳ್ ನಿಲೆ, ವಸ್ತು-ಕವಿ-* ।
ಪ್ರವರ-ಸ್ತುತಮಪ್ಪುದು ತೋಟಕಮೆಂ *
ದವಧಾರಿಸು ನೀನ್ ಅದನಬ್ಜ-ಮುಖೀ*! ॥ 148 ॥

136. Third instance: ⏑—— | ⏑—— | ⏑—*— | ⏑——, the **Bhujaṅgaprayāta; Caesura at 8 (diśā). (Four Bacchicus'.)**

ಭುಜಂಗಪ್ರಯಾತಂ

ಕುಶಂ ವಾರ್ಧಿ-ಪರ್ಯಾಯಮು*ಕ್ಕುಂ; ವಿರಾಮಂ
ದಿಶಾ-ಸಂಖ್ಯೆಯಕ್ಕುಂ; ಪಯೋ*ಜಾಯತಾಕ್ಷೀ, ।
ವಿಶೇಷಂ ಕವೀಂದ್ರ-ಸ್ತುತಂ * ಪಿಂಗಳಂ-ಬೋಲ್
ಪ್ರಶಸ್ತಂ ಸಮಸ್ತಂ ಭುಜಂ*ಗಪ್ರಯಾತಂ. ॥ 149 ॥

137. Fourth instance: ⏑—⏑ | ——⏑ | ⏑*—⏑ | —⏑—, the **Vaṁśastha; Caesura at 7.**

ವಂಶಸ್ಥಂ

ದಿವಾಕರಾಕಾಶ-ದಿ*ನೇಶ-ಪಾವಕರ್;
ಸುವಿಶ್ರಮಂ ಬಂದಿರೆ * ಸಪ್ತ-ಸಂಖ್ಯೆಯೊಳ್, ।

ಸವಿಸ್ತರಂ ನಿಲ್ತಿರೆ,* ಸಂದುದಿಂತುದಾ
ತ್ತ-ವಂಶೆ, ವಂಶಸ್ಥಮಿ*ದುರ್ವಿ-ಭಾಗದೊಳ್. || 150 ||

138. **Fifth instance:** — — ⏑ | — — ⏑ | ⏑ —*⏑ | — ⏑ —, **the Indravaṁśa; Caesura at 8 (digdanti).**

ಇಂದ್ರವಂಶಂ

ವ್ಯೋಮ-ದ್ವಯಂ, ಮುಂತೆ ದಿನೇ*ಶ-ಪಾವಕರ್
ತಾವೊಂದೆ, ದಿಗ್-ದಂತಿಯೊಳಾ*ಗೆ ವಿಶ್ರಮಂ, ।
ಶ್ರೀಮಾನಿನೀ, ಸಯ್ಯಡಿಯಾ*ತನಿಂದಿದಂ
ನಾಮೋಪಮಂ ಮಾಡಿದನಿಂ*ದ್ರವಂಶಮಂ. || 151 ||

139. **Sixth instance:** — ⏑ — | — ⏑ — | — ⏑ — | — ⏑ —, **the Sragviṇi; Caesura not indicated. (Four Amphimacrus'.)**

ಸ್ರಗ್ವಿಣಿ

ಜಾತವೇದೋ-ಗಣಂಗಳ್ ಚತುಃ-ಸ್ಥಾನ-ಸಂ
ಜಾತಮಾಗುತ್ತುಮಿರ್ದಂದಿನಂತಾದೊಡಾ ।
ಜಾತಮಂ ಸ್ರಗ್ವಿಣೀ-ವೃತ್ತಮೆಂಬರ್, ಜಗತ್-
ಖ್ಯಾತಮಂಭೋಜ-ಪತ್ರೋಪಮಾನೇಕ್ಷಣೇ! || 152 ||

140. **Seventh instance:** ⏑ ⏑ ⏑ | — ⏑ ⏑ | ⏑*— ⏑ | — ⏑ —. **the Nirupama; Caesura at 7 (dineśahaya), or 8 (diśâgaja, according to M.).**

ನಿರುಪಮಂ

ಸುರಪುರೇಂದು-ದಿವ್* ಸಾಧಿಪಾಗ್ನಿಗಳ್
ಬರೆ, ದಿನೇಶ-ಹಯ*ದೊಳ್ ವಿರಾಮಮಾ ।
ಗಿರೆ, ಪೆಸರ್ ನೆಗಳೆ* ಪಿಂಗಳೋಕ್ತಿಯೊಳ್
ನಿರುಪಮಂ, ನಿರುಪ್*ಮಾನ-ವಿಭ್ರಮಂ. || 153 ||

141. **Eighth instance:** ⏑ ⏑ ⏑ | — ⏑ ⏑ | ⏑*— ⏑ | ⏑ — —, **the Drutapada; Caesura at 7 (śaila).**

ದ್ರುತಪದಂ

ಶತಮುಖೇಂದು-ರವಿ-*ತೋಯ-ಗಣಂ ಪ
ದ್ಧತಿಯೊಳಾಗೆ, ಯತಿ*ಶೈಲದೊಳಕ್ಕುಂ; ।

ಶತ-ದಳಾಯತ-ಸು*ಲೋಚನೆ, ವೃತ್ತಂ
ದ್ರುತಪದಂ ಮೃದು-ವ*ದೋಕ್ತಿಗಳಿಂದಂ. || 154 ||

142. Ninth instance: ⏑⏑⏑ | ⏑—⏑ | ⏑* —⏑ | ⏑——, the Lalitapada; Caesura at 7 (kulagiri).

ಲಲಿತಪದಂ

ಕುಲಿಶಧರಾರ್ಕ-ಯು*ಗಂಗಳ ಮುಂದಂ
ಜಲ-ಗಣಮೊಪ್ಪಿರೆ*, ಬಂದು ವಿರಾಮಂ ।
ಕುಲಗಿರಿಯೊಳ್ ನಿಲೆ*, ಪಿಂಗಳನಿಂದಂ
ಲಲಿತಪದಂ ಪೆಸ*ರಿಂ, ಲಲಿತಾಂಗೀ! || 155 ||

143. Tenth instance: —⏑— | ⏑⏑⏑* | —⏑⏑ | ⏑⏑—, the Candrike; Caesura at 6.

ಚಂದ್ರಿಕೆ (ಚಂದ್ರಿ)

ರ-ನ-ಭ-ಸಂ || ಉಸಿರ್ ಆಱು ನೆಲೆಯೊಳ್. || 156[1] ||

144. Eleventh instance: —⏑⏑ | —⏑⏑ | —⏑— | ⏑——, the Hamsamatta (Hamsi, Hamsakeḷi?); Caesura not pointed out.

ಹಂಸಮತ್ತಂ

ಭ-ಭ-ರ-ಯಂ. || 157[2] ||

145. Twelfth instance; ⏑⏑— | ⏑—⏑* | ⏑⏑— | ⏑⏑—, the Pravarâkshara (Pravitâkshara); Caesura at 6.

ಪ್ರವರಾಕ್ಷರಂ (ಪ್ರವಿತಾಕ್ಷರಂ)

ಸ-ಜ-ಸ-ಸಂ || ವಿರಾಮಮಾಱನೆಯೊಳ್. || 158[3] ||

146. Thirteenth instance: ⏑⏑⏑ | ⏑⏑⏑ | —* —— | ⏑——, the Puṭa (Ghaṭa); Caesura at 7.

ಪುಟಂ (ಘಟಂ)

ನ-ನ-ಮ-ಯಂ || ಯತಿ ಸಪ್ತಸ್ಥಾನದೊಳ್. || 159[4] ||

1) In M., Rc., D., B. (Candri); the Caesura only in Rc. (and D.). 2) Only in Rc. (Hamsi), H., Ra.; and D. (Hamsa kaḷâ?). 3) Only in Rc. (Pravarâkshara), M. (Pravitâkshara) and D. (Pravarâkshara). 4) Rc. (Puṭa), M., D. (Puṭa).

147. Fourteenth instance: ⏑—⏑ | ⏑⏑— | ⏑—⏑ | ⏑⏑—, the Jaloddhatĕ,—dhata; Caesura not pointed out. (Amphibrachys, Anapaestus, Amphibrachys, Anapaestus.)

ಜಲೋದ್ಧತೆ (ಜಲೋದ್ಧತ)

ಜ-ಸ-ಜ-ಸಂ. || 160 [1] ||

148. Fifteenth instance: ——— | ——*— | ⏑—— | ⏑*——, the Vaiśvadeva (—vi); Caesura at 5 (kâmâstra).

ವೈಶ್ವದೇವಂ (ವೈಶ್ವದೇವಿ)

ಮ-ಮ-ಯ-ಯಂ || ವಿಶ್ರಾಮಂ ಕಾಮಾಸ್ತ್ರದೊಳ್. || 161 [2] ||

149. Sixteenth instance: ⏑⏑⏑ | ⏑—— | ⏑⏑⏑ | ⏑——, the Kusumavičitra; Caesura not pointed out. (Tribrachys, Bacchicus, Tribrachys, Bacchicus.) Cf. v. 808.

ಕುಸುಮವಿಚಿತ್ರಂ

ನ-ಯ-ನ-ಯಂ. || 162 [3] ||

13. Atijagati. Quarters of 13 syllables; (1024×8 *i. e.*) 8192 vṛittas possible

ಅತಿಜಗತಿಯೆಂಬ ಛಂದಸ್ಸಿನೊಳ್ 13 ಅಕ್ಕರಂ ಪಾದಮಾಗಿ ಪುಟ್ಟುವ 8192 ವೃತ್ತಂಗಳೊಳಗೆ

150. First instance: ⏑—⏑ | —⏑⏑ | ⏑⏑— | ⏑—⏑ | —, the Ručira; Caesura not pointed out.

ರುಚಿರಂ

ದಿನೇಶ-ಚಂದ್ರ-ಪವನ-ಭಾನು-ರುದ್ರರೊಂ
ದಿ ನಿಲ್ವುದುಂ, ವಿಳಸಿತ-ಪದ್ಮ-ಪತ್ರ-ಲೋ ।
ಚನೇ, ಕರಂ ಸಕಲ-ಕವೀಂದ್ರರೊಲ್ಮೆಯಿಂ
ಸುನಿಶ್ಚಿತಂ, ರುಚಿರಮಿದಾಗವೋಕ್ತಿಯಿಂ. || 163 [4] ||

151. Second instance: ⏑⏑⏑ | —⏑⏑ | —⏑⏑ | —⏑⏑ | —, the Ačyuta (Abhyudita, Abhyudaya); Caesura at 4 (ambudhi), or 5 (bâṇa, in Rc. and D.; H., Ra. ânanda).

ಅಚ್ಯುತಂ

ನಗಹರೇಂದು-ಗಣ-ತ್ರಿತಯಾಗ್ರ-ಹರಂ
ಸೊಗಸಿ ಕೂಡಿರೆ, ನಿಂದೊಡೆ ವಿಶ್ರಮಣಂ ।

1) Rc., M., D. 2) Only in Rc. and D. 3) Only in Rb.; besides this it has only Nos. 136 and 137. H., Ra. have only Nos. 134. 135. 138. 141. 142. 144. 4) In H., Ra., Rc., M., D., B.

ನೆಗಳಿದಂಬುಧಿಯಲ್ಲಿದು ಪಿಂಗಳನಿಂ,
ಮೃಗ-ನಿಭೇಕ್ಷಣೆ, ನಾಮದೊಳಚ್ಯುತಮುಂ. || 164[1] ||

152. **Third instance:** ⏑⏑⏑ | ⏑—⏑ | ⏑—* ⏑ | —⏑— | —, **the Prabhâta; Caesura at 8 (vasu).**

ಪ್ರಭಾತಂ

ನ-ಜ-ಜ-ರ-ಗಂ || ವಿರಾಮಂ ವಸುವಿಂ. || 165[2] ||

153. **Fourth instance:** —⏑⏑ | —⏑⏑ | —⏑⏑* | —⏑⏑ | —, **the Komalaručira (M. Komala); Caesura at 9 (nidhi). (Four Dactyls and a long syllable.)**

ಕೋಮಲರುಚಿರಂ

ಭ-ಭ-ಭ-ಭ-ಗಂ || ವಿಶ್ರಾಮಂ ನಿಧಿ-ಸಂಖ್ಯೆಯೊಳ್. || 166[3] ||

154. **Fifth instance:** —⏑⏑ | ——⏑ | ⏑* —⏑ | —⏑⏑ | —, **the Saundarî (M. Sundara); Caesura at 7 (muni).**

ಸೌಂದರಿ

ಭ-ತ-ಜ-ಭ-ಗಂ || ವಿಶ್ರಮಂ ಮುನಿ-ಸಂಖ್ಯೆಯೊಳ್. || 167[4] ||

155. **Sixth instance:** —⏑⏑ | ⏑—* ⏑ | ⏑⏑— | ⏑⏑— | —, **the Ambuja; Caesura at 5 (śara).**

ಅಂಬುಜಂ

ಭ-ಜ-ಸ-ಸ-ಗಂ || ಶರದಿಂದೆ ವಿರಾಮಂ. || 168[5] ||

156. **Seventh instance:** ⏑⏑— | ⏑—⏑ | ⏑⏑— | ⏑—⏑ | —, **the Mañjubhâshiṇî (?).**

ಮಂಜುಭಾಷಿಣಿ

ಸ-ಜ-ಸ-ಜ-ಗಂ. || 169[6] ||

157. **Eighth instance:** ——— | ——⏑ | ⏑——* | ⏑⏑— | —, **the Mattamayûra; Caesura at 9 (nidhi).**

ಮತ್ತಮಯೂರಂ

ಎತ್ತಂ ಧಾತ್ರಿ-ವ್ಯೋಮ-ಪಯೋ-ವಾ*ಯು-ಹರರ್ಕಳ್
ಪತ್ತಿರ್ದಾಗಳ್ ಬಂದು, ವಿರಾಮಂ*ನಿಧಿಯೊಳ್ ಮೇ ।

1) H. Ra. (abhyudita), Rb., Rc., M. (abhyudaya), D., B. 2) Not in Rb.; M. has prabhuvitta. 3) Not in Rb. 4) Not in Rb. 5) Only in M. 6) Only in Rb.; it has also a Mangalikâ, but corrupt; its first line has the form: S-J-S-S-G.

ಯ್ತಿತ್ರೊಪ್ಪುತ್ತಂ ಬಂದಿರಲಾಗಳ್ * ಪೆಸರಿಂದು
ವೃತ್ತಂ ಸಂದಿರ್ದಪ್ಪುದು, ಕೇಳ್, ಮ*ತ್ತಮಯೂರಂ. || 170[1] ||

14. *Sakvari.* Quarters of 14 syllables; (2048×8 *i. e.*) 16384 vrittas possible

ಶಕ್ವರಿಯೆಂಬ ಛಂದಸ್ಸಿನೊಳ್ 14 ಅಕ್ಕರಂ ಪಾದಮಾಗಿ ಪುಟ್ಟುವ 16384 ವೃತ್ತಂಗಳೊಳಗೆ

158. First instance: — — ⏑ | — ⏑ ⏑ | ⏑ — ⏑ | ⏑ — ⏑ | — —*, the Vasantatilaka; Caesura at the Quarter's (pada) end (D., B. at 8).

ವಸಂತತಿಲಕಂ

ವ್ಯೋಮೇಂದು-ಭಾನುಗಣಾಯುಗ್ಮದಿನತ್ತಲಕ್ಕಂ *
ಸೋಮೇಶ್ವರ-ದ್ವಿತಯಮಂತವಱಿ*ೊಳ್ ವಿರಾಮಂ * |
ಸಾಮಾನ್ಯಮಲ್ಲದು, ಪದಾಂತದೊಳನ್ವಿತಾರ್ಥಂ*;
ನಾಮಂ ವಸಂತತಿಲಕಂ, ಕಮಲಾಯತಾಕ್ಷೀ*! || 171[2] ||

159. Second instance: ⏑ ⏑ ⏑ | ⏑ ⏑ ⏑ | —* ⏑ ⏑ | ⏑ ⏑ ⏑ | ⏑ —, the Praharaṇakalita (B.); Caesura at 7 (hayatati).

ಪ್ರಹರಣಕಲಿತಂ

ನ-ನ-ಭ-ನ-ಲ-ಗಮೆಂ*ಬಿವು ಗಣ-ನಿಯಮಂ
ಜನಿಯಿಸೆ, ಯತಿ ನಿ*ಲ್ತಿರೆ ಹಯ-ತತಿಯೊಳ್, |
ನಿನಗದನಱಿ*ವಂ*ತಿರೆ ವಿರಚಿಸಿದೆಂ;
ವನರುಹ-ವದನೇ*, ಪ್ರಹರಣಕಲಿತಂ. || 172[3] ||

160. Third instance: ⏑ ⏑ ⏑ | — ⏑ ⏑ | — ⏑ —* | ⏑ ⏑ — | ⏑ —, the Kusumâṅghripa; Caesura at 9 (nidhi).

ಕುಸುಮಾಂಘ್ರಿಪಂ

ತ್ರಿದಶ-ಚಂದ್ರ-ಹುತಾಶನಾ * ನಿಲರುಂ ಲ-ಗಂ
ಪುದಿದು ಕೊಂಡಿರೆ, ವಿಶ್ರಮಂ * ನಿಧಿಯೊಳ್ ಬೆಡಂ |

1) Not in Rb.; Ra., H. have manmathamayûra; D. and Rc. only mayûra. 2) In Ra., Rb., Rc., M., D., B. 3) Instead of ಪ್ರಹರಣಕಲಿತಂ D. has -ಕವಿತಂ, M. and Rc. have -ತಿಲಕಂ, H., Ra., Rb. -ಕಳಿಕೆ.

ಗೊಡವಿ ಬಂದಿರೆ, ನಾಗವ*ರ್ಮನಿನಾದುದ
ಭ್ಯುದಯ-ಕಾರಣವೋಪಳೇ*, ಕುಸುಮಾಂಘ್ರಿಪಂ. || 173[1] ||

161. Fourth instance:—⏑⏑ | ⏑—⏑ | ⏑⏑— | ⏑⏑⏑ | ——*, **the Vanamayûra; Caesura at Quarter's (pada) end.**

ವನಮಯೂರಂ

ಬಂದಿರೆ ಸರೋಜರಿಪು ಭಾನು ಮರುದಿಂದ್ರಂ*,
ಮುಂದಿರೆ ಹರ-ದ್ವಯ-ಗಣಂ, ವಿಮಲ-ಸಂಪೂ* |
ರ್ಣೇಂದು-ವದನೇ, ಯತಿ ಪದಾಂತದೊಳೆ ನಿಂದಂ*
ದೆಂದುಮಿದು, ಕೇಳ್, ಪೆಸರಿನಿಂ ವನಮಯೂರಂ*. || 174[2] ||

162. Fourth instance again:—⏑⏑ | ⏑—⏑ | ⏑⏑— | ⏑⏑⏑ | ——, **the Vanamayûra as Kuṭmala (not Kuḍmala); Caesura at 5 (pañcama, in Rc.; in M. campaka), or at 4 (or 7? vârudhi=vârdhi, in D. and B.).**

ಕುಟ್ಮಲಮೆಂಬ ವನಮಯೂರಂ

ಭ-ಜ-ಸ-ನ-ಗ-ಗಂ || ಯತಿ ಪಂಚಮದೊಳ್, ಅಥವಾ ವಾರುಧಿಯೊಳ್. || 175[3] ||

163. Fifth instance:—⏑⏑ | —⏑⏑ | —⏑— | ⏑⏑— | ⏑—, **the Saundara (M. guṇa saundara), Caesura at mṛigendra (Rc.), anindra (Ra.), anendra (D.), agendra (=kulagiri, 8? H., M.).**

ಸೌಂದರಂ

ಭ-ಭ-ರ-ಸ-ಲ-ಗಂ (ವಿಶ್ರಮಣಂ ಅಗೇಂದ್ರದೊಳ್). || 176[4] ||

15. Atiśakvari. Quarters of 15 syllables; (4096×8 *i.e.*) 32768 vṛittas possible

ಅತಿಶಕ್ವರಿಯೆಂಬ ಛಂದಸ್ಸಿನೊಳ್ 15 ಅಕ್ಕರಂ ಪಾದಮಾಗಿ ಪುಟ್ಟುವ 32768 ವೃತ್ತಂಗಳೊಳಗೆ

164. First instance: ⏑⏑⏑ | ⏑⏑⏑ | ——*— | ⏑—— | ⏑——, **the Mâlini; Caesura at 8.**

ಮಾಲಿನಿ

ಅಮರ-ಗಣ-ಯುಗಂಗಳ್*, ಮುಂತೆ ಭೂ-ತೋಯಯುಗ್ಮಂ
ಕ್ರಮದೆ ನಿಲೆ, ಬೆಡಂಗಂ*ತಾಳ್ದಿ ಬಂದಾ ವಿರಾಮಂ |

1) In H., Ra., Rc., D., M., B. 2) Ra., Rb., Rc., D., B., M.; D. puts the Caesura at gaja, B. at aja. 3) Rc., M., D., B. 4) Not in Rb. and B.

ವಿಮಲಮೆನಿಸಲೆಂಟಱೆ *ಬಲ್ಲಿ ನಿಲ್ತಂದೊಡಕ್ಕುಂ,
ಸಮುದ-ವನಿತೆ, ನೀಂ ಕೇಳ್*, ಮಾಲಿನೀ-ನಾಮ-ವೃತ್ತಂ. || 177[1] ||

165. **Second instance:** ⏑⏑⏑ | ⏑⏑⏑ | ⏑⏑*⏑ | ⏑⏑⏑ | ⏑⏑—, **the Maṇigaṇanikara; (Caesura according to D. and B. at vasumati *i. e.* 8). (Seven Pyrrhichs and a long syllable.)**

ಮಣಿಗಣನಿಕರಂ

ಸುರಪುರ-ಗಣಮೆಸೆ*ದಿರೆ ಜಲನಿಧಿಯೊಳ್,
ಮರುತನುಮವಱೊಳೆ *ಬೆರಸಿರೆ ತುದಿಯೊಳ್, |
ಸುರಚಿತ-ಮಣಿ-ಗಣ-*ನಿಕರ-ವಿಲಸಿತೇ,
ಸುರುಚಿರಮಿದನಱಿ*, ಮಣಿಗಣನಿಕರಂ. || 178[1] ||

166. **Third instance:** ⏑⏑⏑ | ⏑⏑— | ⏑⏑⏑ | —⏑*⏑ | ⏑——, **the Vičitralalita (Palâśadaḷa); Caesura at 11 (hara; according to B. at randhra).**

ವಿಚಿತ್ರಲಲಿತಂ

ತ್ರಿದಶ-ಮರುದಿಂದ್ರಪುರ-ಚಂದ್ರ-*ಸಲಿಲಂಗಳ್
ತುದಿಯೊಳಿರೆ, ತಳ್ತು ಹರರಲ್ಲಿ*ಯತಿ ನಿಲ್ಕುಂ; |
ವಿದಿತಮಿದು ಧಾರುಣಿಯೊಳಬ್ಜ-*ದಳ-ನೇತ್ರೇ,
ಸದಮಲ-ವಿಚಿತ್ರಲಲಿತಂ, ಲ*ಲಿತ-ಗಾತ್ರೇ! || 179[2] ||

167. **Fourth instance:** —⏑— | ⏑⏑⏑ | —⏑⏑ | —⏑⏑ | —⏑—*, **the Maṇivibhûshaṇa; Caesura at Quarter's (pada) end.**

ಮಣಿವಿಭೂಷಣಂ

ಪಾವಕೇಂದ್ರ-ಶಶಿಯುಗ್ಮದಿನತ್ತ ಹುತಾಶನಂ*
ಭಾವಿಸುತ್ತಿರೆ, ಪದಾಂತದೊಳಿರ್ದೊಡೆ ವಿಶ್ರಮಂ*, |
ದೇವಿ, ಚಾರು-ನಯನೇ, ನುತ-ಕೀರ್ತಿ-ಕವೀಂದ್ರ-ಸಂ*
ಭಾವಿತಂ ಮಣಿವಿಭೂಷಣಮೆಂದಱಿ ನೀನ್ ಇದಂ*! || 180[3] ||

168. **Fifth instance:** ⏑⏑⏑ | ⏑—⏑ | —⏑⏑ | ⏑—⏑ | —⏑—*, **the Suraṅga Kesara, Sukesara (M., Ra., H.) or Kesara (Rc.); Caesura at Quarter's end.**

1) H., Ra., Rb., Rc., M., D., B. 2) H., Ra., Rc., M., B. and Rb.; Rb. calls it palâśadaḷa.
3) Ra., Rc., M., D., B., H.

ಸುರಂಗಕೇಸರಂ

ಅಮರ-ಗಣಾರ್ಕ-ಶೀತಕರ-ಭಾನು-ಪಾವಕೋ-*
ತ್ತಮ-ಗಣ-ಪಂಚಕಂ, ಕಡೆಯೆ ಚೆಲ್ವುವೆತ್ತ ವಿ* ।
ಶ್ರಮಮಿದನಾಗಳುಂ ಕವಿಗಳೋದುತಿರ್ಪರೆ*
ನ್ನ ಮನಸಿನೊಪ ಕಾಂತೆಯೆ, ಸುರಂಗಕೇಸರಂ*. ॥ 181[1] ॥

169. Sixth instance: ⏑⏑⏑ | ⏑ — ⏑ | ⏑ — ⏑ | — * ⏑⏑ | —⏑—, the Navanaḷina; Caesura at 10.

ನವನಳಿನಂ

ದಿವಿಜ-ದಿನಾಧಿಪಯುಗ್ಮ-ಶೀ*ತಕರಾಗ್ನಿಯಿಂ
ಬಿವು ನೆರೆದಿಂಬನೆ ಬಂದೊಡಾ* ಯತಿ ಹತ್ತಱಿ ।
ತ್ತವತರಿಸಿದೊರ್ಡಮಂಬುಜಾ*ಯತ-ಲೋಚನೇ,
ನವನಳಿನಂ ಕವಿ-ರಾಜಹಂ*ಸ-ವಿನಿರ್ಮಿತಂ. ॥ 182[2] ॥

16. Ashṭi. Quarters of 16 syllables; 65536 vṛittas possible

ಅಷ್ಟಿಯೆಂಬ ಛಂದಸ್ಸಿನೊಳ್ 16 ಅಕ್ಕರಂ ಪಾದಮಾಗಿ ಪುಟ್ಟುವ 65536 ವೃತ್ತಂಗಳೊಳಗೆ

170. First instance: ⏑⏑⏑ | ⏑⏑⏑ | ⏑⏑⏑ | ⏑ * — ⏑ | ⏑⏑ — | —, the Lalitapada; Caesura at 10.

ಲಲಿತಪದಂ

ಕುಲಿಶಧರ-ಪುರ-ದಿನಪ-*ಮಾರುತ-ಹರಾಂತಂ
ನೆಲಸಿ ನಿಲೆ, ಯತಿ ದಶದೊ*ಳಿರ್ದೊಡೆ ನಿತಾಂತಂ ।
ಸಲೆ ನೆಲಕೆ ಪರೆದುದಿದ* ನೋದಬಲೆ, ಸಂತಂ
ಲಲಿತಪದಮುಚಿತ-ಪದ-*ಯುಕ್ತಮತಿಕಾಂತಂ. ॥ 183[3] ॥

171. Second instance: — ⏑⏑ | — ⏑⏑ | — ⏑⏑ | — ⏑⏑ * | — ⏑⏑ | —, the Jagadvandita; Caesura at 12 (bhâskara). (Five Dactyls and a long syllable.)

ಜಗದ್ವಂದಿತಂ

ಇಂದು-ಗಣಂ ಶರ-ಸಂಖ್ಯೆಯೊಳೊಂದಿರೆ*, ಚಂದ್ರಧರಂ
ಬಂದು ಪದಾಂತದೊಳಿರ್ದೊಡೆ, ಭಾಸ್ಕರ*ರೊಳ್ ಯತಿಯುಂ ।

1) H., Ra. (sukesara), Rc. (heading: suranga kesara), M., D., B. 2) Not in H., Ra., Rb. and M. 3) Ra., Rb., Rc., M., B., D., H.

ನಿಂದು ವಿರಾಜಿಸೆ, ಪಿಂಗಳನಿಂ ಪರಿ*ದತ್ತು ಜಗ
ದ್ವಂದಿತಮಿಂತಿದನೋದುವುದಿಂಬಿನ*ಪದ್ಮ-ಮುಖೀ! || 184[1] ||

172. Third instance: ⏑⏑⏑ | — ⏑⏑ | ⏑ — * ⏑ | ⏑—⏑ | ⏑—⏑ | —, the Maṅgaḷa; Caesura at 8 (danti).

ಮಂಗಳಂ

ನ-ಭ-ಜ-ಜ-ಜ-ಗಂ || ಯತಿ ದಂತಿಯೊಳ್. || 185[2] ||

173. Fourth instance: ⏑—— | ——— | ⏑⏑⏑ | ⏑⏑— * | —⏑— | —, the Vijayânanda; Caesura at 12 (divasakara, dinakara).

ವಿಜಯಾನಂದಂ

ಯ-ಮ-ನ-ಸ-ರ-ಗಂ || ಯತಿ ದಿವಸಕರದೊಳ್. || 186[2] ||

174. Fifth instance: ⏑—⏑ | —⏑— | ⏑—⏑ | —⏑— | ⏑—⏑ | —, the Pañcacâmara.

ಪಂಚಚಾಮರಂ

ಜ-ರ-ಜ-ರ-ಜ-ಗಂ. || 187[3] ||

17. Atyashṭi. Quarters of 17 syllables; 131072 vṛittas possible.

(If the Jagadvandita v. 184 were put under this head and a long syllable added, a true Hexameter would be produced.)

ಅತ್ಯಷ್ಟಿಯೆಂಬ ಛಂದಸ್ಸಿನೊಳ್ 17 ಅಕ್ಕರಂ ಪಾದಮಾಗಿ ಪುಟ್ಟುವ 131072 ವೃತ್ತಂಗಳೊಳಗೆ

175. First instance: ——— | —⏑⏑ | ⏑⏑⏑ | — * —⏑ | ——⏑ | ——, the Mandâkrânta; Caesura at 10.

ಮಂದಾಕ್ರಾಂತಂ

ಕಾಂತೇ, ಧಾತ್ರೀ-ಹಿಮಕ್ಕದಮರಾ*ಕಾಶ-ಯುಗ್ಮೇಶ-ಯುಗ್ಮಂ
ಮುಂತಂ ಬಂದೀ ಪದದ ಕಡೆಯೊಳ್* ಚಲ್ವನಾಂತಿರ್ದೊಡಂ, ವಿ |
ಶ್ರಾಂತಂ ನಿಲ್ಕುಂ ದಶಮದೆಡೆಯೊಳ್*; ಯವ್ವನಾಕ್ರಾಂತೆ, ಮಂದಾ
ಕ್ರಾಂತಂ ವೃತ್ತಂ ನೆಗಳ್ದದಿಳೆಯೊಳ್*ಪಿಂಗಳ-ಪ್ರೋಕ್ತಿಯಿಂದಂ! || 188[4] ||

1) H., Ra., Rc., M., D., B. 2) H., Ra., Rc., M., D., Sb. 3) Only in Rb. 4) Not in Rb.

176. Second instance: ⏑ — ⏑ | ⏑⏑ — | ⏑ — * ⏑ | ⏑⏑ — | ⏑ — — | ⏑ —, the Pṛithvi; Caesura at 8 (vasu; according to M. at yati).

ಪೃಥ್ವಿ

ಇನಾನಿಲ-ದಿನೇಶ-ಮಾ*ರುತ-ಪಯೋ-ಲ-ಗಂಗಳ್ ಬೆಡಂ
ಗನಾಳ್ದು ನಿಲೆ, ವಿಶ್ರಮಂ * ವಸುಗಳಲ್ಲಿ ಚಲ್ವಾದೊಡಂ ।
ದು, ನೀರಜ-ದಳೇಕ್ಷಣೇ*, ಬಗೆದು ಕೇಳ್ ಇದಂ! ಪೃಥ್ವಿಯೆಂ
ಬ ನಾಮದೊಳಿದಲ್ತೆ ಸಂ*ದುದು ನಿರಂತರಂ ಪೃಥ್ವಿಯೊಳ್? ‖ 189[1] ‖

177. Third instance: ⏑ — — | — — —* | ⏑⏑⏑ | ⏑⏑ — | — ⏑⏑ | ⏑ —, the Śikhariṇi; Caesura at 6.

ಶಿಖರಿಣಿ

ಯ-ಮ-ನ-ಸ-ಭ-ಲ-ಗಂ ‖ ವಿಶ್ರಮಂ ಆಱಿಂಬಳ್ಳಿ. ‖ 190[2] ‖

178. Fourth instance: ⏑⏑⏑ | ⏑⏑ —* | — — — | — ⏑ — | ⏑⏑ — | ⏑ —, the Hariṇîpluta; Caesura at 6 (shaṭka).

ಹರಿಣೀಪ್ಲುತಂ

ಕುಲಿಶಧರ-ವಾ*ತೋರ್ವೀ-ವೈಶ್ವಾನರಾನಿಲರಂತದೊಳ್
ನೆಲಸೆ ಹರಿಯುಂ * ಕಾಮಪ್ರಧ್ವಂಸಿಯುಂ, ಯತಿ ಷಟ್ಕದೊಳ್ ।
ನಿಲೆ, ಬಗೆದು ಕೇಳ್*, ಜ್ಯೋತ್ಸ್ನಾ-ಕಾಂತಿ-ಪ್ರಭಾಸಿತ-ಲೋಚನೇ,
ಲಲಿತ-ಹರಿಣೀ-*ನೇತ್ರೇ, ಕರ್ಣಾಮೃತಂ ಹರಿಣೀಪ್ಲುತಂ. ‖ 191[3] ‖

179. Fifth instance: ⏑⏑⏑ | ⏑⏑⏑ | ⏑⏑⏑ | ⏑⏑⏑ | ⏑⏑⏑ | — —, the Vanajadaḷa. (Five Tribrachys' and two long syllables.)

ವನಜದಳಂ

ನ-ನ-ನ-ನ-ನ-ಗ-ಗಂ. ‖ 192[4] ‖

180. Sixth instance: ⏑⏑⏑ | ⏑ — ⏑ | — ⏑⏑ | ⏑ — ⏑ | ⏑ — ⏑ | ⏑ —, the Kanakâbjanîya; Caesura not pointed out.

ಕನಕಾಬ್ಜನೀಯಂ

ನ-ಜ-ಭ-ಜ-ಜ-ಲ-ಗಂ. ‖ 193[5] ‖

181. Seventh instance: the Narkuṭaka (Narkaṭaka)[6], is the same with Kanakâbjanîya (?).

---

1) Also in Rb. 2) Not in Rb. 3) Also in Rb. 4) Only in Rb. 5) Not in Rb. 6) Only in M.; it appears therein in a highly corrupt form; its third line, however, is identical with the Kanakâbjanîya's scheme.

18. Dhṛiti. Quarters of 18 syllables; 262144 vṛittas possible

ಧೃತಿಯೆಂಬ ಛಂದಸ್ಸಿನೊಳ್ 18 ಅಕ್ಕರಂ ಪಾದಮಾಗಿ ಪುಟ್ಟುವ
262144 ವೃತ್ತಂಗಳೊಳಗೆ

182. First instance: —⏑— | ⏑⏑— | ⏑—*⏑ | ⏑—⏑ | —⏑⏑ | —⏑—, the Mallikâmâlĕ; Caesura at 8 (vasu).

ಮಲ್ಲಿಕಾಮಾಲೆ

ಜ್ವಾಲೆ-ವಾಯು-ದಿನೇಶಯು*ಗ್ಮ-ಶಶಾಂಕ-ಪಾವಕರೆಂಬಿವರ್
ಲೀಲೆಯಿಂ ಬರೆ, ವಿಶ್ರಮಂ *ವಸು-ಸಂಖ್ಯೆಯೊಳ್ ನಿಲೆ, ಭಾಮಿನೀ, |
ನೀಲ-ಲೋಲ-ಸಹಸ್ರ-ಕುಂ*ತಳೆ, ಸಂದುದಿಂತಿದು ಮಲ್ಲಿಕಾ
ಮಾಲೆಯೆಂಬುದು ನಿಶ್ಚಯಂ *ಕವಿ-ರಾಜಹಂಸ-ವಿನಿರ್ಮಿತಂ. || 194[1] ||

183. Second instance: ——— | ——*⏑ | ⏑⏑⏑ | ⏑—— | ⏑—— | ⏑——, the Kandarpajâta; Caesura at 5 (kâmâstra).

ಕಂದರ್ಪಜಾತಂ

ಮ-ತ-ನ-ಯ-ಯ-ಯಂ || ವಿರತಿ ಕಾಮಾಸ್ತ್ರದೊಳ್. || 195[2] ||

184. Third instance: ⏑⏑⏑ | ⏑⏑⏑ | ⏑⏑—* | ⏑⏑— | ——⏑ | ⏑——, the Aravinda Caesura at 9 (nidhi).

ಅರವಿಂದಂ

ಸುರಪುರಯುಗ-ಪವನ-*ದ್ವಿತಯಾಕಾಶಾಂಬು-ಗಣಂಗಳ್
ನೆರೆದಿರೆ, ಯತಿ ನಿಧಿಯೊಳ್*ನಿಲೆ, ಕೇಳ್, ಆನಂದದೊಳೆಂದುಂ |
ನಿರತಿಶಯದೊಳಿದನೋ*ದೆಲೆ, ನೀಲಾಬ್ಜೇಕ್ಷಣೆ, ನೀನ್! ಈ
ಸುರುಚಿರಮೆನಿಪದೆ ದಲ್*ಪೆಸರಿಂದಂ ತಾನ್ ಅರವಿಂದಂ. || 196[2] ||

185. Fourth instance: ⏑⏑— | ⏑⏑⏑ | ⏑—⏑ | ⏑⏑⏑ | —⏑⏑ | ⏑⏑—, the Hamsaka.

ಹಂಸಕಂ

ಸ-ನ-ಜ-ನ-ಭ-ಸಂ. || 197[3] ||

---

1) Also in Rb. 2) Not in Rb. 3) Only in Rb.

19. Atidhṛiti. Quarters of 19 syllables; 524288 vṛittas possible

ಅತಿಧೃತಿಯೆಂಬ ಛಂದಸ್ಸಿನೊಳ್ 19 ಅಕ್ಕರಂ ಪಾದಮಾಗಿ ಪುಟ್ಟುವ
524288 ವೃತ್ತಂಗಳೊಳಗೆ

186. First instance: ⏑⏑⏑ | —⏑⏑ | —⏑*— | ⏑⏑— | ⏑—⏑ | ⏑—⏑ | —, the Taraḷa; Caesura at 8 (diśâkari; B., D.: mahîśvara = 16).

ತರಳಂ

ಸುರಪ-ಶೀತಕರಾಗ್ನಿ-*ಮಾರುತ-ಭಾನುಯುಗ್ಮ-ಗಣಂಗಳಿಂ
ಪರದೊಳೊಪ್ಪಿ ಹಿಮಾಂಶು*ಶೇಖರನಾಗೆ, ವಿಶ್ರಮಣಂ ದಿಶಾ ।
ಕರಿಗಳೊಳ್ ನಿಲೆ, ಸುಂದು*ದಿಂತಿದು ನಾಗವರ್ಮ-ವಿನಿರ್ಮಿತಂ,
ತರಳ-ಲೋಚನೆ, ನಾಮ*ದಿಂ ತರಳಂ ಕವೀಂದ್ರ-ಜನ-ಸ್ತುತಂ. ॥ 198[1] ॥

187. Second instance: ⏑—— | ——— | ⏑⏑⏑ | ⏑⏑—* | —⏑— | —⏑— | —, the Meghavisphûrjita; Caesura at 12 (mârtaṇḍa).

ಮೇಘವಿಸ್ಫೂರ್ಜಿತಂ

ಯ-ಮ-ನ-ಸ-ರ-ರ-ಗಂ ॥ ವಿಶ್ರಮಂ ಮಾರ್ತಂಡದೊಳ್. ॥ 199[2] ॥

188. Third instance: ——— | ⏑⏑— | ⏑—⏑ | ⏑⏑—* | ——⏑ | ——⏑ | —, the Śârdûlavikrîḍita; Caesura at 12 (dineśa).

ಶಾರ್ದೂಲವಿಕ್ರೀಡಿತಂ

ಉರ್ವೀ-ಮಾರುತ-ಭಾಸ್ಕರಾನಿಲ-ವಿಯದ್*ದ್ವಂದ್ವಂ, ಪದಾಂತಂಗಳೊಳ್
ಶರ್ವಂ, ವಿಶ್ರಮಣಂ ದಿನೇಶರೆಡೆಯೊಳ್*ನಿಲ್ಕುಂ ಮನಂಗೊಳ್ವಿನಂ, ।
ನಿರ್ವ್ಯಾಜಂ ಭುವನ-ತ್ರಯಂಗಳೊಳಗೀ*ವೃತ್ತಂ ಪ್ರಸಿದ್ಧಂ ಕರಂ,
ಚಾರ್ವಂಭೋರುಹ-ಪತ್ರ-ನೇತ್ರೆ, ಪೆಸರಿಂ*ಶಾರ್ದೂಲವಿಕ್ರೀಡಿತಂ. ॥ 200[3] ॥

189. Fourth instance: —⏑— | ⏑⏑— | ⏑⏑— | ——⏑ | ⏑—⏑ | ⏑—⏑ | —, the Khaĉarapluta; Caesura at paksha.

ಖಚರಪ್ಲುತಂ

ರ-ಸ-ಸ-ತ-ಜ-ಜ-ಗಂ ॥ ವಿಶ್ರಮಣಂ ಪಕ್ಷದೊಳ್. ॥ 201[4] ॥

---

1) Also in Rb.; B. and D. ನಾಗಪಿಂಗಳನಿರ್ಮಿತಂ. 2) Not in Rb. 3) Also in Rb. 4) H., Ra., Rc., D., M., Sb. 'Paksha's meaning in this instance is doubtful; perhaps 15.

20. Kṛiti. Quarters of 20 syllables; 1048576 vṛittas possible

ಕೃತಿಯೆಂಬ ಛಂದಸ್ಸಿನೊಳ್ 20 ಅಕ್ಕರಂ ಪಾದಮಾಗಿ ಪುಟ್ಟುವ 1048576 ವೃತ್ತಂಗಳೊಳಗೆ

190. First instance: ⏑⏑— | —⏑⏑ | —⏑— | ⏑⏑⏑ | —*—— | ⏑—— | ⏑—, **the Mattebhavikriḍita; Caesura at 13; Ra., H. at 10 (daśa).**

ಮತ್ತೇಭವಿಕ್ರೀಡಿತಂ

ಶ್ವಸನೇಂದು ಜ್ವಲನಂ ದಿವಂ ಧರೆ ಜಲಂ*ದೈತ್ಯಾರಿ ಕಾಮಾಂತಕ-
ಪ್ರಸರೋದ್ಯದ್-ಗಣವುಂ, ತ್ರಯೋದಶ-ಯತಿ-*ಪ್ರಸ್ತಾರವಾಗಿರ್ದೊಡೀ ।
ವಸುಧಾ-ಚಕ್ರದೊಳೆಯ್ದೆ ಸಂದುದು ಕರಂ*, ಮತ್ತೇಭವಿಕ್ರೀಡಿತಂ
ಪೆಸರಾಯ್ತಿಂತಿದು ಪಿಂಗಳಾಹಿ-ವರನಿಂ*, ವ್ಯಾಲೋಲ-ನೀಲಾಲಕೀ! || 202[1] ||

191. Second instance: —⏑⏑ | —⏑— | ⏑⏑⏑ | —⏑*⏑ | —⏑⏑ | —⏑— | ⏑—, **the Utpalamâlĕ; Caesura at 11 (rudra).**

ಉತ್ಪಲಮಾಲೆ

ಶೀತಕರಾನಲೇಂದ್ರಪುರ-ಚಂದ್ರ-*ಶಶಾಂಕ-ಹುತಾಶನಂ ಲ-ಗೋ
ಪೇತವೊಡಂಬಡುತ್ತಮಿರೆ, ರುದ್ರ*ರ ಸಂಖ್ಯೆಯೊಳಾಗೆ ವಿಶ್ರಮಂ, ।
ಸಾತಿಶಯೋಕ್ತಿಯಿಂದಿದು ವಿರಾಜಿ*ಸುಗುಂ ಕವಿ-ರಾಜಹಂಸನಿಂ
ಭೂತಳದೊಳ್ ನೆಗಳ್ತೆವಡೆದುತ್ಪ*ಲಮಾಲೆ, ವಿಲೋಲ-ಲೋಚನೇ! || 203[2] ||

192. Third instance: ⏑⏑⏑ | —⏑⏑ | —⏑⏑ | ——*— | ⏑⏑— | ⏑⏑— | ⏑—, **the Anavadya (D. anamadhya, M. anavandya); Caesura at 11 (rudra).**

ಅನವದ್ಯಂ

ನ-ಭ-ಭ-ಮ-ಸ-ಸ-ಲ-ಗಂ || ವಿಶ್ರಮಂ ರುದ್ರನ ಸಂಖ್ಯೆಯೊಳ್. || 204[3] ||

193. Fourth instance: —⏑⏑ | —⏑⏑ | —⏑⏑ | —⏑⏑* | —⏑— | ⏑⏑— | ⏑—, **the Vanamañjari; Caesura at 12 (dinanâtha). It is the Vanavallari of Rb., the Nâgarañjita of Ra., H.**

ವನಮಂಜರಿ (ವನವಲ್ಲರಿ, ನಾಗರಂಜಿತಂ)

ಭ-ಭ-ಭ-ಭ-ರ-ಸ-ಲ-ಗಂ || ವಿಶ್ರಮಂ ದಿನನಾಥರೊಳ್. || 205[4] ||

---

1) Also in Rb.; ಪಿಂಗಳಾಹಿ only in B. and D., the others ನಾಗವರ್ಮ. 2) H., Ra., Rc., Rb., M., D. 3) H., Ra., Rc., M., D. 4) Also in Rb.

21. Prakṛiti. Quarters of 21 syllables; 2097152 vṛittas possible

ಪ್ರಕೃತಿಯೆಂಬ ಛಂದಸ್ಸಿನೊಳ್ 21 ಅಕ್ಕರಂ ಪಾದಮಾಗಿ ಪುಟ್ಟುವ
2097152 ವೃತ್ತಂಗಳೊಳಗೆ

194. First instance: ⏑⏑⏑ | ⏑—⏑ | —⏑⏑ | ⏑—⏑ | ⏑*—⏑ | ⏑—⏑ | —⏑—, the *Campaka*-mālĕ; Caesura at 13.

ಚಂಪಕಮಾಲೆ

ತ್ರಿದಶ-ರವೀಂದು-ಭಾಸ್ಕರ-ಗಣಾ-ತ್ರಿತ*ಯಾಗ್ರದೊಳಗ್ನಿ ಚಲ್ವುವೆ
ತ್ತುದಯಿಪಿನಂ ತ್ರಯೋದಶದೊಳಾಗಿರೆ* ವಿಶ್ರಮಣಂ, ನಿರಂತರಾ ।
ಭ್ಯುದಯಕರಂ ಪರಂ ನಿನಗಶೋಕ-ಮ*ಹೀರುಹ-ಪಲ್ಲವೋಲ್ಲಸತ್- ।
ಪದ-ಯುಗೆ, ನಿಚ್ಚವೋದು, ಗಡ, ಚಂಪಕ*ಮಾಲೆಯನೊಲ್ದು ಲೀಲೆಯಿಂ! || 206[1] ||

195. Second instance: ——— | —⏑— | —*⏑⏑ | ⏑⏑⏑ | ⏑—*— | ⏑—— | ⏑——*, the Sragdharĕ; Caesura at 7 (hayanikara).

ಸ್ರಗ್ಧರೆ

ಭೂಮಿ-ಜ್ವಾಲೇಂದು-ದೇವಾ*ಧಿಪಪುರ-ಗಣದಿಂ*ಮುಂತೆ ತೋಯ-ತ್ರಯಂಗಳ್*
ತಾಮೆತ್ತಂ ಬಂದು ಚಲ್ವಾ*ಗಿರೆ, ಹಯನಿಕರ-*ಸ್ಥಾನದೊಳ್ ನಿಲ್ವಿನಂ ವಿ* ।
ಶ್ರಾಮಂ, ಛಂದಕ್ಕಲಂಕಾ*ರಮಿದೆನೆ ಜನಕಾ*ನಂದಮಂ ಮಾಡುಗುಂ, ಸ್ರಗ್-*
ಧಾಮ-ಪ್ರೋದ್ದಾಮ-ಕೇಶಾ*ನ್ವಿತೆ, ಒಗೆ! ಪೆಸರಿಂ*ಸ್ರಗ್ಧರಾ-ನಾಮ-ವೃತ್ತಂ. || 207[1] ||

196. Third instance: —⏑— | ⏑⏑⏑ | —⏑—* | ⏑⏑⏑ | —⏑— | ⏑⏑⏑ | —⏑—, the Taraṅgama (M. turaṅgama); Caesura at 9 (randhra).

ತರಂಗಮಂ (ತುರಂಗಮಂ)

ರ-ನ-ರ-ನ-ರ-ನ-ರಂ || ಯತಿ ರಂಧ್ರದೊಳ್. || 208[2] ||

197. Fourth instance: ⏑⏑⏑ | ⏑⏑⏑ | ⏑⏑⏑ | ⏑——* | ⏑—— | ——⏑ | ———, the Lalitagati; Caesura at 12 (ravi).

ಲಲಿತಗತಿ

ನ-ನ-ನ-ಯ-ಯ-ತ-ಮಂ || ವಿರಾಮಂ ರವಿಯೊಳ್. || 209[3] ||

1) Also in Rb. 2) Rc., D., M. 3) H., Ra., Rc., M., D.

22. Ākṛiti[1]. Quarters of 22 syllables; 4194304 vṛittas possible

ಆಕೃತಿಯೆಂಬ ಛಂದಸ್ಸಿನೊಳ್ 22 ಅಕ್ಕರಂ ಪಾದಮಾಗಿ ಪುಟ್ಟುವ
4194304 ವೃತ್ತಂಗಳೊಳಗೆ

198. First instance: ⏑⏑– | ––⏑ | ––⏑ | ⏑⏑⏑ | ⏑⏑–* | –⏑– | –⏑– | –, the Mahâsragdharĕ; Caesura at 15 (paksha).

ಮಹಾಸ್ರಗ್ಧರೆ

ಮರುದಾಕಾಶದ್ವಯೇಂದ್ರಾನಿಲ-ಹುತವಹಯು*ಗ್ಮಾಂಗಜನ್ಮಾಂತಕರ್ಗಳ್
ಬರೆ, ಪಕ್ಷ-ಸ್ಥಾನದೊಳ್ ನಿಲ್ತಿರೆ ವಿರತಿ, ಮಹಾ*ಸ್ರಗ್ಧರಾ-ನಾಮ-ವೃತ್ತಂ, |
ಗುರು-ವಿದ್ಯಾ-ಪ್ರೇಮಿ, ಅಭ್ಯಾಸದೆ ವಿಲಸಿತೆ, ಚಾ*ರ್ವಾನನೇ, ಕಾವ್ಯ-ಮೋದಾ
ಸ್ಫುರಿತ-ಪ್ರೋದ್ಭಾಸಿ, ಕಾಂಚೀ-ಖಚಿತ-ರಸನ-ಯು*ಕ್ತಾಂಗನೇ, ಕೇಳ್, ಪ್ರಿಯಾಖ್ಯೇ! ||210[2]||

199. Second instance: –⏑⏑ | –⏑– | ⏑⏑⏑ | –⏑– | ⏑⏑⏑* | –⏑– | ⏑⏑⏑ | –, the Bhadraka; Caesura at 15 (paksha).

ಭದ್ರಕಂ

ಭ-ರ-ನ-ರ-ನ-ರ-ನ-ಗಂ || ವಿರತಿ ಪಕ್ಷದೊಳ್. || 211[3] ||

200. Third instance: –⏑⏑ | –⏑⏑ | –*⏑⏑ | –⏑⏑ | –⏑⏑* | –⏑⏑ | –⏑⏑ | –, the Vanamañjari; Caesura at 7 (hayavrâta, turagavrâta) and 8 (gajavraja, gajavrâta). (Seven Dactyls and a long syllable.)

ವನಮಂಜರಿ

ಭ-ಭ-ಭ-ಭ-ಭ-ಭ-ಭ-ಗಂ || ವಿಶ್ರಮಂ ಹಯವ್ರಾತದೊಳ್ಗಂ ಗಜವ್ರಾತದೊಳ್ಗಂ. || 212[3] ||

201. Fourth instance: ⏑⏑– | ––– | –⏑– | ⏑⏑–* | –⏑⏑ | –⏑– | –⏑– | –, the Cûtakuja; Caesura at 12 (padminîmitra).

ಚೂತಕುಜಂ

ಸ-ಮ-ರ-ಸ-ಭ-ರ-ರ-ಗಂ || ವಿಶ್ರಮಂ ಪದ್ಮಿನೀಮಿತ್ರನೊಳ್. || 213[3] ||

1) From here our MSS., with the exception of B., show irregularities in the headings. B., however, with D., calls class 25 (against M., Rb. and Rc.) Atikṛiti. Class 22 is Akṛiti in D., H.; Ākṛiti in Ra., Rc., and B.; Atikṛiti in Rb.; Vikṛiti in M. 2) Also in Rb. 3) Not in Rb. and B.

23. Vikṛiti[1]. Quarters of 23 syllables; 8388608 vṛittas possible

ವಿಕೃತಿಯೆಂಬ ಛಂದಸ್ಸಿನೊಳ್ 23 ಅಕ್ಕರಂ ಪಾದಮಾಗಿ ಪುಟ್ಟುವ
8388608 ವೃತ್ತಂಗಳೊಳಗೆ

202. First instance: ⏑⏑⏑ | ⏑–⏑ | ⏑–⏑ | ⏑–⏑ | ⏑–⏑ | ⏑–⏑ | ⏑–⏑ | ⏑–, the *Haṁsagati*; Caesura according to H., Ra. and M. at 8 (vasu); according to Rc., B. and D. at 11 (hara). (Proceleusmaticus, six Dactyls and a long syllable.)

ಹಂಸಗತಿ

ದಿವಿಜ-ಷಡಂಬುಜಮಿತ್ರ-ಗಣ-ಪ್ರಕರಂ ಲ-ಗಮುಂ ಕ್ರಮದಿಂ ಪದದೊಳ್
ವಿವರಿಸೆ, ಬಂದು ವಿರಾಜಿಸೆ ವಿಶ್ರಮಣಂ ವಸು-ಸಂಖ್ಯೆಗಳೊಳ್, ನಯದಿಂ ।
ದೆ ವಿಚಲಿತಂ ಪದ-ಘಟ್ಟಿಯನಾಳ್ದೆಸವುತ್ತಿರೆ, ಕೇಳ್ ಕಳ-ಹಂಸ-ಗತೀ,
ಭುವನದೊಳೀ ತೆಱದಿಂದಮೆ ಸಂದುದು ಪಿಂಗಳನಿಂದಿದು ಹಂಸಗತೀ. || 214[2] ||

203. Second instance: ––– | ––– | ––*⏑ | ⏑⏑⏑ | ⏑⏑⏑ | ⏑⏑⏑ | ⏑⏑⏑ | ⏑–, the *Mattâkriḍĕ*; Caesura at 8 (kari).

ಮತ್ತಾಕ್ರೀಡೆ

ಮುನ್ನಂಭೂಮಿದ್ವಂದ್ವಾಕಾಶಂ *ಸುರಪುರ-ಗಣಮೆಸೆದಿರೆ, ಗಣ-ತತಿಯಿಂ
ದಿನ್ನಿತ್ತಲ್ ವೈಕುಂಠೇಶಾನರ್*, ಕರಿಯೊಳೆ ನಿಲೆ ಯತಿ-ತತಿ, ಲಲಿತ-ಪದೋ ।
ತ್ಪನ್ನಂ ವೃತ್ತಂ, ಭಿನ್ನಾಬ್ಜಾಕ್ಷೀ*, ಕವಿ-ವರ-ಮತದಿನಿದತಿಶಯತರಮಿಂ
ತೆನ್ನಿಂದಾಯ್ತೀ ಮತ್ತಾಕ್ರೀಡಾ*ಹ್ವಯಮಿದನಱಿವುದು, ಸರಸಿರುಹ-ಮುಖೀ! [3]
|| 215 ||

204. Third instance: ⏑⏑⏑ | –⏑⏑ | –⏑⏑ | –⏑⏑* | ––– | ⏑⏑– | ⏑⏑– | ⏑–, the *Saundara*; Caesura at 12 (dinanâtha).

ಸೌಂದರಂ

ನ-ಭ-ಭ-ಭ-ಮ-ಸ-ಸ-ಲ-ಗಂ || ವಿಶ್ರಮಣಂ ದಿನನಾಥಸ್ಥಾನದೊಳ್. || 216[4] ||

---

1) Ra. Vikṛiti, Rc. Kṛiti, M. Prakṛiti, D. Kṛiti. In Rb. there is nothing corresponding to Vikṛiti. 2) Not in Rb. 3) Rc., M., B., D. 4) Rc., M., D. In Ra. there is a much mutilated Vidaḷitasarasija, probably the same with No. 211.

24. Saṅkṛiti[1]. Quarters of 24 syllables; 16777216 vṛittas possible

ಸಂಕೃತಿಯೆಂಬ ಛಂದಸ್ಸಿನೊಳ್ 24 ಅಕ್ಕರಂ ಪಾದಮಾಗಿ ಪುಟ್ಟುವ
16777216 ವೃತ್ತಂಗಳೊಳಗೆ

205. First instance: ⏑⏑⏑ | ⏑⏑⏑ | —*⏑⏑ | ⏑⏑⏑ | ⏑—*⏑ | ⏑⏑⏑ | ⏑⏑⏑ | ⏑——, **the Lalita; Caesura at 7 (giri); Alliteration also in the course of the lines.**

ಲಲಿತಂ

ಸುರಪುರ-ಯುಗಳಂ *ಬರೆ, ಶಶಿ-ದಿವಿಜಂ *ಖರಕರ-ಸುರಯುಗ-ತೋಯಂ
ವಿರಚಿಸೆ ಕಡೆಯೊಳ್,* ಬರೆಸಿರೆ ಪದ-ವಿ*ಸ್ತರದೊಳೆ ಗಣ-ನಿವಹಂಗಳ್, |
ಗಿರಿಯೊಳೆ ಯತಿಗಳ್ *ದೊರೆಕೊಳೆ, ಲಲಿತಾ*ಕ್ಷರ-ಪದ-ರಚನೆಗಳಿಂದಂ
ಪರೆದುದು, ಲಲಿತಂ *ಧರೆಗಿದು ಪೆಸರಾ* ಗಿರೆ, ಸರಸಿರುಹ-ದಳಾಕ್ಷೀ! || 217[2] ||

206. Second instance: —⏑⏑ | ——*⏑ | ⏑⏑⏑ | ⏑⏑—* | —⏑⏑ | —⏑⏑ | ⏑⏑⏑ | ⏑——, **the Tanvi; Caesura at 5 and 12 (bâṇa = 5, adri = 7), or simply at 12.**

ತನ್ವಿ

ಇಂದು-ನಭಂಗಳ್ *ಸುರಪುರ-ಪವನೇಂ*ದುದ್ವಯಮಾಗಿರೆ, ಕುಲಿಶ-ಜಲಂಗಳ್
ಮುಂದಿರೆ, ಬಾಣಾ*ದ್ರಿಗಳೊಳೆ ಯತಿಗಳ್ *ನಿಂದಿರೆ, ನೀನ್ ಅಱಿಯತಿಶಯದಿಂ
ದಂ, |
ಸುಂದರಿ, ವೃತ್ತಂ*ದ್ರುತ-ಪದ-ಲಲಿತಂ *ಸಂದುದು ಪಿಂಗಳನುಮತದಿ, ಸಂಪೂ
ರ್ಣೇಂದು-ನಿಭಾಸ್ಯೇ, *ಧರೆಗಿದು ಪರಿದ*ತ್ರೈಲ್ಲಿಯುಮುದ್ಭವಕರಮೆನೆ, ತನ್ವೀ. [3]
|| 218 ||

207. Third instance: ⏑⏑⏑ | ⏑—⏑ | —*⏑⏑ | —⏑⏑ | —⏑⏑ | —⏑⏑ | ⏑—⏑ | —⏑—, **the Arkamarîči; Caesura at 7 (śaila; M. giri).**

ಅರ್ಕಮರೀಚಿ

ನ-ಜ-ಭ-ಭ-ಭ-ಭ-ಜ-ರಂ || ವಿಶ್ರಮಣಂ ಶೈಲದೊಳ್. || 219[4] ||

208. Fourth instance: ⏑⏑⏑ | ⏑—⏑ | —⏑*⏑ | ⏑—⏑ | ⏑—⏑ | ⏑—⏑ | —⏑— | ⏑⏑—, **the Paṅkaja; Caesura at 8 (dikkari).**

ಪಂಕಜಂ

ನ-ಜ-ಭ-ಜ-ಜ-ಜ-ರ-ಸಂ || ವಿರಾಮಂ ದಿಕ್ಕರಿಯೊಳ್. || 220[5] ||

---

1) Ra. Satkṛiti, Rb. H. Samskṛiti, Rc. Samskṛiti, D. Prakṛiti, M. Atikṛiti. 2) M., Rc., D., B.; Rb. calls it Tilaka, but, in a second instance, also Lalita. 3) M., Rc., D., B. 4) M., Rc., D. 5) M.

25. Abhikṛiti[1]. Quarters of 25 syllables; 33554432 vṛittas possible

ಅಭಿಕೃತಿಯೆಂಬ ಛಂದಸ್ಸಿನೊಳ್ 25 ಅಕ್ಕರಂ ಪಾದಮಾಗಿ ಪುಟ್ಟುವ
33554432 ವೃತ್ತಂಗಳೊಳಗೆ

209. First instance: —⏑⏑ | ——*— | ⏑⏑— | —*⏑⏑ | ⏑⏑⏑ | ⏑⏑⏑* | ⏑⏑⏑ | ⏑⏑⏑ | —, the Krauñčapada; Caesura at 5, 5 and 8 (bhûta, śara, âśâgaja); two Alliterations.

ಕ್ರೌಂಚಪದಂ

ಶೀತಕರೋರ್ವೀ-*ವಾತ-ಶಶಾಂಕರ್,*ಯುಗ-ಮಿತ-ಸುರಪುರ-*ನಿವಹದ
ಕಡೆಯೊಳ್
ಭೂತಗಣಾಧೀಶಂ,*ಭೂತ-ಶರಾಶಾ* ಗಜದೊಳೆ ಯತಿಗಳು*ಮೆಸೆದಿರೆ, ಪೆಸರಿಂ, ।
ನೀತಿ-ಯುತೇ, ಕೇಳ್,*ಸಾತಿಶಯೋಕ್ತಿ-*ಕ್ರಮದೊಳೆ ನೆಗಳ್ದದಿ*ದತಿಶಯ-ರಚನೋ
ಪೇತಮಶೇಷೋ*ರ್ವೀತಳಕಂ ಕ್ರೌಂ*ಚಪದಮಿದತಿಶಯ-*ಪದ-ರಚನೆಗಳಿಂ. || 221[2] ||

210. Second instance: ⏑⏑⏑ | ⏑⏑⏑ | ⏑⏑*⏑ | ⏑⏑⏑ | ⏑⏑—* | —⏑⏑ | —⏑⏑ | —⏑⏑ | —, the Hamsapada (M. -gati); Caesura at 8 and 7 (kari, giri).

ಹಂಸಪದಂ

ದಿವಿಜಪುರ-ಯುಗಮು*ವಱಿ ಪರದನಿಲಂ,*ಶೀತಕರ-ತ್ರಿತಯಂ, ಕಡೆಯೊಳ್
ಭವನಿರೆ, ಕರಿ-ಗಿರಿ-*ಗಣನೆಗಳೊಳಗಂ*ತಳ್ತೆಸೆಗುಂ ಪದ-ವಿಶ್ರಮಣಂ, ।
ಭುವನದೊಳತಿಶಯ*ತರಮಿದು ಹೃದಯಾ*ನಂದಕರಂ ಕೃತ-ಸೌಖ್ಯತರಂ
ಕವಿ-ಜನ-ಹಿತಕರ*ಮಿದನಱಿ, ಕೆಳದೀ,*ಹಂಸ-ವಿನಿರ್ಮಿತ-ಹಂಸಪದಂ. || 222[3] ||

211. Third instance: ⏑⏑⏑ | ⏑⏑⏑ | ⏑⏑⏑ | ⏑⏑⏑* | ⏑⏑⏑ | ⏑⏑⏑ | ⏑⏑⏑ | ⏑⏑⏑ | —, the Vidaḷitavanaruha; Caesura at 12 (dinakara). Cf. Note ad v. 216.

ವಿದಳಿತವನರುಹಂ

ನ-ನ-ನ-ನ-ನ-ನ-ನ-ನ-ಗಂ || ಯತಿ ದಿನಕರಕೆಡೆಯೊಳ್. || 223[4] ||

1) Rb., Rc., M. Abhikṛiti; D., B. Atikṛiti. 2) Rb., Rc., M., D., B. 3) Rc., D., B., M. 4) Rb., Rc., M., D.

26. Utkṛiti. Quarters of 26 syllables; 67108864 vṛittas possible

ಉತ್ಕೃತಿಯೆಂಬ ಛಂದಸ್ಸಿನೊಳ್ 26 ಅಕ್ಕರಂ ಪಾದಮಾಗಿ ಪುಟ್ಟುವ
67108864 ವೃತ್ತಂಗಳೊಳಗೆ

212. First instance: — — — | — — — | — — * ⏑ | ⏑⏑⏑ | ⏑⏑⏑ | ⏑⏑⏑ | —*⏑ — | ⏑⏑— | ⏑—, the Bhujaṅgavijṛimbhita; Caesura at 8 and 11 (hari, hara).

ಭುಜಂಗವಿಜೃಂಭಿತಂ

ಆದಿ-ಕ್ಷ್ಮಾಯುಗ್ಮಾಕ್ರಾಶಾಗ್ರಂ * ಪುರ-ಮಿತ-ಸುರಪುರ-ಸಹಿತಂ * ಕೃಶಾನು-ಮರುಲ್-ಲ-ಗಂ
ಪಾದಾಂತಕ್ಕೋರಂತೊರ್ಪ್ಪುತ್ತಂ, * ಹರಿ-ಹರರೊಳೆ ಯತಿ-ನಿಯಮಂ, * ವಿನೂತ-ವಿಭೂತಿಯೊಳ್ |
ಪಾದಾಂತಕ್ಕಾದ್ಯಂತಕ್ಕೊಳ್ಪಂ * ಪಡೆದುದು ಧರೆಗತಿವಿತತಂ * ಕವೀಂದ್ರ-ಸಹಾಯದಿಂ
ದೋದಲ್ ಚಲ್ಪಿಂ ವೃತ್ತಂ, ಕೇಳಾ * ಪ್ರಿಯ-ವದನ-ವನಿತೆ, ಪೆಸರಿಂ*ಭುಜಂಗವಿಜೃಂಭಿತಂ. || 224[1] ||

213. Second instance: — — — | ⏑⏑⏑ | ⏑⏑⏑ | ⏑⏑⏑ | ⏑⏑⏑ | ⏑⏑⏑ | ⏑⏑⏑ | ⏑⏑— | — —, the Apavâha.

ಅಪವಾಹಂ

ಮ-ನ-ನ-ನ-ನ-ನ-ನ-ಸ-ಗ-ಗಂ. || 225[2] ||

214. Third instance: ⏑⏑⏑ | ⏑⏑⏑ | ⏑⏑*⏑ | ⏑⏑⏑ | ⏑⏑⏑ | ⏑*⏑⏑ | ⏑⏑⏑ | ⏑⏑⏑* | — —, the Vanalaté; Caesura at 8 (kari, hari); four Alliterations in each Quarter. (Six Proceleusmaticus' and a Spondeus.)

ವನಲತೆ

ಅದಿತಿಜಪುರಮಿರೆ * ಮದ-ಗಜದೆಡೆಗಳೊ*ಳೊದವಿರೆ ನಯದೊಳೆ * ಬಂದಾ
ತುದಿಗಳೊಳುದಯಿಸೆ * ಸದಮಲ-ಗುರು-ಯುಗ * ಮದು ಕರಿ-ಹರಿ-ಯತಿ * ಯಿಂದಂ |
ವಿದಿತಮಿದವನಿಗೆ * ಪುದಿದಿರೆ ರಸದೊಳೆ * ಪದೆದಿದನತಿಮುದ * ದಿಂದಂ
ಮೃದು-ಪದ-ರಚನೆಯೊ*ಳೊದವಿದೊಡಿದನಱಿ*ವುದು, ಸತಿ, ವನಲತೆ*
ಯೆಂದುಂ. || 226[3] ||

1) H., Ra., Rc., M., D., B. 2) Rb. 3) Rc., M., D., B.; in H., Ra. only a few words.

215. Fourth instance: ⏑⏑⏑ | ⏑—⏑ | ⏑*⏑⏑ | ⏑⏑— | ⏑⏑*⏑ | ⏑⏑⏑ | ⏑⏑⏑* | ⏑—⏑ | ⏑—, the Munimata (M. Munimana); Caesura at 7 (muni). Rb. calls it saraḷa.

ಮುನಿಮತಂ (ಸರಳಂ)

ಅನಿಮಿಷ-ಭಾನು-ದಿ*ವಿಜ-ಪವನಂ ಬರೆ*, ಸುರಪುರಯುಗ-ಪು*ರ-ಭಾನು-ಲ-ಗಂ,
ಘನ-ಯುತೆ, ನಿನ್ನಯೆ*ಮನದನುರಾಗದಿ*ನಿರೆ ಮುನಿ-ತತಿಯೊ*ಳೆ ವಿಶ್ರಮಣಂ, ।
ಮನವೊಸೆದೋದಿದ*ನನುನಯದಿಂದಱಿ*, ವಿನಮಿತ-ಲಲಿತ-*ಪದೋಕ್ತಿಗಳಿಂ
ಜನ-ಹಿತಮಿಂತಿದು*ಮುನಿಮತಮೆಂಬುದು*; ನಿನಗಱುಪಿದೆ, ಕೇ*ಳದೇ, ನಿರುತಂ.
|| 227 [1] ||

216. The Samavṛittas beginning with ukta (uktĕ) and ending in utkṛiti have thus been described.

ಕಂದಂ

ಉಕ್ತಂ ಮೊದಲಾಗಿರೆ ಪೂ
ರ್ವೋಕ್ತದಿನುತ್ಕೃತಿಯನೆಯ್ದೆ, ಸಮವೃತ್ತಮುಮಂ, ।
ವ್ಯಕ್ತತರಮಾಗೆ, ಮೃದು-ಮಧು
ರೋಕ್ತಿಗಳಿಂ ತಿಳಿಯ ಪೇಳ್ದೆನಂಬುಜ-ವದನೇ! || 228 [2] ||

217. Their sum is 67108864. (shaṭka = 6; naga = 7; mṛigadhara = 1; ambara = ⏑; nâga = 8; gaja = 8; ṛitu = 6; yuga = 4.)

ಯುಗ-ಋತು-ಗಜ-ನಾಗಾಂಬರ-
ಮೃಗಧರ-ನಗ-ಷಟ್ಕಮೆನಿಪ ವೃತ್ತದ ಲೆಕ್ಕಂ ।
ಸೊಗಯಿಸಿ ತೋರ್ಕುಂ; ಗಣಿಯಿಪು
ದಗಣಿತ-ಗುಣ-ನಿಲಯ-ನಾಗವರ್ಮನ ಮತದಿಂ. || 229 [3] ||

218. A verse teaching how to find out easily each of the six vṛittas most used in Canarese (utpala, v. 203; śârdûla, v. 200; sragdharĕ, v. 207; mattebha, v. 202; mahâsragdharĕ, v. 210; čampaka, v. 206).

ಮತ್ತೇಭವಿಕ್ರೀಡಿತಂ

ಗುರುವೊಂದಾದಿಯೊಳುತ್ಪಲಂ; ಗುರು ಮೊದಲ್ ಮೂಱಾಗೆ ಶಾರ್ದೂಲಮಾ
ಗುರು ನಾಲ್ಕಾಗಿರಲಂತು ಸ್ರಗ್ಧರೆ; ಲಘು-ದ್ವಂದ್ವಂ ಗುರು-ದ್ವಂದ್ವಮಾ ।

1) Rb. (Saraḷa), M. (Munimana), D., B. In Rb. there appears another, but too mutilated to be recognised; some of its feet, according to the rule of the first line, are Bha-Ja-Sa-Na-Bha-Ya..., after which follows: rañjita-padam....dagradam (idakkum). 2) H., Ra., M., D., B. 3) M., D., B.

ಗಿರೆ ಮತ್ತೇಭ; ಲಘು-ದ್ವಯ-ತ್ರಿಗುರುವಿಂದಕ್ಕುಂ ಮಹಾಸ್ರಗ್ಧರಂ;
ಹರಿಣಾಕ್ಷೀ, ಲಘು ನಾಲ್ಕು ಚಂಪಕಮಿವಾಱು ಖ್ಯಾತಿ-ಕರ್ಣಾಟಕಂ. || 230[1] ||

ಗದ್ಯಂ

ಇದು ಸಮಸ್ತ-ಭಗವದ್-ಅರ್ಹತ್-ಪರಮೇಶ್ವರ-ಚಾರು-ಚರಣಾರವಿಂದ-ಮಂದ-ಮಧುಕರಾಯಮಾನ-ವಿಬುಧ-ಜನ-ಮನಃ-ಪದ್ಮಿನೀ-ರಾಜಹಂಸ-ಶ್ರೀಮತ್-ಕವಿರಾಜಹಂಸ-ವಿರಚಿತಮಪ್ಪ ಛಂದೋಂಬುಧಿಯೊಳ್ ಸಮವೃತ್ತವಿವರಣಂ ದ್ವಿತೀಯಾಶ್ವಾಸಂ.

1) This secondary verse appears in Sa., in a sort of appendix of M., in ch. 6 of Ra., H., as v. 31 in Rd., and as v. 16 in O. In the second line the tu is short though followed by sra (cf. Weber p. 224 seq.); ya before tri, however, is counted as long; ಮತ್ತೇಭ instead of ಮತ್ತೇಭಂ.

III. CHAPTER

ತೃತೀಯಾಶ್ವಾಸಂ

1. Further Sama Vṛittas.

ಇತರಸಮವೃತ್ತಂಗಳ್

219. **The Daṇḍaka:** ⏑⏑⏑ | ⏑⏑⏑ | —⏑— | —⏑— | —⏑— | —⏑— | —⏑— | —⏑— | —⏑—. Quarters of 27 syllables.

ದಂಡಕವೃತ್ತಂ

ಕಂದಂ

ಅಮರ-ಗಣಾ-ಯುಗ್ಮದಿಂ ಮುಂ
ದಮರ್ದೇೞುಂ ಶಿಖಿ-ಗಣಂ ಬರಲ್, ದಂಡಕದ । [M. ದಮರ್ದಿರೆಯುಂ ಶಿಖಿ]
ಪ್ರಮುದಿತ-ಲಕ್ಷ್ಣಮಕ್ಕುಂ;
ಕಮಲ-ಮುಖೀ, ತಿಳಿದು ಕೊಳ್ವುದೆನ್ನಯೆ ಮತದಿಂ! ‖ 231[1] ‖

220. **The Mâlâvṛittas**, that together with the Daṇḍaka use to be counted separately. Cf. v. 235 and No. 55.

ಮಾಲಾವೃತ್ತಂಗಳ್

ಕಂದಂ

ಸದಮಲಮುಖಿ, ಆಂ ಸಮವೃ
ತ್ತದ ತೆಱನಂ ನಿನಗೆ ತಿಳುಪಿದೆಂ; ಮಾಲಾವೃ ।
ತ್ತದ ಪಾಂಗನೆಯ್ದೆ ಕೇಳ್, ಇ
ನ್ನುದಾತ್ತ-ಮತಿ, ವಿಬುಧ-ಜನ-ಮನೋ-ರಂಜನಮಂ! ‖ 232[2] ‖

---

1) In the MSS. it occurs at the end of this Chapter. It is in H.,Ra. (the reading of which is peculiar, but very incorrect), Rc., M., D., B. H. and Ra's verse mentions, so far as it can be made out, that the first Daṇḍaka with seven Amphimacrus' (—⏑—) is called Vṛishṭiprayâta, and that there are altogether six kinds of Daṇḍakas. Then H., Ra. and M. adduce another verse (that cannot be restored) wherein Pracita is mentioned, and which probably wants to state that the other five Daṇḍakas the quarters of each of which increase by one and one Amphimacrus, bear the common name of Pracita. See Weber p. 406.

2) In H., Ra., M., D., B.

221. First instance: —⏑⏑ | ⏑—⏑ | ⏑⏑*— | ⏑⏑⏑ | —⏑⏑ | ⏑*—⏑ | ⏑⏑— | ⏑⏑⏑ | —⏑⏑ | ⏑——, the Lalitapada, Quarters of 30 syllables, Caesura at 8; three Alliterations. (Seven Paeons and a Spondee.)

ಲಲಿತಪದಂ

ತಾನೆ ಶಶಿ-ಸೂರ್ಯ-ಪವ*ಮಾನ-ಸುರ-ಶೀತಕರ-*ಭಾನು-ಮರುದಿಂದ್ರ-ವಿಧು-
ತೋಯದೆ, ವಿರಾಮ-
ಸ್ಥಾನಮೆಸೆಗುಂ ಪದ-ವಿ*ತಾನದೊಳನುಕ್ರಮದೆ*, ನೀನಱಿವುದೀ ಲಲಿತವೃತ್ತ
ಮನಿದುಂ, ಚಂ |
ದ್ರಾನನೆ, ಘನಾತಿಶಯೆ*, ಸೋನ್ನತ-ಕಟಾಕ್ಷ-ಭರೆ*, ಗಾನ-ರಸ-ಜಿಹ್ವಿಕೆ, ವಿಲಾಸವತಿ,
ಕಾವ್ಯ-
ಶ್ರೀ-ನಿಲಯಮಂ ವಿಬುಧ-*ಮಾನಿತಮನುಜ್ಜ್ವಲ-ವ*ಚೋ-ನಿಚಿತಮಂ ರಚಿತಮಂ
ಕವಿಗಳಿಂದಂ. || 233[1] ||

222. Second instance: ⏑⏑⏑ | ⏑⏑⏑ | ⏑⏑⏑ | ⏑*⏑⏑ | ⏑⏑⏑ | ⏑⏑⏑ | ⏑⏑*⏑ | ⏑⏑⏑ | ⏑—⏑ | ⏑⏑— | —, the Kusumaśara, Quarters of 31 syllables, Caesura at 10; 4 Alliterations.

ಕುಸುಮಶರಂ

ಸುಱರ ಪಡೆ ನೆರವಿಯೊಳೆ*ಕರಿಗಳೆನಿತನಿತಱಿೞೊಳೆ*, ಖರಕರ-ಸಮೀರಣ-ಪದಾಂತಂ
ಪುರಮಥನನಿರೆ, ಬಳಿಕೆ*ನೆಱೆದು ಯತಿ ದಶಮದೊಳೆ*ಧರಧರದಿನೊಪ್ಪಿ ನಿಲೆ, ಸಂತಂ|
ಧರೆಯೊಳಿದು ನೆಗೞ್ದ ಕವಿ-*ವರ-ಮತದೆ ಜನ-ನುತದೆ*ಪರಮ-ಪದಮೆಯ್ದುಗಿದ
ನಂತಂ,
ಸರಸಿರುಹ-ದಳ-ನಯನೆ*, ಕರಮೆಸೆವ ಕುಸುಮಶರ-*ನಿರತಿಶಯಮೆಂಬುದು
ನಿತಂತಂ. || 234[2] ||

2. The Ardhasama Vṛittas

ಅರ್ಧಸಮವೃತ್ತಂಗಳ್

223. Now follow the Ardhasama Vṛittas, in which two and two quarters only are formed of the same syllable-feet, viz. the 1st and 3rd, the 2nd and 4th. Cf. v. 239.

---

1) H., Ra., Rc., Rd., M., D., B. 2) H., Ra., Rd. (where it forms the last verse of the MS.), M., D., B.

ಕಂದಂ

ವೃತ್ತ-ಸುಬಾಹವೆ, ಕೇಳ್, ಇ
ರ್ಪತ್ತಾಱುಂ ಛಂದದಿಂದೆ ಪೊಱಗಣ ಮಾಲಾ ।
ವೃತ್ತಮನಱಿಪಿದೆನಿನ್ನು
ವೃತ್ತಿಯನಱಿಪಿದಪೆನರ್ಧಸಮ-ವೃತ್ತಮುಮಂ. ‖ 235[1] ‖

224. **First instance: The A č y u t a k a; number of syllables in the 1st and 3rd quarters 11, in the others 10. The scheme is two times:**

⏑⏑⏑ | ⏑—⏑ | ⏑—⏑ | ⏑—
—⏑⏑ | —⏑⏑ | —⏑⏑ | — |

ಅಚ್ಯುತಕ್ಕುದಾಹರಣಂ

ಶತಮುಖ-ಭಾನುಯುಗಾಗ್ರ-ಲ-ಗಂ,
ಶೀತಕರ-ತ್ರಿತಯಾಗ್ರ-ಹರಂ, ।
ಮತಿ-ಯುತೆ, ಬಂದೊಡಿದಚ್ಯುತಕಂ
ಭೂತಳದೊಳ್ ನೆಗಳ್ದರ್ಧಸಮಂ. ‖ 236[2] ‖

225. **Second instance: the D i v i j a k a l p a l a t ĕ; number of syllables in the 1st and 3rd quarters 11, in the others 12. The scheme is two times:**

—⏑— | ⏑⏑⏑ | —⏑— | ⏑—
⏑⏑⏑ | —⏑⏑ | ⏑—⏑ | —⏑— |

ದಿವಿಜಕಲ್ಪಲತೆಗುದಾಹರಣಂ

ಪಾವಕಾಮರ-ಗಣಾನಲಂ ಲ-ಗಂ,
ದಿವಿಜ-ಚಂದ್ರ-ಕುಮುದಾರಿ-ಪಾವಕಂ; ।
ಭಾವಿಸುತ್ತಮಿರೆ, ಕೋಮಲಾಂಗಿಸೀ,
ದಿವಿಜಕಲ್ಪಲತೆಯಾಯ್ತು ನಾಮದಿಂ. ‖ 237[3] ‖

226. **Third instance: the R a v i p r a b h ĕ (Viraprakara, Viraḥpraka); number of syllables in the 1st and 3rd Quarters (pada) 20, in the others 18. *Sara* = 5. The scheme is two times:**

⏑⏑⏑ | ⏑—⏑ | ⏑—⏑ | ⏑—⏑ | ⏑—⏑ | ⏑—⏑ | ⏑—
—⏑⏑ | —⏑⏑ | —⏑⏑ | —⏑⏑ | —⏑— | ⏑⏑— |

---

1) H., Ra., Rc., M., D., B. 2) H., Ra. (ačyutaka), Rc. and Rd. (aččutaka), M. (abhyudaka), D. (aččutaka), B. (ačyutaka). 3) H., Rc., Rd., M., D., B.

ರವಿಪ್ರಭೆಗುದಾಹರಣಂ

ಅಮರ-ಸರೋರುಹಮಿತ್ರ-ಗಣಂ, ಶರ-ಸಂಖ್ಯೆಯ ಮುಂದೆ ಲ-ಗಂ,
ಸೋಮ-ಗಣಂಗಳೆ ನಾಲ್ಕೆಡೆಯೊಳ್ ಬರೆ, ಪಾವಕಂ ಮರುತಂ ।
ಕ್ರಮದೊಳೆ ಬಂದನುಲೋಮ-ವಿಲೋಮ-ಪದ-ದ್ವಯದಿಂ ನಿಯಮಂ;
ನಾಮಮಿದಕ್ಕೆ ರವಿಪ್ರಭೆಯಾಗಳೆಯಕ್ಕುಮಬ್ಜ-ಮುಖೀ! || 238[1] ||

227. Supplementary description. Pâda=quarter.

ಕಂದಂ

ಪಾದ-ವಿಪರ್ಯಾಸದೊಳೀ
ಭೇದಂಬಡೆದೇಕ-ವರ್ಣ-ಹೀನಾಧಿಕದಿಂ ।
ದಾದಂದರ್ಧಸಮಂ ಪೆಸ
ರಾದುದದಂ ಬಗೆದು ಕೇಳ್ದುದಂಬುಜ-ವದನೇ! || 239[2] ||

3. The Vishama Vṛittas

ವಿಷಮವೃತ್ತಂಗಳ್

228. Here follow the Vishama Vṛittas, in which all quarters (pâda) are more or less different from each other. Pada=verse.

ಕಂದಂ

ವಿಪರೀತ-ಗಣಾಕ್ಷರಮಾ
ಗಿ, ಪದಂಗಳ್ ನಾಲ್ಕು ಪಾದವೊಂದದೆ ನಿಲ್ಕುಂ; ।
ಚಪಲಾಕ್ಷಿ, ವಿಷಮವೃತ್ತಮ
ನುಪದೇಶಿಪೆನವಱ ಭೇದಮಂ ಕ್ರಮದಿಂದಂ. || 240[3] ||

229. First instance: the U d g a t a. The scheme is:

⏑⏑– | ⏑–⏑ | ⏑⏑– | ⏑
⏑⏑⏑ | ⏑⏑– | ⏑–⏑ | –⏑⏑̄ |
–⏑⏑ | ⏑⏑⏑ | ⏑–⏑ | ⏑–
⏑⏑– | ⏑–⏑ | ⏑⏑– | ⏑–⏑ | – ||[4]

1) Rd. (viraprakara), L. (viraḣpraka), Sb. and M. (raviprabhĕ), H. 2) Ra., Ha., M., D., B. 3) H., Ra., M., D., B. 4) The final letters of lines 2 and 4 are doubtful.

ಉದ್ಗತಕ್ಕುದಾಹರಣಂ

ಮರುದರ್ಕ-ವಾಯು ಲಘು ಮುಂದೆ
ಬರೆ ಸುರ-ಮರುದ್-ದಿನೇಶನುಂ ಶಶಿ- | [ದಿನೇಶ-ಪಾವಕಂ]
ವಾರಿಜರಿಪು-ಸುರಪಾರ್ಕ-ಲ-ಗಂ
ಮರುದರ್ಕ-ವಾಯು-ರವಿಯಿಂದಮುದ್ಗತಂ. || 241[1] ||

230. Besides the Udgata there are various Vishama Vṛittas.

ಇಂತು ವಿಷಮವೃತ್ತಮನೇಕ-ಪ್ರಕಾರಮಕ್ಕುಂ.

231. Second instance: the *S*loka or Anushṭup-śloka; quarters of 8 syllables. The scheme, as far as it is fixed, is the following (oja=an odd quarter, 1 and 3; yugma=an even quarter, 2 and 4), the dots denoting the syllables that are not fixed.

1 2 3 4 5 6 7 8
· · · · ⏑ — — ·
· · · · ⏑ — ⏑ · | (generally 5 6 7 8: ⏑ — ⏑ —)
· · · · ⏑ — — ·
· · · · ⏑ — ⏑ · || (generally 5 6 7 8: ⏑ — ⏑ —)

ಇನ್ನು ಅನುಷ್ಟುಪ್-ಶ್ಲೋಕ-ಲಕ್ಷಣಂ

ಶ್ಲೋಕಂ

ಅಕ್ಕರುಂ ನಾಲ್ಕೆರಡಿಂದತ್ತ
ಲಕ್ಕುಂ ಯ-ಗಣವೋಜದೊಳ್; |
ಮಿಕ್ಕ ಯುಗ್ಮಾಂತದೊಳ್ ಸೂರ್ಯ
ನಕ್ಕುಂ ಶ್ಲೋಕೋಕ್ತಿಯೊಳ್, ನಿಜಂ. || 242[2] ||

---

1) H., Ra., Rc., Rd., Sb., M., D., B.; ದಿನೇಶನುಂ ಶಶಿ occurs in Sb., H. and Ra. There is another Udgata in D. and M. after the *C*aturûrdhva, the scheme of which is as follows:

⏑⏑⏑ | ⏑—⏑ | ⏑⏑— | ⏑
⏑⏑⏑ | ⏑—⏑ | —⏑— |
⏑⏑⏑ | ⏑—— | ⏑—
⏑⏑⏑ | ⏑—⏑ | ⏑⏑— | ⏑— ||

2) Rc., D., B.

232. The same statement in a Samskṛit verse (without alliteration).

ಶ್ಲೋಕಂ

ಪಂಚಮಂ ಲಘು ಸರ್ವತ್ರ,
ಸಪ್ತಮಂ ದ್ವಿ-ಚತುರ್ಥಯೋಃ, ।
ಷಷ್ಠೇ ಚ ಗುರು ಜಾನೀಯಾದ್,
ದಿಶ್ಯತೇ ಶ್ಲೋಕ-ಲಕ್ಷಣಂ. || 243[1] ||

233. However elsewhere each seventh syllable of all the quarters of the Śloka is allowed to be long (Weber pp. 335. 336; 5. 6. 7. throughout: ⏑ — —); but such is not the rule given by the author. His rule is that the seventh syllables ought to be alternately long and short. Abdhi=4 or 7. (Karâbdhi=shining or great seven?)

ಕಂದಂ

ಎಯ್ದಾಱೇೞೆಂಬೆಡೆಯೊಳ
ಮೆಯ್ದುಗೆ ಲಘು-ಗುರು-ಕರಾಬ್ಧಿ-ಗುರು!—ಸಪ್ತಕದೊಳ್ ।
ಎಯ್ದೋರ್ ಗುರು-ಲಘು-ಲಕ್ಷಣ
ಮೆಯ್ದುಗೆ! ಪರಿಪೂರ್ಣಮಷ್ಟ-ವರ್ಣ-ಶ್ಲೋಕಂ. || 244[2] ||

234. But as some poets of old have stated that, like each sixth syllable, each seventh one too may be long, all the said syllables may be long.

ಕಂದಂ

ಆಱನೆಯ ತಾಣದೊಳ್ ಗುರು
ತೋಱಿದೊಡಂ, ಶ್ಲೋಕ-ಲಕ್ಷಣಂ ಕೆಡದದುವುಂ ।
ಬೇಱೆ ಪುರಾತನ-ಕವಿಗಳ್
ತೋಱಿದೊಡಂತೆರಡಱೊಳಗೆಯುಂ ಗುರುವುಚಿತಂ. || 245[3] ||

---

1) D., B. A similar verse occurs twice in M. (here and in the first chapter); of its two readings the first is: ಶ್ಲೋಕೇನಷ್ಟಗುರುರ್ಜ್ಞೇಯಂ ಸರ್ವತ್ರಲಘುಪಂಚಮಂ । ದ್ವಿಚತುಃಪಾದಯೋರ್ಹ್ರಸ್ವಂ ಸಮಸ್ತ್ರದೀರ್ಘಮನ್ಯಯೋಃ ।। ; the second one is: ಷಟ್ತ್ರಿಚತುಷ್ಟಯೋರ್ಜ್ಞೇಯಂ ಸರ್ವತ್ರಲಘುಪಂಚಮಂ । ದ್ವಿಚತುಃಪಾದಯೋರ್ಹ್ರಸ್ವ ಖ್ಯಾನುಷ್ಟುಭೋಽಭವೇತ್ ।। For D. and B.'s reading cf. Weber p. 338.

2) Sb., M., H., Ra., L., D. The true reading of this verse is somewhat questionable, as on MS. agrees with the other. 3) H., Ra., Ro., M., L., D., B.

235. Another verse of the common *S*loka in Canarese.

ಶ್ಲೋಕಂ

ಯೋಗಿ-ಯೋಗ-ಚಿದಾನಂದ	[ಯೋಗಿಯೋಗಚಿತಸ್ತೋಮಂ
ಮಾಗಮ-ಜ್ಞನೆ ಮೂಡಿದಂ ।	ಸ್ವಾಗಮಜ್ಞಾನವರಾಧಿಕಂ ।
ರಾಗದಿಂ, ವಿನತಾಪಾಂಗೀ,	ರಾಗದಿಂಬಿನತಂಗಿಗೆ
ನಾಗವರ್ಮ-ಮತಂಗಳಿಂ.	ನಾಗವರ್ಮಬರಂಗಳ್ಗಂ ‖] [1] ‖ 246 ‖

236. Third instance: the Tripadonnati; quarters 1, 2 and 4 contain each 10 syllables; quarter 3 consists of 12 syllables, (having two more, from which peculiarity probably the name of the metre is derived). The scheme:

— ⏑ ⏑ | — ⏑ ⏑ | — ⏑ ⏑ | —
— ⏑ ⏑ | — ⏑ ⏑ | — ⏑ ⏑ | — |
— ⏑ ⏑ | — ⏑ ⏑ | — ⏑ ⏑ | — ⏑ ⏑
— ⏑ ⏑ | — ⏑ ⏑ | — ⏑ ⏑ | — ‖

ತ್ರಿಪದೋನ್ನತಿಯ ಲಕ್ಷಣಂ

ಚಂದ್ರಗಣ-ತ್ರಿತಯಂ, ಕಡೆಯೊಳ್
ಚಂದ್ರಧರಂ ಬರೆ ಮೂಱಿಡೆಯೊಳ್, ।
ಚಂದ್ರ-ಚತುಷ್ಟಯಮಾಗಿರೆ, ಭಾವಿಸು,
ಚಂದ್ರ-ಮುಖೀ, ತ್ರಿಪದೋನ್ನತಿಯಂ! ‖ 247 [2] ‖

237. Fourth instance: the Pada *C*aturûrdhva. Commencing with 8 (kari) syllables it grows by 4 and 4 (cf. the name of *C*aturûrdhva), so that its second quarter has 12 (dinapa), its third quarter 16 (râja), its fourth quarter 20 (râvaṇakara) syllables. (The syllables are generally not ordered to be fixed ones, atra guru-laghu-vibhâgo neshyate, Weber p. 348.)

ಕಂದಂ

ಕರಿ-ದಿನಪ-ರಾಜ-ರಾವಣ
ಕರ-ಪರಿಸಂಖ್ಯಾಕ್ಷರದೆ ಪೊದಳ್ದೆಸೆಯೆ ಗಣಾಂ ।

1) M. D., B. have a similar instance; Ra., H.'s reading too appears above, they calling it Nâṭaka *S*loka. 2) H., Ra., Rc., Rd., M., Sb., L.

ತರಮಪ್ಪುದು ಚತುರೂರ್ಧ್ವಂ [ತೆರದಿಂ ಪದಚ ಇತ್ಯಾದಿ]
ಪರಿಸ್ಫುಟಂ. ಬಗೆದು ಕೇಳ್ವುದಂಬುಜ-ವದನೇ! || 248[1] ||

238. A verse in the Pada *C*aturûrdhva metre. Its scheme is:

⏑⏑⏑ | ⏑—— | ——
⏑⏑— | —⏑⏑ | ⏑—⏑ | ——— |
⏑⏑⏑ | ⏑⏑⏑ | ⏑⏑— | —⏑— | ⏑—— | —
⏑⏑— | ⏑—⏑ | ——⏑ | ⏑—— | —⏑— | ⏑—⏑ | ⏑— ||

ಪದಚತುರೂರ್ಧ್ವಂ

ಅತಿಶಯ-ವಾಕ್-ಸಂಪನ್ನಂ
ಶತಪತ್ರೋದ್ಭವ-ಮಹಾನ್ವಯೋತ್ಪನ್ನಂ ।
ಚತುರ-ಕವಿ-ಕುಲ-ಲಲಾಮಂ ಗುಣೋದಯೋದ್ದಾಮಂ
ಚತುರಾನನೇಂದ್ರ-ವಿಷ್ಣು-ಪ್ರತಿಮಂ ಶ್ರೀ-ನಾಗವರ್ಮನ ಪ್ರತಿಮಂ. || 249[2] ||

B. THE MORA-METRES[3]

ಮಾತ್ರಾಛಂದಂಗಳ್

In the first part of a quarter of a verse in a Mora (mâtrĕ)-Metre there are some not-fixed syllables which do not fall under the category of Feet, but have to represent a certain amount of Moras.

1. The Vaitâḷikĕ (Vaitâḷi)

239. The number of Moras (mâtrĕ) in the Vaitâḷikĕ: in the odd (ojĕ) quarters (pâda) 14, in the even (yuk) 16; the sum of all Moras 60.

ಕಂದಂ

ಮೊದಲೊಳ್ ಪದಿನಾಲ್ಕೆರಡನೆ
ಯದಱೊಳ್ ಪದಿನಾಱು, ಮೂಱಱೊಳ್ ಪದಿನಾಲ್ಕು ।

1) H., Ra., M., D., B. Pada čaturûrdhva must be the true reading. 2) H. Ra. (-ನೇಂದ್ರ-ಮುಕಿ-ಪ್ರತಿಮಂ), D., B. A praise of Nâgavarma! 3) This heading is not in the MSS.

ಗ್ರದ ಪಾದದೆ ಪದಿನಾಱುಂ
ತುದಯಿಪುದಱುವತ್ತು ಮಾತ್ರೆ ವೈತಾಳಿಕೆಗಂ. || 250[1] ||

240. Definition of the Vaitâḷi in a Vaitâḷi verse: in the odd quarters *first* appear 6 (kara) Moras, and in the even ones 8 (kari); *then* an Amphimacrus (marudishṭa, fire, —⏑—) and a short and long syllable are added to each quarter. The scheme of the verse runs as follows:

⏑⏑—⏑⏑ | —⏑— | ⏑— 14 *Moras*
⏑⏑——— | —⏑— | ⏑— | 16 *Moras*
⏑⏑—⏑⏑ | —⏑— | ⏑— 14 *Moras*
⏑⏑——⏑⏑ | —⏑— | ⏑— || 16 *Moras*

ವೈತಾಳಿಕೆ

ಕರ-ಮಾತ್ರೆಗಳಕ್ಕುಮೋಜೆಯೊಳ್, [ಖರ-ಮಾತ್ರೆ]
ಕರಿ-ಸಂಖ್ಯಾತಂ ಮಾತ್ರೆ ಯುಕ್ಕಿನೊಳ್, |
ಮರುದಿಷ್ಟ-ಲ-ಗಂ ತದಂತದೊಳ್
ಬರೆ, ವೈತಾಳಿ, ವಿಲೋಲ-ಲೋಚನೇ! || 251[2] ||

☞ Observe here that at the places where no fixed syllables are ordered, in Canarese always two and two short syllables can be taken separately, either as ⏑⏑ or —, so that ⏑— (Iambus) is excluded.

2. The Aupacčhandasika

241. The Aupacčhandasika differs from the Vaitâḷike only by the circumstance that instead of the short and long syllable a Bacchious (⏑——, toya) is added. The scheme of the following Aupacčhandasika verse is:

— —⏑⏑ | —⏑— | ⏑—— 16 *Moras*
———⏑⏑ | —⏑— | ⏑—— | 18 *Moras*
— ⏑⏑— | —⏑— | ⏑—— 16 *Moras*
———⏑⏑ | —⏑— | ⏑—— || 18 *Moras*

ಔಪಚ್ಛಂದಸಿಕಂ

ಈ ಪೇೞ್ದುದು ವಹ್ನಿ ತೋಯ-ಯುಗ್ಮಂ
ತಾಂ ಪಾದ-ದ್ವಯಕಂತೆ ಬಂದೊಡಕ್ಕುಂ, |

1) D., B. 2) M., H., Ra., D., B.

ಚಾಪಲ-ನೇತ್ರೇ, ವಿರಾಜಿಸುತ್ತಂ
ದೌಪಚ್ಛಂದಸಿಕಂ ಕವೀಶ್ವರೋಕ್ತಂ. || 252[1] ||

242. The Vaitâḷikĕs (the Aupacchandasika being in fact a sub-division of the Vaitâḷikĕ), as they are formed of Mora-feet (mâtrâ gaṇa), have been treated separately.

ಗದ್ಯವಚನಂ

ಇಂತಾದೌಪಚ್ಛಂದಸಿಕಂ ಮೊದಲಾಗಿ ವೈತಾಳಿಕೆಯುಂ, ಪ್ರಾಚ್ಯ-ವೃತ್ತಿಕೆಯುಂ ಪರಾಂತಿಕೆಯುಮೆಂದುಂ ಮಾತ್ರಾಗಣಾಧಿಕಂಗಳೆಂದಂತು ವೈತಾಳಿಕೆಗಳ್ ಬೇಱೆ ಪೇಳಲ್ಪಡೆಗುಂ[2].

3. The Jâti Gâdĕ

(Gâthâ) is introduced. The verse adduced consists of 3 lines (pada) each containing 23 Moras, and shows, to some extent, the peculiarity of the Śloka, (wherein two Amphibrachus' are prescribed), as after the 17th Mora in each line an Amphibrachus (with a long syllable) is to occur.

ಅದಲ್ಲದೆಯುಂ ಜಾತಿಗಾದೆಗಳ ಲಕ್ಷಣಮಂ ಪೇಳ್ವೆಂ—
ಪದಮೂಱಾಗಿಯುಂ ಶ್ಲೋಕದ ಲಕ್ಷಣಮುಮಾಗಿಯುಂ
ವಿದಿತಂ ಜಾತಿಗಾದೆಯೆಂಬುದು. ಸಂದಭಿಧಾನದಿಂ
ದಿದನೋದು, ವಿಲೋಲ-ಷಟ್ಪದ-ಸಂನಿಭ-ಕುಂತಳೇ! || 253[3] || [ದಿದನೋದುಗೆ]

Its scheme:

⏑⏑— — ⏑— — ⏑⏑— ⏑⏑ | ⏑—⏑ | —	23 *Moras*
⏑⏑— — ⏑— ⏑— ⏑⏑— ⏑ | ⏑—⏑ | — |	23 *Moras*
⏑⏑—(⏑)⏑⏑—⏑—⏑⏑—⏑ | ⏑—⏑ | — ‖	23 *Moras*

1) Sb., L., M., Ra., H. 2) Sb., L., M., Ra., H. Their readings differ very much; the one given is the clearest. 3) Sb., H., Ra., M., L. Our reading is that of Sb., H., Ra. and L. M. begins ಪದಮುಲಾಗಿಯುಂ. The first two lines contain each 23 Moras, the third only 22. M.'s otherwise very deficient reading (instead of ದಿದನೋದು) is ದಿದನೋದುಗೆ, and would bring the last line also up to 23 Moras. The Gâdĕ (gâthâ) has been looked upon as the Âryâ (Weber p. 295); but the verse of the text cannot belong to that class, even if M.'s beginning be adopted. Mr. Colebrooke states, p. 446: "The same denomination (gâthâ) is applicable also to stanzas consisting of any number of verses (lines) other than four."

C. THE MORA-FEET[1]

ಮಾತ್ರಾಗಣಂಗಳ್

Introduction

Here feet (gaṇa) of a certain number of Moras (not syllable-feet) are first introduced. Such feet, in the Ragaḷĕs, consist either of three, or of four, or of five syllables. The feet of one of the mentioned three classes in their various shapes are, without any restriction, used one for the other (except in a Canarese vṛitta, for instance, v. 276).

The forms of the feet, for which rule 289 and its exposition are presupposed, are the following:

1. The 2 feet of three Moras

◡◡◡ (Tribach); —◡ (Trochee).

2. The 4 feet of four Moras

◡◡◡◡ (Proceleusmatic); —◡◡ (Dactyl); ◡◡— (Anapaest); —— (Spondee).

3. The 6 feet of five Moras

◡◡◡◡◡; —◡◡◡ (Paeon); ——◡ (Antibacchic); ◡◡—◡; —◡— (Amphimacer); ◡◡◡—.

☞ Observe that no foot dare begin with an Iambus *i. e.* ◡—! This observation is essential as to all the Mora-Feet metres (excepting the peculiar Samskṛit Āryâs to which Kanda, Āryâ, etc. belong, v. 282 seq.).

1. The Raghaṭĕ or Ragaḷĕ

ರಘಟಾಲಕ್ಷಣಂ

248. The Raghaṭĕ is neither built on the system of the syllable-feet nor on that of a mere number of Moras, but on an equal number of Moras (mâtrâ) *included within certain feet* (gaṇa); and harmonises with beating time in music (tâḷa).

ಕಂದಂ

ಗಣ-ನಿಯಮ-ವಿಪರ್ಯಾಸದೊ
ಳೆಣಿಕೆವಡೆದೊಳ್ಪೆಸೆದು ಮಾತ್ರೆ ಸಮನಾಗೆ, ಗಣಾ |

1) This heading is not in the MSS.

ಗ್ರಣಿಯ ಮತದಿಂದೆ ತಾಳದ
ಗಣನೆಗೊಡಂಬಟ್ಟುದದುವೆ ರಘಟಾ-ಬಂಧಂ. || 254 ||[1]

244. There are 3 kinds of Ragaḷĕ, which are frequently used: the Mandânila, Lalitĕ and Utsava (Utsâha).

ಮಂದಾನಿಲ-ಲಲಿತೋತ್ಸವ
ಮೆಂದೇ ರಗಳೆಗಳ ನಾಮಮಕ್ಕುಂ; ಕ್ರಮದಿಂ |
ದೊಂದಕೆ ಪದಿನಾಱಿರ್ಪ
ತ್ತೊಂದಕ್ಕಿರ್ಪತ್ತು ನಾಲ್ಕು ಮಾತ್ರೆಗಳಬಲೇ! || 255 ||[2]

245. The Mandânila has 16 Moras in each quarter, the Lalitĕ 20, the Utsava (utsâha) 24.

ಇಪ್ಪತ್ತು ಮಾತ್ರೆ ಲಲಿತೆಗೆ
ಒಪ್ಪುದು, ಪದಿನಾಱು ಮಾತ್ರೆ ಮಂದಾನಿಲಕಂ |
ತಪ್ಪುದುವುತ್ಸಾಹಕ್ಕಱಿ
ಯೊಪ್ಪುವುದಿಪ್ಪತ್ತು ನಾಲ್ಕು ಮಾತ್ರೆಗಳಬಲೇ! || 256 ||[3]

246. First instance: the **M a n d â n i l a**, with 16 Moras in each quarter, that are enclosed in 4 feet, each of which consists of 4 Moras. The Mandânila verses, like the other Ragaḷĕs, require *at least* two Alliterations (cf. Weber, p. 201. 391), one at the beginning of each quarter and one at the end. A peculiarity also is that the last two quarters' Alliteration generally is different from that of the first two; sometimes each line begins with a different one.

ಮಂದಾನಿಲಕ್ಕುದಾಹರಣಂಗಳ್

The scheme is four times:

⏑⏑⏑⏑ | ⏑⏑⏑⏑ * ⏑⏑⏑⏑ | ⏑⏑⏑⏑

Descriptive verses[4]

ಆ ವೇಳೆಯೊಳತಿ-ಸಂಭ್ರಮಮೆಸೆದಿರೆ,
ಪೂವಲಿ-ಪುರ-ವೀಥಿಗಳೊಳ್ ನೆಱೆದಿರೆ |

1) H., Ra., Rc., M., Sb., L., D., B. Harîśvara, the guru of Râghava, already composed a Sadgirijâ Vivâha in Ragaḷĕs, *Can. Bas. Pur.* 62, v. 55. 2) D., B. 3) Rc., Rd., D., B. There are no instances for the Ragaḷĕs except in D. and B. (for each a praise), but of a character unfit for the object of the present edition. 4) From the 9th chapter of the Râjaśekhara Vilâsa where they occur after the prose-sentence that follows verse 41. Another instance is found XIV., after v. 106. See Râvaṇa digvijaya, Mangalore edition p. 10.

ಪವಳದ ರನ್ನದ ಗುದಿಗಳ ಗುಡಿಗಳ್,
ನವ-ಮೌಕ್ತಿಕ-ರಂಗದ ದಾಂಗುಡಿಗಳ್, || 257 ||

ಮೆಱೆದುವು ಮಿಱುಗುವ ಮಿಸುನಿಯ ತೋರಣ
ಮಱಿಕೆಯ ಪುರ-ಜನದುತ್ಸವದೋರಣ |
ಮಾನೆಯ ಮೇಲಣ ಪಳವಿಗೆ ಮಿಳಿರ್ದಿರೆ,
ನಾನಾ-ವಿಧ-ವಾದ್ಯ-ಧ್ವನಿಯಳುರ್ದಿರೆ, || 258 ||

ಕರೆದುವು ಬಿರುದಿನ ಕಹಳೆಗಳಾಗಳ್,
ಪರೆದುದು ಪಳಹದ ರವಮೆಣ್ದೆಸೆಯೊಳ್,
ಗಿರಿ-ಬಂಧುರ-ಸಿಂಧುರ-ತತಿ ನಡೆ ತರೆ,
ಚರ-ವೃಂದದ ಕುಂದದ ಕಳಕಳಮಿರೆ, || 259 ||

ಪೊಸ ಮೇಳದ ತಾಳದ ಮೃದು-ನಿನದಂ
ಪಸರಿಸೆ ಗೀತ-ರವಂ, ಕಡು ಬಿನದಂ
ಬಡೆದಿದಿರ್ವಂದುದು ರಾಜ-ಪ್ರಚಯಂ,
ಬಿಡದೊಡವಂದುದು ನಾರೀ-ನಿಚಯಂ. || 260 ||

A praise[1)]

ಶ್ರೀಕರುಣೇಶಾ, ಶ್ರುತಿ-ತತಿ-ದೇಶಾ,
ಲೋಕ-ನಿಘರ್ಷಾ, ಲೋಭಿತ-ಹರ್ಷಾ, |
ಪ್ರೇಮ-ನಿವಾಸಾ, ಪ್ರಕಟಾಭಾಸಾ,
ಕ್ಷೇಮ-ವಿಸರಣಾ, ಕ್ಷಮ-ಗುಣ-ಭರಣಾ! || 261 ||

247. Second instance: the Lalitĕ, with 20 Moras in each quarter, that are enclosed in 4 feet, each of which consists of 5 Moras.

ಲಲಿತೆಗುದಾಹರಣಂಗಳ್

The scheme is four times (the Caesura not always being evidently indicated):

◡◡◡◡◡ | ◡◡◡◡◡ * ◡◡◡◡◡ | ◡◡◡◡◡

Descriptive verses[2)]

ಅಲ್ಲಿ ಮಾಮರದಲ್ಲಿ ಮಲ್ಲಿಕಾ-ಲತೆಯಲ್ಲಿ
ಯೆಳೆಯಸುಗೆಮರದಲ್ಲಿ ಜಳರುಹಾಕರದಲ್ಲಿ |

1) An imitation of the only verse occurring in D. and B. 2) Râjaśekhara Vilâsa, 10th chapter, after verse 57.

ಸಂಪಗೆಯ ತರುಗಳೊಳ್ ಸೊಂಪಿಡಿದ ಸುರಯಿಯೊಳ್
ಪಾದರಿಯ ಬನದಲ್ಲಿ ಮಾಧವಿಯ ಲತೆಯಲ್ಲಿ || 262 ||

ತಿಳಕ-ಬಕುಳಾದಿ-ತರು-ನಿವಹದಾರವೆಗಳೊಳ್
ದಳ-ಫಳ-ಕುಸುಮ-ವಿಸರ-ವಿದಿತ-ವಿಟಪಂಗಳೊಳ್ |
ಪೂಗೊಯ್ಯಲೆಂದಬಲೆಯರ್ ನೆರೆದು ಬಗೆದಂದು
ಬೇಗದಿಂ ಪರಿತಂದು ಪರಿತೋಷದಿಂ ನಿಂದು. || 263 ||

Further descriptive verses[1)]

ಸುಧೆ-ದಧಿ-ಘೃತಂ ಮಧು-ಸದ್ಯೈಕ್ಷವ-ರಸಂಗಳಿಂ,
ಮಧುರತರ-ಭಸಿತ-ಮಿಶ್ರಿತ-ಸಿತ-ಜಳಂಗಳಿಂ, |
ಹಿಮ-ವಿಮಳ-ಮಲಯಜ-ಸುಗಂಧಾನುಲೇಪದಿಂ,
ಕಮಳರಿಪು-ಧವಳ-ಕಳಮಾಕ್ಷತ-ಕಳಾಪದಿಂ, || 263 *a* ||

ಪರಿಮಳ-ಮಿಳಿತ-ದಳಿತ-ನಳಿನ-ಕುಮುದಂಗಳಿಂ,
ಸರಸ-ಚಂಪಕ-ವಕುಳ-ತಿಳಕ-ಕುಸುಮಂಗಳಿಂ, |
ದಮನ-ಮರುವಕ-ಬಿಲ್ವ-ಪಲ್ಲವ-ಸ್ತೋಮದಿಂ,
ಕಮನ-ಘೃತ-ಸಹಿತ-ಗುಗ್ಗುಳ-ಧೂಪ-ಧೂಮದಿಂ, || 263*b* ||

ಪ್ರಚುರ-ಶುಚಿ-ರುಚಿರ-ರುಚಿ-ಮಣಿ-ದೀಪ-ಮಾಲೆಯಿಂ,
ರಚಿತ-ರುಚಿ-ನಿಚಿತ-ಶುಚಿ-ಸಾಜ್ಯ-ಭೋಜ್ಯಾಳಿಯಿಂ, |
ನವ-ನಾರಿಕೇಳ-ಕದಳೀ-ಫಳ-ಪ್ರಸರದಿಂ,
ವಿವಿಧತರ-ಸುರಭಿ-ರಸ-ವೀಟಕಾ-ವಿಸರದಿಂ, ಇತ್ಯಾದಿ || 263*c* ||

A praise[2)]

ಸತ್ಯ-ಧರ್ಮ-ಸುಶೀಲ, ಸರ್ವ-ಜನ-ಪರಿಪಾಲ,
ನಿತ್ಯ-ನಿರ್ಮಲ-ಚರಿತ, ನೀತಿ-ಯುತ-ಗುಣ-ಭರಿತ, |
ಭೂರಿ-ರವಿ-ಸಂಕಾಶ, ಭೂ-ದೀನ-ರಕ್ಷೇಶ,
ಕಾರುಣ್ಯ-ವಿಖ್ಯಾತ, ಕಾಮಿತ-ಪ್ರತಿದಾತ! || 264 ||

1) Ráj. Vilása XIII., after v. 51. Other instances occur Ráj. Vilása II., after v. 117; XIV., after v. 169. 2) An imitation of the verse in D. and B.

248. Third instance: the **U t s a v a** or **U t s â h a**, with 24 Moras in each quarter, that are enclosed in 8 feet, each of which consists of 3 Moras. Cf. the Utsâha v. 339.

ಉತ್ಸಾಹಕ್ಕುದಾಹರಣಂಗಳ್

The scheme is four times:

⏑⏑⏑ | ⏑⏑⏑ | ⏑⏑⏑ | ⏑⏑⏑ * ⏑⏑⏑ | ⏑⏑⏑ | ⏑⏑⏑ | ⏑⏑⏑

Descriptive verses

(A rebuke)[1)]

ಯಾರು? ಏಕೆ ಬಂದಿಯೆನೆ ವಿಚಾರವನ್ನು ಮಾಡುವಂಥ
ಪಾರುಪತ್ಯವಿತ್ತವನ್ನ ತೋಱಿ ಕೊಟ್ಟು ನುಡಿಯ ಬೇಕು! |
ಮಂಗನಂತೆ ಪಲ್ಲ ಕಿಸಿದು, ತುಂಗ-ಸಾಸಿಯೆಂದು, ಬಱಿದೆ
ಹಿಂಗದೆನ್ನ ಕೂಡೆ ವಿಕ್ರಮಾಂಗವನ್ನು ಮೆಱಿಸಲೇಕೆ? || 265 ||

ಮೊಗವ ಕಂಡರೀಗ ಮರ್ಕಟಗಳ ವೋಲು ತೋರ್ಪುತಿಹುದು.
ವಿಗಡತನದ ಮಾತುಗಳನೆ ಬೊಗಳ ಬೇಡ! ಸಾಕು! ಸಾಕು! |

(A lamentation)[2)]

ಅಟ್ಟ ಅನ್ನವುಣ್ಣ ಬಿಡನು, ಕೊಟ್ಟ ಸಾಲ ಕೇಳ ಬಿಡನು,
ಪೆಟ್ಟಿಯೊಳಿಹ ಚಿನ್ನದೊಡವೆ ತೊಟ್ಟೆನೆನಲು ಯಮನು ಬಿಡನು; |
ಅಕ್ಕನಿಲ್ಲಿ ಕರೆಯಲಿಲ್ಲ, ಮಕ್ಕಳನ್ನು ಪಡೆಯಲಿಲ್ಲ!
ದುಕ್ಕಗೊಂಡು ಕಣ್ಣ ನೀರನುಕ್ಕಿಸುವರೆ ಯಮನು ಬಿಡನು. || 266 ||

ಹೇಳೆನೆಂಬರಿಷ್ಟರಿಂಗೆ ಬೇಳೆ ಬೆಲ್ಲ ಹೊನ್ನು ತಂದು,
ನಾಳೆ ಮಗನ ಮದುವೆಯೆನಲು, ಕಾಳ ಬೆನ್ನ ಬಿಡನು. ಇದಕೊ! |
ಮಾಳಿಗೆಯದು ಮನೆಯುಮಿರಲಿ, ಜಾಳಿಗೆಯೊಳು ಹೊನ್ನುಮಿರಲಿ,
ಆಳು ಮಂದಿಯಾನೆಯಿರಲಿ, ಕಾಳ ಬೆನ್ನ ಬಿಡನು. ಇದಕೊ! || 267 ||

---

1) From the Râvaṇa digvijaya, Mangalore edition, p. 12; there, however, a new verse begins after two and two lines, and there is no final Alliteration; besides the Canarese is not worthy of imitation, old and new forms being blended.

2) The 41st Dâsa Song in the Mangalore collection; the remarks to verse 265 equally concern these verses; observe also the offences against the rules of Euphony (sandhi)! Verses 265, 266, and 267, though correct with regard to feet and Moras (for the counting of which they are given), are not elegant with regard to form.

1)
A praise

ಪ್ರೇಮ-ವಾಸ, ಸದ್ಗುಣೈಕ-*ಧಾಮ, ಸೂರ್ಯ-ಕೋಟಿ-ಭಾಸ,
ಕೋಮಲಾಂಗ, ಸಂತತಾಭಿ*ರಾಮ, ನಿರ್ಮಲಾಂತರಂಗ, |
ಸಂಕುಲಾರ್ತಿ-ನಿಗ್ರಹಾತ್ಮ*, ಶಂಕಿತಾತ್ಮ-ಧೈರ್ಯ-ಕರ್ತ,
ಕಿಂಕರೀಕೃತೋರ್ವಿ-ರಾಜ*, ಪಂಕ-ವೈರಿ, ಪುಣ್ಯ-ವಾಕ! || 268 ||

249. A fourth instance: the Sîsapadya[2]. Each quarter of this consists of 6 Puruhûta (⏑⏑—⏑) feet (gaṇa) *i. e.* feet of five Moras, to which the two feet pointed out by Sarasijasakha (⏑⏑⏑ . ⏑⏑⏑) *i. e.* 2 feet of three Moras are added.

ಕಂದಂ

ಪುರುಹೂತ-ಗಣಗಳಾಱಿಂ,
ಸರಸಿಜಸಖ-ಗಣಗಳೆರಡು ಸಂಧಿಸಿ ಬರ್ಕುಂ !
ಚರಣಕ್ಕೆ ಸೀಸದಂತದೊ
ಳೊಱಿಗಿಂತಹ ಸರಳ ತನ್ನೊಳೊಪ್ಪುವ ತೆಱಿದಿಂ. || 269 ||

The scheme is four times;

1	2	3	4	5	6	1	2
⏑⏑⏑⏑⏑	⏑⏑⏑⏑⏑	⏑⏑⏑⏑⏑	⏑⏑⏑⏑⏑ *	⏑⏑⏑⏑⏑	⏑⏑⏑⏑⏑	⏑⏑⏑	⏑⏑⏑

ಸೀಸಂ

ತಿಂಗಳಂ ತಳೆದಿತ್ತ, ರಂಗ-ಮಂಗಳ-ಕರ್ತ*, ತುಂಗ-ಸೂರ್ಯ-ಸುಭರ್ತ, ತಮಸ-ನಾಶ!
ಮಂಗಳಂ ಮನವಾಂತ, ಮಧುರತಾ-ಕರುಣಾತ್ಮ*, ಭಂಗ-ನಿಗ್ರಹಿಪಾತ, ಭೀತಿ-ಹರಣ! |

1) An imitation of the verse in D. and B.

2) This is taken from the Kavijihvâbandhana, where the rule and instance form verses 46 and 47 of the 2nd chapter. The Sîsa and Āṭagîtĕ (this name, however, is not given there) *together* form *one* viz. the 47th verse. The instances given in the text are a close imitation (the first line of the Āṭagîtĕ is that of the original), especially with regard to the scheme; the words ಮುನಿಸುರಾಸುರವಂದ್ಯ also belong to the original. The appellations for the two kinds of feet are peculiar.—Regarding the large number of Alliterations being desired in the Ragaḷĕs confer the Lalita (v. 217), the Krauñcapada (v. 221), the Vanalatĕ (v. 226), the Lalitapada (v.233), and the Kusumaśara (v. 234) among the Sama Vṛittas! The Lalitĕ (v. 256) in fact bears the name of at least one of the mentioned Vṛittas. An Utsava occurs again in verse 339. The Dâsa Padas are all composed in Ragaḷĕ metres, but their schemes are somewhat different; for the schemes vary according to the tunes used. Though there be many metrical mistakes in the Dâsa Padas, they can easily be found out and corrected.—There are a number of Sîsapadyas in the *Saraṇalîlâmṛita* (ps. 4. 57. 61. 109. 113. 161. 173. 217. 223. 226.), Beṅgaḷûru, 1871. It is a very imperfect and faulty edition; however, the Sîsas there are built on the scheme of the present text, but the Āṭagîtĕs are of such various forms as to fall under no apparent rule.

ಸಂಗೀತ-ರಸಲೋಲ, ಸಾಹಿತ್ಯದಾನಂದ*, ಪೊಂಗುವರ್ಕಗೆ ಪೋಲಿಪಮಲ-ಕಿರಣ!
ಕಂಗಳುಂ ಮುಗಿಯದ, ಕರಂಗಳುಂ ಬಿಗುವಿಡದ*, ಪಿಂಗದೆ ಸಹಾಯಮಮಂ ಪಡಿಪ ಶರಣ!

|| 270 ||

To this a so-called Āṭagīte, as people call it, is to be added, the scheme of which is two times:

◡◡◡ | ◡◡◡ | ◡◡◡* ◡◡◡ | ◡◡◡◡ | ◡◡◡
◡◡◡ | ◡◡◡ | ◡◡◡* ◡◡◡◡ | ◡◡◡ |

ಆಟಗೀತೆ

ವಿಗತ-ದುಷ್ಕೃತಾಂಗ*, ವಿಮಲ-ಸುಸ್ಥಿರ-ಚಿತ್ತ,
ಗಗನ-ಪೀಠ-ವಾಸ*, ನಮ್ರ-ಪ್ರೀತ! |
ನಗ-ಕುಲಾದಿ-ಧಾತ*, ಮುನಿ-ಸುರಾಸುರ-ವಂದ್ಯ,
ಜಗ-ಪರಿಣುತ-ರಾಜ*, ಕೇವಲ-ದಾತ! || 271 ||

250. A fifth instance: the *Caupadi*. Each quarter consists of 4 feet, the first three consisting each of 5 Moras, the last one of 3. Alliteration is required at the beginning and at the end, and Caesura may occur after the 8th Mora of a quarter.

The schemes appearing in the following two verses are (both are given in full to show, how the feet of the same number of Moras may interchange):

A

◡◡◡ — | ◡◡◡*◡◡ | — ◡ — | ◡◡◡
◡◡◡◡◡ | — ◡*◡◡ | ◡◡◡◡◡ | ◡◡◡ |
◡◡ — ◡ | — ◡*◡◡ | ◡◡ — ◡ | ◡◡◡
◡◡ — ◡ | — ◡*◡◡ | ◡◡◡◡◡ | ◡◡◡ ||

B

— — ◡ | — ◡◡◡ | ◡◡◡◡◡ | — ◡
— — ◡ | — — ◡ | ◡◡◡◡◡ | — ◡ |
◡◡◡◡◡ | — ◡ — | ◡◡◡ — | ◡◡◡
◡◡◡◡◡ | ◡◡◡ — | ◡◡◡ — | ◡◡◡ ||

The Rule

ಚೌಪದಿಯ ಲಕ್ಷಣಂ

ಎಸೆವ ಚೌಪದಿಗೆ* ಪದಿನೆಂಟು ಮಾತ್ರೆಗಳು,
ಸಸಿನೆ ಯತಿಯೆಂಟ*ಱೊಳು ಪಸರಿಸುತಲಿರಲು, |

ಹಸನಾಗಿ ನಾಲ್ಕು* ಪದ ಸಮನಾಗಿ ಬರಲು,
ಬಿಸಜಾಕ್ಷಿ, ಪ್ರಾಸು*, ತಿಳಿ, ಮೊದಲು ಕಡೆಯಿರಲು. || 272[1] ||

A descriptive verse

ಪ್ರಾಚೇತಸಾಖ್ಯ-ಮುನಿ-ಪತಿಯ ಬಲವಂದು,
ವಾಚಸ್ಪತಾಚಾರ್ಯನಡಿಗೆಱಗಿ, ನಿಂದು, |
ಗುರು ಹಿರಿಯರಂಘ್ರಿಯಂ ನೆನೆದು ಮಾನಸದಿ,
ಧರೆಯ ಕವಿಗಳಿಗೆ ಕೆಯ್ ಮುಗಿದು ಸಂತಸದಿ. || 273[2] ||

251. A sixth instance, with the Trivuḍĕ (Triviḍĕ) Tâḷa.

The scheme, in short syllables, is four times:

⏑⏑⏑⏑⏑ | ⏑⏑⏑⏑⏑ | ⏑⏑⏑⏑ | ⏑⏑⏑* | ⏑⏑⏑⏑ | ⏑⏑⏑⏑⏑

or in numbers, four times:

5 . 5 . 4 . 3 * 4 . 5

Verses containing the lamentation of the female Tirukŏḷavinâči whose little son, named *S*aṅkara, had been killed by a horse having kicked it.

ಮಗನೆ, ನೀನ್ ಇಂತಳಿಯೆ, ಸೆಯ್ರಿಪೆನೆಂತೊ? ಪೇಳೆಯ್, ಶಂಕರಾ!
ಸುಗುಣ-ನಿಧಿ, ನೀನ್ ಎನ್ನ ಮೊಱೆಗಳನೊರ್ಮೆ ಕೇಳೆಯ್, ಶಂಕರಾ! |
ಪರಸಿ, ಪಾಡಿ, ಮಹೇಶನಿಂದವೆ ಬೇಡಿ ಮುಂನಂ, ಶಂಕರಾ,
ತುರಗ-ಖುರಕೆಂದಕಟ, ಪೆತ್ತೆನೆ, ಕುವರ, ನಿಂನಂ, ಶಂಕರಾ? || 274 ||

ಎಂತು ಮಱೆವೆನೊ ಸವಿಯ ಪಾಲಿಡುವಮರ್ದು-ನಗೆಯಂ, ಶಂಕರಾ?
ಕಾಂತಿ ಶೋಭಿಸಿ ಮುದ್ದು ವೀಱುವ ಮೊಗದ ಬಗೆಯಂ, ಶಂಕರಾ? |
ಝಣಝಣಿಸೆ ಕಿಱುಗೆಜ್ಜೆ, ಕರತಳ-ತಾಳ-ರವಕೇ, ಶಂಕರಾ,
ಕುಣಿವ ನಿನ್ನಯೆ ಬಿನದಮೊಪ್ಪುಗುಮೆನ್ನ ಮನಕೇ, ಶಂಕರಾ! || 275[3] ||

252. A seventh instance: the Layagrâhi Vṛitta. Observe that this is a Canarese Vṛitta or metre of *Syllable-Feet!* Each foot, however, consists of 5 Moras, and throughout bears the form of the Paeon (—⏑⏑⏑), except at the end of the quarters where a Spondee (— —) occurs.

1) Verse 30 in Rd. It is a verse that lacks elegance; kshi before prâ remains short, cf. note to v. 230; the Caesura at 8 is not recommendable. 2) Râvaṇadigvijaya, p. 2.
3) Râjaśekharavilâsa XIII., 121 seq.

The scheme is four times:

— ◡◡◡ | — ◡◡◡* | — ◡◡◡ | — ◡◡◡* | — ◡◡◡ | — ◡◡◡* | — ◡◡◡ | — —

ಲಯಗ್ರಾಹಿವೃತ್ತಂ

ಧೀರ-ಜನರಿಂ ಶ್ರುತಿ-ವಿಚಾರ-ಪರರಿಂ ಲಸದುದಾರ-ಗುಣರಿಂ ದುರಿತ-ದೂರ-ನಿಜ-ಭಕ್ತ್ಯಾ
ಚಾರ-ಯುತರಿಂ ನಿಗಮ-ಸಾರ-ಮತರಿಂ ಸುಭಗ-ದಾರ-ನುತರಿಂ ಹರಿ-ಕುಮಾರ-ವರ-ಮಾರಾ ।
ಕಾರ-ಮಹರಿಂ ವಿವಿಧ-ವೀರ-ಭಟರಿಂ ವಿಜಿತ-ಶೂರ-ಪರರಿಂ ತುರಗ-ವಾರ-ಗಜ-ಶಿಕ್ಷಾ-
ಭಾರ-ವಹರಿಂ ಮಿಳಿದಪಾರ ಧನರಿಂ ಮೆಱೆಗುವಾ ರುಚಿರ-ಪಟ್ಟಣವಿಳಾ-ರಮಣ-ಯುಕ್ತಂ.[1]
|| 276 ||

253. An eighth instance, that may be called an Ashṭapadi. It has a refrain, and belongs to the Eka Tâḷa class. It is no Vṛitta, so that its feet of 4 Moras are interchangeable.

The scheme in short syllables is eight times:

◡◡◡◡ | ◡◡◡◡

Its refrain is once: ◡◡◡◡ | ◡◡◡◡

(ಅಷ್ಟಪದಿ)

ಹಯಗಳ, ಕರಿ-ಘ
ಟ್ಟೆಯಗಳ, ಬಲಿದೊಂ
ಟೆಯಗಳ, ಮೇಣ್ ಕ
ತ್ತ್ರಿಯಗಳ, ಪನ್ನಗ- |
ಚಯಗಳ, ಬಿಗಿದ
ಶ್ವಯಗಳ ಸಹಿರ
ಣ್ಮಯಗಳ ಸುರಥಾ
ಲಯಗಳೊಳುಲಿವುತ | ನಡೆಯುವರಾಗಳ್. || 277 ||

ತೇರ್ಗಳ ಚಿತ್ಕ್ರುತಿ,
ವಾರ್ಗುಳ ಹಾರ್ಕೆ, ಸು
ರಾರ್ಗಿಳ ಧನು-ಟಂ
ಕಾರ್ಗಳಡಾಯುಧ- |

1) Râjaśekharavilâsa II., 91; another one occurs in XIII, 55.

ಧಾರ್ಗಿಳ ಸೊನ, ಪದ-
ಚಾರ್ಗಿಳ ಬೊಬ್ಬೆಯೊ
ಳೊರ್ಗಳೆದಂಬರ-
ಮಾರ್ಗದೊಳುಲಿವುತ | ನಡೆಯುವರಾಗಳ್. || 278[1] ||

254. A ninth instance, with the **Eka Tâḷa** like the Ashṭapadi; it too is accompanied with a refrain. The feet contain 3 and 4 Moras.

Its refrain is:

```
1     2      3     4
⏑⏑⏑ | ⏑⏑⏑⏑ | ⏑⏑⏑ | ⏑⏑⏑⏑           or  3 | 4 | 3 | 4
⏑⏑⏑ | ⏑⏑⏑⏑ | ⏑⏑⏑ | ⏑⏑⏑⏑               3 | 4 | 3 | 4
⏑⏑⏑ | ⏑⏑⏑⏑ | ⏑⏑⏑ | ⏑⏑⏑⏑               3 | 4 | 3 | 4
⏑⏑⏑ | ⏑⏑⏑⏑ | ⏑⏑⏑ | ⏑⏑⏑⏑ | ⏑ ||        3 | 4 | 3 | 4 | 1 ||
```

The verse-scheme, in its first part, is four times:

```
1     2      3     4      5     6      7     8
⏑⏑⏑ | ⏑⏑⏑⏑ | ⏑⏑⏑ | ⏑⏑⏑⏑ | ⏑⏑⏑ | ⏑⏑⏑* | ⏑⏑⏑ | ⏑⏑⏑⏑ |   or

          3 | 4 | 3 | 4 | 3 | 3* | 3 | 4 |
```

in its second part:

```
1     2      3     4      5     6      7     8
⏑⏑⏑ | ⏑⏑⏑⏑ | ⏑⏑⏑ | ⏑⏑⏑⏑ | ⏑⏑⏑ | ⏑⏑⏑⏑ | ⏑⏑⏑ | ⏑⏑⏑⏑
⏑⏑⏑ | ⏑⏑⏑ | ⏑⏑⏑ | ⏑⏑⏑⏑
⏑⏑⏑ | ⏑⏑⏑ | ⏑⏑⏑ | ⏑⏑⏑⏑
⏑⏑⏑ | ⏑⏑⏑⏑ | ⏑⏑⏑ | ⏑⏑⏑⏑ | ⏑⏑⏑ | ⏑⏑⏑⏑ | ⏑⏑⏑ | ⏑⏑⏑⏑ | ⏑ ||  or

          3 | 4 | 3 | 4 | 3 | 4 | 3 | 4
          3 | 3 | 3 | 4
          3 | 3 | 3 | 4
          3 | 4 | 3 | 4 | 3 | 4 | 3 | 4 | 1 ||
```

1) Râvaṇadigvijaya p. 35. It is scarcely necessary to make the remark that these two verses are full of grammatical blunders; the metre only is to be paid regard to. The Râvaṇadigvijaya's author is Gŏrasappĕ Sântayya; in the last verse he remembers Kshemapura Veṅkaṭa.

ಪಲ್ಲವಂ

ಏನ ಮಾಳ್ಪೆ ದಶಾನನೇಂದ್ರನ
ಹೀನ-ಕೃತ್ಯಕ್ಕಿನ್ನು ಧನಪನ
ಸೂನು-ದುರ್ಮತಿಗಾನು ಪುಗೆ, ಸುಂ
ಮಾನವಳಿದನುಮಾನವಾಯ್ತಿದಕೆ. ||

ಪದಂ

ಏತಕೀ ಪಥವಾತು ಬಂದೆನೊ ಧಾತುಗೆಟ್ಟ ತೆಱದಿ? ಮೇಣ್ ದು
ಷ್ಪಾತುಮಾಧಮನೀತನಿಹ ಸಂಕೇತಮೆಂದು ಭರದಿ ತಿಳಿಯದೆ,
ಭೀತಿಯುಳಿದೀ ರೀತಿಯಿಂದದ್ಭೂತ-ಖಳನ ಕರದಿ ಸಿಲುಕಿ, ವಿ
ಘಾತಿಸಿತು ಸುಪ್ರೀತಗಿತ್ತಿಹ ಮಾತಿದಿಂದುಏಿರದೆ ನುಡಿ ಪ್ರ |
ಖ್ಯಾತವಾಗಿದು ನೀತಿದಪ್ಪಿದ ಪಾತಕದಿ ನೆರೆದೇತಱಿದು ಸುಖ
ಮಾತುರದೊಳು ನಡೆದೆ! ಸತಿಯರ
ಜಾತಿ-ಗುಣವ ಬಿಡದೆ, ನಾಂ ನಿ
ರ್ಹೇತಿಯಿಂದೀ ಯಾತುಧಾನನಿಗಾತಿಶಯದೊಳು ಸೋತೆನಕಟಕಟ! || 279 [1] ||

255. A tenth instance, with the Eka Tâḷa. The feet contain 3 and 4 Moras.

The refrain, in numbers, is:

3 . 4 . 3 . 4 . 3 . 4 * 3

3 . 4 . 3 . 4 . 3 . 4 |

The verse-scheme is twice:

3 . 4 . 3 . 4 . 3 . 4 . 3 * 4

3 . 4 . 3 . 4 . 3 . 4 . 3 |

ಪಲ್ಲವಂ

ಪರರ ಗೊಡವೆಯದಿರದೆ ಹೊಱಿಡಲಿ ನರರ ಕುಲದಿಂ! ಪಿರಿಯ
ಕರುಣೆಯೊಡೆಯಗೆ ಪರಸಿ ಭಜಿಸಿರಿ ಸರಿಸಬಲದಿಂ! |

1) Râvaṇadigvijaya, pp. 43. 44, where occurs another verse; line 4 the ḍi before pra remains short. The verse is at least of use for scanning.

ಪದಂ

ಕಡೆಯ ಕಾಣಿಸು! ತಡಿಸು ವಿಘ್ನವ! ನಡಿಸು ಸುಗತಿಗೆ ನಮ್ಮ! ನೀನೇ
ಒಡೆಯ! ನೀನೆಯ್ ಕೊಡುವದಿಷ್ಟವೆ! ಬಿಡಿಸು ಲೋಕದ ಹಮ್ಮ! ।
ನಡಿಸು ಸತ್ಯವ! ಕೆಡಹು ಮಿಥ್ಯೆಯ! ಸುಡೆಲೆ ಮಲಿನತೆಯೆಲ್ಲ! ಮನವೇ,
ತಡೆಯದೆಡೆವಿಡದೊಡೆಯನಕ್ತಿಯ ನುಡಿದು, ಕೀರ್ತಿಯ ಸೊಲ್ಲ! ॥ 280[1] ॥

256. The author will continue to give instruction about metres which belong to all Indian languages, viz. the Kandas and others. Confer v. 70.

ಕಂದಂ

ಇಂತೀ ಕ್ರಮದಿಂದಂ, ಕೇಳ್,
ಎಂತಾನುಂ ಸರ್ವ-ವಿಷಯ-ಭಾಷಾದಿಗಳಿಂ ।
ಭ್ರಾಂತಿಲ್ಲದೆಯಱುಪಿದೆನಿಂ
ನುಂ ತಿಳಿವುದು ಕಂದದಂದಮುಂ, ಕಮಳ-ಮುಖೀ! ॥ 281[2] ॥

ಗದ್ಯಂ

ಇದು ಭಗವದರ್ಹ-ಪರಮೇಶ್ವರ-ಚಾರು-ಚರಣಾರವಿಂದ-ಮಂದ-ಮಧುಕರಾಯಮಾನ-ವಿಬುಧ-ಜನ-ಮನಃಪದ್ಮಿನೀ-ರಾಜಹಂಸ-ಶ್ರೀಮತ್-ಕವಿ-ರಾಜಹಂಸ-ವಿರಚಿತಮಪ್ಪ ಛಂದೋಂಬುಧಿಯೊಳ್ ತೃತೀಯಾಶ್ವಾಸಂ.

---

1) See the erotic verses in Râvaṇadigvijaya, p. 40. 2) H., Ra. (-ಭಾಷಾದಿಯನಾಂ), M. (-ಭಾಷಾದಿಗಳಂ), D., B.

IV. CHAPTER

(Continuation of the Mora-feet Metres)

ಚತುರ್ಥಾಶ್ವಾಸಂ

257. Now follow the rules regarding the Mora-feet metres comprehensively called Āryĕ's viz. the Kanda, Āryĕ (or Vipuḷĕ), Gītikĕ, Saṅkīrṇa (Saṅkīrṇaka) and Duvayi (Duvadi, Dûvĕ, Duvavi, Duvvĕ).

☞ Observe that in these Āryâ metres feet may begin with an Iambus *i. e.* ◡—! (Cf. the different observations to verse 251 and that introducing the Ragaḷĕ's).

ಕಂದಂ

ಕಂದಕ್ಕಾರ್ಯೆಗೆ ಗೀತಿಕೆ
ಗೊಂದಿದ ಸಂಕೀರ್ಣಕೆಸೆವ ದುವಯಿಗೆ ಮಾತ್ರಾ- ।
ವೃಂದಮುಮಂ ಗಣವಿವರಣಾ
ಯುಂದಮುಮಂ ತಿಳಿಯ ಪೇಳ್ವೆನಂಬುಜ-ವದನೇ! ॥ 282[1] ॥

258. The feet (gaṇa) for the Āryâ metres have the following five forms and names:

◡◡—, giriśam, Anapaestus
—◡◡, dhûrjaṭi, Dactylus
— —, śarvam, Spondeus
◡—◡, purâri, Amphibrachys
◡◡◡◡, śaśipura or makharipu, Proceleusmaticus

The 6th foot (vishaya = 5, adri=1) in each half of an Āryâ verse is to be either a śaśipura (◡◡◡◡) or a purâri (◡—◡). (Mind that when not falling under a special rule, one foot may be put in the place of the other, as in general the number of Moras of the feet only are leading.)

ಕಂದಂ

ಗಿರಿಶಂ ಧೂರ್ಜಟಿ ಶರ್ವಂ
ಪುರಾರಿ ಮಖರಿಪುವೆನಿಪ್ಪವಿಂತೆಯ್ದು ಗಣಂ ।

1) H., Ra. (duvayi), M. (duvadi, duvavi), D. and B. (dûvĕ), L. (duvvĕ).

ಬರೆ, ಶಶಿಪುರ ವಿಷಯಾದ್ರಿಯೊ
ಳಿರದಿರ್ಕೆ ಪುರಾರಿಯೆಂಬ ಗಣಮಬ್ಜ-ಮುಖೀ! || 283[1] ||

2. The Kanda (Skandhaka, Āryâgîti)

ಕಂದಲಕ್ಷಣಂ

259. The first form of the Āryĕs is the Kanda. In it (as well as in the other Āryĕs) each of the mentioned feet contains 4 Moras. (In the Ragaḷĕs, as will be remembered, also feet of 3 and 5 Moras are used.)

ಕಂದಂ

ಇಂತಾದ ಗಣದ ಮಾತ್ರಾ-
ಸಂತತಿ ನಾಲ್ಕಕ್ಕುಮತ್ತವಕೆರ್ಣಂದೊಂದ |
ರ್ಕಂತೆಯ್ದು ಗಣಂಗಳ್ ಬ
ರ್ಕುಂ, ತೊದಳೇಂ, ಕಂದ-ಜಾತಿಯೊಳ್, ಕಮಳ-ಮುಖೀ! || 284[2] ||

260. In the quarters (pada) of the Kanda occur altogether 16 feet (pura=3, bâṇa=5, vahni=3, śara=5), 3 in each odd (ojĕ, 1 . 3) and 5 in each even (yugmĕ, 2 . 4) quarter, or 12 Moras in each odd and 20 in each even one. The scheme of the following Kanda-verse is:

1.	1: ⏑⏑–	2: ⏑–⏑	3: ⏑⏑⏑⏑			12
2.	4: ⏑⏑–	5: –⏑⏑	6: ⏑–⏑	7: –⏑⏑	8: ––	20
3.	1: ⏑⏑–	2: ––	3: ⏑⏑–			12
4.	4: ⏑⏑–	5: ––	6: ⏑–⏑	7: –⏑⏑	8: ⏑⏑–	20

ಕಂದಂ

ಪುರ-ಬಾಣ-ವಹ್ನಿ-ಶರ-ಗಣ
ಮಿರೆ ನಾಲ್ಕುಂ ಪದದೊಳೋಜೆ ಯುಗ್ಮೆಗಳೊಳ್ ಪ |
ನ್ನೆರಡಿರ್ಪತ್ತ್ರೋಳಿಯ ಪ
ನ್ನೆರಡಿರ್ಪತ್ತಕ್ಕೆ ಮಾತ್ರೆಗಳ್, ಮೃಗ-ನಯನೇ! || 285[3] ||

1) H., Ra., Sb., L., M., D., B. 2) H., Ra., Sb., M., L. 3) H., Ra., Sb., M., L.

261. The rule regarding the number of Moras in the Kanda-quarters (aḍi) is repeated in other words.

ಕಂದಂ

ಪನ್ನೆರಡು ಮಾತ್ರೆ ಮೊದಲೊಳ್,
ಸನ್ನುತವಿರ್ಪತ್ತು ಮಾತ್ರೆಯೆರಡನೆಯಡಿಯೊಳ್, ।
ಇನ್ನಿಪ್ಪವುಮಿಾ ತೆಱದಿಂ;
ಬಿನ್ನಣಮೇಂ, ಕಂದ-ಲಕ್ಷಣಂ, ಕಮಳ-ಮುಖೀ! || 286[1] ||

262. (Besides the 6th foot of a Kanda-half falling under a special rule, v. 283) it is to be observed that in the odd places (śaśi=1, pura=3, bâṇa=5, adri=7) of each Kanda-half the foot with the long syllable in the middle, *i. e.* ◡—◡ (purâri), is not allowed to occur. The scheme of the following Kanda-verse is:

1 2 3
◡◡◡◡ | — — | ◡◡—
4 5 6 7 8
◡◡◡◡ | — — | ◡◡◡◡ | — — | — — |
1 2 3
◡◡ — | ◡—◡ | —◡◡
4 5 6 7 8
◡◡◡◡ | ◡◡— | ◡—◡ | ◡◡— | ◡◡— ||

ಕಂದಂ

ಶಶಿ-ಪುರ-ಬಾಣಾದ್ರಿಗಳೊಳ್, [H. Ra. ಶಶಿಪುರವಿಷಯಾದ್ರಿ etc.]
ಬಿಸಜ-ಮುಖೀ, ಮಧ್ಯ-ಗುರುಗಳಾಗಲ್, ಕಂದಂ ।
ಪುಸಿಯಲ್ತೆ? ಗಂಡನಿಲ್ಲದ
ಶಶಿ-ವದನೆಗೆ ಗರ್ಭಮಾದ ತೆಱನೊಳ್ ಕೆಡುಗುಂ. || 287[2] ||

263. A further verse on the Kanda that states the following: An Amphibrachys (◡—◡) ought not to occur at the odd (vishama) places; at the 6th place (of each half) either an Amphibrachys or a Proceleusmaticus (◡◡◡◡) is to occur; three of the even (avishama) places (2 . 4 . 8) do not fall under a particular rule (though it is in fact a stringent rule to conclude each half, at the 8th place, with a long syllable; but cf. v. 27); the number of all the Moras is 64.

ಕಂದಂ

ಜ-ಗಣಂ ವಿಷಮದೊಳಾಗದು;
ಜ-ಗಣಂ ಮೇಣ್ ನ-ಗಣಮಕ್ಕೆಯಾಱನೆಯೆಡೆಯೊಳ್; ।

1) O. (v. 14.), Ra. H. (in chapter 6), Rc., Rd. (v. 19), M., Sb., D., B; Kavijihvâbandhana IV., v. 57. 2) M., Ra. H. (in supplement), Rd. (v. 20), O. (v. 15), M., Sb., D., B.

ತ್ರಿಗಣದೊಳವಿಷಮ-ಸಾಧ್ಯಂ;
ಬಗೆಯೆ, ಚತುಃಷಷ್ಟಿ-ಮಾತ್ರೆ ಕಂದದ ಲೆಕ್ಕಂ. || 288[1] ||

3. The Āryĕ (Vipulĕ)

ಆರ್ಯೆಗೆ ಲಕ್ಷಣಮಂ ಪೇಳ್ವಂ

264. **The Ārye's first quarter (like that of the Kanda) consists of 12 Moras, its second one of 18, its third one again of 12, and its last one of 15, (the special rules for the *first* 6th place, and the odd and even places being to be remembered).**

ಕಂದಂ

ಮೊದಲೊಳ್ ಪನ್ನೆರಡೆರಡನೆ
ಯದಱೊಳ್ ಪದಿನೆಂಟು, ಮೂಱಱೊಳ್ ಪನ್ನೆರಡಂ ।
ತ್ಯದ ಪಾದದಲ್ಲಿ ಪದಿನೆ
ಯ್ದದು ಮಾತ್ರಾ-ನಿಯಮಮಾರ್ಯೆಯೊಳ್, ವನಜ-ಮುಖೀ! || 289[2] ||

265. **The first half of the Āryĕ consists of 7 feet and a long syllable; the second one (padântya, parârdha, padârdha) has a short syllable instead of the foot of the 6th place (rasa).**

ಕಂದಂ

ಮಿಗದೇಳ್ ಗಣಮುಂ ಬೞಿಕಾ
ರ್ಯೆಗೆ, ಮುಂತಂ ತುದಿಯೊಳೊಂದೆ ಗುರು ತಾಂ ಬಂದಿ ।
ನ್ನಗಲದೆ ಪದಾರ್ಧದೊಳ್, ಶಿಶು- [D., B.: ಪರಾರ್ಧ; Ra.: ಪದಾಂತ್ಯ]
ಮೃಗಾಕ್ಷಿ, ಲಘುವೊಂದೆ ಬಂದು ನಿಲ್ಕುಂ ರಸದೊಳ್. || 290[3] ||

A scheme of the Āryĕ:

1	2	3			
⏑⏑⏑⏑ |	⏑⏑⏑⏑ |	⏑⏑⏑⏑			12
4	5	6	7	8	
⏑⏑⏑⏑ |	⏑⏑⏑⏑ |	⏑—⏑ |	⏑⏑⏑⏑ |	— |	18
1	2	3			
⏑⏑⏑⏑ |	⏑⏑⏑⏑ |	⏑⏑⏑⏑			12
4	5	6	7	8	
⏑⏑⏑⏑ |	⏑⏑⏑⏑ |	⏑ |	⏑⏑⏑⏑ |	— ||	15

1) H. Ra. (in supplement), M., Sb. Observe that Na gaṇa in this verse is not the Tribrachys (⏑⏑⏑), but ⏑⏑⏑⏑. 2) H., Ra., Rc., M., D., B., L., Sb. D. and B. call it Āryâgīti, and say that its last quarter contains 18 Moras; H., Ra. and Sb. that its third contains 15, and its last 16 Moras. See, however, next verse. 3) H., Sb., M., Ra., D., B.; D. and B. also: Āryĕ.

4. The Gîtikĕ (Gîtĕ)

266. The Gîtikĕ has the two quarters (pâda) of the *first* half of the Vipuḷĕ (*i. e.* the Āryĕ, the author not paying any regard to the slight difference in Saṁskṛita between the two, that concerns only the Caesura which for this class of metres is not ordered by him) also in its second half.

ಕಂದಂ

ವಿಪುಳಾರ್ಯೆಯ ಪೂರ್ವಾರ್ಧ-
ದ್ವಿಪಾದದಂತಾಗಿ, ಬರ್ಕುಂ ಗೀತಿಕೆ; ಕೇಳ್, ಇಂ ।
ನಪರಾರ್ಧ-ಪಾದ-ಯುಗಮುಮ
ದುಪಮೆಯೆ ಬರೆದೋದು, ಕಲ್ತು ತಿಳಿವ ವೊಲಿಳೆಯೊಳ್. ॥ 291[1] ॥

A scheme of the Gîtikĕ:

```
  1      2      3
◡◡◡◡ | ◡◡◡◡ | ◡◡◡◡                       12
  4      5      6      7     8
◡◡◡◡ | ◡◡◡◡ | ◡◡◡◡ | ◡◡◡◡ | — |          18
  1      2      3
◡◡◡◡ | ◡◡◡◡ | ◡◡◡◡                       12
                6      7     8
◡◡◡◡ | ◡◡◡◡ | ◡—◡  | ◡◡◡◡ | — ||         18
```

5. The Saṅkîrṇaka (Saṅkîrṇa)

267. The Saṅkîrṇaka is formed of the first half (pûrvârdha) of the Kanda and of the second half (aparârdha) of the Āryĕ.

ಕಂದಂ

ಕಂದದ ಪೂರ್ವಾರ್ಧದೊಳನು
ಸಂಧಿಸಲಾರ್ಯಾಪರಾರ್ಧಮದನುಕ್ರಮದಿಂ ।
ಪೊಂದಿದೊಡೆ ಸಂಕೀರ್ಣಕ
ಮೆಂದುಂ ಕವಿ-ರಾಜಹಂಸನಂಬುಜ-ವದನೇ! ॥ 292[2] ॥

1) Sb., M., H., Ra., Rc. Rc.'s reading is the following: ವಿಪುಲಾಯರ್ಾ-ಪೂವಾರ್ಧಾ- | ದ್ವಿಪದಂ ತಾನೆಂತು ಬರೆ ಗೀತಿಗೆಯಿಂ || ನಪರಾರ್ಧಮುಮಾಪಾಂಗೇಂ | ಮುಪದೇಶಮ ಕಲ್ತು ಕೊಳೆ ಜಾಣೇ ||

2) M., Sb., H., Ra., Rc., D., B., L.

A scheme of the Saṅkīrṇaka:

1	2	3			
∪∪∪∪	∪∪∪∪	∪∪∪∪			12
4	5	6	7	8	
∪∪∪∪	∪∪∪∪	∪—∪	∪∪∪∪	∪∪—	20
1	2	3			
∪∪∪∪	∪∪∪∪	∪∪∪∪			12
4	5	6	7	8	
∪∪∪∪	∪∪∪∪	∪	∪∪∪∪	— ‖	15

6. The Duvayi (Duvadi, Duvavi, etc.)

268. (Duvayi is a Tadbhava of Dvipadi *i. e.* a verse with two lines.)

A translation of the reading of No. *a.* is: "In the first (line) 6 Moras occur as well as in the second line (pada); (then) the Kanda-feet (of the second line) nicely appear, and a long syllable (guru) is joined at the end[1]; 28 Moras[2] are ordered for the Duvayi."

A translation of No. *b.* is: "In the first (line) 6 Moras occur as well as in the second line; (then) the Kanda-feet nicely appear; in one and one (*i. e.* in each line) 26 Moras are ordered for the Duvayi."

ಕಂದಂ

a. ಮೊದಲೊಳೆ ಮಾತ್ರೆಗಳಾಱು
ಪ್ಪುದು; ಪದವೆರಡಱೊಳಮಂತೆ; ಕಂದದ ಗಣಮೆ[3] ।
ಯ್ದುದಯಿಸಿ, ಗುರುವೆರಸಿರ್ಕಂ[4]
ತ್ಯದಿನಿರ್ಪತ್ತೆಂಟು ಮಾತ್ರೆ ದುವಯಿಗೆ ನಿಯಮಂ[5]. ‖ 293 ‖

The scheme of this verse is twice:

∪∪∪∪∪∪ * ∪∪∪∪ · ∪∪∪∪ · ∪—∪ · ∪∪∪∪ · ∪∪∪∪ * — | **28 *Moras.***

b. ಮೊದಲೊಳ್ ಮಾತ್ರೆಗಳಾಱು
ಪ್ಪುದು; ಪದವೆರಡಱೊಳಮಂತೆ; ಕಂದದ ಗಣಮೆ ।
ಯ್ದುದಯಿಸುಗುಮೇಕಮೇಕ[6]
ತ್ರದಿನಿರ್ಪತ್ತಾಱು ಮಾತ್ರೆ ದುವವಿಗೆ ನೇಮಂ[7]. ‖ 294 ‖

---

1) The ಗುರುವೆರಸಿರ್ಕಂ is in Sb., H., Ra and L. 2) The ಇರ್ಪತ್ತೆಂಟು in Sb., M., Ra., H. 3) Ra.... ಳಮುಂತೆ; D., B... ಪದದೆರಡಱೊಳೆ ಮುಂತೆ. 4) Ra.... ವೆರಸಿರ್ಕಂ. 5) Ra. ತದಷ್ಟ ತ್ತೆಂಟು ಮಾತ್ರೆ. 6) This is M.'s reading; Ro.... ಗುಮವೇಕತ್ವದ; B... ಗುಮೇಕತ್ರದೊ; D... ಗಿಂತೇ ಕತ್ರದೊ. 7) Ro. ನದುವಿರ್ಪತ್ತಾಱು; B. ಳದುವಿರ್ಪತ್ತಾಱು; D. ಳದುಮಿರ್ಪತ್ತಾಱು; M. ತ್ರದಿನಿರ್ಪತ್ತೆಂಟು.

The scheme of this is twice:

⏑⏑⏑⏑⏑⏑⏑ * ⏑⏑⏑⏑ . ⏑⏑⏑⏑ . ⏑–⏑ ⏑⏑⏑⏑ . ⏑⏑– | 26 *Moras.*

269. An instance of the Duvayi. (Number of Moras: sura = 1; khačara = 1; ravi = 12; garuḍa = 1; vidyâdhara = 12; pannagarâja = 1.)

ದುವಯಿ

ಸುರ-ಖಚರ-ರ*ವಿ-ಗರುಡ-ವಿದ್ಯಾಧರ-ಪನ್ನಗರಾಜವಂತಿಕಂ | 28 *Moras*
ಪರಮ-ಪದಂ*ವಿನಮಿತ-ಜನಮಂ ಪರೀಕ್ಷಣಂ ಗೆಯ್ದೆನಿಂತಿದಂ[1] ||295|| 28 *Moras*

ಗದ್ಯಂ

ಇದು ಭಗವದರ್ಹತ್-ಪರಮೇಶ್ವರ-ಚಾರು-ಚರಣಾರವಿಂದ-ಮಂದ-ಮಧುಕರಾಯಮಾನ-ಮನಃಪದ್ಮಿನೀ-ರಾಜಹಂಸ-ಶ್ರೀಮತ್-ಕವಿ-ರಾಜಹಂಸ-ನಾಗವರ್ಮ-ವಿರಚಿತಮಪ್ಪ-ಛಂದೋಂಬುಧಿಯೊಳ್ ಕಂದ-ಆರ್ಯೆ-ಗೀತಿಕೆ-ಸಂಕೀರ್ಣ-ದುವಯಿಗೆ ಲಕ್ಷಣಂ ಚತುರ್ಥಾಶ್ವಾಸಂ.

1) Only in H. and Ra. It proves the 28 Moras for the line, if the liberty is taken to read in the first line, instead of sura-khača-ravi, sura-khačara-ravi. There is a Dohâ (S. Dvipatha) among the Prâkṛita metres in Colebrooke p. 413; it is a stanza of 4 verses (lines), containing alternately 13 and 11 Moras (and scanned 6+4+3 and 6+4+1).—The first metre of the next chapter is the Tripadi, with regard to which the Duvayi may have been thought to form the connecting link.

D. THE CANARESE MORA-FEET[1)]

ಕನ್ನಡಮಾತ್ರಾಗಣಂಗಳ್

V. CHAPTER

ಪಂಚಮಾಶ್ವಾಸಂ

ಕರ್ಣಾಟಕವಿಷಯಜಾತಿಯಂ, ಕೇಳ್, ಪೇೞ್ವೆಂ

270. The author having finished the languages etc. common to all the countries, now introduces the pure Canarese metres. Cf. verses 70. 281.

ಕಂದಂ

ಅರ್ಣವ-ಜಾತಾನನೆ, ಸಂ
ಪೂರ್ಣತೆಯಿಂ ಸಕಲ-ವಿಷಯ-ಭಾಷಾದಿಗಳಂ ।
ನಿರ್ಣಯಮಾಗಱುಪಿದೆನಾಂ
ಕರ್ಣಾಟಕ-ಭಾಷೆಯುಂದಮಂ, ಕೇಳ್, ಪೇೞ್ವೆಂ. || 296[2)] ||

271. Pure Canarese metres present 3 classes of Mora-feet, viz. the Brahma-, Vishṇu- and Rudra-class, (a foot beginning with or forming an Iambus, *i. e.* ◡ —, being *always excluded;* cf. note to verse 251, and the introduction to the Ragaḷĕs). To form them, two (— —), three (— — —) and four (— — — —) long syllables are each separately in a certain manner interchanged with short ones, so as to obtain 4 (ambunidhi) feet for the Brahma-class, 8 (gaja) for the Vishṇu-class, and 16 (dharaṇīśvara) for the Rudra-class.

ಕಂದಂ

ಎರಡುಂ ಮೂಱುಂ ನಾಲ್ಕುಂ
ಗುರುವಿಂ ಪ್ರಸ್ತರಿಸಲಂಬುನಿಧಿ-ಗಜ-ಧರಣೀ ।
ಶ್ವರ-ಗಣಮೊಗೆಗುಮವರ್ಕಂ
ಸರಸಿಜಭವ-ವಿಷ್ಣು-ರುದ್ರ-ಸಂಜ್ಞೆಗಳಕ್ಕುಂ. || 297[3)] ||

1) This heading is not in the original. 2) M., Ra. (-ಭಾಷಾದಿಗಳಂ), D., B. H. (-ಭಾಷಾದಿಗಳಂ). 3) M., Sb., H., Ra., D., B.

272. The peculiar manner in which the feet of the three classes, viz. those connected with two (kara), three (pura) and four (vârdhi) long syllables, are obtained.

ಚಂಪಕಮಾಲೆ

ಕರ-ಪುರ-ವಾರ್ಧಿಯಾಗೆ, ಗುರುವಾಗಿರೆ ತದ್-ಗುರುವಿಂದಧೋಧಸಾ
ಗಿರೆ ಲಘು-ಯುಗ್ಮಮಾ ಕ್ರಮದೆ ಮುಂತೆ ಸಮಂ. ಕಡೆವಟ್ಟ ಬಿಣ್ಪಿನೊಳ್ ।
ಬರೆ ಲಘುವೊಂದೆ; ಪಿಂತೆ ಲಘು; ಮುಂತೆ ಸಮಂ. ಮೊದಲಿಂ ತಗುಳ್ದು, ಪಂ
ಕರುಹ-ದಳೇಕ್ಷಣೇ, ಗಣಮನಿಂತಿಡು ಸರ್ವ-ಲಘುತ್ವಮಪ್ಪಿನಂ. ॥ 298[1] ॥

273. Exposition of verse 298.

ಬ್ರಹ್ಮಗಣನಾಲ್ಕರ್ಕೆ ವಿವರಂ

a. **The four Brahma-feet, from 3-4 Moras.**

1. — · —, ಬ್ರಹ್ಮ (Spondee) ಎಂತುಂ[2]
2. ◡◡ · —, ಸುರಪಂ (Anapaest) ನೆಗಳ್ದಂ
3. — · ◡, ಧಾತೃ (Trochee) ನಾಕಿ
4. ◡◡ · ◡, ಅಜನೆ (Tribach) ಧರೆಗೆ

ವಿಷ್ಣುಗಣಮೆಂಟರ್ಕೆ ವಿವರಂ

b. **The eight Vishṇu-feet, from 4-6 Moras.**

1. — — · —, ಗೋವಿಂದಂ (Molossus)
2. ◡◡— · —, ಹೃದಯೇಶಂ (Ionicus minor) ನಯದಾಳ್ಕಂ
3. — ◡ · —, ನಾಕಿಗಂ (Amphimacrus)
4. ◡◡◡ · —, ಪರಹಿತಂ
5. — — · ◡, ಕಂಸಾರಿ (Antibacchius)
6. ◡◡— · ◡, ನರಕಾರಿ
7. — ◡ · ◡, ಶ್ರೀಪತಿ (Dactyl)
8. ◡◡◡ · ◡, ಮುರಹರ (Proceleusmatic) ಮುರರಿಪು

1) H. and Ra. (after the exposition), Sb., M., D., B. 2) Different readings of H., Ra.

ರುದ್ರಗಣಪದಿನಾಱಱ್ಕೆ ವಿವರಂ

c. **The sixteen Rudra-feet, from 5-8 Moras.**

1. — — — · —, ಗಂಗಾಧೀಶಂ
2. ◡◡— — · —, ಗಿರಿಜಾನಾಥಂ ಗಿರಿಜಾಕಾಂತಂ
3. — ◡ — · —, ನೀಲಕಂಠಂ
4. ◡◡◡ — · —, ವೃಷಭಲಕ್ಷ್ಮಂ
5. — — ◡ . —, ಕಾಮಾಂತಕಂ
6. ◡◡ — ◡ · —, ಪ್ರಮಥಾಧಿಪಂ ಪ್ರಥಮಾಧಿಪಂ
7. — ◡◡ · —, ಶೂಲಧರಂ (Choriambus)
8. ◡◡◡◡ · —, ಪುರಮಥನಂ
9. — — — · ◡, ಕಂದರ್ಪಾರಿ
10. ◡◡— — · ◡, ಮದನಧ್ವಂಸಿ
11. — ◡ — · ◡, ಚಂದ್ರಮೌಳಿ
12. ◡◡◡ — · ◡, ಭುಜಗಧಾರಿ
13. — — ◡ · ◡, ಭೂತಾಗ್ರಣಿ (Ionicus major)
14. ◡◡ — ◡ · ◡, ತ್ರಿಜಗದ್ಗುರು
15. — ◡◡ · ◡, ಕಾಮರಿಪು (Paeon)
16. ◡◡◡◡ · ◡, ಮದನರಿಪು

☞ Only verses 299-312, *i. e.* 13 metres, occur in the present work, that are constructed with special regard to the feet and their names adduced in this place; besides feet of more than 5 Moras are ordered only for seven of them, viz. čitra, v. 300; čitralatĕ, v. 301; great akkara, v. 302; nice akkara, v. 305; little akkara, v. 306; eḷĕ, v. 307; and gītikĕ, v. 312. After these 13 metres the shaṭpadis begin, a class of metre in which no feet of more than 5 Moras can occur, no feet are called by special names, only *the number of Moras,* and not the form of feet, is taken into account, and *one foot with the same number of Moras,* as in the Ragaḷĕs and to a great extent in the Āryĕs, *may be put for the other.* For the shaṭpadis (and the utsâha, v. 339) only the feet of 3, 4 and 5 Moras (without any reference to classification), as they have been adduced in the introduction to the Ragaḷĕs, p. 76, are used, and they, together with a number of the Vṛittas, the Ragaḷĕs and the Kanda, are the truly popular metres in Canarese. Of the metres of verses 299-312 only tripadi, akkarikĕ and čaupadi are used now-a-days, as being strictly regulated regarding the number of Moras contained in their feet; the rest, of which the editor has never seen any instances elsewhere but akkara and eḷĕ, has been discarded, as it seems for the difficulty of scanning; for though the name of one of the three classes of feet be given, who can know all at once what peculiar foot will suit the circumstances? However by introducing some special rules as to the number of Moras, all of them might prove useful; the equal akkara (v. 303), the middle akkara (v. 304) and the čhandovataṁsa in fact present already some such rule, and the śarashaṭpadi has been rightly referred to its proper place as the first of the shaṭpadis (see note to v. 317). Whether originally there has been more uniformity in all of them, and the forms of the text for some are corrupt (there appear to be two recensions), are questions worthy of consideration. All the different readings at hand have been adduced; cf. Addenda. Observe that none of the feet under No. 273 begins with an Iambus (⏑—), such a foot being foreign to true Canarese metres.

1. The Tripadi (Trivadi, Trivaḷi)

ಪಿಂತೆ ಪೇಳ್ದ ಗಣದ ನೆರವಿಯೊಳ್ ತ್ರಿವಳಿಯ ಲಕ್ಷಣಮಂ ಪೇಳ್ಗೆಂ

274. A Tripadi verse: The first line has 4 feet, each consisting of 5 Moras; in its middle the Caesura and another Alliteration occur. (The second foot of the second line *i. e.*) the 6th (rasa) foot (of the verse) as well as (the second one of the third line *i. e.*) the 10th one (of the verse) are to consist each of a Brahma (Bisaruhodbhava) foot (—⏑, or ⏑⏑⏑, or — —, or ⏑⏑—). The remaining feet contain either 5 Moras, or where the Moras of the Brahma feet chosen do not allow so many, only 4, (the number of Moras for the first line being 20, those for the second one 17, and those for the third one 18).

ತ್ರಿಪದಿ

ಬಿಸರುಹೋದ್ಭವ-ಗಣಂ *ರಸ-ದಶ-ಸ್ಥಾನದೊಳ್,
ಬಿಸರುಹ-ನೇತ್ರೇ! ಗಣಮೆ ಬರ್ಕುಳಿದವು,
ಬಿಸರುಹ-ನೇತ್ರೇ, ತ್ರಿಪದಿಗೇ! ‖ 299[1] ‖

The scheme of the adduced verse:

1	2	3	4	
⏑⏑⏑— |	⏑⏑⏑—*	⏑⏑⏑— |	—⏑—	20 Moras in 4 feet
5	VI	7	8	
⏑⏑⏑⏑ |	— — |	⏑⏑⏑— |	⏑⏑⏑⏑	17 Moras in 4 feet
9	X	11		
⏑⏑⏑⏑ |	— — |	⏑⏑⏑— ‖		18 Moras in 3 feet

To show that not the form but the number of the Moras is essential for the feet (excepting the 6th and 10th where, however, *any one* of the four Brahma-feet may occur), the following schemes of Tripadi verses, occurring in the 11th chapter of the Râjaśekharavilâsa, are given here.

1) M. (Trivadi), Sb. Ra. (Trivaḷi), D., B. The verses of the Râjaśekharavilâsa are of a nature that does not allow them to be quoted here. The number of Moras for the lines, that is not stated in the Canarese text, is in all good instances that which is given in No. 274. Thus the Tripadi bears a decided character, and has therefore not unfrequently been used in Canarese poetry; another circumstance in its favour is that none of its feet contains more than 5 Moras.

v. 89:

1 2 3 4
⏑⏑—⏑ | ⏑⏑—⏑*⏑⏑⏑— | ⏑⏑—⏑
5 6 7 8
⏑⏑⏑⏑ | —⏑ | ⏑⏑—⏑ | ⏑⏑⏑—
9 10 11
⏑⏑—⏑ | ⏑ ⏑ ⏑ | ⏑⏑—⏑ ||

v. 90.

1 2 3 4
⏑⏑—⏑ | ——⏑*⏑⏑—⏑ | —⏑—
5 6 7 8
⏑⏑⏑⏑ | —⏑ | ⏑⏑—⏑ | —⏑⏑⏑
9 10 11
⏑⏑⏑— | ⏑ ⏑ ⏑ | ⏑⏑—⏑ ||

v. 91:

1 2 3 4
⏑⏑⏑— | —⏑—*⏑⏑⏑— | ⏑⏑—⏑
5 6 7 8
⏑⏑⏑— | ⏑⏑⏑ | ⏑⏑⏑— | ⏑⏑⏑⏑
9 10 11
⏑⏑—⏑ | —⏑ | ⏑⏑⏑— ||

2. The *C*itra (Upačitrikĕ, Vičitra)

275. A translation of the *C*itra verse: "When the feet (gaṇa) of the three (śikhibraja = tretâgni) lines (pâda) (each of which is in possession also) of the course of a Rudra-foot (bhujagapaksha = bhujagadhâri), are mixed with a Brahma-foot (aja) at 6 (rasa) and 10, and Vishṇu-feet (adhokshaja), as in the last metre (Tripadi), occur (for the other places), it is the *C*itra."

ಚಿತ್ರಂ

ಭುಜಗಪಕ್ಷ-ಗತಿ-ಶಿಖಿ*ಬ್ರಜ-ಪಾದ-ಗಣವೊಳ
ಗಜ-ರಸ-ದಶದೊಳ್, ಪೆಱಗಣಧೋ
ಕ್ಷಜ-ಗಣಮಾದೊಡದು ಚಿತ್ರಂ. || 300 [1] ||

---

1) This is the editor's tentative reading. Bhujagapaksha recurs in v. 307, where it apparently forms two words: bhujaga = 1, paksha = 2, purposing, at the same time, to represent a Rudra-foot. There may be the possibility of attributing the same meaning to it in this instance, viz. bhujaga = 1, pakshagati (garuḍa) = 1, śikhibraja (sun?) = 1, to denote the three *pâdas*; or bhujaga = 1, pakshagati = 1, śikhi (parvata) = 8, to denote the number of *feet*; (śikhibraja, if dinapa, however, properly denotes 12). The above reading has been framed to avoid, as ordered, the aja at other places but the 6th and 10th; but examining, for instance v. 301, it appears that whilst it *must* occur at the said places, it *may* occur, if not forbidden, also elsewhere.

The scheme of the verse:

```
           1          2          3         4
20 M. ⏑⏑⏑—⏑ | ⏑⏑⏑—*⏑⏑—⏑ | ⏑⏑⏑⏑
           5         VI        7
14 M. ⏑⏑⏑⏑  | ⏑⏑—  | ⏑⏑⏑⏑—
           8         9         X
18 M. ⏑⏑⏑⏑  | —⏑⏑ ' | ——||
```

ಚಿತ್ರಂ

H. ಭುಜಗಪಕ್ಷ-ಗತಿ ಶಿಖಿ
ಬ್ರಜ-ಪಾದ-ಗಣಮೊಳಗಿರೆ ರಸ-ದಸಮದೊಳ್ ಪೆಱಗಣಧೋ
ಕ್ಷಜ-ಗಣಮಾದೊಡದು ಚಿತ್ರಂ. ||

ಉಪಚಿತ್ರಿಕೆ

D., B. (& L. for the 1st line) ಭುಜಪಕ್ಷ-ಯುಗ-ಧೂಮ
ಧ್ವಜ-ಪಾದ-ಗುರುವಿನೊ [L. ಧ್ವಜ ಪಾಳ ಗಣವಿಗ]
ಳಜನಿರ್ದ ರಸದೊಳಂ ಪೆಱವೆಡೆಗಳೊಳಧೋ
ಕ್ಷಜ-ಗಣಮಾದೊಡದುಪಚಿತ್ರಿಕೆ. ||

ವಿಚಿತ್ರಂ

K., M. ಭುಜಪಕ್ಷ-ಯುಗಳ-ಧೂಮ
ಧ್ವಜ-ಪಾದ-ಗಣದೊ
ಳಜನಿರ್ದಂ ರಸದೊಳ್ ನಿಜ ಪೆಱವೆಡೆಗಳೊಳಧೋ [K. ಬೆಸರವಿಚೆ]
ಕ್ಷಜ-ಗಣಮುಮಾದೊಡದು ವಿಚಿತ್ರಂ, ಕೆಳದೀ! || [K. ದೊಡದುವಿಚಿ]

ಚಿತ್ರಂ

Sb., Ra. (=H.) ಭುಜಗಪಕ್ಷ-ಗತಿ-ಶಿಖಿ
ವ್ರಜ-ಪಾದ-ಗಣಮೊಳಗಿರೆ ರಸ-ದಶಮದೊಳ್ ಪೆಱಗಣಧೋ [Sb. ಗಣವಿನೊಳ್ಗಿರೆ]
ಕ್ಷಜ-ಗಣಮಾದೊಡದು ಚಿತ್ರಂ. || [Ra. ಚಿತ್ರಾ]

3. The Citralatĕ (Učita, Vičitra, Citra)

276. "When at the beginning (tudi) a Rudra-foot occurs, and the whole verse (pada) bears the variegated form of the preceding (metre, the *Citra*, wherein the Rudra-feet are intermixed with those of the two other classes), it is the *Citralatĕ*" (the Brahma after the Rudra of the first line happening only on account of the Rudra chosen).

H. (=Ra., & nearly Sb.) ತುದಿಯೊಳೀಶ್ವರ-ಗಣಾ
ಮೊದವಿರೆ, ಪದವೆಲ್ಲಂ, |
ಮದಗಜ-ಗಮನೆ, ಪೆಱಗಣಾ ಚಿತ್ರಲತೆಯಂ
ದದೊಳಿರ್ದೊಡದೆ ಚಿತ್ರಲತೆಯಕ್ಕುಂ. || 301[1] ||

The scheme of the verse:

```
                 1        2
9 M.       ⏑⏑⏑–⏑ | ⏑⏑⏑
                 3        4
10 M.      ⏑⏑⏑⏑ | ⏑⏑–– |
                 5        VI
18 or 19 M. ⏑⏑⏑⏑ | ⏑ ⏑ ⏑̄ | ⏑⏑⏑⏑– | ⏑⏑⏑–
                          X
16 or 17 M. ⏑ ⏑ –  | ⏑ ⏑ ⏑̄ | –⏑⏑⏑ | ––||
```

D., B. ತುದಿಯೊಳೀಶ್ವರ-ಗಣಂ
ಮೊದಲೊಳಿರೆ, ಪದಮೆಲ್ಲಂ, |
ಮದಗಜ-ಗಮನೆ, ಪೆಱಗಣ ಚಿತ್ರದಂ
ದದಿನಿರ್ದೊಡದು ತಾಂ ಚಿತ್ರಮಕ್ಕುಂ. || [B. ದದಿನಿರ್ದೊಡೆ ಚಿತ್ರಮಕ್ಕುಂ]

K., M. ತುದಿಯೊಳೀಶ್ವರ-ಗಣಮುಂ
ಮೊದುಂ, ಗಜ-ಗಮನೆ, ಪೆಱಗಣೆಂದಂ ಚಿತ್ರಂ | [K. ಮೊದಲಿಂ ಗಜ]
ಮದದೊಳಗಿರ್ದೊಡಮದವುಂ [K., for the two lines, only: ಮದದೊಳ್ಗಿರ್ದಂತು ಚಿತಂ ನಯದಿಂ]
ವಿದಿತಮಿರ್ದೊಡಂತುಚಿತಂ ನಯದಿಂ. ||

Sb. ತುದಿಯೊಳೀಶ್ವರ-ಗಣ [identical with L.]
ಮೊದವಿರೆ, ಪದಮೆಲ್ಲಂ, |
ಮದಗಜ-ಗಮನೆ, ಪೆಱಗಣ ಚಿತ್ರೆಯಂ
ಗದೊಳಿರ್ದೊಡದೆ ಚಿತ್ರಲತೆಯಕ್ಕುಂ. || [L. ದೊದವಿರ್ದೊಡದು ವಿಚಿತ್ರಮಕ್ಕುಂ]

Ra. ತುದಿಯೊಳೀಶ್ವರ-ಗಣ
ಮೊದವಿರೆ, ಪದವೆಲ್ಲಂ, |
ಮದಗಜ-ಗಮನೆ, ಪೆಱಗಣ ಚಿತ್ರಲತೆಯಂ
ದದೊಳಿರ್ದೊಡದೆ ಚಿತ್ರಲತೆಯಕ್ಕುಂ. ||

1) The ನೆ of foot vi. and ದೆ of x. may be taken either as short or long; the second line may be joined to the first.

4. The Five Akkaras

ಎಯ್ದಕ್ಕರಲಕ್ಷಣಮಂ ಪೇಳ್ವೆಂ

277. The *great* (piri) *Akkara.* At the beginning of the first line an aja; then five vishṇus; at the end (tudi) a rudra. At the beginning of the second line an aja; then four vishṇus; at the 6th place an aja; then a rudra. The feet of the third line are in name the same as those of the first; and those of the fourth line in name the same as those of the second.

ಪಿರಿಯಕ್ಕರಂ

ಮೊದಲೊಳಜ-ಗಣಂ ಕುಂದದೆ ಬಕ್ಕತ್ತಮೆಯ್ದು ಗಣಂಗಳ್ ವಿಷ್ಣುವಕ್ಕುಂ;
ತುದಿಯೊಳೆಂಬ ತಾಣದೊಳೆಲ್ಲಿಯುಂ ಕಂದರ್ಪರಿಪು-ಗಣಂ ನೆಲಸಿ ನಿಲ್ಕೆ; ।
ಪದದೊಳೆರಡೆಂಬ ಸಂಖ್ಯೆಯೊಳಾಱಱೊಳಜ-ಗಣಂ ಸಮವಾಯಮಪ್ಪೊಡಕ್ಕುಂ,
ಸದಮಳೇಂದು-ನಿಭಾನನೇ, ಕರ್ತೃವಿನಿಷ್ಟದಿನರಿದು ಪಿರಿಯಕ್ಕರಂ. || 302 ||

The scheme of the verse:

	1	2	3	4	5	6	7
32 M.	⏑⏑⏑	⏑⏑⏑—	—⏑⏑	——⏑	—⏑⏑	—⏑⏑	—⏑——
	1	2	3	4	5	VI	7
32 M.	⏑⏑⏑	—⏑—	⏑⏑—⏑	———	⏑⏑⏑⏑	—⏑	⏑⏑⏑—⏑ |
	1	2	3	4	5	6	7
33 M.	⏑⏑⏑	⏑⏑—⏑	—⏑⏑	—⏑⏑	⏑⏑⏑—	⏑⏑—⏑	—⏑——
	1	2	3	4	5	VI	7
30 or 29 M.	⏑⏑⏑	—⏑⏑	—⏑⏓	—⏑⏑	—⏑⏑	⏑⏑⏑	⏑⏑—⏑— ‖

Sb. ಮೊದಲೊಳಜ-ಗಣಂ ಕುಂದದೆ ಬಕ್ಕ ತಲೆಯ್ದು ಗಣಂಗಳೆ ವಿಷ್ಣುವಕ್ಕುಂ;
ತುದಿಯೊಳೆಂಬ ತಾಣದೊಳೆಲ್ಲಿಯುಂ ಕಂದರ್ಪರಿಪು-ಗಣ ನೆಲಸಿ ನಿಲೆ, ।
ಪದದೊಳೆರಡೆಂಬ ಸಂಖ್ಯೆಯೊಳಾಱಱೊಳಜ-ಗಣಂ ಸಮವಾಯಮಪ್ಪುದಕ್ಕುಂ,
ಸದಮಳೇಂದು-ನಿಭಾನನೆ, ಕರ್ತೃವಿನಿಷ್ಟದಿನಿಂತಿದು ಪಿರಿಯಕ್ಕರಂ. ||

Ra. ಮೊದಲೊಳಜ-ಗಣಂ ಕುಂದದೆ ಬಕ್ಕತ್ತಲೆಯ್ದು ಗಣಂಗಳೆ ವಿಷ್ಣುದಕ್ಕುಂ;
ತುದಿಯೊಳೆಂಬ ತಾಣದೊಳೆಲ್ಲಿಯುಂ (ಕಂ)ದರ್ಪರಿಪು-ಗಣಂ ನೆಲಸಿ ನಿಲೆ, ।
ಪದದೊಳೆರಡೆಂಬ ಸಂಖ್ಯೆಯೊಳಾಱಱೊಳಜ-ಗಣಂ ಸಮವಾಯಂಮಪ್ಪೊಡಕ್ಕು,
ಸದಮಳೇಂದು-ನಿಭಾನನೆ, ಕರ್ತೃವಿನಿಷ್ಟದಿನಿಂತತಿದು ಪಿರಿಯಕ್ಕರಂ. ||

K., M. ಮೊದಲೊಳೆ ಜಗಣಂಗಳ್ ಕುಂದದೆ ಬಕ್ಕು ಮತ್ತಮೆಯ್ದು ಗಣಂಗಳು ವಿಷ್ಣುವಕ್ಕುಂ;
ತುದಿತುದಿಯೊಳೆಂಬ ತಾಣದೊಳೆಲ್ಲಿಯುಂ ಕಂದರ್ಪಹರ-ಗಣಂ ನೆಲಸಿ ನಿಲ್ಕೆ; ।

ಪದಾಂತ್ಯದೊಳೆರಡೆಂಬ ಸಂಖ್ಯೆಯೊಳಂ ನಾಲ್ಕುಂ ಜಗಣಂ ಸಮವಾಯಮಪ್ಪುದಕ್ಕುಂ;
ಸ . . . . ಕರ್ತೃವಿನಿಷ್ಟದೊಳಿಂತಿದು ಪಿರಿಯಕ್ಕರಂ. ||

H. ಮೊದಲೊಳ್ ಜಗಣಂ ಕುಂದದೆ ಬಕ್ಕತ್ತಮೆಯ್ದು ಗಣಂಗಳ್ ವಿಷ್ಣುವಕ್ಕುಂ;
ತುದಿಯೊಳೆಂಬ ತಾಣದೊಳೆಲ್ಲಿಯುಂ ಕಂದರ್ಪರಿಪು-ಗಣಂ ನೆಲಸಿ ನಿಲೆ, |
ಪದದೊಳೆರಡೆಂಬ ಸಂಖ್ಯೆಯೊಳಾಱಿಱೊಳಜಗಣಂ ಸಮವಾಯಂಮಪ್ಪೊಡಕ್ಕುಂ,
ಸದಮಳೇಂದು-ನಿಭಾನನೆ, ಕರ್ತೃವಿನಿಷ್ಟದಿನಿಂತರಿದು ಪಿರಿಯಕ್ಕರಂ. ||

L. ಮೊದಲೊಳು ಅಜ-ಗಣಮಕ್ಕುಂ, ಏತ್ತವೆಯ್ದು ಗಣ ವಿಷ್ಣುವಕ್ಕುಂ;
ತುದಿಯೊಳೆಂಬ ತಾಣದಲ್ಲಿ ಕಂದರ್ಪರಿಪು-ಗಣಂ ನೆಲಸಿ ನಿಲ್ಕೆ; |
ಪದದೊಳೆರಡೆಂಬ ಸಂಖ್ಯೆಯೊಳ್ ನಾಲ್ಕಱಿಱೊಳಜ-ಗಣಂ ಸಮವಾಯುತಕಂ,
ಸದಮಳೇಂದು-ವಿಭಾನನೆ, ಕರ್ತೃವಿನಿಷ್ಟದಿನಿಂತಿದು ಪಿರಿಯಕ್ಕರಂ. ||

278. **The *equal* (dŏrĕ) *Akkara*. Each line has the following 6 feet: two sarasijodaras (vishṇus, only of four or five Moras), then an aja, then again two sarasijodaras, and another aja (the final of which is long). So far it is a regular metre, and would be fully so, if for all the places respectively feet of the same number of Moras were selected.**

ದೊರೆಯಕ್ಕರಂ

ಸರಸಿಜೋದರ-ಗಣಮೆರಡಜನುಮಲ್ಲಿ ನೆರೆದಿಕ್ಕೆ, ಮತ್ತಂ
ಸರಸಿಜೋದರ-ಗಣಮೆರಡಜನುಮಕ್ಕೆ, ಗಣಮುಮಾಱಕ್ಕುಂ. |
ಸರಸಿಜ-ಲೋಚನೆ, ದೊರೆವೆತ್ತ ಗಣದಿಂ ದೊರೆವೆತ್ತ ಪೆಸರಿಂ
ದೊರೆಯಾಗಿ ಸಂದುದು ದೊರೆಯಕ್ಕರಮಿದನಱಿವುದೀ ತೆಱದಿಂ. || 303 ||

The scheme of the verse:

	1	2	III	4	5	VI	
26 M.	⏑⏑⏑—	⏑⏑⏑⏑	⏑⏑⏑	⏑⏑—⏑	⏑⏑—⏑	——	
26 M.	⏑⏑⏑—	⏑⏑⏑⏑	⏑⏑⏑	⏑⏑—⏑	⏑⏑⏑—	——	|
26 M.	⏑⏑⏑⏑	—⏑⏑	⏑⏑—	⏑⏑⏑—	⏑⏑—⏑	⏑⏑—	
26 M.	⏑⏑—⏑	—⏑⏑	⏑⏑—	⏑⏑⏑⏑	⏑⏑⏑—	⏑⏑—	‖

or in numbers:

5 . 4 . 3 . 5 . 5 . 4
5 . 4 . 3 . 5 . 5 . 4 |
4 . 4 . 4 . 5 . 5 . 4
5 . 4 . 4 . 4 . 5 . 4 ||

K., M. ಸರಸಿಜೋದರ-ಗಣಮೆರಡಜನುಮಲ್ಲಿ ನೆರದಿಕ್ಕೆ, ಮತ್ತಂ
ತಿರೆರಡು ಸೂಳ್ ಬಂದಾಗಮಿಂತೊಪ್ಪೆಯಿಂದ್ರವಿಖ್ಯಾತಂ, ।
ಸರಸಿಜ-ಲೋಚನೆ, ದೊರೆವೆತ್ತ ಪೆಸರಿ
ದೊರೆಯಾಗಿ ಸಂದುದಿದುರುತರ ದೊರೆಯಕ್ಕರಮಿದನಱಿ'ದೀ ತೆಱದಿಂದಂ, ಕಾಂತೇ! ॥

Ka. ಸರಸಿಜೋದರ-ಗಣಮೆರದೆರಡುನಮಲ್ಲಿ ನೆರದಿಕ್ಕೆ, ಮೊತ್ತಂ
ಸರಸಿಜೋದರ-ಗಣಮೆರಡುಮಕ್ಕೆ, ಗಣಮುಮಾಱಿಕ್ಕಂ, ।
ಸರಸಿಜ-ಲೋಚನೆ, ದೊರೆವೆತ್ತರಧಿದೊರೆವೆತ್ತ ಪೆಸರಿ
ದೊರೆಯಾಗಿ ಸಂದುದು ದೊರೆಯಕ್ಕುಮಿದನಱಿ'ವುದೀ ತೆಱದಿಂ. ॥

Sb. ಸರಸಿಜೋದರ-ಗಣವೆರಡನುಮಲ್ಲಿ ನೆರದಿಕ್ಕೆ, ಮತ್ತಂ
ಸರಸಿಜೋದರ-ಗಣವೆರಡಜನುಮಕ್ಕೆ, ಗಣಮುಮೂಱಿಕ್ಕುಂ. ।
ಸರಸಿಜ-ಲೋಚನೆ, ದೊರೆವೆತ್ತ ಗಣದಿಂ ದೊರೆವೆತ್ತ ಪೆಸರಿಂ
ದೊರೆಯಾಗಿ ಸಂದುದು ದೊರೆಯಕ್ಕರಮಿದನಱಿ'ವುದೀ ತೆಱದಿಂ. ॥

L. ಸರಸಿಜೋದ್ಭವ-ಗಣಮೆರಡುಜನುಮಲ್ಲಿ ನೆರದಿಕ್ಕು, ಮಾತ್ರಂ
ಸರಸಿಜೋದರ-ಗಣಮೆರಡುಂಜನಿಮಲ್ಲಿಂ ಕೆಳಗವು ಮೂಱಿಕೆ, ।
ಸರಸಿಜ-ಲೋಚನೆ, ದೊರೆವೆತ್ತ ಗಣದಿಂದಂ
ಧರೆಯೊಳಗಿರಿ ಸಂದಿರೆ ದೊರೆಯಕ್ಕರವಿದನಱಿ'ವುದೀ ತೆಱದಿಂ. ॥

H. ಸರಸಿಜೋದರ-ಗಣಮೆರಡೆರಡುಮವಲ್ಲಿ ನೆರದಿಕ್ಕೆ; ಮತ್ತಂ
ಸರಸಿಜೋದರ-ಗಣಮೆರಡುಮಕ್ಕೆ, ಗಣಮುಮಾಱಿಕ್ಕುಂ. ।
ಸರಸಿಜ-ಲೋಚನೆ, ದೊರೆವೆತ್ತ ಪೆಸರಿ
ದೊರೆಯಾಗಿ ಸಂದುದು ದೊರೆಯಕ್ಕರಮಿದನಱಿ'ವುದೀ ತೆಱದಿಂ. ॥

279. **The *middle* (naḍu) *Akkara*. Each line is as follows: One jalajasambhava (bramha), three jalaruhodaras (vishṇus), and one kâmântaka (rudra, the final of which is long). The number of feet, therefore, is five (kâmabâṇâvaḷi).**

ನಡುವಣಕ್ಕರಂ.

ಜಳಜಸಂಭವ-ಗಣಮಕ್ಕೆ ಮೊದಲೊಳ್; ನಡುವೆ ಮೂಱುಂ
ಜಳರುಹೋದರ-ಗಣಮಕ್ಕೆ; ಕಾಮಾಂತಕ-ಗಣಮಕ್ಕುಂ, ।
ತಿಳಕದಂತಿರೆ ತಲೆಯೊಳ್ ಬಂದಿಕ್ಕೆ; ಕಾಮಬಾಣಾ
ವಳಿಯ ಪಾಂಗೆಯ್ದೆ ಗಣಮಕ್ಕೆ ನಡುವಣಕ್ಕರಕೆ, ಸಖೀ! ॥ 304 ॥

The scheme of the verse:

	1	2	3	4	5	
24 M.	⏑⏑⏑	— ⏑ ⏑	⏑⏑—⏑	⏑⏑⏑—	⏑⏑⏑——	
24 M.	⏑⏑⏑	— ⏑ ⏑	⏑⏑—⏑	——⏑	⏑⏑⏑——	|
24 M.	⏑⏑⏑	— ⏑ ⏑	⏑⏑⏑—	——⏑	—⏑——	
24 M.	⏑⏑⏑	——⏑	⏑⏑—⏑	⏑⏑⏑—	⏑⏑⏑⏑—	||

or in numbers:

3 . 4 . 5 . 5 . 7

3 . 4 . 5 . 5 . 7 |

3 . 4 . 5 . 5 . 7

3 . 5 . 5 . 5 . 6 ||

H. ಜಳಸಂಭವ-ಗಣಮಕ್ಕೆ ಮೊದಲೊಳೆ, ನಡುವೆ ಮೂಱಿಂ
ಜಳರುಹೋದರ-ಗಣಮಕ್ಕೆ, ಕಾಮಾಂತಕ-ಗಣಮಕ್ಕು |
ತಿಳಿದಂತಿರೆ ತಲೆಯೊಳೆಂಬ ತೆಕ್ಕೆ, ಕಾಮಬಾಣಾ
ವಳಿಯಾ ಪಾಂಗೆಯ್ದು ಗಣಮಕ್ಕೆ ನಡುವಣಕ್ಕರಕ್ಕೆ, ಸಖೀ! ||

M. ಜಳಜಸಂಭವ-ಗಣಮಕ್ಕೆ ಮೊದಲೊಳು, ನಡುವೆ
ಜಳರುಹೋದರ-ಗಣಮಕ್ಕೆ, ಬಳಿಕ್ಕ ಕಾಮಾರಿ-ಗಣಂ |
ತಿಳಕದಂತಿರೆ ಕಡೆಯೊಳ್ ಬಂದುಯಿಕ್ಕೆ, ಕಾಮಬಾಣಾ
ವಳಿಯಂ ಪಾಂಗೆಯ್ದೆ ಗಣವಕ್ಕೆ ನಡುವಣಕ್ಕರಕ್ಕೆ; ಪೆಸರಿಂತು, ಸಖೀ! ||

Sb. ಜಳಜಸಂಭವ-ಗಣಮಕ್ಕೆ ಮೊದಲೊಳೆ, ನಡುವೆ ಮೂಱಿಂ
ಜಳರುಹೋದರ-ಗಣಮಕ್ಕೆ, ಕಾಮಾಂತಕ-ಗಣಂ ಬಕ್ಕುಂ, |
ತಿಳಕದಂತಿರೆ ತಲೆಯೊಳೆ ಬಂದಿಕ್ಕೆ, ಕಾಮಬಾಣಾ
ವಳಿಯ ಪಾಂಗೆಯ್ದೆ ಗಣವಕ್ಕೆ ನಡುವಣಕ್ಕರಕ್ಕೆ; ಪೆಸರಿಂತು, ಸಖೀ! ||

Ra. ಜಳಸಂಭವ-ಗಣಮಕ್ಕೆ ಮೊದಲೊಳೆದಮೊಳೆ, ನಡುವೆ ಮೂಱಿಂ
ಜಳರುಹೋದರ-ಗಣಮಕ್ಕೆ, (ಕಾ)ಮಾಂತಕ-ಗಣಮಕ್ಕುಂ |
ತಿಳಿದಂತಿರೆ ತಲೆಯೊಳೆಂಬ ತೆಕ್ಕೆ, ಕಾಮಬಾಣಾ
ವಳಿಯಾ ಪಾಂಗೆಯ್ದು ಗಣಮಕ್ಕೆ . . . . . ||

L. ಜಲಸಂಭವ-ಗಣಮಕ್ಕು ಮೊದಲೊಳು, ನಡುವೆ ಮೂಱಿಂ
ಜಲರುಹೋದರ-ಗಣಮಕ್ಕೆಂ, ಬಳಿಕ ಕಾಮಾರಿಗಣಂ ।
ತಿಲಕದಂತಿರೆ ಲತೆಗಳೊಳು ಬಂದಿಕ್ಕೆಮಾ ಕಾಮಬಾಣಾ
ವಳಿ ಪಾಂಗಿಯೆಡೆಗಕ್ಕೆ . . . . ||

280. The *nice* (ಒಳ್ಳೆ) *Akkara*. Each line consists of four feet in the following order: a vanajasambhava (brahma), two vanaruhodaras (vishṇus), and a rudra.

ಎಡೆಯಕ್ಕರಂ

ವನಜಸಂಭವ-ಗಣಮಕ್ಕೆ ಮೊದಲೊಳತ್ತಲ್
ವನರುಹೋದರ-ಗಣ-ಯುಗಳಮದಕ್ಕೆ, ರು ।
ದ್ರನದಚಿಂತ್ಯದೊಳ್ ಬಂದಿಕ್ಕೆ, ನಾಲ್ಕೆ ಗಣ
ವಿನಿತೆ, ವನಿತೆ, ಕೇಳ್, ಎಡೆಯಕ್ಕರಕ್ಕಿನಿಸುಂ. || 305 ||

The scheme of the verse:

	1	2	3	4	
19 M.	∪∪∪	–∪∪	∪∪–∪	∪∪∪––	
18 M.	∪∪∪	–∪∪	∪∪∪∪	∪∪–∪–	।
18 M.	∪∪∪	–∪–	––∪	–∪∪∪	
19 M.	∪∪∪	∪∪∪–	∪∪–∪	–∪∪–	॥

or in numbers:

3 . 4 . 5 . 7
3 . 4 . 4 . 7 ।
3 . 5 . 5 . 5
3 . 5 . 5 . 6 ॥

H. ವನಜಸಂಭವ-ಗಣಮಕ್ಕೆ ಮೊದಲೊಳತ್ತಲು
ವನರುಹೋದರ-ಗಣ-ಯುಗಮಕ್ಕೆ, ರು ।
ದ್ರನಿಂತದಚಿಂತೆದೊಳಂ ಬಂದು, ನಾಲ್ಕೆಡೆ ಗಣ
ವಿನತೆ, ವನಿತೆ, ಕೇಳ್, ಎಡೆಯಕ್ಕರಕ್ಕೆನಿಸುಂ. ||

Sb. ವನಜಸಂಭವ-ಗಣಮಕ್ಕೆ ಮೊದಲೊಳತ್ತಲ್
ವನರುಹೋದರ-ಗಣ-ಯುಗಮಕ್ಕೆ, ರು ।
ದ್ರನಂತದಚಿಂತ್ಯದೊಳಂ ಬಂದು, ನಾಲ್ಕೆ ಗಣ
ದನಿತೆ, ಕೇಳ್, ಎಡೆಯಕ್ಕರಕ್ಕೆನಸುಂ. ||

K., M. ವನಜಸಂಭವ-ಗಣಮಕ್ಕೆ ಮೊದಲೊಳೆತ್ತಲ್
ವನರುಹೋದರ-ಗಣ-ಯುಗಳಮವಕ್ಕೆ, ರು |
ದ್ರನದಱಿಂತ್ಯದೊಳ್ ಬಂದಿಕ್ಕೆ, ನಾಲ್ಕು ಗಣ
ಮನಿತುಮೆಸೆವ ಕಡೆಯಕ್ಕರಕ್ಕೆ ಮಾತ್ರೆಗಳ್. ||

Ra. . . . .
. . . . ರು |
ದ್ರನಿಂತದಱಿಂತ್ಯದೊಳಂ ಬಂದು ನಾಲ್ಕೆಡೆ ಗಣ
ಏನಿತೆ, ಕೇಳ್, ಎದೆಯಕ್ಕರಕ್ಕೆನಿಸುಂ. ||

281. The *little* (kiṟi) *Akkara.* Each line consists of the following three feet: two pŏḍĕyalars (vishṇus) and a śaṅkara (rudra).

ಕಿಱಿಯಕ್ಕರಂ

ಪೊಡೆಯಲರಿರ್ಬರುಂ ಮೊದಲೊಳಿಕ್ಕೆ,
ಜಡೆಯ ಶಂಕರನೊರ್ಬಂ ತುದಿಯೊಳಿಕ್ಕೆ, |
ಮಡದಿ, ಕೇಳ್, ಮೂಱು ಗಣಮೆಸೆದಿಕ್ಕೆ;
ಗಡ, ಕಿಱಿಯಕ್ಕರಕ್ಕಿದೆ ಲಕ್ಷಣಂ! || 306 ||

The scheme of the verse:

	1	2	3
15 M.	⏑⏑⏑⏑	– ⏑ –	⏑⏑⏑–⏑
17 M.	⏑⏑⏑–	⏑⏑– –	⏑⏑⏑–⏑ |
15 M.	⏑⏑⏑–	– ⏑ ⏑	⏑⏑⏑–⏑
16 M.	⏑⏑⏑⏑	– ⏑ –	⏑⏑–⏑– ||

or in numbers:

4 . 5 . 6
5 . 6 . 6 |
5 . 4 . 6
4 . 5 . 7 ||

H. ಪೊಡೆಯಲರಿರ್ಬರ್ ಮೊದಲೊಳಿಕ್ಕೆ,
ಜಡೆಯ ಶಂಕರನೊಬ್ಬಂ ತುದಿಯೊಳಿಕ್ಕೆ, |
ಮಡದಿ, ಕೇಳ್, ಮೂಱಿಡೆ ಗಣಮೆಸೆದಿಕ್ಕೆ;
ಗಡ, ಕಿಱಿಯಕ್ಕರಕಿದೆ ಲಕ್ಷಣಂ! ||

D., B. ತಡೆಯದೆ ಹರಿ-ಯುಗಂ ಮೊದಲೊಳಿರ್ಕೆ,
ಜಡೆಯ ಶಂಕರನೊರ್ವಂ ತುದಿಯೊಳಿರ್ಕೆ, |
ಮಡದಿ, ಕೇಳ್, ಮೂಱು ಗಣಮೆಸೆದಿರ್ಕೆ; [D. ಕೇಳಿ ಗುರುಗಣಮೆಸೆದಿರ್ಕೆ]
ಗಡ, ಕಿಱಿಯಕ್ಕರಕ್ಕಿದು ಲಕ್ಷಣಂ! ||

K., M. ತಡೆಯದೆ ಹರಿ-ಯುಗಂ ಮೊದಲೊಳಿಕ್ಕೆ,
ಜಡೆಯ ಶಂಕರನೊರ್ವಂ ಕಡೆಯೊಳಿಕ್ಕೆ, | [L. ಕಡೆಯೊಳಿಕ್ಕುಂ]
ಮಡದಿ, ಕೇಳ್, ಸುರ-ಗಣಮೆಸೆದಿಕ್ಕೆ; [Sb.-ಮೂಱಿದೆ ಗಣಮೆಸೆದಿಕ್ಕೆ]
[L. -ಮೂಱು ಗಣಮೊಸದಿಕ್ಕುಂ]
ಕಡ, ಕಿಱಿಯಕ್ಕರಕ್ಕಿದುವೆ ಲಕ್ಷಣಂ! || [Sb.-ಕ್ಕಿದೆ ಲಕ್ಷಣಂ] [L.-ಕ್ಕಿದು ಲಕ್ಷಣಂ]

Ra. ಪೊಡೆಯಲದಿರ್ಬ ಮೊದಲೊಳಿಕ್ಕೆ,
ಜಡೆಯ ಶಂಕರನೊಬ್ಬಂ ತುದಿಯೊಳಿಕ್ಕೆ, |
ಮೊಡದಿ, ಕೇಳ್, ಮೂಱಿಡೆ ಗಣಮೆಸೆದಿರೆ,
ಗಡ, ಕಿಱಿಯಕ್ಕರಕಿದೆ ಲಕ್ಷಣಂ! ||

5. The Elĕ[1]

282. The Elĕ. There occur 6 (bhujaga=1, paksha=2, pura=3) feet (of which two are bhujagapakshas *i. e.* bhujagadhâris); the 6th foot forms an aja.

ಏಳೆಯ ಲಕ್ಷಣಮಂ ಪೇಳ್ವೆಂ
ಭುಜಗ-ಪಕ್ಷ-ಪುರ-ಗಣಾ-*
ಬ್ರಜದೊಳಾಱಿಱೊಳಪ್ಪು
ದಜಗಣಾಳಿಳೆ, ಭವತೀ! || 307 ||

The scheme of the verse:

1 ⏑⏑⏑—⏑ | 2 ⏑⏑⏑— * 3 ⏑⏑⏑— | 4 ⏑⏑—⏑
5 ⏑⏑⏑—⏑ | VI ⏑⏑— ||

Sb. ಭುಜಗ-ಪಕ್ಷ-ಪುರ-ಗಣ-
ಬ್ರಜದೊಳಾಱಿಱೊಳಪ್ಪು
ದಜ-ಗಣೆಳೆಸಿಭವತಿ! ||

1) The reading of the last line of the verse in the MSS. is doubtful; eḷĕ (not ēḷĕ), however, is the form given in v. 68. Cf. the note to v. 300.

K., M. ಅಜ-ಪಕ್ಷ-ಸುರ-
ವ್ರಜದೊಳಾಜಿಯೊಳಪ್ಪು
ದು ಜಗದೊಳೆಳೆನಿಭವತಿ! ||

Ra. ಭುಜಗ-ಪಕ್ಷ-ಪುರ-ಗಣ-
ಬ್ರಜದೊಳಾಜಿಜಿಯೊಪ್ಪು
ದಜ-ಗಣೆಳೆಸಿಭಗತಿ! ||

H. ಭುಜಗ-ಪಕ್ಷ-ಪುರ-ಗಣ-
ಬ್ರಜದೊಳಾಜಿಜಿಯೊಪ್ಪು
ದಜ-ಗಣೆಳೆನಿಭಗತಿಂ. ||

6. The Akkarikĕ

ಅಕ್ಕರಿಕೆಯ ಲಕ್ಷಣಮಂ ಪೇಳ್ಗೆಂ

283. The Akkarikĕ is a Canarese Samavṛitta (cf. v. 276), somewhat connected with the Kusuma vicitra of v. 162. Each line shows the following 6 (khara or kara, see v. 244) feet: a Proceleusmatic (muraripu), a Spondee (bomma), a Proceleusmatic, a Spondee, a Proceleusmatic, a Choriambus (*i. e.* a Dactyl and a long syllable). At every 6th syllable occurs Caesura, and after it another Alliteration.

The scheme is four times:

⏑⏑⏑⏑ | — — * ⏑⏑⏑⏑ | — — * ⏑⏑⏑⏑ | —⏑⏑.—

or in numbers:

4 . 4 . * 4 . 4 * 4 . 4 . 2

ಅಕ್ಕರಿಕೆ

ಮುರರಿಪು, ಬೊಮ್ಮಂ, ಮುರರಿಪು, ಬೊಮ್ಮಂ, ಮುರರಿಪು, ಶೂಲಧರಂ
ಸರಸದೆ ನಿಲ್ಕುಂ; ಖರ-ಗಣಮಕ್ಕುಂ ಸುರುಚಿರ-ಮಾತ್ರೆಗಳಿಂ; |[1)]
ನಿರುಪಮದಿಂದಂ ಪರಿಮಿತಮಪ್ಪಂತಿರೆ, ಯತಿಯಾಱಱೊಳಂ[2)]
ಬರೆ, ತರಳಾಕ್ಷೀ, ಧರೆಯೊಳಿದೆತ್ತಂ ಕರಮೆಸೆವಕ್ಕರಿಕೇ. || 308 ||

1) H. ಶಿರದೊಳೆ ನಿಲ್ಕಂ ಖರ-ಗಣಮಕ್ಕ ಸುರಚಿರ-ಮಾತ್ರಗಳಿಂ; Ra. ಸರಸದೆ ನಿಲ್ಕಂ ಖರ-ಗಣಮಕ್ಕಂ . . . ; K. M . . . . ಖಗ-ಗಣಮಕ್ಕಂ; D. B. ಸರಸದೆ ನಿಲ್ಕಂ ಕರಿ-ದಳ-ಸಂಖ್ಯಾ-ಸುರುಚಿರ-ಮಾತ್ರಗಳಿಂ.

2) H. ಯತಿ ರಿತುಯೆತ್ತಂ; Ra. ಯತಿ ರಿತುಯತ್ತಂ; M. ಯತಿ ಎತುಸಾರದೊಳ್; K. ಯತಿ ಋತುಸುರರೊಳ್; L. ಯತಿ ಋತುಶರದೊಳ್; D. B. ಯತಿ ಷಟ್-ಶರದೊಳ್. ಋತು = 6.

7. The Caupadi (Caupadigĕ)

ಚೌಪದಿಯ (ಚೌಪದಿಗೆಯ) ಲಕ್ಷಣಮಂ ಪೇೞ್ಗುಂ

284. The *Caupadi* too is to be considered a Canarese Samavṛitta according to the author's views (else he would somewhere have introduced a Dactyl instead of the Proceleusmatic, etc.). Each line consists of a Proceleusmaticus (madanapitṛi) and a Choriambus (śaṅkara, *i. e.* in practice a Dactyl and a long syllable).

The scheme is four times:

⏑⏑⏑⏑ | —⏑⏑ . —

or in numbers:

4 . 4 . 2

ಚೌಪದಿ

ಮದನನ ತಂದೆಯ ಮುಂ
ದೊದವಿದ ಶಂಕರನೊಳ್ |
ಪುದಿದಿರೆ, ಸಂದುದು, ನೋ
ಡಿದು, ಸತಿ, ಚೌಪದಿಗೇ. [D., B. ಸರಿ ಚೌಪದಿ ಕೇಳ್] || 309 ||

K., M. ಮದನನ ತಂದೆಯ ಮುಂ
ದುದಯಿಸೆ ಶಂಕರನೊಳ್ |
ಪೊದವಿರೆ, ಸಂದುದು, ನೋ
ಡಿದು, ಸತಿ, ಚೌಪದಿಗೇ. ||

Rs., H. ಮದನನ ತಂದೆಯ ಮುಂ
ದುದಯಿಸೆ ಶಂಕರನೊಳ್ |
ಪಾದವಿರೆ, ಸಂದುದು, ನೋ
ಡಿದು, ಸತಿ, ಚೌಪದಿಗೇ. ||

8. The Chandovataṁsa (Chandovasanta)

ಛಂದೋವತಂಸಕ್ಕೆ ಲಕ್ಷಣಮಂ ಪೇೞ್ಗುಂ

285. The *Chandovataṁsa*. Each line contains first three mandaradharas (vishṇu), then a bisaruhajanma (brahma) in its end.

ಛಂದೋವತಂಸಂ

ಮಂದರಧರ-ಗಣಮೆಸೆದಿರೆ ಮೊದಲೊಳ್,
ಬಂದಿರೆ ನಾಲ್ಕಕೆ ಬಿಸರುಹಜನ್ಮಂ; |
ಸಂದುದು ಲಕ್ಷಣಮೀ ತೆಱದಿಂದಂ
ಛಂದೋವತಂಸಕೆ, ಮದಗಜ-ಗಮನೆ! || 310 ||[1]

The scheme of the verse:

	1	2	3	4
16 M.	—⏑⏑	⏑⏑⏑⏑	⏑⏑⏑⏑	⏑⏑—
16 M.	—⏑⏑	—⏑⏑	⏑⏑⏑⏑	—— |
16 M.	—⏑⏑	—⏑⏑	—⏑⏑	——
16 or 17 M.	——⏑	—⏑⏑	⏑⏑⏑⏑	⏑⏑⏓ ||

H. ಮಂದರಧರ-ಗಣಮೆಸೆದಿಕ್ಕೆ ಮೊದಲೊಳೆ;
ಬಂದಿಕ್ಕು ನಾಲ್ಕೆ; ವಿಸಮುಹಂ ಜನ್ಮಂ |
ಸಂದುದು; ಲಕ್ಷಣಮಿಾ ತೆಱಿದಿಂ
ಛಂದೋವಸಂತಕ್ಕೆ ಸಂದುದು, ಮದಗಜ-ಗಮನೆ! ||

Ra. ಮಂದರಧರ-ಗಣಮೆಸೆದಿಕ್ಕೆ ಮೊದಲೊಳೆ;
ಬಂದಿಕ್ಕುಂ ನಾಲ್ಕೆ; ವಿಸಮುಹುಂ ಜನ್ಮಂ |
ಸಂದುದು; ಲಕ್ಷಮಿಾ ತೆಱಿದಿಂ
ಛಂದೋವಸಂತಕ್ಕೆ ಸಂದುದು, ಮದಗಜ-ಗಮನೆ! ||

Sb. ಮಂದರಧರ-ಗಣಮೆಸೆದಿಕ್ಕೆ ಮೊದಲೊಳೆ;
ಬಂದಿಕ್ಕುಂ ನಾಲ್ಕೆ; ಬಿಸರುಹ-ಜನ್ಮಂ |
ಸಂದುದು; ಲಕ್ಷಣಮಿಾ ತೆಱಿದಿಂದಂ
ಛಂದೋವತಂಸಕ್ಕೆ ಪಂದುದು, ಗಜ-ಗಮನೆ! ||

1) The *meaning* of the readings of K., M. and L. only well agrees with the construction of this metre as far as it appears in the verses; according to it this verse is presented. If we read "gamane" instead of "gamanĕ", the last line contains a Mora in excess, occasioned by the first foot "čhandóva" (——⏑) that is the reading of all the MSS. The ನಾಲ್ಕೆ, ನಾಲ್ಕುಂ must refer to the number of the feet of a line.

K., M. ಮಂದರಧರ-ಗಣಮೆಸೆದಿರೆ ಮೊದಲೊಳ್,
ಪೊಂದಿರೆಯುಂ ಕಡೆಯೊಳಜಂ, |
ಸಂದುದು ಲಕ್ಷಣಮವನಿಯೊಳೆಂದುಂ
ಛಂದೋವತಂಸಮಂಬುಜ-ವದನೆ! ||

L. ಮಂದರಧರ-ಗಣ ಬಂದಿರೆ ಮೊದಲೊಳು;
ಕುಂದದೆ ಬಂದಿರೆ ನಾಲ್ಕುಂ; ತುದಿಯೊಳು ವಿಷರುಹ-ಜಲ್ಮಂ |
ಸಂದುದು; ಲಕ್ಷಣಮವನಿಯೊಳೀ ತೆಱದಿಂದಂ
ಛಂದೋವಸಂತಕೆ ಸಲೆ ಗಜ-ಗಮನೆ! ||

9. The Madanavati

ಮದನವತಿಲಕ್ಷಣಂ

286. **The Madanavati.** "When there are 5 (vishaya) madanapitṛi (vishṇu) feet and afterwards a long syllable occurs" (it is the Madanavati); "the same line is formed, when a harapada (rudra) is found after 4 upendras" (vishṇus); or "when a hari stands at the end of 3 madanaharas" (rudras, and is followed by the long syllable), "it is the Madanavati". Feet of the same number of Moras interchange.

ಮದನವತಿ

ಮದನನ ತಂದೆಯ ಗಣಮವು ವಿಷಯದೊಳಿರೆ, ಗುರು ಮುಂ
ದೊದವಿರೆ; ಪದದೊಳಮದಱ ಪೊಲಪ್ಪುದು ಹರ-ಪದಮುಂ |
ವಿದಿತಮುಪೇಂದ್ರ-ಚತುಷ್ಟಯದಿತ್ತಲಬುಜ-ವದನೇ,
ಮದನಹರ-ತ್ರಯದಿಂ ಹರಿ ಕಡೆ ಪಡೆ, ಮದನವತೀ. || 311 ||

The scheme of the metre as to Moras is four times either:

22 M. ⏑⏑⏑⏑ (1) | —⏑⏑ (2) | ⏑⏑⏑⏑ (3) | ⏑⏑⏑⏑ (4) | ⏑⏑⏑⏑ (5) | —

or

⏑⏑⏑⏑ (1) | —⏑⏑ (2) | ⏑⏑⏑⏑ (3) | ⏑⏑⏑⏑ (4) | ⏑⏑⏑⏑— (5)

or

⏑⏑⏑⏑— (2) | ⏑⏑⏑⏑⏑ (2) | ⏑⏑⏑⏑⏑ (3) | ⏑⏑⏑⏑ (4) | —

The first structure in numbers:

4 . 4 . 4 . 4 . 4 . 2 (i. e. one long)

H. ಮದನನ ತಂದೆಯ ಗಣಮೂರ್ವಿಷಯದೊಳಿರೆ, ಮುಂ
ದೊದವಿರೆ, ಪದದೊಳಮದಟಿ ಪೊಲಪ್ಪುದು ಹರಪದಮುಂ |
ವಿದಿತಮುಪೇಂದ್ರ-ಚತುಷ್ಟಯದಿಂದಬುಜಜನುಂ
ಮದನಹರ-ತ್ರಯದಿಂ ಪಂ ಕಡೆ ಪಡೆದ ಮದನವತಿ. ||

Sb. ಮದನನ ತಂದೆಯ ಗಣಮವು ವಿಷಯದೊಳಿರೆ, ಗುರು ಮುಂ
ದೊದವಿರೆ, ಪದದೊಳಮದಟಿ ಪೊಲಪ್ಪುದು ಹರಪದಮುಂ |
ವಿದಿತಮುಪೇಂದ್ರಂ ಚತುಷ್ಟಯದಿಂದಬುಜಜನುಂ
ಮದನಹರ-ತ್ರಯದಿಂ ಪರಿವಡೆ ಪಡೆದ ಮದನವತಿ. ||

Ra. ಮದನನ ತಂದೆಯ ಗಣಮೌ ವಿಷಯದೊಳಿರೆ, ಮುಂ
ದೊದವಿರೆ ಪದದೊಳಮದಟಿ ಪೊಲಪ್ಪುದು ಹರಪದಮುಂ |
ವಿದಿತಮುಪೇಂದ್ರಂ ಚತುಷ್ಟಯದಿಂದಬುಜಜನುಂ
ಮದನಹರ-ತ್ರಯದಿಂ ಪರಿ ಕಡೆ ಪಡೆದ ಮದನವತಿ. ||

K., M. ಮದನನ ತಂದೆಯ ಗುಣಮುಂ ವಿಷಯದೊಳಿರೆ, ಗುರುವೊಂ
ದೊದವಿರೆ, ಪದದೊಳುಮವಟಿ ಪೊಲಪ್ಪುದು ಗುರುತರ-ಪದಮುಂ |
ವಿದಿತಮೆ ವಿದಿತಮೆಚಂದ್ರ-ಚತುಷ್ಟಯದಿಂದತ್ತಂಬುಜ-ವದನೆ,
ಮದನಹರ-ತ್ರಿತಯಂ ಹರಿ ಕಡೆ ಪಡೆ, ಮದನವತಿ. ||

L. ಮದನನ ತಂದೆಯ ಗಣಮವು ಷಯದೊಳಿರೆ, ಗರುವೊಂ
ದೊಂದಂಗನೆವಿರೆ, ಪದದೊಳಿಮರ ಪೊಲಪ್ಪುಡು ಗುರುಪಾದಮುಂ |
ವಿದಿತಮುಚಂದ್ರ-ಚತುಷ್ಟಯದಿಂದತ್ತಬ್ಜಮಂ
ಮದನಹರ-ತ್ರಿತಿಯಕ್ಕಂ ಹರಿ ಕಡೆ ಪಿಡೆದುದನ ಪೊಲೆ. ||

10. The Gîtikĕ (Gîtigĕ, Gîta)

ಗೀತಿಗೆಯ ಲಕ್ಷಣಮುಂ ಪೇಳ್ವೆಂ[1)]

287. The Gîtikĕ; the 6th foot of every second line is to be a Brahma (padmabhava); the other feet are not ordered, but according to K., M. are Vishṇus.

1) Sb., Ra., H. here ಗೀತಿಗೆ, in the verse ಗೀತ; M. ಗೀತಿಕೆ, also in the v.

ಗೀತಿಗೆ

H., Ra. ಎರಡಱೊಳಾಱೆಂಬ ಸಂಖ್ಯೆಯೊಳ್
ಬರೆ ಪದ್ಮಭವನುಳಿದವು ಮೆಚ್ಚುವ ತೆಱದಿಂ ।
ದಿರೆ, ಬಳಿಕಿನ್ನೆರಡಂ ಮುನ್ನಿನಂತೆ
ಕರಮೆಸೆದೊಪ್ಪುಗೀತ-ಗಣಂ. ॥ 312 ॥

The scheme of the verse:

1 2 3
⏑⏑⏑⏑ | – – ⏑ | – ⏑ –
4 5 VI 7
⏑⏑–⏑ | ⏑⏑⏑⏑ | ⏑⏑– | ⏑⏑⏑⏑– |
1 2 3
⏑⏑⏑⏑ | –⏑⏑– | –⏑–⏑
4 5 VI
⏑⏑⏑⏑ | –⏑– | ⏑⏑– ||

That of K. and M.:

1 2 3
⏑⏑– | ⏑⏑⏑ | –⏑–
4 5 VI 7
⏑⏑–⏑ | ⏑⏑⏑⏑ | ⏑⏑⏑ | –⏑– |
1 2 3
⏑⏑– | ⏑⏑⏑– | –⏑–
4 5 VI 7
⏑⏑⏑– | –⏑⏑ | –– | –⏑⏑ ||

or in numbers:

14 M. 4 . 5 . 5
19 M. 5 . 4 . 4 . 6 |
16 M. 4 . 6 . 6
18 M. 4 . 5 . 4 ||

or in numbers:

12 M. 4 . 3 . 5
17 M. 5 . 4 . 3 . 5 |
14 M. 4 . 5 . 5
17 or 18 M. 5 . 4 . 4 . 4 or 5 ||

Sb. ಎರಡಱೊಳಾಱೆಂಬ ಸಂಖ್ಯೆಯೊಳ್
ಪರೆ ಪದ್ಮಭವನುಳಿದವು ಮೆಚ್ಚುವ ತೆಱದಿಂ ।
ದಿರೆ, ಬಳಿಕವೆರಡುಂ ಮುನ್ನಿನಂತೆ
ಕರಮೆಸೆದೊಪ್ಪುವ ಗೀತ-ಗಣಂ. ॥

Ra. ಎರಡಱೊಳಾಱೆಂಬ ಸಂಖ್ಯೆಯೊಳ್
ಬರೆ ಪದ್ಮಭ(ವ)ನುಳಿದೌ ಮೆಚ್ಚುವ ತೆಱದಿಂ ।
ದಿರೆ, ಬಳಿಕಿನ್ನೆರಡಂ ಮುನ್ನಿನಂತೆ
ಕರಮೆಸೆದೊಪ್ಪುಗೀತ-ಗಣಂ. ॥

K., M. ಎರಡಾಱೆನಿಪ ಸಂಖ್ಯೆಯೊಳ್
ಬರೆ ಬ್ರಹ್ಮನುಳಿದೆಡೆಗಳೊಳು ವಿಷ್ಣು ಮುಂ ।
ದಿರೆ, ಮುಂದಣ ಪದಂ ಮುನ್ನಿನಂ
ತುರುತರಂ ಗೀತಿಕೆಗಿಂತಕ್ಕುಂ, ಸಖಿ! ॥

L. ಎರಡಱೊಳಱೆಂಬ ಸಂಖ್ಯೆಯೊಳ್
ಬರೆ ಪದ್ಮಭವನುಳಿದವು ಮೆವೆಂಬ ತೆಱದಿಂ |
ದಿರೆ, ಬಳಿಕ್ಕಿರೆ ನಗಣಮುಂ ಮುನ್ನಿನಂತೆ
ಕರಮೆಸೆದೊಪ್ಪುವ ಗೀತಿಕೆಗೆ, ಕೇಳು, ಗಣಮಕ್ಕುಂ. ||

☞ Here end the metres that are based upon a more or less indefinite number of Moras in the respective feet. With the Shaṭpadis a class begins that is excellent for exactness; for each foot, as is the case with regard to the Ragaḷĕ s, and Āryĕ s, is to consist of a definite number of Moras at a given place. *The feet used are those mentioned in connection with the Ragaḷĕ s*, p. 76; no foot, as observed there and p. 77, dare begin with an Iambus (⏑—). The various readings have been given not so much for elucidating the rules (that are exact enough) as for throwing some light on the history of prosody.

11. The Six Shaṭpadis

ಷಟ್ಪದಿಯ ಲಕ್ಷಣಂ

288. There are six (ṛitu) Shaṭpadis: In each class the first two lines (pâda, pada) of half a verse are equal; each third line has half a line (arĕ) in excess, and a long syllable (indudhara; v. 315 tâ; v. 317 madanahara; see v. 29) at its end. No. 289

ಕಂದಂ

ಒಂದಿದ ಋತು ಷಟ್ಪದಿಗಳೊ
ಳೊಂದೇ ತೆಱನೆರಡು ಪಾದಮುಂ; ಮೇಣ್ ಮುಂದ |
ಕ್ಕೊಂದರೆ ಬರ್ಕುಂ; ತುದಿಯ
ಲ್ಲಿಂದುಧರಂ ಬಂದೊಡಱಿಗೆ ಷಟ್ಪದಿಯ ತೆಱಂ. || 313[1] ||

289. The same statement in other words.

ಮೊದಲೆರಡು ಪದದ ಲೆಕ್ಕದೊ
ಳೊದವಿದ ವರ್ಣಂ ಸಮಾನ; ಮೂಱನೆಯ ಪದ |
ಕ್ಕದಱರ್ಧಮನೊಡಗೂಡು
ತ್ತದಱೊಳ್ ಗುರುವೊಂದನಿರಿಸೆ, ಷಟ್ಪದಿಯಕ್ಕುಂ. || 314[2] ||

1) Rc.'s concluding verse; D., B; M.'s verse 73 and Sb.'s verse 75 of their first chapter.
2) Rd. verse 22.

290. The same again, adding only that there are six lines (aḍi); (the number of Moras is stated in v. 316).

ತೋಱುವ ಮಾತ್ರೆಯ ಷಟ್ಪದಿ
ಗಾಱಾಱಡಿಯೆರಡಱಲ್ಲಿಯೊಂದೇ ನಿಯಮಂ; |
ಮೂಱಱಕ್ಕೊಂದು ತದರ್ಧಂ;
ಬೇಱೇಱಂ ಕಡೆಯೊಳೆಲ್ಲಮಿಾ ತೆಱನಕ್ಕುಂ. || 315[1] ||

291. The six Shaṭpadis are: *S*ara, Kusuma, Bhoga, Bhâmini, Parivardhini, Vârdhika (Vârtika). The first has 8 (kari) Moras in its first line, the second 10, the third 12 (ravi), the fourth 14 (manu), the fifth 16 (râja), the sixth 20.

ಶರ-ಕುಸುಮ-ಭೋಗ-ಭಾಮಿನಿ-
ಪರಿವರ್ಧಿನಿ-ವಾರ್ಧಿಕಂಗಳೆಂದಾಱು ತೆಱಂ; |
ಕರಿ-ದಶ-ರವಿ-ಮನು-ರಾಜರ್
ಬರೆ, ವಿಂಶತಿ-ಮಾತ್ರೆಯಿಂದೆ ಷಟ್ಪದಿ ನಡೆಗುಂ. || 316[2] ||

292. The *S*arashaṭpadi. Feet of 4 Moras. (The wording, however, refers it to the foregoing class of metres, stating that it consists of mandaradharas *i. e.* vishṇus, with a madanaharam *i. e.* rudra at their end; see note. Accordingly it might appear as if only vishṇus and rudras were allowed; in practice, however, a brahma of 4 Moras is looked upon as equally fit, and the rudra is represented by any foot of 4 Moras plus the guru. Examine verses 318-321, and the *ś*arashaṭpadis in the Râvaṇadigvijaya, ps. 16. 30. 36. 43. 46. 48).

The scheme is twice:

⏑⏑⏑⏑ | ⏑⏑⏑⏑
⏑⏑⏑⏑ | ⏑⏑⏑⏑
⏑⏑⏑⏑ | ⏑⏑⏑⏑ | ⏑⏑⏑⏑ | — |

or in numbers:

4 . 4
4 . 4
4 . 4 . 4 . 2 |

1) M.'s v. 75 and Sb.'s v. 77 of their first chapter; D., B.

2) Rc.'s one but last verse; Ra., H. have it after their 6th chapter (on algebraic computations, etc.) in an appendix; M.'s v. 74 and Sb.'s v. 76 of their first ch.; Rd. v. 23; D., B.; Kavijihvâbandhana, iv., 55; its following verse is: ಆಱಡಿಯಾಱಕ್ಕೆಷ್ಟಪದ | ಮೂಱೆರಡು ಪದಕ್ಕೆ ಕರಿಯು ದಶ-ರವಿ-ಮನುವುಂ || ಮೀಱಿದ ಷೋಡಶ-ವಿಂಶತಿ | ತೋಱಿದ ಲಘುವಿರ್ದ್ದಗಳಿಗೆ ಷಟ್ಪದಿ-ಕ್ರಮಮಂ ||. The ರಾಜರ್ ಬರೆ of the text is only in Rc.; the others have ಷೋಡಶ-ವರ. Sb. has ವಾರ್ತಿಕಂಗಳ್.

ಶರಷಟ್ಪದಿ

ಮಂದರಧರ-ಗಣಾ
ಮೊಂದಿರೆ, ಕಡೆಯೊಳ್
ಕುಂದದೆ ನೆಲಸುಗೆ ಮದನಹರಂ; ।
ಇಂದು-ನಿಭಾನನೆ,
ಮುಂದಣಾ ಪದನೀ
ಯಂದದೊಳಿರೆ, ಶರಷಟ್ಪದಿಯೀ! || 317[1] ||

293. In each of its first lines (âdi, čaraṇa) it has 8 (kari) Moras (laghu); its third and sixth line consist each of 14 (manu) Moras; number of all Moras 60.

ಶರಷಟ್ಪದಿ

ಮೆಱೆವೆರಡಡಿಯು
ತ್ತರದೆರಡಡಿಯೊಳ್
ಕರಿ-ಲಘುಗಳ್; ಮೂಱಾಱನೆಯಾ ।
ಚರಣದೆ ಮನುವಿಂ
ತಱುವತ್ತು ಲಘುವು
ಶರಷಟ್ಪದಿಗಂಬುಜ-ನಯನೇ! || 318[2] ||

294. The Kavijihvâbandhana's rule (iv., 56). *S*aradhi = 4; yuga = a couple of laghus (in the form of the guru).

ಶರಷಟ್ಪದಿ

ಚರಣಗಳೆರಡಕೆ
ಕರಿ-ಲಘುಗಳು ಬರೆ,
ನಿರುತದಿ ಮೂಱನೆಯಡಿಗಳಿಗೇ ।
ಶರಧಿ-ಯುಗಂ ಪೆ
ರ್ಚಿರೆ, ಶರಷಟ್ಪದಿ,
ಸರಸಿಜ-ನಯನೆ, ಸುರಮ್ಯ-ನಿಧೀ. || 319 ||

1) D., B.; in H., Ra., Sb. and M. it stands between the Eḷĕ and Akkarikĕ (being simply called S h a ṭ p a d i), which circumstance accounts for the use of madanahara and mandaradhara; these words do not occur in any of the other rules cited with reference to the śarashaṭpadi.

2) Only in D., B.

295. The rule of another author.

ಶರಷಟ್ಪದಿ

ಶರಕಂ ನಾಲುಕು
ಚರಣ-ಸುಮಾತ್ರೆಗ
ಳಿರುತಿರ್ಪವು ದ್ವಾತ್ರಿಂಶಗಳೂ; |
ಎರಡನೆಯಂಘ್ರಿಂ
ಗೆರಡು ಚತುರ್ದಶ
ಮಱುವತ್ತಾಗಿಹುದುರು-ಮಾತ್ರೇ. || 320 ||[1]

296. Another form of it. Manu = 14.

ಶರಷಟ್ಪದಿ

ಶರಷಟ್ಪದಿ-ಮೊದ
ಲೆರಡು ಪದಂಗಳು
ಸರದಲ್ಲೆಂಟು ಸುಮಾತ್ರೆಗಳೂ; |
ಪಿರಿಯ ಪದದ ಮೊದ
ಲಿರೆ, ಮನು-ಮಾತ್ರೆಗ
ಳುರುತರದಱುವತ್ತು ಗಣನೆಯೂ. || 321 ||[2]

297. The Kusumashaṭpadi. Feet of 5 Moras (mâtrë, laghu); number of all Moras 74.

The scheme is twice:

⏑⏑⏑⏑⏑ . ⏑⏑⏑⏑⏑
⏑⏑⏑⏑⏑ . ⏑⏑⏑⏑⏑
⏑⏑⏑⏑⏑ . ⏑⏑⏑⏑⏑ . ⏑⏑⏑⏑⏑.— |

or in numbers:

5 . 5
5 . 5
5 . 5 . 5 . 2 |

1) In Sa. 2) In Rd. v. 24.

ಕುಸುಮಷಟ್ಪದಿ

ಒಸೆಯೆ ಮೊದಲೆರಡು ನಾ
ಲ್ಕೆಸೆವೆಯ್ದನೆಯ ಪದದೆ
ದಶ-ದಶ-ಸುಮಾತ್ರೆ, ಮೂಱಱನೆಯೊಳೂ ।
ಮಿಸುಪ ಪದಿನೇಳು ಲಘು;
ರಸದಿನೆಪ್ಪತ್ನಾಲ್ಕು
ಕುಸುಮಷಟ್ಪದಿಗಿಂತು, ಕಮಲ-ನಯನೇ! || 322[1] ||

298. The Kavijihvâbandhana's reading (iv., 57).

ಕುಸುಮಷಟ್ಪದಿ

ಸೊಗಸುವೆರಡಡಿಗಳೊಳು
ಪೊಗಳೆ ದಶ-ಲಘುಗಳಿರೆ,
ಮಿಗೆ ಮೂಱನೆಯ ಪದಕೆ ಮೇಲೆಯೇಳೂ ।
ಪೊಗಲೊಡನೆ ಮೆಱೆವುತಿರೆ,
ಮೃಗ-ನೇತ್ರೆ, ಆ ಮತದಿ
ಜಗದೊಳದು ಕುಸುಮಷಟ್ಪದಿಯೆನಿಪುದೂ. || 323 ||

299. Another reading. The first two lines in the first and second half contain together 40 Moras; the third lines each 16 plus 1.

ಕುಸುಮಷಟ್ಪದಿ

ಝಂಪೆತಾಳಂ

ಧರೆಯೊಳಗೆ ಕುಸುಮಕ್ಕೆ
ಚರಣಗಳು ನಾಲ್ಕಕ್ಕೆ
ನೆಱೆ ಮಾತ್ರೆ ನಾಲ್ವತ್ತು; ಮಿಕ್ಕೆರಡಕೇ ।
ಎರಡೆಂಟು, ಮೇಲೊಂದು
ವರ-ಮಾತ್ರೆ ಕೂಡಿ, ಸಂ
ಚರಿಸುತಿಹುದೆಪ್ಪತ್ತು ನಾಲ್ಕು ಮಾತ್ರೇ. || 324[2] ||

1) D., B. 2) Sa. It is said that chiefly the jhampe tâḷa is used for the Shaṭpadis.

300. A fourth reading.

ಕುಸುಮಷಟ್ಪದಿ

ಕುಸುಮಷಟ್ಪದಿಯ ಮೊದ
ಲೆಸೆವ ಪದ-ಯುಗ್ಮಕ್ಕೆ
ದಶ-ಮಾತ್ರೆಗಳು; ಮೇಲಣೊಂದೊಂದಱೊ ।
ವಿಷಮ-ಪದ-ಯುಗ್ಮಕ್ಕೆ
ಸಸಿನೆ ಹದಿನೇಳು; ಭಾ
ವಿಸಿ ನೋಡಲೆಪ್ಪತ್ತು ನಾಲ್ಕು ಮಾತ್ರೇ. || 325[1] ||

301. The Bhogashatpadi. Feet of 3 Moras (kaḷe); number of all Moras 88. Arka=12. Pada, Carana, Anghri=line.

The scheme is twice:

⏑⏑⏑ . ⏑⏑⏑ . ⏑⏑⏑ . ⏑⏑⏑
⏑⏑⏑ . ⏑⏑⏑ . ⏑⏑⏑ . ⏑⏑⏑
⏑⏑⏑ . ⏑⏑⏑ . ⏑⏑⏑ . ⏑⏑⏑ . ⏑⏑⏑ . ⏑⏑⏑.— ।

or in numbers:

3 . 3 . 3 . 3
3 . 3 . 3 . 3
3 . 3 . 3 . 3 . 3 . 3 . 2 ।

ಭೋಗಷಟ್ಪದಿ

ಪೊಳೆವ ಮೊದಲಿನೆರಡು ಪದದೆ,
ಬಳಿಕ ಚರಣದೆರಡುವೆಡೆಗೆ
ಕಳೆಗಳರ್ಕ-ಸಂಖ್ಯೆಯಾಱು ಮೂಱಱಂಘ್ರಿಗೇ ।
ತಿಳಿಯಲಿರ್ಪ-ತಿರ್ಪ-ತಿಂತು
ಕಳೆಗಳೆಂಬತೆಂಟಱಿಂದೆ
ತೊಳೆಪುದಾಗಲೊಡನೆ, ಲಲನೆ, ಭೋಗಷಟ್ಪದೀ. || 326[2] ||

1) Ed. v. 25. 2) D., B.

302. The Kavijihvâbandhana's verse (iv., 58). The first two lines (čaraṇa) have each 12 (bhânu) Moras (laghu); the third line (pâda, also v. 329) comprises exactly 8 Moras in excess.

ಭೋಗಷಟ್ಪದಿ

ಭಾನು-ಲಘುಗಳೆಸೆವ ಚರಣ
ತಾನವೆರಡಕಕ್ಕು; ಮುಂತ
ನೂನಮೆಂಟು ಮಾತ್ರೆ ಮಿಗಲು ಕಡೆಯ ಪಾದಕೇ; ।
ಭಾನು-ತತಿ-ಸುರಮ್ಯಮಪ್ಪ
ದೇನನೆಂಬೆ? ಭೋಗ-ನಾಮ-
ಸಾನುರಾಗಮಪ್ಪದಿಂದು, ಸರಸಿಜಾನನೇ! || 327 ||

303. A third reading. Aṅghri, aḍi, pada = line.

ಭೋಗಷಟ್ಪದಿ

ಮುನ್ನಿನಂಘ್ರಿಗಳ್ಗೆ ಮಾತ್ರೆ
ಪನ್ನೆರಡು ವಿರಾಜಿಸುವದು;
ಚನ್ನೆ, ಮೇಲಣಡಿಗೆ ಮಾತ್ರೆ ಪತ್ತುಮೆರಡುಮಂ ।
ಸನ್ನಿಸಲ್ಕೆ, ಭೋಗದಾಯಿ
ಚನ್ನ ಪದಗಳೊಂದುಗೂಡಿ,
ಸನ್ನುತಾಂಗಿ, ಅಷ್ಟಕೋತ್ತರಾಷ್ಟದಶಕ, ಕೇಳ್! || 328[1] ||

304. A fourth reading. Arka = 12.

ಭೋಗಷಟ್ಪದಿ

ಭೋಗಷಟ್ಪದಂಗಳೊಳಗೆ
ಬೇಗ ಮೊದಲ ಪಾದ-ಯುಗ್ಮ
ಕಾಗಳಕ್ಕುಮರ್ಕ-ಮಾತ್ರೆ ಲೆಕ್ಕಸಂಖ್ಯೆಯೂ; ।
ಮೇಗಣೊಂದಱೊಂದು ಪಾದ
ಕಾಗಳಿಪ್ಪತುಗಳು ಕೂಡ
ಲಾಗಳೆಂಬತೆಂಟು ಮಾತ್ರೆ-ಗಣನೆ ರಂಜಿತೂ. || 329[2] ||

1) Sa. 2) Ed. v. 26.

305. The **Bhâminishaṭpadi**. Feet alternately of 3 and 4 Moras; number of all Moras 102. Manu = 14. Pada, pâda = line.

The scheme is twice:

◡◡◡ | ◡◡◡◡ | ◡◡◡ | ◡◡◡◡
◡◡◡ | ◡◡◡◡ | ◡◡◡ | ◡◡◡◡
◡◡◡ | ◡◡◡◡ | ◡◡◡ | ◡◡◡◡ | ◡◡◡ | ◡◡◡◡ | — |

or in numbers:

3 . 4 . 3 . 4
3 . 4 . 3 . 4
3 . 4 . 3 . 4 . 3 . 4 . 2 |

ಭಾಮಿನಿಷಟ್ಪದಿ

ಮೊದಲೆರಡು ನಾಲ್ಕೆಯ್ದನಿಪ ಸತ್-
ಪದದೆ ಮನು-ಸಂಖ್ಯಾತ-ಮಾತ್ರೆಯು;
ತುದಿಯ ಮೂಱಱನೆಯೊಳಿರ್ಪತ್ತು ಮೂಱು ಮಾತ್ರೆಗಳೂ; |
ಒದವಿದೀ ಪರಿಯಾಱು ಪಾದಕೆ
ಪುದಿದ ಮಾತ್ರೆಯು ನೂಱೆರಡು; ಕೇಳ್,
ಇದುವೆ ಭಾಮಿನಿಯೆಂದೆನಿಪ ಷಟ್ಪದಿಯ ಲಕ್ಷಣವೂ. || 330[1] ||

306. Half a verse from the Kavijihvâbandhana (iv. 59). Aṅga = line.

ಭಾಮಿನಿಷಟ್ಪದಿ

ಏಳೆರಡು ಮಾತ್ರೆಗಳು ಚರಣಗ
ಳೋೞಿಯೆರಡಱೊಳಿರ್ಕೆ; ಸಂತತ
ವಾಳೆ ನವ-ಲಘುಗಳನೆ ಮೂಱನೆಯಂಗ; ವೆಗ್ಗಳಿಸೀ[2] || 331 ||

307. Another version.

1) D., B. 2) Herewith concludes our copy of the work.

ಭಾಮಿನಿಷಟ್ಪದಿ

ತ್ರಿವುಡೆತಾಳಂ

ಚಂದದಲಿ ಭಾಮಿನಿಯ ಷಟ್ಪದಿ
ಗಂದಮಾದಿಯ ಪಾದಗಳಿಗಾ
ನಂದದಿಂ ಮನು-ಮಾತ್ರೆ; ಮೇಲಣ ಪಾದಕೊಂದೊಂದೂ ।
ಕುಂದದಿಹುದಿಪ್ಪತ್ತು ಮೂಱಿಂ
ತೊಂದುಗೂಡಿಸುವಾಱು ಪಾದಕೆ,
ಮಂದ-ಗತಿ, ನೂಱೆರಡು ಮಾತ್ರೆಯ ಗಣನೆ ಗೆಯ್ದಿಹುದೂ. ‖ 332[1] ‖

308. A fourth reading.

ಭಾಮಿನಿಷಟ್ಪದಿ

ಭಾಮಿನಿಯ ಷಟ್ಪದಿಯ ಮೊದಲೊಳ
ಗಾ ಮಹಾ-ಪಾದ-ದ್ವಯಂಗಳು,
ನೇಮಿಸಲು, ಮನು-ಮಾತ್ರೆ; ಮೇಲಣ ಪಾದಮೊಂದೊಂದೂ ।
ನೇಮದಿಂದಿಪ್ಪತ್ತು ಮೂಱಱ
ನಾಮಗಳನೊಂದೊಂದು ಕೂಡಲು,
ಭೂಮಿಯೊಳು ನೂಱೆರಡು ಮಾತ್ರೆಯ ಗಣನೆ ರಂಜಿಸುಗೂ. ‖ 333[2] ‖

309. The **Parivardhinishaṭpadi**. Feet of 4 Moras (mâtrĕ, laghu); number of all Moras 116. Pâda, aḍi = line.

The scheme is twice:

⏑⏑⏑⏑ . ⏑⏑⏑⏑ . ⏑⏑⏑⏑ . ⏑⏑⏑⏑
⏑⏑⏑⏑ . ⏑⏑⏑⏑ . ⏑⏑⏑⏑ . ⏑⏑⏑⏑
⏑⏑⏑⏑ . ⏑⏑⏑⏑ . ⏑⏑⏑⏑ . ⏑⏑⏑⏑ . ⏑⏑⏑⏑ . ⏑⏑⏑⏑ . — |

or in numbers:

4 . 4 . 4 . 4
4 . 4 . 4 . 4
4 . 4 . 4 . 4 . 4 . 4 . 2 |

1) Sa. 2) Rd. v. 27.

ಪರಿವರ್ಧಿನಿಷಟ್ಪದಿ

ಪಾದಗಳೆರಡಱೊಳುತ್ತರದೆರಡುಂ
ಪಾದದೆ ಷೋಡಶ-ಷೋಡಶ-ಮಾತ್ರೆಯು;
ಭೇದಿಸಿ, ಮೂಱನೆಯಾಱನೆಯಡಿಯೊಳ್ ಲಘುವಿರ್ಪತ್ತಾಱೂ; |
ಸಾದರಮಿಂತಾಱಡಿಯೊಳ್, ಗುಣಿಯಿಸೆ,
ಶೋಧಿತ-ಲಘು ನೂಱುಂ ಪದಿನಾಱಲೆ,
ಕಾದಲೆ, ಕೇಳ್, ಇಂತಿದು ನಿಶ್ಚಯ ಪರಿವರ್ಧಿನಿಷಟ್ಪದಿಗೇ. || 334[1] ||

310. Another version. *Ritu*=6. Pada, *Caraṇa*=line.

ಪರಿವರ್ಧಿನಿಷಟ್ಪದಿ

ಮೊದಲ ಚರಣಗಳಿಗೊದವಿದ ಮಾತ್ರೆಯು
ಪದಿನಾಱನಿಸುಗುಮುಪರಿ-ಪದಗಳಿಗೆ
ಸದಮಳ-ಋತು-ಯುಗ-ವಿಂಶತಿ-ಮಾತ್ರೆಗಳತಿಶಯದಿಂದೆಸೆಗುಂ; |
ಮುದದಿಂದಾಱು ಪದಂಗಳಿಗಾಗಿಹು
ದಿದು ಪರಿವರ್ಧಿನಿ ಷೋಡಶ-ಶತದಿಂ
ದುದಿತ-ಸುಮಾತ್ರೆಗಳೊಪ್ಪುಗು ಜಗತೀ-ವಲಯದಿ ಕವಿ-ಮತದಿಂ. || 335[2] ||

311. A third version.

ಪರಿವರ್ಧಿನಿಷಟ್ಪದಿ

ಪರಿವರ್ಧಿನಿಷಟ್ಪದಿಗಾ ಮೊದಲಲಿ
ಯೆರಡು ಪದಂಗಳು ಷೋಡಶ-ಮಾತ್ರೆಗ
ಳುರುತರದಿಂ ಮೇಲೊಂದೊಂದುಂ ಷಡ್ವಿಂಶತಿ-ಮಾತ್ರೆಗಳೂ; |
ನಿರುತಂ ಪದವಾಱುಂ ಕೂಡಲು, ಶತ
ಮಿರೆ, ಮೇಲಧಿಕಂ ಷೋಡಶ-ಮಾತ್ರೆಗ
ಳುರುತರಮೀ ತೆಱದಿಂ ನೆಱೆ ಬಲ್ಲವರಾಲಿಪುದೊಲವಿಂದಾ. || 336[3] ||

312. The **Vârdhikashaṭpadi** (Vârdhikya-, Vârtika-). Feet of 5 Moras; number of all Moras 144. (The same verse, with the only difference of "Vârtika," occurs in Sa.) Pada, pâda=line.

1) D., B. 2) Sa. 3) Rd. v. 28.

The scheme is twice:

◡◡◡◡◡ . ◡◡◡◡◡ . ◡◡◡◡◡ . ◡◡◡◡◡

◡◡◡◡◡ . ◡◡◡◡◡ . ◡◡◡◡◡ . ◡◡◡◡◡

◡◡◡◡◡ . ◡◡◡◡◡ . ◡◡◡◡◡ . ◡◡◡◡◡ . ◡◡◡◡◡ . ◡◡◡◡◡ . — |

or in numbers:

5 . 5 . 5 . 5

5 . 5 . 5 . 5

5 . 5 . 5 . 5 . 5 . 5 . 2 |

ವಾರ್ಧಿಕಷಟ್ಪದಿ

ಲೀಲೆಯಿಂ ವಾರ್ಧಿಕದ ಷಟ್ಪದಿಯ ಮೊದಲ ಪದ
ದೇಳಿಗೆಯುಮಿರ್ಪತ್ತು ಮಾತ್ರೆಯಿಂದೆಸೆದಿರ್ಕು
ಮಾಲಲಿತಮೆನಿಪ ಮೂಱುಱನೆಯ ಪಾದಗಳ್ ಮೂವತ್ತೆರಡು ಮಾತ್ರೆಯಿಂ |
ಮೇಲೆನೆ ವಿರಾಜಿಸುಗುಮಿಂತಾಱು ಪಾದಂಗ
ಳಾಲಿಸಲ್, ಮಾತ್ರೆಗಳ್ ನೂಱ ನಾಲ್ವತ್ತಱಿಂ
ಮೇಲೆ ನಾಲ್ಕೆಸೆದಪುವು ಛಂದೋಂಬು-ರಾಶಿಯೊಳ್. ನೀಂ ಕೇಳ್ಪುದಿಂದು-ವದನೇ!
|| 337[1] ||

313. **Another version.** (Though it does not mention the long syllable at the end of each third line, its Moras are included in the total.) Battisa = 32.

ವಾರ್ಧಿಕಷಟ್ಪದಿ

ವಾರ್ಧಿಕ್ಯಷಟ್ಪದಮದೆಂತೆನಲು, ಮೊದಲ ಪಾ
ದ-ದ್ವಯಂ ವಿಂಶತಿಂ-ವಿಂಶತಿಂ-ಮಾತ್ರೆ; ಮೇ
ಲಿರ್ದುದೊಂದೊಂದು ಪಾದಂಗಳಂ ಬತ್ತೀಸ-ಬತ್ತೀಸ-ಮಾತ್ರೆಯಿಂದೇ |
ಪೊರ್ದಿರ್ದ ಷಟ್ಪದಂಗಳ ಕೂಡಿ ಮೇಳಯಿಸೆ
ಯಿರ್ದುದದು ನೂಱ ನಾಲ್ವತ್ತು ನಾಲುಕು ಮಾತ್ರೆ;
ಸಿದ್ಧಿಯಿಂದಲಿ ರಾಜ-ಸಭೆಯೊಳುಂ ತಪ್ಪದೋದಿದನು, ವಿದ್ಯಾಧಿಕನೆಲೋ! || 338[2] ||

---

1) Sa., D., B.; B. reads ವಾರ್ಧಿಕ್ಯ-ಷಟ್ಪದಿಯು. After this Sa., D. and B. adduce the first verse of the Canarese Jaimini Bhârata as an instance (ಶ್ರೀವಧುವಿ etc.); an eminent forgery!

2) Rd.; in the beginning it has ವಾರ್ಧಿಕ that is against the metre; ವಾರ್ಧಿಕ್ಯ or ವಾರ್ಧಿಕದ must be the reading.

12. The Utsâha

314. The Utsâha is composed of the two Brahma-feet of 3 Moras, i. e. of Trochees and Tribachs, of which each line comprises seven; besides each of its 4 lines has a long syllable in its end. Confer the Utsâha of the Ragaḷe's vs. 256; 265; 266; 267; 268.

The scheme (in Tribachs) is four times:

⏑⏑⏑ . ⏑⏑⏑ . ⏑⏑⏑ . ⏑⏑⏑ . ⏑⏑⏑ . ⏑⏑⏑ . ⏑⏑⏑ . —

or in numbers:

3 . 3 . 3 . 3 . 3 . 3 . 3 . 2

ಉತ್ಸಾಹದ ಲಕ್ಷಣಂ

ಭೂ-ಹಿತಾರ್ಥಮೆನಿಸುವಜನ ಗಣಮವೆರಡು ಸಪ್ತ-ಸಂ
ದೋಹಮಾಗಿ, ಕಡೆಗೆ ಗುರು ಬೆಡಂಗನಾಳ್ದು ನಿಲೆ, ಲಯ ।
ಗ್ರಾಹಿಯಾಗಿ, ಮಧುರ-ವಚನ-ರಚನೆವೆತ್ತು, ಬಂದೊಡು
ತ್ಸಾಹಮೆಂಬ ಪೆಸರೊಳೆಸೆವುದಬ್ಜ-ಪತ್ರ-ಲೋಚನೇ! || 339[1] ||

ಇತಿ ಪಂಚಮಾಶ್ವಾಸಂ

1) Sb., M., D., B., Ra., H.

VI. CHAPTER

ಷಷ್ಠಾಶ್ವಾಸಂ

E. THE SIX SOLUTIONS[1]

ಷಟ್ಪ್ರತ್ಯಯಂಗಳ್

315. **The author is going to teach the *six solutions* (pratyaya) regarding the syllable-feet metres, so far as he understands them. (These so-called solutions are of no practical value. The English headings are given according to A. Weber.)**

ಕಂದಂ

ಬಯಸಿದ ದೇವಾಕ್ಷರದ
ಪ್ರಯೋಗತರವಾದುದೆಲ್ಲಮಂ ಪೇಳ್ದಂ; ನಿ ।
ರ್ಣಯಮಾಗಿಲ್ಲಿಂ ಷಟ್-ಪ್ರ
ತ್ಯಯಮಂ ಚಲ್ವಾಗಿ ಪೇಳ್ವೆನೆಂಗಱಿವನಿತಂ. || 340[2] ||

316. **The first solution: a first rule showing how to attain to "the enumeration or exhibition of the possible combinations" of a metre (čhandas), or P r a s t â r a. (This verse has appeared already as verse 30 of the text.)**

ಪ್ರಸ್ತಾರಮಿಂತಕ್ಕುಂ

ಕಂದಂ

ಗುರುಗಳನಿಟ್ಟವಱಾದಿಯ
ಗುರುವಿಂದಂ ಕೆಳಗೆ ಲಘುವನಿಡು! ಮುಂತೆ ಸಮಂ ।

---

1) **This heading is not in the original.** **2)** **M., Ra., H.**

ಗುರು; ಮಾಣಿಣಾಕೆ ಪಿಂತೆ; ನಿರಂ
ತರ-ಲಘುಗಳನೆಯ್ದುವಂನೆಗಂ, ಮೃಗ-ನಯನೇ! || 341[1] ||

317. The second solution: a rule showing "how to find out the form (scheme) of a certain combination of a metre, the combination's *place* in the respective prastâra being known", or Nashṭa. (Weber, p. 439. 440.) rûpa=unit.

ನಷ್ಟಮಿಂತಕ್ಕುಂ

ಚಂಪಕಮಾಲೆ

ಮೊದಲೊಳು ಛಂದದೀಯೆಡೆಯ ಲೆಕ್ಕದಿ[2] ಕೆಟ್ಟುದು ವೃತ್ತಮೆಂದು ಪೇ
ಳ್ದುದು; ಬಗೆ ಬಂದೊಡಾಗಳವಱಂಕಮನರ್ಧಿಸಿ ಬಿಣ್ಪನಿಟ್ಟು[3] ಕೊ ।
ಳ್ದುದು; ಸಮ-ಭಾಗವಿೞ್ದೊಡೆ ರೂಪು-ಯುತಾರ್ಧದೆ[4] ಬಿಣ್ಪನಿಟ್ಟು ಕೊ
ಳ್ದುದು; ಗಡ, ಸೂತ್ರಮೀ ತೆಱದೆ ಕಾಣ್ಬುದು ನಷ್ಟಮನಂಬುಜಾನನೇ! || 342 ||

318. The third solution: a rule teaching "how to assign a certain combination of a metre to its proper place in the prastâra, the combination's *form* being known", or Uddishṭa. (Weber, p. 441-444.)

ಉದ್ದಿಷ್ಟಮಿಂತಕ್ಕುಂ

ಮತ್ತೇಭವಿಕ್ರೀಡಿತಂ

ಬಗೆದಾ ವೃತ್ತ-ಪದಾಂತಮೆಯ್ದುವಿನೆಗಂ ಸಂಖ್ಯಾತಮಂ ಸೂಕ್ಷ್ಮದಿಂ[5]
ದ್ವಿಗುಣಂಗೆಯ್ದು, ಲಘು-ವ್ರಜಂಗಳೆಡೆಯೊಳ್ ನಿಂದಂಕಮಂ ಕೂಡಿ, ಮೆ ।

---

1) Sb., D., B.; before it B. adduces again vs. 296 and 297 of the text, and the following prose-sentence: ಛಟ್ಟೀವೃತ್ತವ ಬರೆಯೆಂದರೆ ಹೇಳಿದ ಲೆಕ್ಕ ಸಮವಾದರೆ ಅರ್ಧವ ಮಾಡಿ ಲಘುವನಿಕ್ಕುವದು, ವಿಷಮವಾದರೆ ಒಂದು ಕೂಡಿ ಕೊಂಡು ಅರ್ಧವ ಮಾಡಿ ಗುರುವನಿಕ್ಕುವದು, ಒಂದು ಉಳಿದರೆ ಲಘುವನಿಕ್ಕಿ ಆ ಮೇಲೆ ವೃತ್ತಪೂರ್ತಿಪರಿಯಂತರ ಗುರುವನಿಕ್ಕುವದು ಉದ್ದಿಷ್ಟಕ್ಕೆ ಲಕ್ಷಣ. ಇದು ಎಷ್ಟನೆ ವೃತ್ತವೆಂದು ಕೇಳಿದರೆ ವೃತ್ತದ ಒಂದು ಪಾದವನು ಗುರುಲಘುಸಂಜ್ಞೆಯಿಂ ಬರದು ದ್ವಿಗುಣಿಸಿ, ಗುರುಲಘುವಿನ ಕೆಳಗೆ ಲೆಕ್ಕವನಿಕ್ಕಿ, ಲಘುವಿನ ಕೆಳಗಣ ಲೆಕ್ಕವನ್ನು ವಟ್ಟು ಮಾಡಿ, ಒಂದು ಕೂಡಿ ಕೊಂಡು ಎಣಿಸಿ, ಛಟ್ಟೀವೃತ್ತವೆಂದು ಹೇಳುವದು.

2) D. ಛಂದದೊಂದೆಡೆಯ ಛಂದದ; B. ಛಂದವೊಂದೆಯಾ ಛಂದದೆ; M. ಛಂದದಿಂದೆಡೆಯ ಲೆಕ್ಕದ; Sb. ಛಂದಮಾಯೆಡೆಯ ಲೆಕ್ಕದ; H. Ra. ಛಂದವಿಾಯಿಡೆಯ ಲೆಕ್ಕ. 3) B. ....ಱಂಕಮನಿಂದದನೊಳ್ಪನಿಟ್ಟು; Ra. ಬಂದೊಡಾಗಳಕ್ಕರಮನರ್ಧಿಸಿ ಬಿಳ್ಪನಿಟ್ಟು; Sb. ....ಱಂಕನುನರ್ಧಿಸಿ ಬೆಳ್ಪಟ್ಟು; M. ....ಱಂದಮನರ್ಧಿಸಿ ಬಿಣ್ಪನಿಟ್ಟು; D. ....ಸಿಯೊಪ್ಪವಿಟ್ಟು. 4) B. ರೂಪ ಯಥಾರ್ಥದೆ; H. Ra. ರೂಪ-ಯುತಾರ್ಥದ ಬಿಳ್ಪನಿಟ್ಟು; M. ರೂಪ ಯಥಾರ್ಥತೆ ಬಿಣ್ಪವಿಟ್ಟು. 5) The text's reading is B.'s. D. ಸಂಖ್ಯಾಂಕಮಂ ಸೂಕ್ಷ್ಮದಿಂ; H., Ra., Sb. ಸಂಖ್ಯಾಂಕಮಂ ಸೂಕ್ತದಿಂ; M. ಸಂಖ್ಯಾತಮಂ ಸೂತ್ರದಿಂ. Before this verse M. has the following: ಇನಿತಱ ಛಂದವಿಾಸನೆಯ ವೃತ್ತಮದೆಂತುಟದೆಂಬ ಲೆಕ್ಕಮಂ | ತನಿತೆಯರ್ಧಿಸಲ್ಕೆ ಲಘು ತದ್ವಿಷಮಕ್ಕಿರದೊಂದನೊಂದಿಸಿ || ರ್ದನಿತೆಯೆ ಬಿಣ್ಪವಂ ಗುರುವನೊಳೆತ್ತಿ ನಷ್ಟಮಾ | ಯ್ತನಿಸಿದ ವೃತ್ತಮಾ ತೆಱದ ಬಣ್ಪುದು ತಪ್ಪದಿದಂಬುಜಾನನೇ. ||

ಲ್ಲಗೆ ಮತ್ತೊಂದನೆ ಕೂಡಿ, ಬಿಣ್ಪಿನೆಡೆಯೊಳ್ ನಿಂದಂಕಮಂ ಕೂಡದಿರ್!
ನೆಗಳ್ದದ್ದಿಷ್ಟ-ವಿಧಾನಮೀ ತೆಱನುಮಕ್ಕುಂ ಪದ್ಮ-ಪತ್ರೇಕ್ಷಣೇ! || 343 ||

319. The fourth solution: a rule for calculating "the respective relation in number between the long and short syllables in the prastâra or various combinations of a metre", or La-ga-kriyĕ. (Weber, p. 455-457.) ŏndaṛaṅka, ŏndu = a unit.

ಏಕ-ದ್ವ್ಯಾದಿ-ಲ-ಗ-ಕ್ರಿಯೆಯಿಂತಕ್ಕುಂ

ಚಂಪಕಮಾಲೆ

ಅನುಗತವೊಂದಱಂಕಮನೆ ಛಂದದ ಲೆಕ್ಕದೊಳೂರ್ಧ್ವಮಿಟ್ಟು,[1] ಮೆ
ಲ್ಲನೆ ಬಳಿಕೊಂದನಿಟ್ಟದನೆ[2] ಕೂಡುವುದೊಂದಱೊಳೊಂದನಿಟ್ಟು, ಮು |
ನ್ನಿನ ತೆಱನಂತದಂ ತಳೆವುದಪ್ಪುದು[3] ತತ್-ಕ್ರಮಮೆಯ್ದುವನ್ನೆಗಂ.
ವನಜ-ದಳಾಕ್ಷಿ, ನೀನಱಿವುದೇಕ-ಯುಗ-ತ್ರಿ-ಲಘು-ಕ್ರಮಂಗಳಂ.[4] || 344 ||

320. The fifth solution: a rule "for finding out the number of the possible combinations of a metre without exhibiting them one by one", or Saṅkhyâsa (Saṅkhyâ). (Weber, p. 444-452.)

ಸಂಖ್ಯಾಸಮಂ ಪೇಳ್ವೆಂ

ಚಂಪಕಮಾಲೆ

ದೊರೆಕೊಳೆ ವೃತ್ತ-ಸಂಖ್ಯೆಗಳನೋಳಿಯನಿಟ್ಟವಱಾದಿ[5] ಮುನ್ನಿನಂ
ತಿರೆ ಬಳಿಕಕ್ಕರಂಗಳೊಳವನ್ನಿರದರ್ಧಿಸಿ[6] ವಹ್ನಿ-ವಾರ್ಧಿಯಂ |
ಶರದೊಳೆ ಕೂಡಿ ಕೊಂಡು ಗತಿಯ ಕ್ರಮದಿಂದಮೆ ಸೂತ್ರದಿಪ್ಪದೊಳ್[7]
ವಿರಚಿಸು[8] ವೃತ್ತ-ವರ್ಣ-ಲಘು[9]-ಮಾತ್ರೆಗಳೆಲ್ಲಮನಂಬುಜಾನನೇ! ||345||

1) H. Ra. ಲೆಕ್ಕದೊಳೂರ್ಧ್ವಮಿಟ್ಟು; Sb. ಲೆಕ್ಕದೊಳೂರ್ಧ್ವಮಿದ್ದು; D. ಲೆಕ್ಕದೊಳೂರ್ಧ್ವಮಿಟ್ಟು; M. ಲೆಕ್ಕದೊಳಂಕವಿಟ್ಟು. 2) M. ಬಳಿಕೊಂದನಿಟ್ಟು ಬರೆ; B. ಬಳಿಕೊಂದನಿಟ್ಟರೆ; H. Ra. ಬಳಿಕೊಂದನಿಟ್ಟದರೆ. 3) H. Ra. ತೆಱನಂತವಂತರಳದಿಪ್ಪುದು; D. ತೆಱದಿಂದೆಯುಂತರದನಪ್ಪುದು; Sb. ತೆಱನಂತವಂತಳದಿಪ್ಪುದು; M. ತೆಱನಂತದಂತಳವುದಿಪ್ಪುದು. 4) Sb. ನೀನಱಿವುದ್ಯೈಕಯುಗತ್ರಿಲಗಕ್ರಮಂಗಳಂ; M. ನೀನಱಿವುದೇಕಯುಗಕ್ರಿಯೆಲಘುಕ್ರಮಂಗಳಂ; Ra. ನೀನಱಿವುದೇಕಯುಭಗತ್ರಿಲಘುಕ್ರಮಂಗಳಂ; B... ದೇಕಕರತ್ರಿಲಘು. Before this verse M. has the following: ಪುದಿಯದೆ ಛಂದವೀಾಯಿಡೆಯೊಳುಮೆ ಕೆಟ್ಟುದಿದೆಂಬ ವೃತ್ತಮಂ | ಪದೆ ಬಗೆ ಬಂದೊಡಾಗಳವಱಕ್ಕರಮಂತವನರ್ಧಿಸಿಟ್ಟು ಸಂ || ಮುದದೊಳೆ ಸೇರಿಸಿದಸೂಗಣದ ಲೆಕ್ಕದೊಳಾಗಳೆಯೊಪ್ಪವಿಟ್ಟು ಕೊ | ಳ್ವುದು ಗಣಸೂತ್ರವೀಾ ತೆಱದ ಬಪ್ಪುದು ತಪ್ಪದದಂಬುಜಾನನೇ. || 5) D., B.....ದಱಾದ; M.... ವಱಾದ; H. Ra... ನೋಳಿಯೊಳಿಯ್ದುದಱಾದ. 6) Ra. ಬಳಿಕಕ್ಕರಂಗಳೊಳವಂನಿರೆದರ್ಧಿಸಿ; D. ಬಳಿಕಕ್ಕರಂಗಳವಿವಂಯಿರದರ್ಧಿಸಿ; Sb. ಬಳಿಕಕ್ಕರಂಗಳೊಳವಂನಿದರ್ಧಿಸಿ; M. ತಿರಲವಱಕ್ಕರಂಗಳಿನವಂನರಿದ್ಧರ್ಧಿಸಿ.

7) H. Ra. ಕ್ರಮದಿಂದ ಸೂತ್ರದಿಪ್ಪದೊಳ್; M., Sb. ಕ್ರಮದಿಂದಮೆ ಸೂತ್ರದಿಪ್ಪದಿಂ. 8) H., Ra., M., Sb., ವಿರಚಿಸು; B. D. ವಿರಚಿಸ. 9) M., Sb. ವೃತ್ತ-ವರ್ಣ-ಲ-ಗ.

321. The sixth solution: a first rule "calculating the space which would be requisite for writing down all the combinations of metres," or the A d h v a. (Weber, p. 434.)

ಅಧ್ವಕ್ಕೆ[1)]

ಕಂದಂ

ದ್ವಿಗುಣಿಸಿ ವೃತ್ತಮನದಱೊಳ್
ತೆಗೆದೊಂದಂ[2)] ಕಳೆದೊಡಕ್ಕುಮಂಗುಲಿಗಳನುಂ[3)] ।
ಮಿಗಿಲಾಗಲಧ್ವಯೋಗಂ[4)];
ನೆಗಳ್ದುವದೇಶದೊಳಪರಿಮಿತಂ ಪ್ರಸ್ತಾರಂ.[5)] || 346 ||

---

1) In M.; others have ಅಧ್ವಯೋಗಮಿಂತಕ್ಕಂ. 2) B. ತೆಗೆದೊದದಂ; Sb. ಬಗೆಗೊಂದಂ; M. ತೆಗೆದೊಂದುಂ; H. Ra. ಬಗೆದೊಂದಂ. 3) D...ಕ್ಕಮುಂಗುವಿಗಣನಂ; Sb... ಕ್ಕಮುಂಗುಳಿಗಳದಂ; M... ಕ್ಕಮುಗುಳೀಗಳದಂ; H. Ra...ಕ್ಕಂ ಮಂಗುಳಿಗಳಮಂ. 4) D., B. ಮಿಗಲಾದ ದಧ್ವಯೋಗದೆ; Ra. ಮಿಗಿಲಾಗದಧ್ವಯೋಗಂ; M. ಮಿಗಲುಗದಧ್ವಯೋಗಂ; Sb., H. ಮಿಗಿಲಾಗಲಧ್ವಯೋಗಂ.

5) H., Ra., Sb. ನೆಗಳ್ದು ಪ್ರಯೋಗದೊಳೆ ಪರಿಮಿತಂ ಪ್ರಸ್ತಾರಂ; M. ನೆಗಳ್ದಾದೆಡೆಯೊಳಗೆ ಪರಿಮಿತಪ್ರಸ್ತಾರಂ; D. ನೆಗಳ್ದುಪದೇಶದೊಳೆ ಪರಿಮಿತು ಪ್ರಸ್ತಾರಂ. This forms the last verse of M., after which it says: ಷಟ್ಪ್ರತ್ಯಯಸಂಪೂರ್ಣಂ. In H., Ra. follows: ಮಾತ್ರಾಪಿಂಡಮಿಂತಕ್ಕಂ|| ನೆಗಳ್ವಕ್ಕರಂಗಳಂ ಮಾತ್ರೆಗಳೊಳ್ ಕಳೆದಿಕ್ಕಿ ನಿಂದವೆಲ್ಲಂ ಗುರು ಮೆಲ್ಲನೆ ಗುರುಗಳಕ್ಕರದಂತಿಗೆ ಮಿಕ್ಕಮೆಲ್ಲ ಲಘುಗಳುಮಕ್ಕುಮಲಘುನಿತಂಬೇ ||ತ್ರಿಪದಿ|| ಸಲೆ ಗುರುಲಘುಗಳ ಕಲಸಿದಕ್ಕರದ ಪಿಂದಂ ನೆಲಸಿದ ಗುರುವಂ ದ್ವಿಗುಣಿಸಿ ಲಘು ಕೂಡಿ ನಿಲೆ ಮಾತ್ರಾಪಿಂಡಂ ಮೃಗನೇತ್ರೇ || Then after some verses (see Addenda) they introduce three on the good and bad qualities of the syllable-feet, the last of which is v. 36 of the text. Then follow our vs. 271, 230, 347, and || ಗದ್ಯ || ಇದು ಅಷ್ಟಾಧಿಕಾರಸಮಾಪ್ತಃ || In the MSS.' former portion ಅಧ್ಯಾಯ is used to mark the divisions; ಅಷ್ಟಾಧಿಕಾರ is most probably a mistake for ಷಷ್ಠಾಧ್ಯಾಯ. Afterwards there occurs an Appendix containing our vs. 35, 29 (here: ನಿಯತಂ ಗುರುವೆಂಬುದು); eight verses about the forms of the 8 syllabical feet, their colours (M. white, Y. darkblue, R. red, S. dhûmra, T. black, J. bandhûka, Bh. sphaṭika, N. yellow), their presiding deities (dharĕ, varuṇa, marutsakha, mâruta, vyoma, bhâskara, čandra, indra), their castes (dvija, śûdra, pitṛi, bhujaga, bhûta, ṛishi, vaiśya, kshatriya), and their good and bad effects; our vs. 183 (that occurs also there in Ra.), 43; five verses on the effect of the 6 alliterations, feet, and some letters; our vs. 282, 316; seven superstitious verses again as to planets, days, feet and devis, also our v. 288. The said miscellaneous verses of the Appendix, more or less, occur in chapter 1 of M., Sb., Rc., B., D.; D. has two of them in an appendix. Cf. p. 12, note; p. 16, note 1. The Appendix of H., Ra. is marked neither as an adhyâya nor as an adhikâra. The last words of the two MSS. are: ಇಂತಿ ನಾಗವರ್ಮಛಂದಸು ಸಮಾಪ್ತಃ.—MS. D., after our v. 346, in the prastára, adduces, with B., the verse: ಇನಿತನೆಯ ಛಂದದಿಂದೊಳ್ವನಿತಕ್ಕಂ (-ಳ್ವನಿತಕ್ಕಂ) ವೃತ್ತ-ಸಂಖ್ಯೆಯಿಂದನಿತನೆ ವಂ । ದನೆ ವಿಷಮ ಮಾಡೊಗವ್ರಸಂತನೊಳರ್ಧಿಸಿ ಬರೆದ ಸೊನ್ನೆಯಿಂ ಕ್ರಮದಿಂದಂ ||; and then in its appendix a sort of *Sânta* prâsa (ಶಾಂತಪ್ರಾಸಂ, v. 51), in which ಪಂತಿ-ನತ್ಯ-ಮತ್ತೆ-ಪುತ್ರಿ are the first syllables of the four Kanda lines; certainly no beautiful alliteration! Thereafter follow superstitious notions regarding letters, etc. Its concluding verse is v. 23 of the text.

322. Good wishes, also one for the great Nâgavarma.

ಮತ್ತೇಭವಿಕ್ರೀಡಿತಂ

ಅಱಿನಂ ಪಾಳಿಯುಮಂ ಪ್ರದುಂಗೊಳಿಸಿ ಕೊಂಡೀ ಭೂಮಿಯುಂ ಭೂಮಿಪರ್
ನೆಱೆಯೋಳ್ಗೆಂದುಮಿಳಾತಳಂ ಬಳೆವುದಕ್ಕೊಳ್ಗಾಲಮುತ್ಕೀಳ್ದಱಿಂ
ಬಱಿನಂ ಪಿಂಗುಗೆ! ನಾಗವರ್ಮ-ಕವಿತಾ-ಮಾಹಾತ್ಮ್ಯಮೀ ಛಂದದೊಳ್
ನೆಱೆಗೊಳ್ಗಂ! ಕವಿರಾಜಹಂಸನ ಮತಂ ಪರ್ವಿಕ್ಕೆ ಭೂಚಕ್ರದೊಳ್! || 347[1] ||

ನಾಗವರ್ಮಛಂದಸ್ಸಮಾಪ್ತಂ | ಶ್ರೀ |

1) H., Ra.

Additions.

P. xiii: According to a MS. of the Kâvyâvalokana which L. Rice Esq. has favored us with, Nâgavarma, in verses 24 and 25 of para. 1 (regarding the mârgadarśana in the guṇaviveka) of ch. iii., mentions the dakshiṇadeśavartikavirâjimârga and the vaidarbhagauḍamârgabheda; and in v. 3 of the next para. the four śabdâlaṅkâras: yamaka, anuprâsa, sanĉitaviĉitraviĉhitti, and vakroktiviśesha. Arthâlaṅkṛiti follows in the course of the chapter. P. xxi: In Kâvyâvalokana iv., v. 8, a quotation in which the army of a king is described, occurs "the infantry that had assembled from Vĕṅgi, Vaṅga, Kaḷiṅga and Koṅga." P. xxviii: Karavûr's Coḷa râja appears also in Bas. P. 47, 36; and a Narasimha Mŏnĕyâr Coḷa nṛipa who is connected with Bâhûr (cf. 47, 37), in 24, 77 seq. P. xxxii: Sindu Ballâḷa is mentioned also in Bas. P. 11, 37; and Kumârapâlaka Gurjara also in chs. 43 and 44, and 54, 75. Basava is stated to have caused a śâsana to be engraved at Kalyâṇa, Bas. P. 59, 56. P. xxxiii: In Bas. P. 19 it is related of Mâdi râja or Mâdarasa, surnamed Sakaḷeśa (sakaḷeśa M.), that he was a Nâdavidyâpaṇḍita, a Sakalakaḷâvida, and a bharatâdiśâstraviĉakshaṇa; that his capital was the beautiful town Ambĕ; and that he knew the thirty-two (battisu)[1] and other râgas, and could play the guitar (vîṇâ) well. There occurs there also an enumeration of various subjects belonging to music, *e. g.* 7 svaras, 22 sutis (śrutis), 7 gamakas. It is interesting to observe that the science of music occupied the mind of the people in S. India in 1369 A. D., or according to the author of the Purâṇa, already at Basava's time. About legends and literary works the existence of which the Purâṇa refers also to Basava's period, see *e. g.* 48, 78 seq.; 53, 7; 54. Sakaḷeśa Mâdarasa occurs again in ch. 47. P. xxxvi: In the one but last, mutilated verse of the Kâvyâvalokana it is said that Dâmodara's son (tanaya) taught this ornament of composition; the last verse of iii., 3 mentions Nâkiga, as does also the fragment of a verse towards the end of the work. P. xxxvii: Kâvyâvalokana iii., 1 (mârgadarśana in the guṇaviveka), sûtra 8 Nâgavarma teaches that there are 10 kṛitiguṇas, viz. sama, samślishṭa, arthavyakti, madhura, kânta, prasanna, sukumâra, ojas, samabhimatodâra, samâdhi. In sûtras 4-21 he separately treats on the first nine, and in sûtra 22 defines samâdhi. This very sûtra (a kanda verse) is quoted by Keśi râja p. 118 (ಪೆಱವಱ etc.), also according to the Mûḍabidar MS.; a fact which proves without doubt that Nâgavarma has preceded Keśi râja. Ps. xxxvii and lxiii: Baḷamardu occurs in Toṭa ârya's nighaṇṭu v. 40, where he explains it by aṅka-aushadha; the commentator gives "war-powder" as the meaning of the last term. One of aṅka's meanings in Reeve's Canarese Dictionary is "war". If we are not mistaken, baḷamardu does not occur in the kabbigakaipiḍi. P. xxxviii: The MS. of the Kâvyâvalokana received from Mr. Rice, commences, instead of "śrîviśveśvara", with "śrîvardhamâna". P. xl: Kâvyâvalokana iii., 2, v., 171 states that the Khyâtiyaśa and Kavitâguṇodaya (Nâgavarma) taught all about the arthâlaṅkṛiti. P. xlv: Dr. Burnell writes to us from Tanjore, 10th January, 1875: "As far as I can judge there is no resemblance in style between the Canarese Râmâyaṇa of Pampa (Hampa)[2] and the Tamiḷ of Kamban[3], as the last is exclusively in verse. Kamban's R. gives its own date as 733

1) Battisu is a Hindusthâni term. 2) Dr. Burnell appears to mean the Râmaĉandraĉarita purâṇa mentioned in p. xli., note 2. 3) With regard to masculine nouns ending in a, it is customary in Tamiḷ and Malĕyâḷa to add to them the sign of the nominative, *i. e.* n, instead of using their crude form; in Kannaḍa only the latter form is employed. In Tamiḷ one letter is used to express p and b. If Tamiḷ Kampa is=Kannaḍa Hampa, the initial k (g) must have had the force of h, though in Tamiḷ as a rule k represents h only in the middle of words (bakula=bahula). Initial h is either omitted in Tamiḷ (asta=hasta), or in words of cognate languages represented by p (pâl=Canarese hâl, milk).

A. D.; but Dr. Caldwell (Comp. Gr. 88) shows that it belongs to about 1030 A. D."[1]). The Tamiḷ Kamba (Kampa), therefore, may be an Abhinava Hampa; his writing exclusively in verse, a custom of later days for legendary compositions at least in Karṇâṭaka, (his being a Vaishṇava, Murdoch, p. 194), and the date assigned to him by Dr. Caldwell seem to favour this supposition. **P. xlvi:** Like Rudrabhaṭṭa the **śaivas** *Iś*varakavi and Maṅgarâja admire the **Jaina** Nâgavarma.—**Vema** ayya, -ârya, **Vemana**, -âčârya, -ârâdhya, -ârya appears in Bas. P. ch. 46; **Mallikârjuna Paṇḍita** also in 46, 36. **P. xlix,** note: That the Tuḷu country is called **Canara** *i. e.* Kannaḍa (Karṇâṭa) is also founded on the Kannaḍa dynasty of Vidyânagari having ruled there. Cf. p. lix. and Ind. Ant. ii., 353. **P. l:** The term "bŏlla" is met in Bas. P. 59, 40. **P. lv:** "**Terasa**" together with the shoḍaśagaṇa is mentioned in Bas. P. 54, 76. **Ps. lvi. and lvii:** In Bas. P. ch. 9, 36-48 Basava calls, among others, the following his illustrious people (mahanta, v. 49, as being śaivas): **vâgîśa** nayinâr (*i. e.* ayyâr, master), **jṅânasambandhi, kulaččari,** keśi râja, the guitar-player mâdi râja, maḷĕ râja (also 47, 36), paṇḍita ayya, ekânta râma ayya, and kŏḍagûsu (also ch. 14). **Ps. lviii. and lx:** In p. 66 of his C. T. Mr. Brown refers Mummaḍi **Prauḍha** R. to 1435-1480 A. D. **Ps. lxii. and lxiii.,** the two **dâsapadas:** A. ಚಿತ್ತೈಸಿದ ವ್ಯಾಸರಾಯ ಚಿತ್ತಜನಯ್ಯನ ದಿವ್ಯಮುಕ್ತಿಯೋಲಗಕಾಗಿ ಮುದದಿ ಚಿತ್ತೈಸಿದರು ॥ ಪಲ್ಲ ॥ ಏರಿದರತುನಕೇರು ಭೇದಿಸಿ ಸೂರ್ಯಮಂಡಲವ । ಸಾರೆ ಸತ್ಯಲೋಕಾರೆ ಸಂಭ್ರಮದಿಂದ । ಭೋರವೆಮ್ರುದಂಗ ಕಹಳೆ ಸುರಿಯೆ ಹೂವಿನ ಮಾಳೆ । ಆರತಿಯನೆತ್ತಿದರು ಸುರರಂಗನೆಯರೆಲ್ಲ ॥ 1 ॥ ವಿಳಂಬಿ-ಸಂವತ್ಸರದಲ್ಲಿ ವಿಜಯನಗರದಲ್ಲಿ । ಪಾಲುಗುಣ-ಬಹುಳ-ಚವುತಿ-ಶ್ರೀವಾರದಲ್ಲಿ । ಬೆಳಗಿಂ ಜಾವದೊಳೆದ್ದು ಕುಳಿತು ಸಿಂಹಾಸನದಿ । ನಳಿನಾಕ್ಷನಾರಾಯಣನೆಂದು ಕರವ ಮುಗಿದರು ॥ 2 ॥ ಭಕ್ತಿಯಿದ್ದಲ್ಲಿಗೆ ಉಕುತಿಸಾತ್ವಿಕರಿಗೆ ಅಖಿಳಾಂಕ (ಅಕಳಂಕ?) ಚರಿತೆಯ ಅನುಮಿಕಾನಂತಾರಿಖಿಳಾಂಕಚರಿತೆಯ ಅಸಿಮಿಕಾನಂತಾ (ಆ ಶೀಮೋಕನಂತಾ?) ಪುರಂದರವಿಟ್ಟಲನ ಬಳಿಗೆ ಚಿತ್ತೈಸಿದರು ॥ 3 ॥

B. ತೆರಳಿದರು ವೈಕುಂಠಕೆ ದಾಸರು ತೆರಳಿದರು ವೈಕುಂಠಕೆ ॥ ಪಲ್ಲ ॥ ರಕ್ತಾಕ್ಷಿ-ನಾಮ-ಸಂವತ್ಸರದ ಪುಶ್ಯ-ಬಹುಳ ಅತಿಶಯದಮಾವಾಸೆಯಂದವರ ॥ 1 ॥ ಅಷ್ಟಗನ್ನಿಕೆಯರು ಆರತಿಯನೆತ್ತಲು ಅಷ್ಟಕಾಗಿದ್ದೆಡೆಗತಿ-ಸಾಮಿಪ್ಯದಿ ತಾವು ॥ 2 ॥ ವೈಕುಂಠಕೆ ಭೂಮಿಗೆ ನಾಮಲ್ಲಿ ಸವುಪಾನವ ಮಾಡಿ ಭಕ್ತರಿಗೆ ಮಾರ್ಗವ ತೋರಿ ॥ 3 ॥ ಗುರು ಮಧ್ವಪತಿ-ವಿಠಲನ ಸ್ಮರಿಸುತ್ತ ಪುರಂದರದಾಸರು ಮೆರೆದು ವೈಕುಂಠಕ್ಕೆ ತೆರಳಿದರು ವೈಕುಂಠದಾಸರು ॥ 5 ॥ There is no v. 4. **P. lxiv.,** No. 21: It is necessary to add that the Purâṇa treats of the sayings and doings of Basava's nephew *C*anna Basava whose miraculous birth at Kalyâṇa of Basava's sister (*C*an. Bas. P. 3, 31 seq.) **Nâgalâmbĕ** (Nâgalâmbikĕ, Nâgâmbĕ) is already referred to in Bas. P. ch. 7. Jainas use to say that *C*anna Basava was the illegitimate son of Bijjaḷa and Basava's sister. **P. lxviii:** Drâkshârâma is called **Dâkshârâma** in Bas. P. 58, 34; see the peculiarity mentioned in p. xiii., note 4. **P. lxxiv:** Regarding the **Bâliyâ** treasure compare Dr. Burnell's statement in p. liii., note 9. **P. lxxx:** The verses from the **Aksharamâlâ** are in Ragaḷĕ, the scheme of each being: 4.4.4.4*4.4.4.1.

P. 20, No. 50, add "v. 183."

P. 22; cf. p. vii. List of 45 **lands** that are adduced in Basava Purâṇa, 6, 18. 19, as containing *S*aivas: lâḷa, mâḷava, sindhu, si*m*haḷa, gauḷa, gurjara, muru, magadha, pâṅčâḷa, matsya, kuraṅga, vaṅga, kaḷiṅga, baṅgâḷa, kâḷava, andhra, turushka, kuru, nepâḷa, kuntaḷa, kukura, barbara, čoḷa, pâṇḍya, tuḷuva, malĕya, malĕyâḷa, karṇâṭa, čâru, kŏṅkaṇa, pallavaka, hammîra, jâḷândra, draviḷa, kâśmîra, bâhḷika, bhoṭa, bhû, kâmbhoja, kannoja, sûrasena, varâḷa, kharpara, pâriyâtra, keraḷa. (Here Veṅgi is not mentioned, but Pallavaka occurs. In the list of Rottler that has been taken from Beshi's čatur akârâdi nighaṇṭu of about A. D. 1729, Veṅgi and Pallava are met.)

List of the **čappanna lands** that are adduced in *C*anna Basava Purâṇa, 6, 48. 49, as containing *S*aivas: aṅga, maḷĕyâḷa, mâḷava, magadha, barbara, kaḷiṅga, kâśmîra, kŏṅkaṇa, sindhu, hammîra, vaṅga, hŏyisaḷa, tuḷava, čoḷa, čârama, pâṇḍya, yavana, samvîra, matsya,

1) Cf. Murdoch p. lxxxvi.

bangâḷa, jaina, bonĕga (conĕga or jonĕga?), sagara, haiviga, tĕlunga, gurjara, gauḷa, nepâḷa, saurâshṭra, singaḷa, draviḍa, kâmbhoja, lâṭa, pancâla, vaidarbha, kuma, kukura, karahâṭa, karpara, yavantika, pâriyâtra, karṇâṭa, kosala, manda, bhadra, kuntaḷa, mahâjinaka, videha, bhoṭaka, turushka, ŏḍḍiya (Orissa), pârasika, mahâghoṭaka, puḷindaka, strîrâjya, kŏngu, mârâṭa. (Neither Vengi nor Pallava.)

List of the cappanna lands in Nijaguṇa's Vivekâcintâmaṇi (prose): anga, vanga, kaḷinga, tĕlunga, kŏnga, lâṭa, bangâḷa, coḷa, keraḷa, gauḷa, pâncâḷa, simhaḷa, kuntaḷa, nepâḷa, malayâḷa, tuḷava, saindhava, kŏnkaṇa, kuru, magadha, matsya, vidarbha, kosala, śûrasena, kâśmîra, mahârâshṭra, karṇâṭa, kirâta, turushka, sankara, barama, trigarta, nishadha, madhya, jaina, barbara, bâhlîka, lâṭa, caina, karâḷa, oḍra, ghûrjara, kâmbhoja, saurâshṭra, sauvîra, pâṇḍya, hûṇa, yavana, mlećcha, haihaya, âryâvarta, bhoja, dvaipa, amaraka, uttarakuru, graiṭi. (Neither Vengi nor Pallava.)

P. 23, No. 55, before the Akkaras, insert "Madanavati (v. 311)".

P. 24, after v. 69 of the text, H. and Ra. have the following two verses, the first being somewhat mutilated:

ಕಂದಂ

ಛಂದಮನಱಿಯದನೋದುಂ [-ನೊಂದುಂ]
ಮುಂದಿರ್ದಾ ತಾಳಮನವಱಿಯದ ಹಾಡು ।
ಬಂದುದಗೆಡೆವನನುಡಿಯು
ಪೊಂದಕ್ಕುಂಬಾರ್ತೆಯಿಲ್ಲ ಕೇಳ್ ಇಂದುಮುಖೀ ॥

ಉತ್ಪಲಮಾಲೆ

ಛಂದಮನೋದದೋದಿದವರೋದುಗಳೇ ನೆಱೆ ಹಾಸ್ಯಲೋಕದೊಳ್
ಸಂದಯಮಿಲ್ಲ ಛಂದಮೆನೆ ಪೂರ್ವಪರಂ ನೆಱೆಯೋದಿದಂದು ನಿಃ ।
ಸಂದಯಮಪ್ಪುದೋದುವ ಪದಂಗಳೞಗೆಲ್ಲೆಡೆಯುಂ ವಿಚಾರಿಸಲ್
ಛಂದಮನೋದಿಯೋದುದುೞದೋದುಗಳೆಂಬಿವನಂಬುಜಾನನೇ ॥

P. 27. In writing the foot-note 2, the editor entertained the opinion that Rb. really was a work of Nâgavarma. But as this is more than improbable, the remark about the different readings looses somewhat of its importance; and the vṛittas only extant in Rb. are foreign to N.'s work.

P. 28, note 3. From what at first sight seemed to be a Mangaḷa verse of Rb. the editor afterwards has learned that Rb.'s Pratishṭhâ includes also the Surataru, and a Nâmânka which as to form is like the Kâmânga.

P. 53, No. 174, add to the scheme: or eight Iambus'.

P. 55, No. 182, add to the scheme of the Mallikâmâlĕ: or Trochæus, Dactylus; Trochæus, Dactylus; Trochæus, Dactylus; Trochæus, a long syllable.

P. 75, note 3, add to Mr. Colebrooke's statement: Weber p. 425.

P. 94. About the Duvayi see p. xvi.

P. 102. We adduce two of the four verses that in our copy of Nâgavarma's Nighaṇṭu, the Vastukosha, are marked as Akkaras; it is difficult to say how far their scheme is correctly represented by their present forms.

ವದನಮಾನನಮಾಸ್ಯಂ ಮುಖಂ ತುಂಡಂ ಲಪನಂ ವಕ್ತ್ರಂ ಮೊಗಕ್ಕೆ ನಾಮಂ
(ರದನ)ದಂತಂ ರದಂ ದಶನಂ ದ್ವಿಜಂ ನಾಲಗೆ ರಸನೆ ರಸಜ್ಞೆ ಜಿಹ್ವೆ ।
ಕದಪು ಗಲ್ಲಂ ಕಪೋಳಂ ಗಂಡಸ್ಥಳಂ ದಂತಚ್ಛದಾಹ್ವಯಮಧರಮೋಷ್ಠಂ
ತದುಪೇತಮಂತದು ಸೃಕ್ವಾಭಿಧಾನಕಮಧರದದಸ್ಥಳಂ ಚಿಬುಕಮೆಂಗೆ ॥
ಒಂದು ಸಾಮಜಮೊಂದು ತೇರ್ ಮೂಱಶ್ವಮೆಯ್ದು ಕಾಲ್ಗಳ್ ಪತ್ತಿಯಕ್ಕುಂ
ಸಂದ ಪತ್ತಿ ಮೂಱಾಗೆ ಸೇನಾಮುಖಂ ಮೂಱಱಿಂ ಗುಲ್ಮಂ ಮೂಱು ಗುಲ್ಮ ।

ಕ್ಕೊಂದು ಗಣಮವು ಮೂಱು ವಾಹಿನಿ ತತ್ತ್ರಯಂ ಪೃತನಾಖ್ಯೆ ಪೃತನೆಗಳ್ ಮೂ
ಱೊಂದಿ ತೋಱೆ ಚಮು ಮೂಱುಮನೀಕಿನಿ ಪತ್ತನೀಕಿನಿಯಕ್ಷೌಹಿಣಿಯೆನಿಕ್ಕುಂ॥

P. 108, No. 282: Mr. Brown has an Ela (ಏಲ) in his Dictionary: "a hurra, or hoop; a carol, or catch: such as this, ಏಟೀಗಟ್ಟಗುಡಿಕೇವಶಾಂ ಯೇರುವಸ್ತೇಕೂಡಾಪೋದಾಂ | ಓ ಓ ಗೊಲ್ಲಭಾಮಾ ||" *i.e.* — — — ⏑⏑⏑ — ⏑ — * — ⏑ — — — — — — — | — — — ⏑ — — || or 40 Moras.

In the Bĕngaḷûr edition of the *Saraṇalîlâmṛita* p. 118. 119. 170. 171 there appear verses called Yâla (*i.e.* Ela), *e.g.* ಇಷ್ಟರಿಂದೆ ಫಣಿತಿವಡದು | ಅಷ್ಟ ತೈಲವ ಪರಿಬತ್ತಿ | ಯಿಷ್ಟು ಅಲ್ಲದೆ ಬಯಲನ್ಯೆದೀತು * ಬೆಳಗುವ ಜೋತಿ | ಅಷ್ಟಮೂರ್ತಿಯೊಳಗೆ ಬೆರದೀತು || *i.e.* — ⏑ — ⏑⏑⏑⏑⏑⏑ | — ⏑ — ⏑⏑⏑⏑ — ⏑ | — ⏑ — ⏑⏑⏑⏑⏑ — — ⏑ * ⏑⏑⏑⏑ — ⏑ | — ⏑ — ⏑⏑⏑⏑⏑⏑ — ⏑ || or 12. 12. 22. 14; or 60 Moras.—ಕೆಟ್ಟಿತು ಕಲ್ಯಾಣವಿನ್ನು | ನಷ್ಟವಾಗಿ ಹೋಗುತ್ತಿದೆ | ಸೃಷ್ಟಿಯೊಳಗಣ ಶರಣರೆಲ್ಲರು * ಅಲ್ಲಮಪ್ರಭುವೇ | ಇಷ್ಟಲಿಂಗದೊಳಗೆ ಬೆರದೀತು || *i.e.* 12. 12. 22. 14.—ಒಂದು ದಿನ ಬಸವರಾಜನು | ಬಂದು ವೋಲಗದೊಳು ಯಿರಲು | ವೊಂದು ಕೌತುಕವನೇ ಹಣ್ಣಿದ * ಬಿಜ್ಜಳರಾಯನು | ಇಂದುಧರನು ತಾನೇ ಬಲ್ಲನು || or 12. 12. 22. 14.

Ps. 95-115. 126-130. Facsimile of MS. K., belonging to the recension of M.

ಶ್ರೀಗೆ ಸುಖಜೀವನಮಲಶ್ರೀಗನುಪಮಭುವನಭವನನಧಿಕಂ ಶ್ರೀಸೌಖ್ಯಾಗಾರಜಗದ್ವಂದಿತನೀಗೆ ನಾಗವರ್ಗನುಪಮಸುಖಮಂ॥ ಅರ್ಣವಜಾತಾನನೆ ಸಂಪೂರ್ಣತೆಯಂ ಸಕಲ-ವಿಷಯ-ಭಾಷಾದಿಗಳಂ ನಿರ್ಣಯಮಾಗರುಪಿದೆನಾಂ ಕರ್ನಾಟಕ-ಭಾಷೆಯಂದಮ ಕೇಳ್ ಪೇೞ್ವೆಂ॥ ಎರಡುಂ ಮೂರುಂ ನಾಲ್ಕುಂ ಗುರುವಿಪ್ಪ ಸ್ಥಾನಮಾಗೆ ಯುಗ-ಗಜ-ಧರಣೀಶ್ವರ-ಪರಿಸಂಖ್ಯೆಯುವಕ್ಕುಂ ಸರಸಿಜಭವ-ವಿಷ್ಣು-ರುದ್ರ-ಸಂಜ್ಞೆಗಳಿಂದಂ॥ ಅದೆಂತೆನೆ॥ ಬ್ರಹ್ಮಗಣಮೆಂತೆಂದೊಡೆ॥ ಯಂತುಂ | ನೆಗಳ್ಗಂ | ನಾರಿ | ಧರೆಗೆ | ಇಂತ್ತುಂ | ನೆಸರುತಿ | ಧರೆಗೆ | ಇದಿ ಬ್ರಹ್ಮಗಣಂ || ವಿಷ್ಣುಗಣವೆಂತೆಂದರೆ | ಗೋವಿಂದಂ | ಮನದಾಣ್ಮಂ | ನಾಕಿಗಂ | ಪರಹಿತಂ | ನಂಸಾರಿ | ನರಕಾರಿ | ಶ್ರೀಪತಿ | ಮುರರಿಪು | ಇವು ವಿಷ್ಣುಗಣಂ || ರುದ್ರಗಣವೆಂತೆಂದರೆ | ಗಂಗಾಧಾರಂ | ಗಿರಿಜಾನಾಥಂ | ನೀಲಕಂಠಂ | ವೃಷಭಲಕ್ಷ್ಮಂ | ಕಾಮಾಂತಕಂ | ಪ್ರಮಥಾಧಿಪಂ | ಶೂಲಧರಂ | ಪುರಮಥನಂ | ಕಂದರ್ಪಾರಿ | ಮದನಧ್ವಂಸಿ | ಚಂದ್ರಮೌಳಿ | ಭುಜಗಧಾರಿ | ಭೂತಾಗ್ರಣಿ | ತ್ರಿಜಗದ್ಗುರು | ಕಾಮರಿಪು | ಮದನರಿಪು || ಇನ್ನು ಗಣಸೂತ್ರಂ | ಕರಪುರವಾರ್ಧಿಯಾಗೆ ಗುರುವಾಗಿರೆ ತಂದುರುವಿಂದದಸ್ತಮಾಗಿರೆ ಲಘು-ಯುಗ್ಮದಿಂ ಕ್ರಮದಿ ಮುಂತೆಸಮಂ ಕಡೆ ಷಟ್ಕ ಬಿಣ್ಪಿನೊಳ್ ಬರೆ ಲಘುವಿಂದ ಮುಂತೆ ಬರೆ ಪಿಂತೆ ಸಮಂ ಮೊದಲಿಂ ತಗುಳ್ದು ಪಂಕರುಹದಳೇಕ್ಷಣೆ ಗಣಮನಿಂತಿದು ಸರ್ವ-ಲಘುತ್ವಮಪ್ಪಿನಿಂ॥ ತ್ರಿಪದಿಗು | ವಿಸರುಹೋದ್ಭವ-ಗಣಂ ರಸ-ದಶ-ಸ್ಥಾನದೊಳ್ ವಿಸರುಹನೇತ್ರ ಗಣನೆ ಬಕ್ಕುಳಿದವು ವಿಸರುಹನೇತ್ರ ತ್ರಿಪದಿಗೆ॥ ಭುಜಪಕ್ಷ್ಮಯುಗಳಧೂಮಧ್ವಜಪಾದಗಣದೊಳಜನಿರ್ದಂ ರಸದೊಳ್ ನಿಜ ಪೆಸರವೆಡೆಗಳೊಳಧೋಕ್ಷಜಗಣಮುಮಾದಡದುವೆ ಚಿತ್ರಂ ಕೆಳದೀ ॥ ತುದಿಯೊಳೀಶ್ವರಗಣಮುಂ ಮೊದಲಿಂ ಗಜಗಮನೆ ಪೆರಗಣಂದಂ ಚಿತ್ರಂ ಮದದೊಳಗಿರ್ದಂತುಚಿತಂ ನಯದಿಂ॥ ಅಕ್ಕರಕ್ಕೆ ಲಕ್ಷಣಂ॥ ಮೊದಲೋಳೆ ಜಗಣಂಗಳ್ ಕುಂದದೆ ಬಕು ಮತ್ತಮೈದು ಗಣಂಗಳು ವಿಷ್ಣುವಕ್ಕುಂ ತುದಿಯೊಳೇಳೆಂಬತಾಣದೊಳೆಲ್ಲಿಯು ಕಂದರ್ಪಹರಗಣಂ ನೆಲಶಿ ನಿಲಕ್ಕೆ ಪದಾಂತ್ಯದೊಳೆರಡೆಂಬ ಸಂಖ್ಯೆಯೊಳು ನಾಲ್ಕುಂ ಜಗಣಂ ಸಮವಾಯಮಪ್ಪುದಕ್ಕುಂ ಸದಮಳೇಂದುನಿಭಾನನೆ ನಾಕಿಗನಿಪ್ಪದೊಳಿಂತಿದು ಪಿರಿಯಕ್ಕರಂ॥ ಸರಸಿಜೋದರಗಣ ಮೆರಡಜನುಮಲ್ಲಿ ಸೆರದಿಕ್ಕೆ ಮತ್ತಂತಿರೆರಡು ಸೂಳ್ ಬಂದಾಗಮಿಂತೊಪ್ಪೆಯಿಂದ್ರವಿಖ್ಯಾತಂ ಸರಸಿಜಲೋಚನೆ ದೊರೆವೆತ್ತ ಪೆಸರಿ ಥೊರೆಯಾಗಿ ಸಂದುದಿದುರುತರದೊರೆಯಕ್ಕರಮಿದನರಿವು ತೆರದಿಂದಂ ಕಾಂತೆ॥ ಜಲಜಸಂಭವಗಣಮಕ್ಕೆ ಮೊದಲೊಳು ನಡುವೆ ಜಲರುಹೋದರಗಣವಕ್ಕೆ ಬಳಿಕ್ಕ ಕಾಮಾರಿ ಗಣಂ ತಿಲಕದಂತಿರೆ ಕಡೆಯೊಳ್ ಬಂದು ಯಿಕ್ಕೆ ಕಾಮಬಾಣಾವಳಿಯಂ ಪೊಗೆಯ್ದಿ ಗಣವಕ್ಕೆ ನಡುವಣಕ್ಕರಕ್ಕೆ ಪೆಸರಿಂತು ಸಖಿ॥ ವನಜಸಂಭವಗಣಕೆ ಮೊದಲೊಳೆತ್ತಲ್ ವನರುಹೋದರಗಣಯುಗಳಮವಕ್ಕೆ ರುದ್ರನದರಂತ್ಯದೊಳ್ ಬಂದಿಕ್ಕೆ ನಾಲ್ಕು ಗಣಮನಿತುಮೆಸೆವ ಕಡೆಯಕ್ಕರಕ್ಕೆ ಮಾತ್ರೃಗಳ್ ॥ ತಡೆಯದೆ ಹರಿಯುಗಂ ಮೊದಲೊಳಿಕ್ಕೆ ಜಡೆಯ ಶಂಕರನೊರ್ವಂ ಕಡೆಯೊಳಿಕ್ಕೆ ಮಡದಿ ಕೇಳ್ ಸುರರಣಮೆಸದಿಕ್ಕೆ ಕಡ ಕಿರಿಯಕ್ಕರಕ್ಕಿದುವೆ ಲಕ್ಷಣಂ॥ ಯಳೆಯ ಲಕ್ಷಣಂ | ಅಜಪಕ್ಷ್ಮಸುರವಜ್ರದೊಳಾರೊಳಪ್ಪ ಜಗದೊಳೆಳೆ ನಿಭವತಿ॥ ಷಟ್ಪದಿಯ ಲಕ್ಷಣಂ | ಮಂದರಧರಗಣ ಬಂದರೆ ಕಡೆಯೊಳ್ ಕುಂದದೆ ಹರಸಾ ಕಡೆಯೊಳಗಿಂದುನಿಭಾನನೆ ಮುಂದಣ ಪದನಿಯಮಮಂ ಮೊದಲಾದಂದು ಷಟ್ಪದಿಯನಿಕ್ಕುಂ॥ ಅಕ್ಕರಿಕೆಯ ಲಕ್ಷಣಂ | ಮುರರಿಪುಬ್ರಹ್ಮಂ ಮುರರಿಪುಬ್ರಹ್ಮಂ ಮುರರಿಪುಶೂಲಧರಂ ಸರಸದಿ ನಿಲ್ಕುಂ ಖಗಗಣಮಕ್ಕುಂ ನಿರುಪ

ಮಛಂದಾಪರಿಮಿತಿಮಪ್ಪಂತಿರೆ ಯತಿ ರುತು ಸುರರೊಳ್ ಬರೆ ತರಳಾಕ್ಷಿ ಧರೆಯೊಳಗೆತ್ತಕ್ಕರಮೆಸವಕ್ಕರಿಗೆ॥ ಚೌಪದಿಯ । ಮದನನ ತಂದೆಯ ಮುಂದುದಯಿಸೆ ಶಂಖರನೊಳ್ ಪೊದವಿರೆ ಸಂದು ನೋಡಿದು ಸತಿ ಚೌಪದಿಗೆ । ಮಂದರಧರಗಣಮೆಸದಿರೆ ಮೊದಲೊಳ್ ಪೊಂದಿರೆಯುಂ ಕಡೆಯೊಳಜಂ ಸಂದುದು ಲಕ್ಷಣಮವನಿಯೊಳೆಂದುಂ ಛಂದೋವತಂಸವದನೆ॥ ಮದನವತಿಯ ಲಕ್ಷಣಂ । ಮದನನ ತಂದೆಯು ಗುಣಮುಂ ವಿಷಯದೊಳಿರೆ ಗುರುವೊಂದೊದವಿರೆ ಪದದೊಳುಮವರ ಪೊಲಿಪ್ಪುದು ಗುರುಪದಮುಂ ವಿದಿತಮೆ ವಿದಿತಮೆ ಚಂದ್ರಚತುಷ್ಟಯದಿಂದತ್ತಂಬುಜವದನೆ ಮದನಹರತ್ರಿತಯಂ ಹರಿ ಕಡೆ ಪಡೆ ಮದನವತಿ॥ ಗಣನಿಯಮಂಗಳಗಣಿತಮೆನಲ್ಕದೆಗಣೆಯಪ್ಪುದಿಪ್ಪತ್ತೆರಡು ಮಾತ್ರೆಗಳಕ್ಕುಂ ಗುಣಯುತೆ ಮದನವತಿಗೆಂದುಂ॥ ಗೀತಿಕೆಯ ಲಕ್ಷಣಂ । ಎರಡಾರೆನಿಪ ಸಂಖ್ಯೆಯೊಳ್ ಬರೆ ಬ್ರಹ್ಮನುಳಿದೆಡೆಗಳೊಳು ವಿಷ್ಣು ಮುಂದಿರೆ ಮುಂದಣ ಪದಂ ಮುನ್ನಿನಂತುರುತರಂ ಗೀತಿಕೆಗಿಂತಕ್ಕುಂ ಸಖೀ॥ ಉತ್ಸಾಹಲಕ್ಷಣಂ । ಜಯದೇವತಾಕ್ಷರಧವಳಪ್ರಯೋಗತರವಾದುದೆಲ್ಲವಂ ಪೇಳ್ದ ನಿರ್ಣಯಮಾಗಿರೆಯುಂ ಷಟ್ಪ್ರತ್ಯಯಮುಂ ಚೆಲ್ವಾಗಿ ಪೇಳ್ವೆನಂಬುಜವದನೆ॥ ಷಟ್ಪ್ರತ್ಯಯಂ॥ ಶ್ಲೋಕಾ॥ ಪ್ರಸ್ತಾರೋ ನಷ್ಟ ಉದ್ದಿಷ್ಟ ಯೇತದ್ವ್ಯಾದಿಲಗಕ್ರಿಯಾ । ಸಂಖ್ಯಾನಾಮಧ್ವಯೋಗಾಚ ಷಟ್ಪ್ರತ್ಯಯಮಿತಿ ಸ್ಮೃತಃ॥ ನಷ್ಟಕ್ಕೆ । ಮೊದಲೊಳ್ ಛಂದದಿಂದೆಡೆಯ ಲೆಕ್ಕದಿ ಕೆಟ್ಟುದು ವೃತ್ತಮೆಂದು ಪೇಳ್ವುದು ಬಗೆ ಬಂದಡಾಗಳವರಂದಮನರ್ಧಿಸಿ ಬಿಟ್ಟಿಟ್ಟು ಕೊಳ್ವುದು ಸಮಭಾಗಮಿಯ್ಯದೊಡೆ ರೂಪು ಯಥಾರ್ಥತೆ ಬಿಳ್ಪುವಿಟ್ಟು ಕೊಳ್ವುದು ಗಡ ಸೂತ್ರಮಿಾ ತೆರದಿ ಕಾಣ್ಬುದು ನಷ್ಟಮನಂಬುಜಾನನೆ॥ ಇನಿತರ ಛಂದಮಿಾಸನೆಯ ವೃತ್ತಮದೆಂತುಟದೆಂಬ ಲೆಕ್ಕಮಂತನಿತನಯರ್ಧಿಸಲ್ಕೆ ಲಘುತದ್ವಿಷಮಕಿರದೊಂದನೊದಿಶಿರ್ದನಿತೆಯೆ ಬಿಳ್ಪುವಂ ಗುರುವಿನೊಳೆತ್ತಿ ನಷ್ಟಮಾಯ್ತೆನಿಶಿದ ವೃತ್ತಮಿಾ ತೆರದಿ ಬಪ್ಪುದು ತಪ್ಪದಿದಂಬುಜಾನನೆ॥ ಉದಿಷ್ಟಕೆ । ನೆಗಳಾನತಪದಾಂತ್ಯಮೆಯ್ದುದಿನೆಗಂ ಸಂಖ್ಯಾತಮುಂ ಸೂತ್ರದಿಂ ದ್ವಿಗುಣಂಗೆಯ್ದು ಲಘು ವಜ್ರಂಗಳಿಡೆಯೊಳ್ ನಿಂದಂಕ್ರಮಂ ಕೊಡುಮೆಲ್ಲನೆ ಮತ್ತೊಂದನೆ ಕೂಡಿ ಬಿಟ್ಟಿನೆಡೆಯೊಳ್ ನಿಂದಂಕಮಂ ಬಿಟ್ಟೊಡಾ ನೆಗದುದಿಷ್ಟವಿಧಾನವಿಾ ತೆರದಿ ಕಾಣ್ಬುದು ನಷ್ಟಮನಂಬುಜಾನನೆ॥ ಪುದಿಯದೆ ಛಂದಮಿಯೆಡೆಯೊಳುಮೆ ಕೆಟ್ಟುದಿದೆಂಬ ವೃತ್ತಮಂ ಪದೆಬಗೆ ಬ ದೊಡಾಗಳವರಕ್ಕರಮಂತವನರ್ಧಿಸಿಟ್ಟುಸಂಹುದದೊಳೆಸೆರಿ ದಿಕಾಗಣದ ಲೆಖ್ಖದೊಳಾಗಳೆಯೊಪ್ಪವಿಟ್ಟು ಕೊಳ್ವುದು ಗಣಸೂತ್ರಮಿಾ ತೆರದಿ ಬಪ್ಪುದು ತಪ್ಪದಿಂದಂಬುಜಾನನೆ॥ ಏಕದ್ವಿಲಗಕ್ರಿಯೆ॥ ಅನುಗತಮೊಂದರಂಕಮನೆ ಡಂದದ ಲೆಖದೊಳಂಕವಿಟ್ಟು ಮೆಲ್ಲನೆ ಬಳಿಕೊಂದನಿಟ್ಟು ಬರೆಕೂಡುವುದೊಂದರೊಳೊಂದನೆಯ್ದೆ ಮುನ್ನಿನ ತೆರನಂತ್ತೆದಂತಳರದಿಪ್ಪುದು ತತ್ರಮಮೆಯ್ದುವಂನೆಗಂ ವನಜದಳಾಯತಾಕ್ಷಿ ನೀನರಿವುದೆಕಯುಗಕ್ರಿಯೆ ಲಘುಕ್ರಮಂಗಳಂ ಶ್ರೀನಾಗವರ್ಮಂ ಸಂಪೂರ್ಣಂ॥ ಕರಕೃತಮಪರಾಧಂ ಕ್ಷಂತುಮರ್ಹಂತಿ ಸಂತಃ ॥ ಶ್ರೀರಸ್ತು ॥

P. 130, note 5, (see Addenda):

ಚಂಪಕಮಾಲೆ (*corrupt*)

ಇನಿತು ಪ್ರಮಾಣದದು ಕೆಟ್ಟುದು ಕಂದಮದಂದು ಬಕ್ಕುಮಿಂ
ಬಿನೊಳೆದೆಬಬವೆತ್ತ[1] ಗಣಸಂಖ್ಯೆಯನೊಂದನೆ ಕೂಡಿ ಲಬ್ಧದಿಂ ।
ಜನನುತಶೇಷದಿಂದಮರಿದೀ ಗಣಮೆಂದದನಿಟ್ಟು ಕೊಂಡು ಮುಂ
ನಿನ ತೆಱದಿಂದವೆತ್ತು ಪದಿನಾಲ್ಕು ಗಣಂಗಳುಮೆಯ್ದುವನ್ನೆಗಂ॥

1) ನೆಬಬಲೆತ

ಮಹಾಸ್ರಗ್ಧರೆ (*cor.*)

..ಯಿೞ ಕಾಣಲ್ಪದೀ ಕಂದದ ಪರಿಮಿತಮಂ ಪೇಳೆ ನಾಲ್ಕೊಂದು ಬೇಗಂ
ಪದಿನಾಱುಂ ತಾಣದೊಳ್ ಪುಟ್ಟುವ ಗಣತತಿಯಂ ತಮ್ಮೊಳೊಂದೊಂದನಾಹ್ಕ[1] ।
ದದಿ ಮಚ್ಚಲ್ಕಲ್ಲಿ ಕಂಡಾ ಗಣದ ಕೆಳಗೆ ನಿಂದಾ ಗಣವ್ರಾತಮಂ ತ
ಪ್ಪದೆ ಬಕ್ಕುದ್ದಿಷ್ಟಮಿಂತೀ ತೆಱವನಱಿವುದಂಭೋಜಪತ್ರಾಯತಾಕ್ಷೀ॥

1) ಷ್ಟಾ

ಚಂಪಕಮಾಲೆ (*cor.*)

ದಿವಸಕರಾಂಬುಧಿಮರುದಂಬರಭೂಮಿಶಶಾಂಕವಹ್ನಿಯಿಂ
ಬಿವು ನೊರೆಕೊಂಡು ಬಂದ ಗಣಮೆಂಟಱೊಳಂ ನೆಗಳ್ದರ್ಕನಾದಿಯಾ ।

ಗವನೆಣೆಸಿಟ್ಟ ಲೆಕ್ಕಮುಮಱಿಂತಿದು ತಪ್ಪದೆ ನಾಗವರ್ಮನಿಂ
ಭುವನದೊಳಂ ಉಕಿ[1]) ಕಲ್ಲಮಱಿವಂತು ಮನೋಹರಮಾಗೆ ಮಾಡಿದಿದಂ[2]) ||

1) ಬುವನದೊಳಂ (a blank)ಳೆ 2) ಮಾಡಿದದಿಂದಂ

ಕಂದಂ (*cor.*)

ಪದಿನಾಱು ಕಲ್ಲನೋಳಿಯು
ಮೊದಲಿಂ ಬರೆಟ್ಟು ಮೂಱು ಸೂಳೆತ್ತಿ ಮನೋ |
ಮುದದ ಗಣಮನೆರಬಪಿರದ[1])
ಪದದೊಳಿನಿಂ ಪೇಳ್ದುದಂಟ್ಟು[2]) ಕಲ್ಗಳನಬಲೇ ||

1) ಮುದದಿಲಗಣಮನೆರದ 2) ದಟ್ಟು

ಕಂದಂ (*cor.*)

ಪ್ರಣಥನರನಾಥ[1]) ಸಿಡೆಯುದೆ
ಮಣಿರ್ವ ಪರಿದೆಯ್ದಿ ಸಂದರಂ[2]) ನಿಂಗೆವಿದ್ಯೆ |
ಸೆಣಸಿ ಬರೆ ಕಂಡು ತಡೆಯದೆ
ಹಣರ್ದು ಮನೆರೆದರನೆ ಕೊಂದು ನೆಲು[3]) ತುಂಗಯಶಾ ||

1) ಪ್ರಣಧನದನಾಥ 2) ಸಂಧರಂ 3) ಮನೆಗೆದರನೆ ಕೊಂದುಗೆಲು

ವಚನಂ

ಅಲ್ಲಿಯ ಪುರಜನಬಂದಂ ಗೋಮೂತ್ರಿಕಂ (-ಮೂತ್ರಿಕಂ) ಸರ್ವತೋಭದ್ರುವದಕ್ಕರಂ ಷಟ್ಪದಂ ತ್ರಿವಧಿ ಚತುಃಪದಿಯೇಳೆ ಮೊದಲಾದೈದು ಸಾವಿರದೆಂಟುನೂಱು ವೃತ್ತಜಾತಿಯ ನಾನಾಛಂದಗಳಕ್ಕುಂ || Then follows the first of the 8 verses about the śubhāśubha of the different gaṇas.

INDEX

FOR THE CANARESE TEXT

ಒತ್ತು, ŏttu (i. e. doubling). A double consonant. 26. 42.

ಓಜ, ಓಜೆ, oja, ojĕ. Odd line. 242. 251. 285.

ಔಪಚ್ಛಂದಸಿಕ, aupacchandasika. Name of a Mora-metre. 252. p. 75.

ಕಂಸಾರಿ, kaṁsâri. The Can. foot— — ⏑. p. 96.

ಕನಕಾಬ್ಜನೀಯ, kanakâbjanîya. Name of a vṛitta. 193.

ಕನ್ದ, kanda (skandhaka). Name of a Mora-feet metre. 281. 282. 284-288. 293. 294. Cf. p. 23 gaṇaniyama kanda.

ಕನ್ದರ್ಪಜಾತ, kandarpajâta. Name of a vṛitta. 195.

ಕನ್ದರ್ಪರಿಪುಗಣ, kandarparipugaṇa. A class of pure Canarese feet. 302.

ಕನ್ದರ್ಪಾರಿ, kandarpâri. The foot — — — ⏑. p. 97.

ಕಪರ್ದಿ, kapardi. Sign for a long letter. 132.

ಕಮಲ, kamala. Name of a vṛitta. 101.

ಕರ, kara. The number 2. 298.

ಕರ, kara. The number 6. 251. 308 (?). Cf. khara.

ಕರಾಬ್ಧಿ, karâbdhi. 244 (?).

ಕರಿ. kari. The number 8. 215. 222. 226. 234. 248. 251. 316. 318. 319.

ಕರಿಪ್ರಾಸ, kariprâsa. A kind of alliteration. 42.

ಕರ್ನಾಟಕ, karnâṭaka. The karṇâṭaka vishaya bhâshâ jâti p. 22; karṇâṭaka vishaya jâti p. 95; karṇâṭaka bhâshĕ anda (i. e. manner) 296; the six vṛittas especially used for the karnâṭaka 230.

ಕಲ್ಯಾಣ, kalyâṇa. Name of a vṛitta. 131.

ಕಳೆ, kaḷĕ. A Mora. 326.

ಕಾಂಚನಮಾಲೆ, kâñcanamâlĕ. Name of a vṛitta. 87.

ಕಾಮಪ್ರಧ್ವಂಸಿ, kâmapradhvaṁsi. Sign for a long letter. 191.

ಕಾಮಬಾಣ, kâmabâṇa. The number 5. 304.

ಕಾಮರಿಪು, kâmaripu. The foot —⏑⏑⏑. p. 97.

ಕಾಮಹರ, kâmahara. Sign for a long letter. 91.

ಕಾಮಾಂಗ, kâmâṅga. Name of a vṛitta. p. 28, *note*.

ಕಾಮಾಂತಕ, kâmântaka. Sign for a long letter. 202.

ಕಾಮಾಂತಕಗಣ, kâmântakagaṇa. A class of pure Canarese feet. 304.

ಕಾಮಾಂತಕಂ, kâmântakam. The foot — — ⏑ —. p. 97.

ಕಾಮಾರಿಗಣ, kâmârigaṇa. A class of pure Canarese feet. p. 105; p. 106.

ಕಾಮಾಸ್ತ್ರ, kâmâstra. The number 5. 161. 195.

ಕಾಮೋದ್ಭವ, kâmodbhava. Name of a vṛitta. 84.

ಕಿಱು ಅಕ್ಕರ, kiṟi akkara. Name of a pure Canarese metre. 306.

ಕುಟ್ಮಲ, kuṭmala. Name of a vṛitta. 175.

ಕುಮುದ, kumuda. Name of a vṛitta. 97. 98.

ಕುಮುದಾರಿ, kumudâri. The foot ⏑—⏑. 237.

ಕುಲಗಿರಿ, kulagiri. The number 7. 155; cf. 140. 178.

ಕುಲಿಶ, kuliśa. The foot ⏑⏑⏑. 99. 218.

ಕುಲಿಶಧರ, kuliśadhara. The foot ⏑⏑⏑. 155. 183. 191.

ಕುಶ, kuśa. The foot ⏑— —. 149.

ಕುಸುಮವಿಚಿತ್ರ, kusumavicitra. Name of a vṛitta. 161.

ಕುಸುಮಶರ, kusumaśara. A name of one of the mâlâvṛittas. 234.

ಕುಸುಮಷಟ್ಪದಿ, kusumashaṭpadi. Name of a pure Canarese metre. 316. 322-325.

ಕುಸುಮಾಂಘ್ರಿಪ, kusumâṅghripa. Name of a vṛitta. 173.

ಕೃತಿ, kṛiti. Name of a type of metres. p. 23. 202-205.

ಕೃಶಾನು, kṛiśânu. The foot —⏑—. 224.

ಕೊಂಕು, kŏṅku (i. e. crookedness). A long syllable (the form to denote a long syllable being a crooked line; cf. vakra). 33.

ಕೊಂಕು ಗೆರೆ, kŏṅku gĕrĕ (i. e. crooked line). The sign for a long syllable. 25.

ಕೋಕನದವೈರಿ, kokanadavairi. The foot —⏑⏑. 119.

ಕೋಮಳ, komaḷa. Name of a vṛitta. 106.

ಕೋಮಳ, komaḷa. Name of a vṛitta. 166.

ಕೋಮಳರುಚಿರ, komaḷarucira. Name of a vṛitta. 166.

ಕ್ರೌಂಚಪದ, krauñcapada. Name of a vṛitta. 221.

ಕ್ಷೋಣಿ, kshoṇi. The foot — — —. 131.

ಕ್ಷ್ಮಾ, kshmâ. The foot — — —. 224.

ಖಚರ, khacara. The number 1. 295.

ಖಚರಪ್ಲುತ, khacarapluta. Name of a vṛitta. 201.

ಖರ, khara. The number 6. 308. cf. kara.

ಖರಕರ, kharakara. The foot ⏑—⏑. 217. 234.

ದಿವಸಾಧಿಪ, divasâdhipa. The foot ⏑—⏑. 158.

ದಿವಸಾಧಿಪ, divasâdhipa. The number 12. 148.

ದಿವಾಕರ, divâkara. The foot ⏑—⏑. 150.

ದಿವಿಜ, divija. The foot ⏑⏑⏑. 136. 138. 139. 182. 214. 217. 227. 237.

ದಿವಿಜಕಲ್ಪಲತೆ, divijakalpalatĕ. Name of a vṛitta. 237.

ದಿವಿಜಪುರ, divijapura. The foot ⏑⏑⏑. 222.

ದಿಶ್, diś. The number 8. 137.

ದಿಶಾಕರಿ, diśâkari. The number 8. 198.

ದಿಶಾಗಜ, diśâgaja. The number 8. 139. 153.

ದಿಶೆ, diśĕ. The number 8. 149.

ದೀರ್ಘ, dîrgha. A syllable with a long vowel. 27. 42. 43.

ದುವದಿ, duvadi. *See* duvayi.

ದುವಯಿ, duvayi (*i. e.* dvipadi). Name of a Mora-feet metre. 282. 293-295.

ದುವವಿ, duvavi. *See* duvayi.

ದೇವ, deva. Sign for a long syllable (H., Rs. in v. 115).

ದೇವ, deva. The foot ⏑⏑⏑. p. 12, *note*. p. 16, *note*. 36.

ದೇವರಮ್ಯ, devaramya. Name of a vṛitta. 97.

ದೇವಾಕ್ಷರ, devâkshara. The feet measured by the names of Brahma, Vishṇu and Rudra. 340.

ದೇವಾಧಿಪಪುರ, devâdhipapura. The foot ⏑⏑⏑. 207.

ದೇಶಿ, deśi. The language of the Canarese country. 16. Cf. adeśi.

ದೈತ್ಯಾರಿ, daityâri. Sign for a short syllable. 202.

ದೊರೆ ಅಕ್ಕರ, dŏrĕ akkara. Name of a pure Canarese metre. 303.

ದೋಧಕ, dodhaka. Name of a vṛitta. 185.

ದ್ರುತಪದ, drutapada. Name of a vṛitta. 154.

ದ್ರುತಪೂರ್ವವಿಲಂಬಿತ, drutapûrvavilambita. Name of a vṛitta. 147.

ದ್ವಂದ್ವಪ್ರಾಸ, dvandvaprâsa. A kind of alliteration. 64.

ದ್ವಿಪ್ರಾಸ, dviprâsa. A kind of alliteration. 64. 65.

ಧರಣಿ, dharaṇi. The foot — — —. 28.

ಧರಣೀಶ್ವರ, dharaṇîśvara. The number 16. 297.

ಧರೆ, dharĕ. The foot — — —. 32. 202.

ಧಾತೃ, dhâtṛi. The Can. foot —⏑. p. 96.

ಧಾತ್ರಿ, dhâtri. The foot — — —. 33. 103. 128. 170. 188.

ಧೂಮಧ್ವಜ, dhûmadhvaja (*i. e.* agni or śikhibraja). The number 3. p. 100.

ಧೂರ್ಜಟಿ, dhûrjaṭi. The Mora-foot —⏑⏑. 283.

ಧೃತಿ, dhṛiti. Name of a type of metres. p. 23. 194-197.

ನ, na. The foot ⏑⏑⏑. 24. 29. 34. 35. 90. 93. 107. 108. 118. 122. 123. 147. 172.

ನ, na. The foot ⏑⏑⏑⏑ of the five Mora-feet. 288.

ನಗ, naga. The number 7. 229.

ನಗಹರ, nagahara. The foot ⏑⏑⏑. 164.

ನಡು ಅಕ್ಕರ, naḍu akkara. Name of a pure Canarese metre. 304.

ನನ್ದ, nanda. Name of a vṛitta. 89.

ನನ್ದಕ, nandaka. Name of a vṛitta. 86.

ನಭ, nabha. The foot — —⏑. 218.

ನರಕಾರಿ, narakâri. The Can. foot ⏑⏑—⏑. p. 96.

ನರಗ, naraga. Name of a vṛitta. 107.

ನರ್ಕುಟಕ, narkuṭaka. Name of a vṛitta. 193*b*.

ನವನಳಿನ, navanaḷina. Name of a vṛitta. 182.

ನಷ್ಟ, nashṭa. A kind of calculation. 342.

ನಾಕ, nâka. The foot ⏑⏑⏑. 32. 33. 35. 126.

ನಾಕಿ, nâki. The Can. foot —⏑. p. 96.

ನಾಕಿಗಂ, nâkigam. The Can. foot —⏑—. p. 96.

ನಾಗ, nâga. The number 8. 229.

ನಾಗರಂಜಿತ, nâgarañjita. Name of a vṛitta. 205.

ನಾನ್ದಿ, nândi. A prayer or eulogium at the commencement of a work. p. 16, *note*.

ನಾಮಾಂಕ, nâmâṅka. Under this appellation the kâmâṅga appears in Rb.

ನಿಜ, nija. A short syllable. 42. 43.

ನಿಧಿ, nidhi. The number 9. 166. 170. 173. 196.

ನಿರುಪಮ, nirupama. Name of a vṛitta. 153.

ನೀತಿಕೆ, nîtikĕ (gîtikĕ?). Name of a vṛitta. 145.

ನೀಲಕಂಠ, nîlakaṇṭha. Sign for a long letter. 89.

ಬೃಹತಿ, bṛihati. Name of a type of metres. p. 23. 117-125.

ಬೃಹತಿ, bṛihati. Name of a vṛitta. 125.

ಬೊಮ್ಮಂ, bŏmmam (i. e. brahmam). The Can. foot ——. 308.

ಬ್ರಹ್ಮಗಣ, brahmagaṇa. A class of pure Can. feet. p. 96. p. 114.

ಬ್ರಹ್ಮಾ, brahmâ. The Can. foot ——. p. 96.

ಭ, bha. The foot —⏑⏑. 24. 29. 34. 35. 147. 172.

ಭದ್ರಕ, bhadraka. Name of a vṛitta. 120.

ಭದ್ರಕ, bhadraka. Name of a vṛitta. 211.

ಭವ, bhava. Sign for a long syllable. 108. 222.

ಭಾನು, bhânu. The foot ⏑—⏑. 132. 163. 171. 174. 181. 198. 227. 233. 236.

ಭಾನು, bhânu. The number 12. 327.

ಭಾಮಿನಿಷಟ್ಪದಿ, bhâminishaṭpadi. Name of a pure Canarese metre. 316. 330-333.

ಭಾಷಾಜಾತಿ, bâshâjâti. The 56 various daughter-languages. p. 22.

ಭಾಸ್ಕರ, bhâskara. The foot ⏑—⏑. 200. 206.

ಭಾಸ್ಕರ, bhâskara. The number 12. 184.

ಭುಜಂಗಪ್ರಯಾತ, bhujangaprayâta. Name of a vṛitta. 149.

ಭುಜಂಗವಿಜೃಂಭಿತ, bhujangavijṛimbhita. Name of a vṛitta. 224.

ಭುಜಂಗಶಿಶುಪದ, bhujangaśiśupada. Name of a vṛitta. 122.

ಭುಜಂಗಶಿಶುಪರಿ, bhujangaśiśupari. Name of a vṛitta. 122.

ಭುಜಂಗಶಿಶುಸೃತ, bhujangaśiśusṛita. Name of a vṛitta. 122.

ಭುಜಗ, bhujaga. The number 1. 307.

ಭುಜಗಧಾರಿ, bhujagadhâri. The Canarese foot ⏑⏑⏑—⏑. p. 97.

ಭುಜಗಪಕ್ಷಗಣ, bhujagapakshagaṇa. A class of pure Canarese feet. 300. 307.

ಭೂ, bhû. The foot ———. 99. 126. 177.

ಭೂತ, bhûta. The number 5. 130. 221.

ಭೂತಗಣೇಶ, bhûtagaṇeśa. Sign for a long syllable. 221.

ಭೂತಾಗ್ರಣಿ, bhûtâgraṇi. The Can. foot ——⏑⏑. p. 97.

ಭೂಮಾಲೆ, bhûmâlĕ. Name of a vṛitta. p. 40, note.

ಭೂಮಿ, bhûmi. The foot ———. 35. 76. 85. 140. 207. 215.

ಭೋಗಷಟ್ಪದಿ, bhogashaṭpadi. Name of a pure Canarese metre. 316. 326-329.

ಭ್ರಮರವಿಲಸಿತ, bhramaravilasita. Name of a vṛitta. 138.

ಮ, ma. The foot ———. 24. 29. 34. 35. 122.

ಮಂಗಲಿಕೆ, mangalikĕ. Name of a vṛitta. p. 48, note.

ಮಂಗಳ, mangaḷa. Name of a vṛitta. 185.

ಮಂಜುಭೂಷಿಣಿ (?ಮಂಜುಭಾಷಿಣಿ), manjubhûshiṇi (? manjubhâshiṇi). Name of a vṛitta. 169.

ಮಖರಿಪು, makharipu. The Mora-foot ⏑⏑⏑⏑. 283.

ಮಣಿಗಣನಿಕರ, maṇigaṇanikara. Name of a vṛitta. 178.

ಮಣಿರಂಗ, maṇiranga. Name of a vṛitta. 130.

ಮಣಿವಿಭೂಷಣ, maṇivibhûshaṇa. Name of a vṛitta. 180.

ಮತ್ತ, matta. Name of a vṛitta. 128.

ಮತ್ತಮಯೂರ, mattamayûra. Name of a vṛitta. 170.

ಮತ್ತಾಕ್ರೀಡೆ, mattâkrîḍĕ. Name of a vṛitta. 215.

ಮತ್ತೇಭ, mattebha. *See* mattebhavikrîḍita. 230.

ಮತ್ತೇಭವಿಕ್ರೀಡಿತ, mattebhavikrîḍita. Name of a vṛitta. 202. 230.

ಮದಗಜ, madagaja. The number 8. 226.

ಮದನತಂದೆ, madanatandĕ (i. e. madana's father, in this case Vishṇu). A class of pure Canarese feet. 309-311.

ಮದನಧ್ವಂಸಿ, madanadhvamsi. The Can. foot ⏑⏑——⏑. p. 97.

ಮದನರಿಪು, madanaripu. The Can. foot ⏑⏑⏑⏑⏑. p. 97.

ಮದನವತಿ, madanavati. Name of a pure Can. metre. 68. 311.

ಮದನಹರ, madanahara. A class of pure Can. feet. 311.

ಮದನಹರ, madanahara. Sign for a long syllable. 317.

ಮಧುಮತಿ, madhumati. Name of a vṛitta. 108.

ಮಧ್ಯಮೆ, madhyamĕ. Name of a type of metres. p. 23. 75-78.

ಮನು, manu. The number 14. 316. 318. 321. 330. 332. 333.

ರುದ್ರ, rudra. Name of a class of pure Canarese feet. 297. p. 97. 305.

ಲ, la. Sign for a short syllable. 24. 29. 86. 90. 113. 134. 136-138. 172. 173 189. 203. 214. 224. 227. 236-238. 241. 251.

ಲಗಕ್ರಿಯೆ, lagakriyĕ. A kind of computation. 344.

ಲಘು, laghu. A short syllable. 25. 28-34. 230. 241. 244. 290. 298. 341. 343.

ಲಘು, laghu. A Mora. 318. 319. 322. 323. 327. 331. 334.

ಲಯ, laya. Tempo. 120.

ಲಯಗ್ರಾಹಿ, layagrâhi. Name of a vṛitta. 143.

ಲಯಗ್ರಾಹಿ, layagrâhi. Name of a Canarese Samavṛitta of 30 syllables. 276.

ಲಲಿತ, lalita. Name of a vṛitta. 217.

ಲಲಿತಗತಿ, lalitagati. Name of a vṛitta. 209.

ಲಲಿತಪದ, lalitapada. Name of a vṛitta. 155.

ಲಲಿತಪದ, lalitapada. Name of a vṛitta. 183.

ಲಲಿತಪದ, lalitapada. Name of one of the Mâlâvṛittas. 233.

ಲಲಿತೆ, lalitĕ. One of the Ragaḷĕ metres. 255. 256. 262-264.

ವಂಶಸ್ಥ, vaṁśastha. Name of a vṛitta. 150.

ವಕ್ರ, vakra. A long syllable (see kŏṅku). 33.

ವನಜ, vanaja. Name of a vṛitta. 121.

ವನಜದಳ, vanajadaḷa. Name of a vṛitta. 192.

ವನಜಸಂಭವಗಣ, vanajasambhavagaṇa. A class of pure Canarese feet. 305.

ವನಮಂಜರಿ, vanamañjari. Name of a vṛitta. 205.

ವನಮಂಜರಿ, vanamañjari. Name of a vṛitta. 212.

ವನಮಯೂರ, vanamayûra. Name of a vṛitta. 174.

ವನರುಹೋದರಗಣ, vanaruhodaragaṇa. A class of pure Canarese feet. 305.

ವನಲತೆ, vanalatĕ Name of a vṛitta. 226.

ವನವಲ್ಲರಿ, vanavallari. Name of a vṛitta. 205.

ವರ್ಗ ಅಕ್ಕರ, varga akkara. Classified consonants. 55.

ವರ್ಗಪ್ರಾಸ, vargaprâsa. A kind of alliteration. 51. 55-57.

ವಸಂತತಿಲಕ, vasantatilaka. A kind of vṛitta. 171.

ವಸು, vasu. The number 8. 165. 189. 194. 214.

ವಹ್ನಿ, vahni. The foot —⏑—. 32. 86. 117. 120. 252.

ವಹ್ನಿ, vahni. The number 3. 285.

ವಾತ, vâta. The foot ⏑⏑—. 35. 191. 221.

ವಾಯು, vâyu. The foot ⏑⏑—. 32. 36. 119. 131. 170. 194. 241.

ವಾರಿಜರಿಪು, vârijaripu. The foot —⏑⏑. 241.

ವಾರುಧಿ, vârudhi (vârdhi). The number 4. 175.

ವಾರ್ತಿಕಷಟ್ಪದಿ, vârtikashaṭpadi=vârdhikyashaṭpadi. 337.

ವಾರ್ಧಿ, vârdhi. The number 4. 149. 298.

ವಾರ್ಧಿಕಷಟ್ಪದಿ, vârdhikashaṭpadi. Name of a pure Canarese metre. 316. 337. 338.

ವಾರ್ಧಿಕ್ಯಷಟ್ಪದಿ, vârdhikyashaṭpadi= vârdhikashaṭpadi. 337. 338.

ವಿಕೃತಿ, vikṛiti. Name of a type of metres. p. 23. 214-216.

ವಿಚಿತ್ರ, vičitra. Name of a vṛitta. 95.

ವಿಚಿತ್ರ, vičitra. Name of a vṛitta. 100.

ವಿಚಿತ್ರ, vičitra. Name of a pure Canarese metre. 300. 301.

ವಿಚಿತ್ರಲಲಿತ, vičitralalita. Name of a vṛitta. 179.

ವಿಜಯಾನಂದ, vijayânanda. Name of a vṛitta. 186.

ವಿದಳಿತವನರುಹ, vidaḷitavanaruha. Name of a vṛitta. 228. cf. p. 60, *note* 4.

ವಿದ್ಯಾಧರ, vidyâdhara. The number 12. 295.

ವಿದ್ಯುನ್ಮಾಲೆ, vidyunmâlĕ. Name of a vṛitta. 111.

ವಿದ್ರುಮ, vidruma. = vinuta. p. 38, *note*.

ವಿಧು, vidhu. The foot —⏑⏑. 233.

ವಿನಮ್ರ, vinamra. Name of a vṛitta. 102.

ವಿನುತ, vinuta. Name of a vṛitta. 123.

ವಿನುತಪ್ರಾಸ, vinutaprâsa. Name of an alliteration. 51. 52.

ವಿಪರ್ಯಾಸ, viparyâsa. Reverse, change. 54. 239. 254.

ವಿಪುಳೆ, vipuḷĕ. Name of a Mora-feet metre. 289-294.

ವಿಭೂತಿ, vibhûti. Name of a vṛitta. 104.

ವಿಯತ್, viyat. The foot ——⏑. 200.

ವಿರತಿ, virati. Caesura. 195. 210. etc.

ವಿರಾಮ, virâma. Caesura. 132-135. 149. 153. 155. 158. etc.

ವಿರಾಮ, virâma. Name of a vṛitta. 102.

ವಿಲೋಮ, viloma. *See* anuloma.

ವಿಶ್ರಮ, viśrama. Caesura. 131. 136. 150. 151. 167. 173. etc.

ವಿಶ್ರಮಣ, viśramaṇa. Caesura. 137. 164. 176. etc.

ಸಂಕೀರ್ಣ, ಸಂಕೀರ್ಣಕ, saṅkîrṇa, saṅkîrṇaka. Name of a Mora-feet metre. 282. 292.

ಸಂಕೃತಿ, saṅkṛiti. Name of a type of metres. p. 23. 217-220.

ಸಂಖ್ಯಾಸ, saṅkhyâsa. A kind of computation. 345.

ಸಂಸ್ಕೃತ, saṁskṛita. Sanscrit. p. 22.

ಸದಮಲ, sadamala. Name of a vṛitta. 100.

ಸಮವೃತ್ತ, samavṛitta. p. 22. 71-234. 228. 232. Cf. vṛitta.

ಸಮೀಪಪ್ರಾಸ, samîpaprâsa. A kind of alliteration. 51. 57-59.

ಸಮೀರಣ, samîraṇa. The foot ⏑⏑—. 234.

ಸಮ್ಬಂಧಾಕ್ಷರ, sambandhâkshara. Perhaps identical with yogâkshara. 58.

ಸರಗ, saraga. Name of a vṛitta. 107.

ಸರಸಿಜಭವಗಣ, sarasijabhavagaṇa. A class of pure Canarese feet. 297.

ಸರಸಿಜೋದರಗಣ, sarasijodaragaṇa. A class of pure Canarese feet. 303.

ಸರಸಿರುಹ, sarasiruha. Name of a vṛitta. 90.

ಸರಸಿಸಖಗಣ, sarasisakhagaṇa. The foot ⏑⏑⏑ of the Sîsa. 269.

ಸರಳ, saraḷa. Name of a vṛitta. 105.

ಸರಳ, saraḷa. Name of a vṛitta. 227.

ಸರೋಜರಿಪು, sarojaripu. The foot —⏑⏑. 174.

ಸರೋರುಹಮಿತ್ರ, saroruhamitra. The foot ⏑—⏑. 238.

ಸರ್ವವಿಷಯಭಾಷಾದಿ, sarvavishayabhâshâdi. 70. 281. 296.

ಸರ್ವವಿಷಯಭಾಷಾಜಾತಿ, sarvavishayabhâshâjâti. p. 22. p. 23, *note* 2.

ಸಲಿಲ, salila. The foot ⏑——. 179.

ಸವರ್ಣ, savarṇa. The letter sa. 57.

ಸಾನ್ದ್ರಪದ, sândrapada. Name of a vṛitta. 142.

ಸಿಂಗಪ್ರಾಸ, siṅgaprâsa. A kind of alliteration. 43. 44.

ಸೀಸ, sîsa (sîsapadya). 269-271.

ಸುನಾಮ, sunâma. Name of a vṛitta. 109.

ಸುನ್ದರ, sundara. Name of a vṛitta. 167.

ಸುಪ್ರತಿಷ್ಠೆ, supratishṭhĕ. Name of a type of metres. p. 23. 86-91.

ಸುಪ್ರಾಸ, suprâsa (vinutaprâsa). A kind of alliteration. 54.

ಸುಮಾಲತಿ, sumâlati. Name of a vṛitta. 116.

ಸುಮುಖಿ, sumukhi. Name of a vṛitta. 144.

ಸುರ, sura. The foot ⏑⏑⏑. 78. 120. 217. 233. 234. 241.

ಸುರ, sura. The number 1. 295.

ಸುರಗಣ, suragaṇa (?). p. 109.

ಸುರಂಗಕೇಸರ, suraṅgakesara. Name of a vṛitta. 181.

ಸುರತರು, surataru. Name of a vṛitta. 83.

ಸುರಪ, surapa. The foot ⏑⏑⏑. 198. 241.

ಸುರಪಂ, surapaṁ. The Can. foot ⏑⏑—. p. 96.

ಸುರಪುರ, surapura. The foot ⏑⏑⏑. 153. 178. 196. 215. 217. 218. 221. 224. 227.

ಸುಲಭ, sulabha. Name of a vṛitta. 108.

ಸುಲಲಿತ, sulalita. Name of a vṛitta. 99.

ಸೂತ್ರ, sûtra. 342. 345.

ಸೂರ್ಯ, sûrya. The foot ⏑—⏑. 32. 81. 233. 242.

ಸೈತುಗೆರೆ, saitugere (*i. e.* straight line). The sign for a short syllable (cf. ṛiju). 25.

ಸೈನಿಕ, sainika. Name of a vṛitta. 134.

ಸೈಯ್ ಅಕ್ಕರ, say akkara. A short syllable. 26.

ಸೋಮ, soma. The foot —⏑⏑. 91. 238.

ಸೋಮೇಶ್ವರ, someśvara. Sign for a long syllable. 171.

ಸೌನ್ದರ, saundara. Name of a vṛitta. 80.

ಸೌನ್ದರ, saundara. Name of a vṛitta. 176.

ಸೌನ್ದರ, saundara. Name of a vṛitta. 216.

ಸೌನ್ದರಿ, saundari. Name of a vṛitta. 167.

ಸ್ಕನ್ಧಕ, skandhaka (kanda). p. 23, *note* 2.

ಸ್ರಗ್ಧರೆ, sragdharĕ. Name of a vṛitta. 207. 230.

ಸ್ರಗ್ವಿಣಿ, sragviṇi. Name of a vṛitta. 152.

ಸ್ವರ, svara. A vowel. 54.

ಸ್ವರ್ಗ, svarga. The foot ⏑⏑⏑. 83.

ಸ್ವಾಗತ, svâgata. Name of a vṛitta. 138.

ಹಂಸಕ, haṁsaka. Name of a vṛitta. 197.

ಹಂಸಕೇಳಿ, haṁsakeḷi. Name of a vṛitta. 157.

ಹಂಸಗತಿ, haṁsagati. Name of a vṛitta. 214.

ಹಂಸಪದ, haṁsapada. Name of a vṛitta. 222.

ಹಂಸಮತ್ತ, haṁsamatta. Name of a vṛitta. 157.

ಹಂಸಮಾಲೆ, haṁsamâlĕ. Name of a vṛitta. 110.

ಹಂಸಿ, haṁsi. Name of a vṛitta. 157.

ಹಯಪ್ರಾಸ, hayaprâsa. A kind of alliteration. 43.

ಹಯತತಿ, hayatati. The number 7. 172.

ಹಯನಿಕರ, hayanikara. The number 7. 207.

ಹಯವ್ರಾತ, hayavrâta. The number 7. 212.

ಹರ, hara. Sign for a long syllable. 102. 105. 112. 127. 139. 164. 170. 174. 179. 183. 236.

ಹರ, hara. The number 11. 214. 224.

ಹರಗಣ, haragaṇa. A class of pure Canarese feet. 311.

ಹರಿ, hari. Sign for a short syllable. 88. 91. 191.

ಹರಿ, hari. The number 8. 224. 226.

ಹರಿಗಣ, harigaṇa. A class of pure Canarese feet. p. 108. 311.

ಹರಿಣೀಪ್ಲುತ, hariṇîpluta. Name of a vṛitta. 191.

ಹರಿಪ್ರಾಸ, haripràsa. A kind of alliteration. 42.

ಹರಿವರ, harivara. Name of a vṛitta. p. 26, *note*.

ಹಲಮುಖಿ, halamukhi, halâmukhi. Name of a vṛitta. 118.

ಹಲಾಯುಧ, halâyudha = halamukhi. 118.

ಹಿಮಕೃತ್, himakṛit. the foot —◡◡. 188.

ಹಿಮಾಂಶುಶೇಖರ, himâ*m*śuśekhara. Sign for a long syllable. 198.

ಹುತವಹ, hutavaha. The foot —◡—. 210.

ಹುತಾಶನ, hutâśana. The foot —◡—. 178. 180. 203.

ಹೃದಯೇಶಂ, hṛidayeśa*m*. The Canarese foot. ◡◡——. p. 96.

INDEX TO THE PREFACE, ESSAY AND ADDITIONS.

CORRECTIONS

REGARDING THE TEXT.

Page 1, *note*, *l.* 2, from bottom, *not* "v. 80" and "v. 34", *but* "v. 79" and "v. 35"; and *ibid.* *last l.*, *not* "v. 34", *but* "v. 35".

P. 5, No. 11, *not* "v. 124 seq.", *but* "v. 147 seq."

P. 6, *note* 2, *l.* 4, f. b., *not* "v. 121" "v. 151", *but* "v. 123" "v. 153"; *l.* 5, f. b., *not* "v. 131", *but* "v. 133"; *l.* 6, f. b., *not* "vs. 111. 115. 137. 147. 153. 181. 215. 286", *but* "vs. 139. 155. 164. 184. 214. 218. 302".

P. 7, No. 14, *not* "v. 28", *but* "v. 29"; *note*, *l.* 2, f. b., *not* "v. 269 seq.", *but* "v. 284 seq."

P. 9, No. 19, *not* "v. 23", *but* "v. 24"; No. 20, *not* "v. 325", *but* "v. 341".

P. 10, heading 5, *not* "v. 27", *but* "v. 28".

P. 12, *note*, *l.* 9, f. b., *not* "v. 35", *but* "v. 36"; *l.* 12, f. b., *not* "v. 32", *but* "v. 36".

P. 14, *note*, *l.* 3, f. top, *not* "v. 124", *but* "v. 126".

P. 15, *note*, *l.* 5, f. t., *not* "v. 42", *but* "v. 43".

P. 16, *note*, *l.* 4, f. t., *not* "Verses 43-48", *but* "Verses 44-49"; *l.* 7, f. t., *not* "v. 41", *but* "v. 42".

P. 18, No. 40, 3, *not* "v. 330", *but* "v. 346".

P. 23, *note*, *l.* 2, f. t., put a stop after "(cf. v. 235)"; *l.* 7, f. t., *not* "66", *but* "67"; *l.* 3, f. b., *not* "of Mâtrâ gaṇas", *but* "of Mâtrâs and Mâtrâgaṇas"; in the Kanda verse strike out the comma after ಮದನನತಿ.

P. 24, *note* 3, *not* "as they are repeated", *but* "as they, with the exception of our v. 288, are repeated".

P. 27, *note* 2, *not* "contain, if required, nothing but a dry enumeration of the gaṇas of", *but* "contain nothing but a dry enumeration of the gaṇas, if required, of".

P. 38, *note* 2, *not* "v. 123", *but* "v. 125".

P. 71, *note* 2, *not* "on MS.", *but* "no MS.".

P. 75, No. 242, (though against the common use of "mâtrâgaṇa"), *not* "Mora-feet", *but* "Moras and feet".

P. 76, Introduction, *l.* 5, *not* "rule 289", *but* "rule 298".

P. 88, No. 257, remark, *not* "observations", *but* "observation". About śaśipura see the remarks in P. vi.

P. 95, No. 270, *not* "common to", *but* "of".

P. 97, remark, *l.* 1, f. t., *insert* "(excepting the śarashaṭpadi)" *after* "13 metres".

P. 109, No. 283, *not* "(bŏmma)", *but* "(bŏmmam)".

P. 112, beginning of scheme 3, *not* "⏑⏑⏑[2]⏑—", *but* "⏑⏑[1]⏑⏑—".

P. 115, remark, *l.* 5, f. t., *not* "p. 77", *but* "p. 74".

P. 128, *note*, *l.* 1, f. t., *not* "vs. 296 and 297", *but* "vs. 297 and 298".